Freddie Mercury: The Man Behind The Showman

Dr Maria Szili

Copyright © 2021 Dr Mária Szili

All rigths reserved.

ISBN-13: 979-8-76859-940-9

Dedication

I want to dedicate this book to the memory of the beloved Freddie Mercury and his loved ones, those wonderful people who cared for and stood by him in his finest hours and in his most difficult times.

Above all, to the amazing members of Queen: Brian May, Roger Taylor and John Deacon; the late Montserrat Caballé, Freddie's family and second family, especially the late Jim Hutton and Joe Fanelli, the always-smiling Peter Freestone, and last but not least to Mary Austin, and the fans all over the world.

I want to express my gratitude and appreciation, and thank them for all they did for Freddie.

Getting to know them was one of the most beautiful gifts of my life. They were and are all great human beings who have set an example of human greatness for all of us to follow.

Contents

Introduction	1
Part One	8
1. The Ultimate Showman	9
2. When I Was a Lad	12
3. Back to Zanzibar	32
4. Moving to London	34
5. Freddie Arrived in London at the Best Time	47
Part Two	49
6. Friends – Freddie, Tim, Brian and Roger	50
7. Freddie and Roger on Death Row	52
8. 'Smile. Makes Sense For a Dental Student'	59
9. Queen's Time Has Finally Come	63
10. Mary Is My Best Friend in The World	74
11. At Last, a Good Bass Guitarist	80
12. Queen and Trident	83
13. *Queen and Queen II* Albums (1973 and 1974)	89
14. *Sheer Heart Attack* Album (1974)	118
15. Break-up with Trident	130
16. Freddie's Relationship with David Minns	132

17. *A Night at the Opera* Album (1975)	137
Part Three	167
18. 'Freddie Never Was the Same Again' (Mick Rock)	168
19. *A Day at the Races* Album (1976)	178
20. Running Amok	
News of the World Album (1977)	187
21. *Jazz* Album (1978)	203
22. *Live Killers* Album (1979)	211
23. *Game and Flash Gordon* Albums (1980)	218
24. *Greatest Hits* Album (1981)	223
25. *Hot Space* Album (1982)	229
26. A Year Without a New Queen Album (1983)	235
27. *The Works* Album (1984)	249
28. *Mr Bad Guy* Album (1985)	261
29. He Is the One, Jim Hutton	267
30. Live Aid (13 July 1985)	270
31. After Live Aid	
A Kind of Magic Album (1986)	281
32. Magic Tour (1986)	299
33. A Holiday for Life	313
34. *Live Magic* Album, 1986	317

35. "The Great Pretender"	319
36. Montserrat Caballé	322
37. Jim's Final Test	327
38. The Treacherous Paul Prenter	328
39. The Ibiza '92 Festival	329
40. Freddie's Heroic Efforts	333
41. Queen Back Together Again (1988)	336
42. Festival 'La Nit', *Barcelona* Album (1988)	338
43. *The Miracle* Album (1989)	354
44. Life in Garden Lodge, 1988-1989	361
45. *Innuendo* Album (1991)	369
46.'Sweet Mother Love'	382
47. Last Hugs and Kisses	387
48. Freddie's Will	400
49. The Biggest Send-Off in History (20 April, 1992)	407
50. The Hollywood Film: Bohemian Rhapsody (2018)	411
51. The Happy Ending	412
Special Thanks	415
Select Bibliography	416

Ady, Endre

I want to be loved

I am no heir, no proud ancestor,
I have no friend, no brother, sister,
I have never belonged,
I have never belonged.

I am, like every human: Highness,
Iceberg, enigma, strange and timeless,
Distant will-o'-the-wisp,
Distant will-o'-the-wisp.

But, oh, I can't remain unspoken,
I have to bare myself wide open,
Behold me, everyone,
Behold me, everyone.

In all self-torture, in every song,
I want to be loved, to belong.
Belong to somebody,
Belong to somebody.

Zollman, Peter (Translated from Hungarian)

Introduction

The devastating loss

Regarded by millions as the most colourful and attractive personality in the world of pop and rock music, and one of the most remarkable musical geniuses of all time: singer, songwriter, musician and charismatic Queen frontman Freddie Mercury passed away at a tragically young age, at the peak of his career, in his Kensington (London) home on 24 November, 1991. He had released a statement the day before he died announcing that he had AIDS.

In the years leading up to his death, his health had gradually deteriorated and - although he kept this fact secret from the public almost until the last moment - his close friends knew the inevitable was about to happen.

His death constituted an enormous loss to his family, band members, friends, the art world and fans. The admiration and love that his loved ones and fans felt for him in their hearts can never be erased, and he lives on as a legend who has become immortal, as he no doubt would have wished. Thirty years after his death, we can say with confidence that his songs have stood the test of time.

Based on his unique legacy, Freddie was ranked 58th in the *100 Greatest Britons* (BBC Poll, 2002) survey of public opinion compiled by the BBC. This ranks him alongside Sir Winston Churchill, Diana Princess of Wales, Queen Elizabeth I, John Lennon, Sir Isaac Newton, Oliver Cromwell, Admiral Nelson, Sir Paul McCartney, Queen Elizabeth II, David Bowie and Stephen Hawking.

There can't be many people in the civilised world who haven't heard of the names mentioned above, all of whom were world-famous historical figures, musicians or scientists that made a significant contribution to Great Britain's cultural, scientific and political heritage.

Freddie Mercury fully deserves his position on this list, he was one in a million.

His lifetime achievements are truly outstanding, representing excellence in the world of rock and pop music. His masterpieces are still known, played and sung virtually all over the world today. Official videos of him and the band have been watched more than seven billion times, with *Bohemian Rhapsody* alone generating more than one billion views.
Brian May, the band's lead guitarist, believes that 'Freddie was a miracle.'
Brian is right; Freddie practised the art of excellence like a Zen master giving his music beauty and quality.
He started writing his songs in the spirit of eternal beginners, put his intellect to one side, and allowed the brain's emotional regions to take control. Most of his songs send messages straight to our hearts and generate a whole range of emotional reactions.

The members of Queen announced the news of Freddie's death as follows:

'We have lost the greatest and most beloved member of our family. We feel overwhelming grief that he has gone, sadness that he should be cut down at the height of his creativity, but above all, great pride in the courageous way that he lived and died. It has been a privilege for us to have shared such magical times.'

One of God's angels must have been holding the hand of whoever wrote this tribute; it perfectly conveys Brian, Roger and John's devastating loss and the gratitude they felt to him. They were left stunned and unable to comprehend the news. Having worked hard together for so long to become successful, when they had achieved everything and should have been in a position to enjoy making music together, Freddie became incurably ill. Then this bright shining star faded away, leaving behind a vacuum that can never be filled.

'In September 2010 (coincidentally, around Freddie's 64th birthday), a poll carried out among rock fans saw him named the Greatest Rock Legend Of All Time, beating Elvis Presley to claim the title, and ahead of David Bowie, Jon Bon Jovi, Jimi Hendrix and Ozzy Osbourne.'
(queenonline.com/freddie-mercury)

Freddie would have been very proud to have beaten his greatest role model, Jimi Hendrix, in popularity, and not by accident. He really would have deserved to have experienced this for himself, but fate took no mercy on him.

One of his close friends, David Evans, wrote this tribute in his book:

'So now he's gone... It's hard to believe, but we have to believe it as we are left behind without him, and we shall never be touched by stardom like this again... He achieved just about everything he wanted, and above all, he went out on top of his world, not sinking, not sliding, not skidding and slithering but fixed firmly on top, exactly where he put himself, and it is inconceivable to think of him as being anywhere else. His star will never become tawdry or tarnished, or slurred by failure and odious comparison. It will always shine as brightly as he left it.' (David Evans and David Minns):

Every fan is grateful to the 2018 Hollywood film *Bohemian Rhapsody*.
The film commemorated the legendary band, Queen and Freddie. His fans loved him and still love him for his art and magical personality, which sparkled in a thousand different colours.

As a result of the film, interest in CDs, DVDs and books about Freddie and Queen has increased many times over; the thousands of comments below the videos prove that a new fan base has been created. The film affected some viewers like an initiation rite or spiritual awakening; those who weren't previously aware of Queen were shocked to discover the difference between the music of today and the music of Queen. Many people rave about the film, as if they have caught a glimpse of heaven. That magical 20 minutes at the end of the film made quite an impression.

My book is intended for anyone who won't settle for just knowing the story of Freddie and Queen, but would like to understand what the mysterious songs were about. I am talking about *'Seven Seas Of Rhye'*, *'My Fairy King'*, *'March of the Black Queen'*, *'Killer Queen'*, *'Bohemian Rhapsody'*, and all the other less puzzling songs. I also wrote about the background to Freddie's unavoidable tragedy, and about who he was, the voice, music and exceptional performance style that attracted crowds of hundreds of thousands to stadiums. What was his secret?

As I learned the story of his life, and as pieces of the puzzle fell into place, I became increasingly sad and in the end felt deep pain, real grief. It was scary enough to know why he couldn't avoid HIV infection, which led to his death.

I became sadder, yet I felt it was better, to untie the knot than simply cut it in half, and I am glad I did it. I just couldn't give up, I needed to finish what I started, I couldn't help but deal with it, despite my sadness. I think it was the only way for me to accept what happened to Freddie. I know it sounds very strange, but that's what happened.

Just watching or seeing Freddie, perceiving or sensing his presence, is dramatically different to just hearing the music; by understanding his songs, we begin to see his world from a more exciting and beautiful perspective.

When I understood *'Bohemian Rhapsody'*, it was like I had been magically transported to Freddie's inner world and had an exceptional discussion with him. I was able to relate the song to everyday life; it had lost its mystical nature, yet I appreciated it more than ever, and now I don't just listen to the song, but I also hear Freddie's message in it.

Freddie wanted to keep his private life to be a secret from prying eyes, but he was the one who told everything about himself, in his songs, with his behaviour, and the interviews he gave.

Many authors have written the story of his tragically short life in some excellent books objectively, right down to the smallest detail, except for books by his friends and loved ones, who remember him with love and respect. It seems Freddie had an almost miraculous effect on his out-of-the-ordinary 'family' members, Jim, Joe and Peter. And this is understandable. For them, Freddie was like a rainbow. When Freddie shined, he was captivating, and when he left, their lives suddenly became dull and their souls frosty. Anything that happened seemed pointless, remote and worthless, as if Freddie had taken the meaning of their lives with him.

Most of his songs of Freddie are classic masterpieces, timeless and unique, both in instrumentation and lyrics, full of deep and rich content. His improvisation and singing technique are fantastic, and his voice is stunning. His original style and glistening, suggestive delivery can evoke heaven and hell, and make hearts beat faster. He can lift you and shake you up, make you laugh or bring tears to your eyes, giving unforgettable moments of joy.

He insisted he didn't write songs for specific people. Many of his lyrics are just mere fantasy, while others are for everyone, because they deal with universal subjects, such as love.

I graduated as a mental hygiene specialist (counsellor) from the University of Debrecen (Hungary) 20 years ago. Still, this fact alone wouldn't be anything like enough to take on the task of writing such an analysis. Even before university, I was interested in psychology, especially personal psychology, personality development and depth psychology. During my studies and after graduating from university, I read the major works of the greatest psychoanalysts. I learned the importance of symbols in mental processes mainly from the works of Carl Gustav Jung. I am a qualified expert in the psychological interpretation of drawings learned from the world-famous Hungarian professor, Dr Zoltán Vass.

Freddie and the other band members always said they didn't like interpreting their songs; everyone should understand them as they want to, and connect with them if they are willing or able to do so.

In this book, I'd like to share how I have interpreted the songs of Freddie.

If only I had known about Queen earlier, but sadly I was aware of them only superficially. However, when I heard that nobody had managed to interpret *'Bohemian Rhapsody'*, my curiosity got the better of me, and I wanted to know what the song was about. I was wondering whether it was really a meaningless malarkey.

At first, it was just a puzzle, but I was soon shocked to realise that suffering is another sentient behind this song. Then events began to move faster, as if a tornado had carried me along. I bought all the relevant books on the market and read them all. I listened to the songs, some for what seemed like a million times. I deciphered each piece in turn, in the order in which the albums arrived, and started writing this book even though that hadn't been my original intention.

For me, Freddie was born, grew up, became a musician, found success, fell ill and passed away in four months. It all happened so quickly. I felt as if I had just had a bad dream. Sometimes I laughed while reading the books and listening to Freddie, but I cried more than I laughed, and from now on, I think this is how it will be whenever I think of him or hear him. I'm always smiling through my tears when I listen to him sing. Freddie captivated me, just as he did so many other people in the world.

But even today, many people simply reject and condemn him – which he dreaded all his life – because they are unable or unwilling to accept the fact that he was bisexual, or in fact, gay. Homophobia persists today, especially among the older age group.

This attitude primarily comes from religions and the general condemnation of diversity and lawful discrimination that remains in some areas of the world.

HIV and AIDS also represented a terrible stigma for gay men in Freddie's life.

The Titanic sank, even though its architect thought it was unsinkable, but he was wrong. The ship lies in the depths of the Atlantic Ocean and can no longer be brought to the surface; she had to be left to her fate. For the sake of the film, director James Cameron went down to a depth of five kilometres to study the ship that had broken into two because he wanted to reflect the truth as far as possible. And he succeeded wonderfully.

I have learned from the story of the giant, magnificent ship that nobody should ever believe their ship is unsinkable. Freddie's story is similar to that of the Titanic.

Getting to know the real Freddie Mercury was a devastating, shocking and unforgettable experience for me, just as traumatic and unbelievable as the sinking of the Titanic. But there was one huge difference, the fate of the Titanic was in the hands of others, whereas it appears that Freddie drove his ship into the iceberg. The question is whether or not this is true, and if so, why? This book aims to answer this question.

In his song, *'The Golden Boy'*, Freddie, through Sir Tim Rice, clearly and understandably described how he saw himself at that time. The song is on Freddie's *Barcelona* album (1988).

'The boy had a way with words, he sang, he moved with grace
He entertained so naturally, no gesture out of place
His road in life was clearly drawn, he didn't hesitate
He played, they saw, he conquered as master of, as the master of his fate.'
......
'His rise was irresistible (yeah) – he grew into the part
His explanation simply that he suffered for his art
No base considerations of some glittering reward
The prize was knowing that his work was noticed and adored.'

Part One

A Kind of Magic

1. The Ultimate Showman

Freddie didn't like people discussing his private life. He especially hated the press because they twisted his words and harassed him with rude questions that usually had nothing to do with music, but instead with sensationalism. At the end of Freddie's life, the paparazzi overran the area around his house, blatantly sniffing around and stealthily following him to take pictures of him when he was ill and barely able to drag himself around.

During his lifetime, he and Queen were often crudely and unfairly criticized, put down and ridiculed in the press, but all to no avail, the public loved them and still do.

Brian May, the band's lead guitarist, said: *'We have never been fashionable. We were popular.' (YouTube: Days of Our Lives documentary)*

Brian thought the music press was upset that it wasn't their positive criticism that made them great. He was probably right, as we will see later.

Queen released 15 albums between 1973 and 1995, selling more than 150 million copies on the global market until 1991, and the growth in sales has by no means come to a standstill.

Freddie wanted to entertain because he loved the stage, adored performing and always appreciated the audience. He craved recognition and to be loved, and this was what he got, right from the start.

Fans worshipped his captivating performance style and the exciting, beautiful songs – and still do so today, even though he left us 30 years ago.

This world was magical to him; he was the sparkle, the scenery, the light and the sound on stage. He was transfigured, becoming a magician instead of just an ordinary man. He made us believe he was the centre of the world, and he was, as long as he was on stage, and this is probably how he felt. Crowds of hundreds of thousands filled the stadiums, sang along with him, clapped, waved their arms around, and screamed in rapture during the concerts.

He gave us his best, showing his authentic self, beautiful spirit, the free, happy, creative man who wanted to entertain with his art. He had become - the ultimate showman, and Queen had become the ultimate rock band. He was one of the biggest stars in the entertainment industry. His music and voice were so unique and inimitable, and his songs were so original as if he created a standalone genre.

This was what he thought about his stage presence:

*'It becomes an out-of-body experience for me up there. It's like I'm looking down on myself and thinking, "F*ck me…that's hot".'* (Lesley-Ann Jones)

He enjoyed this freedom, enjoyed the fact that he could dress as he liked, sparkle in sequined, very sexy clothes, put on the most striking stage costumes, and play all kinds of roles. He could be a serious or cheerful rocker, and at other times a singer in love. He could dominate the stage, rampage, fool around and most importantly for him, he could sing and make music. He could bathe in the unconditional love and devotion, which he craved in such a heartfelt fashion.

'I am really a simple man who is reserved and quiet. I'm not anything like how I appear on stage.' Freddie said about himself.

He was right – as Shakespeare said, 'all the world's stage', and all the men and women merely players, and we all play many parts throughout our lifetime.

Freddie's public roles were, singer, songwriter and musician, but there was also Freddie the private man. He was honest in his personal life; at times, he was gentle, full of love and desire, and at other times insulting and offensive. His emotions were intense and unbalanced; he went through a lot of pain and disappointment, and throughout his life, he just craved someone who would love him for who he was. At the end of his life, he found a faithful companion with whom he was finally happy. He deserved it and had suffered for it.

While on stage or in the studio, he worked obsessively, focusing and creating, which consumed all his energy.

He acted in the same way at concerts. Every minute was planned in detail. He knew which song was coming next, the moment when he would appear on stage, when he would change clothes, and so on. When the music began to play, the emotional artist replaced the rational man.

You can't sing and 'dance' with abandon while your attention is elsewhere; you can't fall out of character, and he never did.

If something disrupted the interaction between the band and the audience, the lighting broke down, or anything else wasn't right, he'd become annoyed and understandably frustrated and anxious. It was because he always aspired to perfection and never wanted to settle for second best, and nor did he have to settle for second, as he had a perfect dream: *'I am not going to be a star, I'm going to be a legend!'*

The perfect dream came true, and he did become a legend. Many people still haven't come to terms with his heartbreakingly premature death, although if he were still alive, he would be over 75. I think he would still be singing, just like Brian May or Roger Taylor.

His inspirational life's work put him at the top of the podium, and those of us who believed in him, who knows who Freddie Mercury was, will keep him at the top as long as our hearts are still beating. Freddie Mercury's name merged with Queen's name, and I'm convinced the band's members didn't meet by chance. Only legendary musicians, like *lead guitarist* and singer Brian May, drummer and singer Roger Taylor, and last but not least, bass guitarist John Deacon can achieve a legendary career.

2. When I Was a Lad

The smile that conquered the whole world

In his book, Mark Hodkinson quotes Freddie's old schoolmate, Derrick Branche:

'Whenever I think of Freddie at school, I always remember him smiling. He seemed to be perpetually smiling, and thinking of that makes me smile too.'

Farrokh Bulsara, who later became Freddie Mercury, was born on 5 September, 1946 in Stone Town Public Hospital on the larger Unguja Island of the exotically named Zanzibar.

(I'll call him Freddie, which is how we all know him, even though he got this name later.)

Freddie was photographed as a baby in a photography studio in Zanzibar that is still there. It's the same today as it was when the photo was taken of little Freddie. The father of the current photographer at this studio took the picture. Freddie was already a star back then, as the photograph won the *Baby of the Year* award. And with that beautiful, happy smile, it's no wonder. (You can find the photo on Pinterest.)

Zanzibar is now part of Tanzania, but at the time, it was a British colony. The long-awaited child was registered as an Indian British citizen on his birth certificate.

Freddie's father was Bomi Bulsara. His mother, Jer Bulsara, gave birth to him at the age of 18, on the day of the Parsi New Year. Bomi was very happy that he had a son who would carry on the Bulsara name. He was born in a small town called Bulsar, to the north of Bombay (Mumbai today) where he lived with his family. The family took its name from this town.

Bomi and Jer were followers of Zoroastrianism, an ancient Persian religion that dates back to 2000 BC. Followers of this faith are called Parsees in India, and many are descendants of ancient Persians.

The couple married for love and were happily looking forward to their blessed child, who they named Farrokh, which was a relatively common name, and fashionable among Persians.

Bomi could not find suitable employment in India, so he moved to Zanzibar – before their marriage - where he took a position as treasurer for the British Government, working at the Supreme Court in Stone Town. At that time there were regular shipping services between Zanzibar and Bombay. The distance between the terminals was 3000 miles.

Persians escaped to India in the 7th and 8th centuries AD due to brutal Islamic religious persecution. Even centuries later, they continue to live according to ancient traditions and practice their religion, which plays an essential role in their lives. Their main prophet is Zoroaster, and their holy book is called Avesta.

According to a Zoroastrian priest, this religion is about a celebration of life. The prophet Zoroaster taught the Persians to *'Seek your happiness in the happiness of all.'*

The Bulsara family belonged to the upper-middle class. Bomi Bulsara's income meant the family could afford to employ some staff, so Freddie also had a nanny, a black African woman called Sabine.

One of Freddie's uncles, on his father's side, had a house in Dar es Salaam (previously the capital of Tanzania), just metres from the Indian Ocean, which Freddie often enjoyed. Freddie's family lived in a two-storey house on the busy Shangani Street. The end of their street looked out onto the ocean. So Freddie spent a lot of time on the beach gazing into the distance, watching the boats go by.

If you're planning to visit the island, you'll find that the residents of Stone Town will be happy to show you where the Bulsara family lived. The building is a hotel now, however, the words *'Freddie Mercury's home'* appear above the main door in large letters. There are photos of Freddie in a showcase on both sides of the main entrance. The island has an agreeable climate, so back then, their lives, in relative terms, could be viewed as an idyllic paradise.

This was how Freddie remembered it: *'...in the morning I'd be woken by the servant. Clutching an orange juice. I'd literally step out onto the beach. In a way, I've been very fortunate, even in the early days.'* (Freddie Mercury)

His mother explained that Freddie started attending a missionary school on the island at five, where he was taught by nuns. The Parsees, and certainly Freddie's family, were happy to lead a British lifestyle, and his parents paid great attention to their son's intellectual development. His father was at home in the afternoons and spent a lot of time with the family. He told Freddie many stories, such as the Tales of the Arabian Nights, and others about legendary mythological heroes, which captured his childish imagination.

Freddie's love for music and his desire to perform were already apparent. He loved listening to records and singing; no matter what kind of music; folk, classical or Indian.

His parents often went to parties and took their son with them, where the young Freddie could hardly wait to perform and entertained everyone with songs. It gave him great pleasure and a sense of pride to bring joy to people through his performance.

Freddie loved looking after his younger sister, Kashmira, who was born in 1952. The two children were only able to spend a few years together before the family 'banished' Freddie, or at least, that was how Freddie saw it.

'They thought boarding school would do me good.' (Freddie Mercury).

Freddie had only just turned eight when his parents sent him to boarding school in February 1955 to get the best possible education at the time and to make sure their son had a predictable future.

The school was in Panchgani, India, where they followed traditional, strict disciplinary principles, with outstanding educational results.

St Peter's School was founded by the Church of England in 1902. Its motto was 'Ut Prosim', which can be translated as 'That I may serve', or in other words, if I do my best, I can get a traditional British education which will prepare me for university.

Freddie talked about these years later when he was an adult:

'Of course, there were feelings of being sent away from my parents and sister – feelings of loneliness, feelings of rejection – but you had to do what you were told... So the sensible thing was to make the most of it. One thing boarding school taught me was to fend for myself.' (Freddie Mercury)

Freddie spent eight years in this school. His parents couldn't visit, but during the summer break – though not every year – he travelled home for a month.

These eight years left their mark on Freddie's life. School years are crucial for every child, and the school did its job, making sure Freddie could make the most of his abilities. The school was well known for having genuine concern for children and tried to create a cheerful, family atmosphere. There was a time to study and time for having fun.

The initial integration must have been challenging for the young Freddie, who had been brought up in a protected environment, surrounded by care and attention at home.

He was no doubt homesick and worried about his little sister's well-being on arriving. He was anxious about the unknown and didn't know what to expect. He was very sad and lonely as he didn't have any real moral support in a completely alien environment, someone who could have helped him work through his everyday challenges. Freddie later paid a very high price for the high standard of education.

A school can't replace a family, which is the essential platform for socialisation, it can only be a supplement. Whereas school prepares children for social interaction, it is mainly the family that helps develop intimate relationships.

Freddie's family could not completely fulfil this role, even in the early years that he spent at home. As a result of their religious practices, physical contact, such as hugging, stroking or caressing, were not considered normal. His nanny looked after him continually, but it is not known what her emotional relationship with him was like.

Love should come pouring from the parents' warm words, looks, touches and hugs. The unconditional love of a mother and father assures the child that they deserve to be loved. With the parents' constant presence and emotional support, the child knows they can always rely on their parents and learns to trust people. There is no fear of being abandoned. The message from parental love is, 'I love you, and I'm there for you. You can trust me.' At the same time, parents should teach their children there are limits and expectations, which they gradually accept as they develop.

In her old age, Freddie's mother appeared in several videos talking with pride about Freddie; they loved him very much, which was why they sent him to a good school. However, they made that decision with a cool head; it seemed logical at the time, and they focused on what would become of Freddie when he grew up. Like some of his cousins, they would have liked him to have a professional career as a lawyer or an accountant.

No doubt it wasn't an easy decision, the separation and absence would also have been difficult for them, but they didn't consider that Freddie, who was a very sensitive child, would need the emotional security of a warm, loving home.

Consequently, Freddie was an emotionally neglected child, and that was why he turned out to be a shy, insecure and love-starved adult with low self-esteem.

In his pre-school years, his parents' constant presence and care and attention gave him a sense of security, but during his boarding school years, they were unable to properly take care of his emotional upbringing. I want to stress this wasn't because they didn't love Freddie, but they just were not able to show their emotions.

Good thoughts, good words and good deeds were the essential teachings of their religion. In contrast to Jesus' words, this does not include positive emotions, such as non-judgmental love.

Freddie was a sensible, intelligent child with a well-developed sense of fairness.

One day he wrote this letter to his parents:

'Panchgani, 15 March, 1962.

Dear Mom and Dad!

As I write this letter to you, I am so angry because a terrible injustice happened to me.

Let me tell you. We were all in the dormitory, Victory, Farang, Derrick and all the other boys. Suddenly Bruce started to hit me:

- Let's box, Bucky - he said. Although I said no, he just started.

Within just a few more moments against my will, a boxing match was going on, and I was in the middle of it.

The boys were all screaming and shouting and throwing pillows at us.

Because of the noise, Mr Davis suddenly entered the dormitory and stopped the fight.

Bruce lied and said I was the one who started the fight, and he was just defending himself. All the boys backed him up. So Mr Davis, the principal, decided I had to be punished and what a terrible punishment they did to me. I had to go to the barbershop and have my hair cut very short. I hated Bruce for that.

You know how much I love my hair, it will never be the same again. I am so sad and angry.

Farrokh'

Freddie wrote this letter in distress. He was 15 at the time and still felt the need to turn to someone about being wronged. We can only imagine how he felt about similar ordeals when he was younger.

Another of Freddie's letters radiates concern, courtesy and respect, partly attributed to his school upbringing and partly to parental influence.

Children who grow up with a lack of affection believe their feelings don't matter, as nobody pays attention to them. Children's main confidantes when they are young are their mother and father. Later, adolescents turn away from their parents and open up to their contemporaries and the world. Freddie was at a disadvantage from the start; it must have seemed to him that he wasn't important to anyone, and so his self-esteem and emotional life were on shaky ground. He must have felt lonely and abandoned. In any case, adolescence is one of the most critical periods in a child's life, which is why Freddie would have needed the continual emotional support of his parents more than ever, and no doubt he missed this.

Emotional neglect in childhood - in this case, physical absence - leads to emotional immaturity, which causes excessive emotional intensity, excessive love, aggression, inability to delay satisfaction and shyness in adulthood. The feeling that 'I'm not good enough' causes a tendency to overcompensate and a desire to stand out. Emotions in children who grow up in this way are generally extreme, and they don't know the golden-mean. These personality traits stayed with Freddie until the end of his life and often made his life hell. The instability of his emotional life and his talent brought him to the stage, where he could forget about himself, where he could step into a beautiful dream world that he had constructed, where he was the star, where he deserved and received everybody's attention and admiration. But the admiration of fans was not enough; it didn't fill the void caused by loneliness.

Concerts and recordings made him happy and satisfied, though only as long as he was on stage or in the studio, but except for a few periods, his private life wasn't dream-like.

Freddie himself thought the lack of affection he experienced in his childhood might have caused the excessive need for the love he felt in adulthood. The desperate sense of lack led to trivial, transient sexual relationships, which did not bring emotional satisfaction, but even more misery and even more desire for physical contact.

Freddie behaved very respectfully towards his parents and cared about them throughout his life, but secretly resented them for leaving him to his fate.

In his song, *'My Fairy King'* on Queen's first album, Freddie sang about his most severe childhood trauma. I will soon be interpreting the lyrics.

The school fulfilled its role. Freddie was taught that demands would be made on him during his life, which he would have to comply with; he would have to take responsibility, share things with others, and cooperate with his partners. School also enhanced his self-confidence to a certain extent.

His performance was recognised and praised; he was awarded a prize for his outstanding sporting achievements, which gave him great pleasure and pride.

Years later, Freddie's friend, David Evans, wrote as follows about Freddie's school years:

'At St. Peter's, Freddie had the benefit of caring teachers, specifically Mr David and Mr Rowe, his housemaster, the sort of teachers that hopefully, we have all had at one time or the other, who introduced him to the joys of Shakespeare, recordings read by English actors such as Olivier and of classical music, neither of which would have been likely to come his way in Zanzibar because he continued to learn to play, mostly self-taught, at St Peter's.

However, most subjects on the curriculum eluded him. His maths was always decidedly dodgy. In later life, when paying restaurant bills, he would always get someone else to check the total. As far as other lessons, the journeying of his own life was the only geography lesson he needed, history touched him only insofar as he always thought of himself as British and English language and literature came naturally insofar as he ever read a book.

Interestingly, he had the attention span of a hummingbird. He had the hardest time concentrating on anything which didn't interest him immediately. Anything that wasn't to do with his own creativity, he had little interest in, and he must have exasperated his teachers who would have seen this behaviour in such an able and intelligent pupil as almost wilful. Like a butterfly, he couldn't wait to be off to the next source of nectar.'

The above description is indicative of attention-deficit hyperactivity disorder (ADHD).

Hyperactivity can be attributed to several causes. In Freddie's case, both a poorly functioning family and high stress (separation from parents, alien environment, increased requirements and strictness) were potential factors.

Based on his friend's description, Freddie's adult behavioural problems, temper tantrums, impulsiveness, outbursts of anger, and underperforming in educational terms - compared to his abilities - are understandable.

In light of the above, we can appreciate Freddie's extraordinary efforts to acquire friends and integrate, all the more, because the vast majority of children with ADHD are incapable of doing so, and are therefore rejected by other kids.

Freddie was popular with his classmates at all the schools he attended because he was kind, attentive, generous and gentle. These attributes helped him to integrate, despite his problems, and he was always capable of making people love him to such an extent that not many could resist his attractive personality.

Freddie wrote the following letter to his parents at the age of 11 about winning the annual school sports trophy:

'Dear Mum and Dad, I hope you are all well, and Kashmira's cold is better. Don't worry, I am fine. Me and my friends at the Ashleigh House are like a second family. The teachers are very strict, and discipline is most important here at St. Peter's. I am very happy to tell you that I was awarded the big trophy, Best All Rounder Junior. I received a big trophy, and they even took a photograph which will appear in the annual school magazine. I'm very proud, and I hope you are too. Send my love to Kash. I love my little sister as I love you all. Farrokh.'

(Matt Richards and Mark Langthorne)

So he was able to find some good friends who he regarded as his second family.

Freddie was a talented, aspiring child, and his character developed positively. He was outstanding in all sports, but excelled at boxing and table tennis, and was unbeatable in both. Sport gave him self-discipline, perseverance, fighting ability and the intoxicating pleasure of victory. These experiences of success proved to him that he could achieve anything he really wanted.

On one occasion in the ring, he had blood all over his face, and pouring from his mouth, and his friend in the corner urged him to give up. However, a steely light flashed in Freddie's eyes, and he fought on with even greater determination. He never gave up and won every bout by knockout. Even back then, he was a stubborn and persistent individual with an ability to fight. He literally had to fight for success and defend himself from violent attacks.

Fortunately, his aunts on both his Mum's and Dad's side lived in Bombay, so Freddie was able to spend holidays with them in those years when he couldn't make it home. His maternal aunt noticed his musical talent and persuaded his mother to pay for private piano lessons at school. His teacher was an elderly Irishman who liked Freddie very much. At first, Freddie just practised from a sense of duty, but later the piano became his inseparable partner.

During adolescence, he and his friends spent an increasing amount of time listening to the radio, enjoying rock and pop music. Freddie's favourites were Little Richard, Fats Domino, Cliff Richard and Elvis Presley. He could play any song flawlessly on the piano on first listening, and even began improvising with them.

Although he studied music theory, he never learned to read sheet music, and nor did he need to.

At the initiative of one of his friends, they formed a band called The Hectics. Their musical style meant they soon became very popular both at school and in the city.

Freddie modestly stayed in the background behind the piano, sang backing vocals, and also sang in the choir.

The Hectics were considered stars at every school event, so Freddie received further confirmation of his musical talent.

Some of his old schoolmates say there were times when he was teased about his protruding front teeth. He was given an associated nickname, which indicates that the teasing was probably regular rather than occasional.

Although he wore a brace, which resulted in constant pain, the fault couldn't be corrected. He had four extra incisors, which were probably the cause.

Freddie's protruding teeth always bothered him, and he tried to cover them with his hand, often drawing in his bottom lip and tightly closing his mouth.

His schoolmates also reported that he began to scream indiscriminately when he felt rejected, indicating that he had difficulty controlling his emotions.

Freddie's close friends from school also provided further valuable information concerning his character. One of them believed there was some kind of charm in Freddie's shyness. Despite his timidity, he participated very actively in events at school and with friends; he tried his best to be accepted and to integrate to alleviate his loneliness. He was happy to learn, but was only interested in his favourite subjects, music and the arts.

According to another friend's statement, his first impression was that Freddie seemed pretty shy, but he liked him because he was sensitive and caring. He could tell Freddie had a different cultural background; he was well-mannered, intelligent and highly respectful, continually aspired to be better and to do more, and wanted to conform to expectations.

Since he had grown up in a different culture than his schoolmates, he was unaware of Indian norms. This might have made him clumsy and awkward, which was enhanced by his shyness and lack of self-confidence, not to mention that adolescents are often clumsy and awkward, even under normal circumstances.

His close friends started to call him Freddie because they found it difficult to pronounce Farrokh. Freddie was pleased about his new name, because he was attracted to Western culture.

He also acted in school plays and got very nervous before the shows. The nerves before each performance were a sign that he took his performances seriously and gave everything he had to perform well. He was good at acting and happy to play female characters. He usually enjoyed performing and the attention he received.

Regarding his homosexuality, many of his contemporaries thought it was obvious he was gay, whereas others disagreed.

In Freddie's words:

'All the things they say about boarding schools are more or less true, about all the bullying and everything else. I had the odd schoolmaster chasing me, but it didn't shock me because somehow, at boarding school, you're not confronted by it, you are just slowly aware of it. There were times when I was young and naive. I had a crush on a Master and would have done anything for him. It's a thing that schoolboys go through, and I had my share of schoolboy pranks, but I'm not going to elaborate any further!' (Freddie Mercury)

He also said he was looked on as gay at school. He was the pretty boy everyone wanted to go to bed with.

This statement implies that, in that environment, it was not unusual to go to bed with pretty boys.

Freddie's art teacher's daughter recalls that he spontaneously started calling his male friends 'darling' one day. Freddie didn't find this strange at all, but the adults were shocked because, at the time, it was unusual for a boy to openly call a girl darling, let alone another boy. Evidently, he must have learned this from someone else who had called him or somebody else by this term. So, it is highly unlikely that it just happened spontaneously. Children generally imitate adults and older children they like, seeing them as role models and wanting to resemble them.

Early adolescence is accompanied by an identity crisis; children are searching for their place in the world, and want to learn how to integrate and start to explore themselves. In that environment, childhood sexual games were only possible among boys, and it could have defined his sexual orientation, especially if he had been abused.

We can be sure of one thing: sexual orientation is not a disease, and neither is it an imperfection or mental disorder. At this point, there is no scientific evidence that specific genes are responsible for a person's sexual orientation.

In their book, Matt Richards and Mark Langthorne cite a quotation from the article *Boarding school: The trauma of the 'Privileged child'* by Joy Schaverien (Journal of Analytical Psychology, 49, 2004, pp 683-705):

'Naturally, a boarding school environment can sometimes be associated with bullying and sexual abuse, and such actions can often shape the individual in their adult life. Jungian analyst, psychotherapist and supervisor Joy Schaverien PhD suggests that the psychological damage suffered particularly by boys at boarding school, primarily as a result of loss when the family is replaced by many same-sex strangers, can have a dramatic effect on sexual development too. She writes: 'Warmth may be sought with the available other, as a new form of sibling group emerges. Sexual experiments may offer solace but may also lead to abuse. This may lead to confusion in the development of sexual identity, and some boys become uncertain of their primary sexual orientation. Whilst initiating the child into the pleasures of homosexuality, the institution proclaims its dangers. This may set a person on a path of covert homosexuality or of proclaimed heterosexuality and emphatic disavowal of homosexuality.'

'My Fairy King'

Freddie sings heartbreakingly in *'My Fairy King'* about a trauma he suffered at school.

In the first two verses, Freddie describes what the world was like before he went to school:

'Aah, aah
In the land where horses born with eagle wings
And honey bees have lost their stings
There's singing forever, ooh yeah
Lion's den with fallow deer
And rivers made from wine so clear
Flow on and on forever
Dragons fly like sparrows thru' the air
And baby lambs where Samson dares
To go on on on on on on

My fairy king can see things
He rules the air and turns the tides
That are not there for you and me
Ooh yeah he guides the winds
My fairy king can do right and nothing wrong'

The young Freddie built a dream world for himself, where anything could happen. However, there was an unexpected, radical twist when everything was suddenly destroyed one 'night':

'Ah, then came man to savage in the night
To run like thieves and to kill like knives
To take away the power from the magic hand
To bring about the ruin to the promised land, aah, aah
They turn the milk into sour
Like the blue in the blood of my veins
Why can't you see it
Fire burning in hell with the cry of screaming pain
Son of heaven set me free and let me go

*Sea turns dry, no salt from sand
Seasons fly no helping hand
Teeth don't shine like pearls for poor man's eyes, aah*

*Someone, someone has drained the colour from my wings
Broken my fairy circle ring
And shamed the king in all his pride
Changed the winds and wronged the tides
Oh, Mother Mercury
Look what they've done to me*

*I cannot run, I cannot hide
La la la la la la la la la la la la'*

These lyrics are among the most beautiful and painful symbolic descriptions ever written of how an innocent, daydreaming child, who believed in fairies and trusted in goodness, was shaken out of his childhood world, and how dramatically he felt this drastic change. A cruel person, or persons, suddenly came on the scene and didn't shrink from killing to take power away from Freddie – the Fairy King. Suddenly, everything was destroyed, ruining the promised land.

Freddie needed strength to feel safe and to believe he could defend himself. As a child, he imagined he could do anything with the help of his fairy ring. He was strong and could control anyone and anything; he was the king among the fairies.

The promised land symbolizes Freddie's trust, founded on the faith he had in his parents, and reinforced by a safe home and school environment in Stone Town.

The phrase, *'Fire burning in hell with the cry of screaming pain'* is about a severe trauma that had afflicted him, as indicated by the words *'someone, someone has drained the colour from my wings.'* In this song, the colour of his wings symbolizes a beautiful childhood world, which had suddenly disappeared, and the world became colourless. He had endured the torments of hell, and would have screamed and shouted in pain, but gripped with fear, he doesn't even dare to shout.

Sexual abuse cannot be ruled out completely, but his school behaviour later contradicts this possibility. He was shy, but not overly so. He could mix in the company of others, and was happy to play the piano, participate in sports, and integrate with his peers; he reported on how satisfied he was in the letter to his parents.

If someone had beaten him up, he would undoubtedly have complained about it. He wouldn't have been ashamed to tell his parents; he had done so previously on other matters, for example, when he wrote to his parents telling them about being forced to have his hair cut.

In any case, there was no apparent reason for anyone to beat up an innocent, good-natured child.

In the song, he turns to the Son of Heaven for help in setting him free and letting him go. Everything has fallen apart, even the sea has run dry (his favourite childhood place disappears), and as time goes by, nobody offers him a helping hand.

It's not enough that the dreamworld that he'd built up had been destroyed, but even the proud king had been shamed. This pain was so deep he needed to complain to his mother; at least he could do this in this song.

Freddie sang the part in a child's voice, describing his childhood dreams. His voice is distorted as the dreamworld becomes twisted and gets tougher when the 'attack' occurs. Then after the 'attack', the sound of his broken heart is childish again, frightfully soft and distressing.

The song's lyrics, and music change in tone, and overlapping voices generate a sense of confusion, sadness and dramatic unrest. Freddie sings at a rapid tempo, almost hurriedly, as if he wants to get it over with as soon as possible, and as if he is compelled to tell the story, but slows down when singing about the consequences, starting from, *'Someone, someone has drained the colour from my wings.'* The slowdown signals that you should listen here; this is the essential part of the story, so pay attention! Roger's astonishing scream at the start of the song indicates that they will be presenting some kind of unusual, strange and shocking story.

The musical composition is ingenious. Roger's introductory scream is breathtaking. Simultaneously, the powerful drums make the heart beat faster, you can only finally draw breath at the start of the section accompanied by the piano, but the brain wants to know what happens after the attack. In the end, the heart is broken, and tears are flowing. Simultaneously, in the final quarter, where the singing has stopped, we can only hear the music at an ever-faster tempo, the sound of the piano, guitar and drum in harmony, yet, creating a maddening tension; only the last few notes allow us to relax, signalling the end of the song when the pressure finally comes to an end.

The lyrics and musical background are in perfect harmony. The degree to which the arrangement has been worked on indicates that the story played a vital role in Freddie's life, as did *'Bohemian Rhapsody'*, which he wrote two years later.

The lyrics of this song constitute one of the finest verses in world literature. He describes a child's world so beautifully and the tragic event so terribly that it would break anyone's heart. This little boy felt he had lost his magic power, and no longer knew what was right and wrong, and didn't even have his mum close by to offer him some comfort, or complain to about his anguish.

'Someone, someone has drained the colours from my wings.' Freddie sings this part in such a painfully beautiful way that anyone who knows what the song is about will reach for their heart. The vocals are beautiful; it sounds like an innocent angel is singing in church.

This song convinced me that Freddie suffered unspeakably and still found the strength to keep going without any compromise, to please his parents and somehow survive this period. He was forced to tolerate this mental torment until he got tougher and grew armour plating, but until the day he died, the wounds never healed. He had no option but to deal with it in this way because he could not run away or hide from the expectations placed upon him, or from the sharp, intimidating gaze of his strict, authoritarian teachers. So it's hardly surprising that Freddie didn't want to remember his childhood years, even if he was more relaxed later. On the other hand, he likely considered the possibility that his parents had 'betrayed' him and exposed him to the torments of hell, which would have filled him with sadness again and again. He couldn't change the past, so he believed it was better not to think about it, but the fact that he revealed it in the song means the trauma was raw and impacted his everyday life.

But in the end, if he wasn't a victim of sexual abuse, what kind of trauma could have afflicted Freddie, resulting in him enduring agony? One of the phrases in the song is, 'Seasons fly no helping hand', which made me realize what could have happened. If seasons went by without help, it probably meant this song is about the time in school when Freddie realised there was no way back to his family. He was unprotected from ridicule and completely alone with his fears, which would have made him even more homesick. The first few years must have been a shocking ordeal for him.

For a young child, the anxiety of trying to cope with separation leads to lifelong trauma; the fact that Freddie was so afraid of being alone as an adult is no coincidence. It's reasonable to assume he went through this mental torment quite often. His irrational fear of being alone and the panic attacks he experienced as an adult would suggest this was the case.

He must have felt that he had lost his parents, and what worse trauma could there be for an eight-year-old child, to whom nobody offered a helping hand or any comfort? He was dropped into a completely alien world, where he couldn't trust anyone because everyone was strange to him.

'That background (the boarding school) helped me a lot because it taught me to fend for myself from a very early age and to be responsible. It was an upheaval of an upbringing, which seems to have worked, I guess.' (Freddie Mercury)

In the above statement, Freddie looked back on his school years very rationally, in adult fashion, thinking it was beneficial for him to believe he could only ever rely on himself. This proved to be a huge disadvantage when he didn't heed friendly warnings, and instead exposed himself to the risk of bars in the night-time.

The word upheaval means a violent and sudden change or disruption to something. So, as an adult, this was how he evaluated this change to his life. A violent and sudden change was what he was dealing with in the song, and a sense of rejection, which also made him afraid. As a sensitive child, this is entirely understandable.

Freddie seriously hated anyone staring at him or a stranger speaking to him; throughout his life, he remained shy in the company of strangers.

Freddie addresses his mother in this song and would now like her to ask, 'Tell me, son, what happened to you?' It would have been an excellent opportunity for them to get closer to each other, but this was impossible because Freddie no longer trusted her, or hardly anyone else. However, this appeal to her reveals that he still resented her, and how vital genuine maternal care and love would have been to him. How important it would have been back then for his mother to say she wouldn't allow her son to go to boarding school, and that he needed his family more than an elite education. This is what she should have done. She cried when they left Freddie in India, knowing deep in her soul that they were exposing him to torment. The other Indian children at Freddie's new school, who had been less pampered at home, may have responded less sensitively to the change of environment. Their homes and families were not 3000 miles away, so they probably suffered less than Freddie.

3. Back to Zanzibar

Freddie left school at the age of 16 in February 1963, without a school-leaving certificate because he had failed, despite achieving good results in his studies the previous year.

After Freddie's death, one of his teachers said in an interview in 2008. (Hindustan Times) that 'one of his homosexual relationships had been discovered, with drastic consequences'. (Mark Blake)

According to David Evans – Freddie's close friend - Freddie was already aware he was attracted to men at the time.

I assume that the above story was true. Otherwise, his parents couldn't have known that Freddie had been involved in a relationship with a male, which they considered unacceptable because their religion strictly condemned homosexuality, as did Christianity.

Later on, the parents only mentioned homosexuality to Freddie as 'other business'.

His parents were incapable of handling this matter properly, which caused Freddie to withdraw. He craved acceptance, but probably received rigid rejection and a lack of understanding instead, as his parents were very strict. This added to the emotional distance between Freddie and his parents, making him even more lonely, reserved and shy. He must have felt ashamed and rejected by his family. And yet, he still adhered to the family traditions and behaved respectfully and affectionately.

His positive attitude was due to his love for his family, but his strict upbringing and high expectations could have played their role in this too.

However, after what had happened, he probably thought he had to be even better to meet his parents' expectations. His desire to conform came from his natural desire to be loved, and his upbringing probably made him believe that homosexuality was a sin. After leaving school and re-entering the big wide world again, he couldn't see any gay couples on the streets or elsewhere, which must have made him wonder.

A farewell letter to one of his friends convinced me that Freddie's intellect was already outstanding and mature for his age. The letter read: *'Modern paintings are like women, you can't enjoy them if you try to understand them.'*

I should point out that I don't think Freddie coined this phrase; he probably heard it from someone, an older, mature-minded artist, for example, but it does reveal a few things about him.

He knew very little about women, and was only close to very few of them; he hadn't had a sexual relationship with a girl, and yet his opinion was that they couldn't be understood. The phrase is surreal and somewhat cynical. I think he was aware of that too. In any case, the phrase is witty.

However, there was a huge gulf between Freddie's intellectual and emotional maturity.

4. Moving to London

I'm going to die at the age of 45

In December 1963, following the elections held earlier that year, Zanzibar gained independence from Britain. However, a disputed election and a failed harvest caused significant unrest. In 1964 the new Arab Sultan was stripped of the throne in a violent political coup, and the leader of the black African party was elected president in his place. This resulted in significant political tension and general chaos.

Several thousand were killed during the bloody uprising, and thousands of intimidated civilians escaped from the island.

During this period, Freddie was having his regular walk on the street with his friend when his friend unexpectedly asked him about death, 'What do you think, how long are you going to live?'

Freddie replied, 'For some reason, the number 45 comes to mind.'

It was not a coincidence that Freddie passed away at the age of 45. Although there is never just one cause of an incident, it does sound like a self-fulfilling prophecy.

Self-fulfilling prophecies usually come true through hypnosis or self-hypnosis. Contrary to popular belief, a hypnotic state is not an unusual experience, but a completely natural condition that we often experience without being aware of it. Freddie was probably startled by the unexpected question. The word 'death' itself induces fear in us, and would have done so for the young Freddie due to his close proximity to the violent uprising and subsequent massacres.

When we experience fear or panic, our emotional state allows words to enter our subconscious, and they start to function as direct hypnotic commands. If we are asked something that doesn't have an obvious answer, we turn 'inwards' for a brief period, focusing our attention intently on the question. This 'faraway' condition is also a kind of hypnotic state.

Hypnosis can be traced back several thousand years to the Lama monasteries in Tibet and the Aryan Hindus, and constitutes the study of the art of suggestion and telepathy. Today, this therapy is also recognised in Western medical science. It is employed along with positive suggestions to treat various diseases, however, negative emotions and thoughts that create fear can destroy us just as effectively, triggering illnesses, accidents and discomfort.

Let me quote a modern hypnotist:

'Can someone get accidentally hypnotized?

Yes, It happens to people on a daily basis.

Hypnosis is simply being in a state of trance. Something we all go through.

Ever driven a long journey, arrived safely at your destination, and realised you don't remember driving part of it? You were in trance.

Ever been reading a good book and got so engrossed you forgot where you were or lost track of time or were oblivious to someone entering the room until they spoke? You were in trance.

Many years ago I knew of a neighbour who accidentally put themselves into a trance when they were sitting listening to a record and they were watching the record going round and round and round and... they went into trance.

So yeah, everyone can, and does, go into trance and thus hypnosis accidentally, and a lot more frequently than one might at first imagine!'
(Keith Blakemore-Noble, Master hypnotist & trainer)

It was no coincidence that the number 45 came to Freddie's mind. In truth, whatever happens in our lives is always a consequence of our conscious or subconscious thoughts, attitudes or words. We are affected by many things during our lives, which find their way into our subconscious without us realising it. Childhood experiences are especially defined from this perspective, because children are more receptive to external stimuli.

Naturally, proving the above is impossible, however, the possibility cannot be dismissed because its effect later appeared in Freddie's behaviour, and I will deal with this when the opportunity arises, but for the time being, let's stay on the subject of the fate of Freddie's family.

The insurgents made a serious threat to his father's life, saying they would cut his head off if they didn't leave the island. The family would have been frightened by this.

Presumably, the sin was that Bomi had worked for the British, and the family had an above-average lifestyle, compared to local families who made a living from manual work.

As the violence in Zanzibar escalated, the Bulsara family was forced to leave in March 1964; they escaped to Britain, carrying only a few suitcases, and settled in Feltham, near Heathrow Airport, to the west of London.

It was quite a big ordeal for the family to adapt to the modest circumstances, the bleak environment and the unusual cold. (Freddie enjoyed sitting around in his own home, wrapped in blankets while watching television.) Later, he would refuse to talk about Zanzibar, his birthplace, and once told a confidante that it was a filthy place.

Freddie's parents, Bomi and Jer, found work in London, and so the family's livelihood was assured, though modestly.

Freddie was on a high; he was pleased his family had moved to Britain and tried to keep their spirits up. He kept saying that they had moved to the best possible place.

As he had been unable to finish his studies in Zanzibar due to the uprising, Freddie had to study for another two years to complete secondary school. To enrol for the art college that he aspired to, he first had to complete two years' preparatory training at Isleworth Polytechnic. He was already 18 when he enrolled here.

His friends here considered him slightly awkward and shy, but liked him because he was sensitive, kind and friendly, and blessed with good humour.

During breaks, he played the piano for his classmates and was happy to play their favourite songs, creating a bond between them.

One of his schoolmates said that it wasn't necessary to be an excellent student in this school; it was enough for someone to show interest in the subjects. Freddie was only interested in music and was happy to act in plays.

One of his classmates mentioned in an interview that when Freddie appeared in a play called *The Kitchen*, he was somewhat nervous and uncertain before the performance, but acted surprisingly well on the school's stage and enjoyed the attention he attracted. (*The Kitchen* was a BBC TV series.)

Freddie's parents objected to him going out in the evenings, not just because they were worried about him, but they would have liked him to continue his studies and to obtain a university degree. Freddie felt he wasn't clever enough, or at least, that's what he told his parents.

Freddie kept telling his parents he would be a musician, but they hoped it was just a daydream, which he would grow out of, and they never encouraged him.

Although his parents didn't like it, he continually went out socializing in the evenings, even at the expense of an argument or being told off by his parents. Freddie hadn't yet started working, and he couldn't move out of their home, but his inner turmoil increased because he wanted to learn as much as possible about the British way of life, especially the music scene.

He took a job during school holidays to earn some pocket money. His colleagues ridiculed him because he wasn't a typical worker: his hands were delicate and well-groomed. He stopped people from mocking him by telling them he would be a musician and only worked out of necessity.

In Zanzibar, it took weeks or months for a magazine to arrive, but everything in London was close and easily accessible, and Freddie only needed a bit of money and independence to start living his own life.

Isleworth Polytechnic taught a range of subjects, including music, drama, films and fashion. During these two years, he had the opportunity to listen to live performances by emerging young musicians, such as The Rolling Stones and guitarist, Jeff Beck, who Freddie liked.

He liked going out and enjoying himself with his friends on Saturday evenings but went home sober and on time because he wanted to conform to his parents' wishes. He also enjoyed playing the piano at home.

One of his friends remembered Freddie as someone who absorbed new experiences like a sponge, including films and exhibitions. He enjoyed this new cultural climate, which he aspired to become part of, yet he didn't like receiving attention at this time. He didn't want to be in the spotlight.

According to one of his friends, after finishing his studies, he decided to form a band, and interviewed around 40 aspiring band members. His friend didn't know any more details about the result of the interviews.

By the time Freddie obtained the desired qualifications, he could breathe easily because he had come one step closer to a career that he yearned for.

After finishing polytechnic, he was finally able to enrol and continue his studies at Ealing Technical College and School of Art, where it was quite difficult to gain admission at the time. Freddie knew that many musicians had come out of this school, so he wasn't interested in any other school. Pete Townshend, the multiple award-winning British rock guitarist, singer, songwriter, composer and author also studied there. He was guitarist and main songwriter for the popular band The Who in the 1960s.

Freddie's sister, Kashmira, talked about his appearance at that time as follows:

'Freddie was very fastidious about his appearance. Whereas he looked neat and tidy, and his hair swept back, everyone else wore their hair long and looked scruffy. I used to walk behind him because I didn't want people to think I was with him.

But he changed his appearance very quickly…. He always used to take hours in front of the mirror looking after his locks.' (Lesley-Ann Jones)

Freddie was always very vain. Regardless of how different people saw him, he began to identify with the pop star he wanted to become. He was already consciously preparing for the role, but for the time being was searching for his style and for what would make him attractive, unique and captivating.

After he had seen Jimi Hendrix for the first time, he tried to imitate him in every way. He wore a bright, flowery jacket over black or multi-coloured shirts, tight, colourful drainpipe trousers with Chelsea boots, and a chiffon scarf tied to his Adam's apple, with large silver rings on his fingers as accessories.

'Art school teaches you to be more fashion-conscious…Always that one step ahead.' (Freddie Mercury)

His college friends liked him as well; they saw him as a guy with a good sense of humour, kind, friendly, polite, attentive and well-mannered.

They thought it was funny when, during breaks, he sat on a bench singing with Tim Staffell, who later went on to be the singer in the band Smile.

Tim Staffell remembered Freddie as follows:

'I guess if I hadn't stepped aside, the world might have been a very different place.'

(YouTube: Freddie Mercury – The Untold Story, a film by Rudi Dolezal and Hannes Rossacher – (DoRo Production)

I'm sure this statement made him very popular with Freddie's fans, and deservedly so. It's not as if he wasn't a good singer, but just that Freddie turned out to be far better than anyone else.

He and Freddie were great friends in school, they sang vocals together, even in the men's toilets, and later Freddie accompanied him to wherever Smile was performing.

Freddie remembered the period when he finished college as follows:

'When I had finished with the illustrating course, I was sick of it. I'd had it up to here. I thought, I don't think I can make a career of this, because my mind just wasn't on that kind of thing. So I thought I would just play around with the music side of it for a while. Everybody wants to be a star, so I just thought that if I could make a go of it, why not?' (Freddie Mercury)

He studied first fashion design, but later on switched to graphic design and illustration at art college, but was only interested in music. Even though he was very talented at drawing, he preferred to seize every opportunity to listen to live performances of the best musicians.

He often drew portraits of his classmates or his favourite people at college. A few of his drawings appear in the film *Freddie Mercury: The Untold Story,* mentioned earlier. Most of them were very good, but the best ones depicted Jimi Hendrix.

I am sure that he took great care with this drawing, as Jimi was his role model. His visual talent helped him significantly to design stage sets and costumes during his career.

John Taylor was one of his best friends in college, and later became the bass guitarist in a band called Ibex, in which Freddie sang for the first time. John said in an interview that Freddie was an excellent artist. He drew a lot of brilliant pictures of Hendrix and other pop musicians.

Brian May, who was later to become Queen's guitarist, already knew Freddie at the time, and this was his view:

'He behaved like a star, he was always dressed immaculately, rather outrageously, sort of being a local character. His core was very shy but using these devices, he cloaked this persona as being rather larger than life, and everyone treated him as a star. He wasn't the leader of the gang, and his nature was very kind and gentle.

...Because everyone wanted to be a musician, they didn't take too seriously Freddie's ambitions. In the beginning, I didn't realize how serious he was. He was a rather flamboyant character. He was obviously a very good artist, but I thought music was a hobby for him, and he would become an artist.' (YouTube: Freddie Mercury: The Untold Story – DoRo Production)

I should add that Brian May and Roger Taylor knew Freddie, but they hadn't heard him sing. Roger and Freddie were also good friends.

(It was on 31 July, 1969, when Freddie first met Brian and Roger in Kensington Pub.)

Freddie first heard Eric Clapton and Jimi Hendrix in December 1966. Hendrix's virtuoso guitar playing, laid-back, utterly original style and energy impressed the audience. Freddie was so taken by Hendrix that he would have gone anywhere to see his favourite musician.

'Jimi Hendrix was just a beautiful man, a master showman and a dedicated musician.'

'I would scour the country to see him whenever he played because he really had everything any rock'n'roll star should have: all the style and the presence. He didn't have to force anything. He'd just make an entrance, and the whole place would be on fire. He was living out everything I wanted to be.' (Freddie Mercury)

Freddie needed inspiration. Jimi Hendrix could play the guitar with his teeth, and even when holding it the wrong way round. Freddie was taken by his mastery of the instrument and the fact that he had perfected his art. Given that Freddie was also a perfectionist, he dreamed of being like Jimi Hendrix, perfect and inimitable.

'So captivated was he by Hendrix that Freddie went to see him perform 14 times, including nine nights in a row at pubs all around London.' (Matt Richards & Mark Langthorne)

I have watched videos of Jimi Hendrix's live performances. In my opinion, Freddie learned three essential things from him: firstly, be original and be yourself, don't try to imitate anyone, either with your performance style or dress sense. Secondly, be the best at what you do, and thirdly, if you're a star, you control the stage. The spotlight is on you.

Jimi played with the guitar, as Freddie did later with the piano and his voice. Freddie's clothes on stage couldn't be compared to anyone else's. His movements were never choreographed. Freddie was original and never content to settle for second best; he aspired to be the best possible in his field. He demanded absolute attention and wanted to be first at everything.

I've had a close look at Freddie's other favourite performer. I scrutinised Elvis Presley to see if Freddie took anything from him. I found some recordings of a Las Vegas concert in 1970. Elvis was singing the final number. It was a real struggle; hardly any sound was coming out of his mouth, but he pulled himself together and sang the song, as expected. He was continually improvising. He was 42 at the time. His clothes were pure white, embellished with silver, the upper part of his chest was open, and a hand-sized section of his bare torso was visible. His movements were theatrical, similar to Freddie's later, when he beckoned the band like a conductor in the final bars, signalling the end of the song with perfect timing, and then spinning around, getting down on one knee and finally taking a bow. The curtain dropped, and the crowd applauded. Elvis crouched down behind the curtain, lifted it and peeked out underneath.

(YouTube: Elvis Presley – Can't Help Falling In Love, Live in Las Vegas 1970.)

In another performance in 1968, Elvis was singing, dressed from head to toe in black, shiny, tight-fitting, leather clothes. Part of his hairy chest was visible. Sometimes getting the lyrics wrong, clowning around, laughing, and the audience laughed with him, enjoying the playfulness; they were utterly mesmerised by the slim, handsome man in good shape and dressed in black. He was 40 years old at the time of this recording.

(YouTube: Elvis Presley – Love Me Tender ('68 Comeback Special 50th Anniversary HD Remaster)

There is no sign of Elvis Presley's influence in Freddie's songs, except in Crazy Little Thing Called Love, a rock'n'roll track. Freddie said he never tried to imitate Elvis. His performance was theatrical from the very beginning, and his bowing was ceremonious, just like Elvis's, but his performance and songs were absolutely different in style.

In any case, Freddie was often dressed entirely in black or white, tight-fitting clothes and leather trousers. However, as we will see later, he had a reason for doing this, he wasn't imitating Elvis.

No matter what Freddie wore on stage, his chest was almost always exposed, or he only covered his upper body with a tie. Elvis Presley is and was seen as the king. Nevertheless, nobody has been able to compete with Freddie's versatility, and, as I mentioned earlier, Freddie even overtook Elvis on a popularity list compiled after he had died.

Little Richard, one of Freddie's childhood favourites, performed the rock'n'roll track *Good Golly Miss Molly* spectacularly on Muhammad Ali's 50th birthday. His voice was gravelly and powerful. He communicated well with the audience, and played the piano like a virtuoso. And he 'played' with his voice, screaming and improvising. His music was vibrant too, and he smiled broadly all the time. His entrance was surprising, his movement feminine. He greeted Muhammad Ali with a whining, girly voice, and kissed him on the cheek saying, '*Happy birthday, baby.*' Little Richard's behaviour was typical of gay men. Apart from the shiny sequins on his black clothes, his dress sense was masculine, and his singing style sensational. Watching his behaviour, there is no similarity to Freddie in any way; after the show, he even spoke to Muhammad Ali with a slightly condescending, stilted voice.

(YouTube: Little Richard – Good Golly Miss Molly - Muhammad Ali's 50th Birthday)

In 1957, Little Richard played the piano standing up (as Freddie did in college), when he and the band played the track, *Lucille*. His singing style was energetic and his voice powerful as he improvised and screamed at times while singing.

(YouTube: Little Richard – Lucille (1957) Long Version, High-Quality Sound)

Queen introduced a rock'n'roll medley into their performances. At the end of 1975, they performed it at Hammersmith Odeon. Freddie's singing and performance style were so exclusive, he did not need to imitate anyone. The music was phenomenal, and so was Freddie's rock'n'roll voice. His stage entrance was terrific: he arrived in a Japanese kimono, but soon started a striptease. He sang in a silk shirt and shorts. The silk shirt hinted, 'Touch me; my skin is silky.' The young audience was delighted, and Freddie got them to sing along with him.

I have always been bored by this version of rock'n'roll music, but the amazing stunts performed by Queen's musicians and Freddie, his rock voice and energy, made the songs exciting. They could add something even to the best artists (Elvis Presley, Little Richard), the kind of originality to spice up these great, old hits. Freddie's characteristic performance style was, *'I'm sexy and want to conquer.'* The conquest was successful, and this was no coincidence.

(YouTube: Queen – Rock'n'Roll Medley (Live at Hammersmith Odeon, London)

Freddie became a defining rock music figure in the second half of the 20th century; he died decades ago, but still has no peer.

Freddie was already good at playing the piano as a child. He captivated everyone. Later, his playing style was simply frenetic; like Jimi on the guitar, he played effortlessly and impressively, yet he never felt he played the piano remarkably well.

His close friends from art college didn't notice any signs that Freddie was gay. He went out on dates with a few girls and showed interest in them.

During his college years, he was involved in a 20-month relationship with one of his fellow students, Rosemary Pearson. They were very close friends and had an intimate relationship. Rosemary later wrote a book entitled *Life, Art and Freddie Mercury*.

During their relationship, Rosemary claims that Freddie often fantasised about what it would be like to have an intimate relationship with a man.

In one section, she writes:

'Freddie was instantly fraught and uncontainable: 'I can't... I'm just strung out in the middle of it.. you're the only one who really knows about this side of me and what I go through all the time. It's such an agony, and everyone thinks my needs are a joke, a fiction.' He had cried and cried.'

Rosemary loved Freddie, but was incapable of accepting a man who daydreamed about other men while having intimate relations with her.

Freddie tried to make her understand that he wasn't able to decide what was best for him. He wanted to see what it was like to have sex with a same-sex partner again. Eventually, Rosemary broke up with Freddie, which upset him; he cried and was inconsolable, as he had been very close to her. He was gentle, kind and protective towards her, as if he were her older brother.

After Freddie's death, Rosemary gave some more revealing information about their relationship to The Times Magazine in 2004.

'He was a terrific clown, a great laugh and very caring. He'd sit next to me in the canteen and be terribly attentive and brotherly. I was an only child, I could trust him. We confided in each other for ages, though nobody dwelt on the past. I did find him attractive.'

Later on, in a documentary Rosemary talked about him again under the name Dr Rose Rose:

'I think I was Freddie's first girlfriend. We had a physical relationship, and he was an ardent lover. He was different. Freddie did see himself as an outsider, and it gave him a kind of freedom. He didn't have to toe the line like other people because he was from a different culture, although

he was as English or more English than most people. That was a contradiction about him.'

(YouTube: 13 Moments That Made Freddie Mercury and Queen 2019)

Rosemary erased Freddie from her life, and they never met again.

After Rosemary left, Freddie missed the gentleness, warmth, love, trust and intimacy. She was the only friend he had who was a trusted confidante. Their intimate relationship brought warmth to his life, but it inevitably rekindled his sexual desires and fantasies about men and a sense that something was lacking

Freddie was already at a stage in his life when young people usually choose a career, start dating looking for a partner. This process was delayed because of the grinding internal conflict. He didn't yet dare to try and find out who and what it was that could make him truly happy.

At the time, Freddie still wasn't a hundred per cent certain about his own sexual identity; but he was certain that his parents condemned homosexuality. He also knew that religion and most people considered it a sin and repulsive. Having said that, I wouldn't rule out the possibility that he was convinced he was attracted to men, but believed he had to choose between a career and a gay partner. His parents' expectations would have put tremendous pressure on him, and his future was totally insecure, causing him to feel terrible. It was quite a chaotic situation for a young adult. There were just too many problems to be solved, all alone and emotionally unstable, and with almost nothing to cling to at the time.

5. Freddie Arrived in London at the Best Time

Freddie was part of the baby boomer generation, becoming an adult in the second half of the 1960s.

A seismic revolution was underway in British popular culture in the 1960s, in the world of music, theatre and politics, and more generally in people's everyday lives. Young people defied conventional social, political and economic traditions. Their views were fundamentally opposed to the established political system, reflecting their growing demands for a freer, more permissive society.

As a result of the general prosperity, almost every household had a radio, the number of televisions increased explosively, and newspapers reached more families. Therefore, the music was accessible to everyone, along with the news.

The Beatles defined music in the 1960s, both in Britain and America. By 1964 the Beatles had sold approximately 80 million records worldwide. The band was formed in 1960 and made music until 1970.

Alongside the Beatles, the most popular British bands, which also conquered America, were The Rolling Stones, The Kinks, The Who and The Animals.

BBC radio also adapted to this demand, with Radio 1 playing only pop music.

The fashion world also changed. Freddie was a regular visitor to the popular Biba store, where cool musicians and other young people could find items that followed the new fashion.

Freddie wanted everything at once. He avidly threw himself into fashion boutiques, record and book shops, and was a regular visitor to venues where musicians met.

In his college years, Freddie often slept at his friends' homes, sometimes on the floor, to avoid his parents' constant rebukes. After he graduated from college he did this more often as he began to prepare for his new life. He wanted to be around others who were aiming for a musical career or playing in a band.

Part Two

Miracles Do Exist and Manifest Themselves

6. Friends – Freddie, Tim, Brian and Roger

The first band that was formed by Brian May with one of his friends was called 1984, after George Orwell's book. Brian heard Tim Staffell, singing and playing harmonica at a concert. As they were looking for a singer, they asked him to join the band. Tim joined and the new band, 1984, played its first gig in October 1964.

Brian was a young man with a great mind and a very strong interest in astronomy. In 1965 he won a scholarship to the prestigious Imperial College of Science and Technology. He studied university-level physics, earned a postgraduate degree in astronomy (later called astrophysics), and later obtained a PhD in astrophysics. At the same time, Tim enrolled at Ealing Technical College & School of Art to study graphic design, as did Freddie.

The band continued to play concerts, and one of their most important gigs was in 1967 when they appeared as a warm-up act for Jimi Hendrix at Imperial College.

Brian was just as fascinated by Jimi as Freddie was.

Brian began playing the guitar at the age of six and lived just a few streets away from Freddie, but the two didn't know each other at the time.

The band, 1984, broke up because Brian was too busy with his studies.

Tim and Brian kept in touch, and both of them really missed music, so they decided to form a new band. Brian wasn't satisfied with the previous band because they hadn't written their own songs, but played those written by other popular groups.

There was a third guy at Freddie's college, Chris Smith, who was good at playing keyboard instruments, and he was happy to join the new band, so now they were only missing a drummer. Brian was the lead guitarist, while Tim was the lead singer and bass guitarist.

Roger Taylor, a young drummer from Cornwall, who played in two bands, came to London in the same year. Both bands were quite successful, but Roger was training to be a dentist, and enrolled at London Hospital Medical School, although he had already decided to be a rock musician by this time. He kept going back to his old band for an occasional concert, but wanted to play in London.

One of the friends he shared a flat with found an advertisement on the Imperial College notice board, saying that a band was looking for a Ginger Baker/Mitch Mitchell style drummer. Roger didn't hesitate and called the person named in the advertisement: Brian May.

They met within a few days, and Tim and Brian listened with surprise to Roger, who was clearly an experienced and outstanding drummer, so they immediately reached an agreement. Brian even enjoyed hearing Roger tune the drums, and thought he was unique in comparison with the other applicants.

The time for miracles had begun in the lives of Freddie, Brian and Roger.

The new band was called Smile, and in the days after Brian's graduation ceremony, they appeared ahead of Pink Floyd at Imperial College. This was the first time Roger and Brian had performed together and launched their fabulous career without realising it. In February 1969, Chris left the band, and just the remaining three played gigs. Their first appearance was a charity gala in the Royal Albert Hall.

Around this time, Tim took Freddie to a Smile rehearsal for the first time. That year, Freddie often met Brian, Roger and Tim in the Kensington Pub. Freddie attended Smile's concerts and, without being asked, gave them sincere and enthusiastic advice on their dress sense, movement and style.

The band didn't take offence at the advice, but didn't take Freddie seriously either.

Brian recalled this:

'He offered suggestions in a way that couldn't be refused. At that time, he hadn't really done any singing, and we didn't know he could. We thought he was just a theatrical rock musician.' (Freddie Mercury – The Untold Story DoRo Production)

Freddie said:

'I was saying to Brian and Roger, 'Why are you wasting your time doing this? You should do more original material. You should be more demonstrative in the way you put the music across. If I was your singer, that's what I'd be doing!' (Freddie Mercury)

By being more 'demonstrative', he meant original songs, improving the way the emotions came across, more passion, appropriate dress and stage presence. Freddie knew what he was talking about, but the others didn't follow up on his advice at the time.

Tim later said he was never really a star like Freddie; he loved to sing, but that kind of movement and style of dress and the theatrical performance wasn't his world and never became his world. This meant Freddie's suggestions fell on deaf ears, as far as Tim was concerned.

7. Freddie and Roger on Death Row

Freddie has changed his style

As we know, Freddie had no intention of working as a graphic designer. He wanted to focus on his future career as a musician with every fibre of his body.

Roger didn't manage to complete his medical training because he – just like Freddie - wanted to build his career as a musician. Later, he graduated as a biologist, though he could never imagine working in a lab.

Freddie and Roger ended up working as fashion traders on a stand at Kensington Market. This part of the market was called Death Row, and many artists sold their products here. The name might have come from the fact that the stuff they sold here was 'dead good', at least according to the vendors.

First, they traded in Freddie's and his fellow students' works of art, but later changed their profile. They began selling dandy clothes and dressed in the same garments themselves to advertise the 'business'.

They enjoyed selling things and having fun; they unloaded junk on their customers as highly-priced 'fashion items'. The joke was that they had created this fashion themselves by hanging around wearing these often ridiculous goods. Roger, with his pretty, girlish face, and Freddie, with his striking appearance, were soon given the name 'queens' by their friends and acquaintances due to their extravagant dress sense. At the time, they couldn't have had any idea what this word meant to Freddie.

When Roger returned to his studies, Freddie closed the stand and began to help another trader. He started using a nearby public phonebox as his office.

According to, Ken Testi, voluntary manager of Ibex - Freddie's first band:

'You could call Freddie on that phone, and he'd answer.' (Mark Blake)

Freddie was brilliant; he always noticed opportunities, and exploited them. Don't forget, he was a survivor who had always been able to cope. Irrespective of the fashion sold at this market stall, Freddie changed his style. His first girlfriend, Rosemary, wrote about this period, when he began to dress in the style of Jimi Hendrix, and started playing the role of a star.

His change of style would have started something like this:

'One morning, Chris Smith encountered him sitting at his desk, his eyes glazed. 'So I put my hands in front and said, "Come on, Fred, you're miles away!"

He just looked up and said, "I am going to be mega! You have no idea how mega I am going to be!"

I said, "Oh, yeah, as mega as Hendrix?"

"Oh, yes!"

I was like, "Well, good luck with that one."'

(Mark Blake)

Chris didn't take him seriously at that point. He even teased Freddie apparently unaware of how determined he was.

An interesting article by a psychiatrist, Nick Duffel, in the magazine, *Therapy Today* (April 2011), explains Freddie's grandiose desires.

'The dissociative, defensively organised personality structure typical of the ex-boarder, which I have named the 'strategic survival personality', is developed as a protective mantle, under duress, often in the very first moments of the child having to survive alone at boarding school. Over time it tends to crystallise into masochism, pathological rebellion or grandiosity – or a combination of all three – as well as intimacy avoidance. It is very hard to shed. Many boarders grow up feeling their parents are strangers, unable to rely on anyone but themselves. They want desperately to be loved but cannot surrender to trust and perversely end up embodying the self-reliance that public schools promote above all things.

Game set and match to the boarding habit, and hence why it seems so indestructible. But bad news for relationships and families. Even those who know they were hurt by it may unconsciously become players of the *game of one, threatened rather than made safe by the beckoning of intimacy, safe only in the arms of the strategic survival personality.'*

Unfortunately, the above description was perfect for Freddie.

Grandiose desires really did materialise in Freddie's life, but not just because he wanted to be a star. Around that time, many people wanted to be musicians and stars. Instead, Freddie wanted to be a megastar, a legend. He announced to Chris Smith that he would be a star after Chris had found him lost in thought at college. Given that Freddie was concentrating intensely on his desire, this condition was a hypnotic state. From that time on, Freddie kept saying to his friends that he would be a star. Whenever he looked in the mirror and adjusted his clothes or hair, he wanted to see whether he looked like a star. If the answer was no, he kept fiddling with his appearance until he was satisfied. His friends were shocked by how often Freddie completed this 'practice'. Freddie continuously spoke about being a megastar, drove some of his friends crazy with this 'mania'. At this time, Freddie was building his star image, and continually practising self-hypnosis, but without realising it. He knew he wanted to be a star, and that's what happened; he believed in it so much that nobody could have stopped him.

(Freddie said, 'You just have to believe in yourself and must never give up, and then you'll get where you want to go to.')

Freddie had two contradictory character traits. On the one hand, he was tender, friendly, generous and compassionate. But he could also be extremely stubborn, inflexible and aggressive. There was no middle ground.

Since childhood, delicate features had characterized Freddie, whereas the toughness was part of a defence strategy. His pathological need for love was well suited to the soft, gentle, caring part of his personality, which everyone found attractive. However, if he felt under attack, he hit back really hard, as he did in the boxing ring during his childhood.

He was alienated from his parents and incapable of building a trusting relationship with them, and this wasn't just his fault. It wasn't that Freddie didn't love his parents; on the contrary, he would have done anything for them, just as he would for anyone else he loved.

He took on the style and attitude of a star; he walked the streets in stage costumes, acted out roles, and sang and practised the part. The legendary stardom – as far as he was concerned - was a symbol of strength, worship, power, control and wealth, with all that comes with it. These factors were missing from his life.

His stage persona was the embodiment of abnormal self-confidence (he had previously referred to himself as a monster). He thought of himself as a star capable of behaving like one on stage, but when he came off stage, he was often in despair and felt defenceless; he constantly needed company and couldn't cope with being alone. The company gave him protection and, at the same time, diverted his attention from his fear of being abandoned and from his pathological fear of being alone.

When he became rich, he could afford to keep an army of friends and staff around him, who constantly buzzed around and fulfilled his every wish without delay. If he said 'cigarette', some boxes soon landed at his fingertips. If he said, 'wee-wee', they escorted him to the toilet, and so on. Did he need any more than this? He definitely did.

The purpose was to attain a sense of control. He could have felt that, if he was the boss, everything depended on him. If he was in control, he was not at the mercy of someone else. In contrast, when he was alone, he couldn't control himself and panicked, and that's why he surrendered to risky adventures, which were still better than being alone. When he became a true star, the star persona also provided security in his private life, the army of friends and employees prevented strangers from making contact unexpectedly. Firstly he didn't trust strangers and secondly, he wanted to decide when to spend his time, with whom and on what.

Before the longed stardom, he was able to relax in the company of friends and acquaintances, was happy to make friends and looked for the opportunity to play music and sing.

Let's go back to Chris and Freddie for a bit. According to Chris, Freddie was practising a lot on the college piano and even began to sing – although not very well, he says – and then Freddie started to get annoyed because he couldn't write his own songs at the time, so he decided to give it a try.

Freddie made a start and one day showed Chris part of a song he had written, called *'Cowboy Song'*. This was how it began:

'Mama, I just killed the man...'

When Chris heard *'Bohemian Rhapsody'* on the radio, seven years later, he thought, *'seems like Freddie has finished the song.'* (Mark Blake)

In the interview Rosemary gave to The Times in 2004, she confirmed Freddie's change of style:

'Freddie spent most of his time rehearsing with his rock band, then called Smile. To Rosemary's embarrassment, he would burst into song in the street, and he wore theatrical clothes, often bought by her at a theatrical costumier who had a second-hand stall on Portobello Road market. She remembers a pirate's outfit and a fur coat Freddie wore over a bare chest and jeans. 'He'd strut around in an open-top — there wasn't much difference between on stage and off, he was always practising, everywhere, lots of big movements and gestures. I just thought he was obsessed with what he wanted to do. It was theatre, a visual expression.

He liked to be a drama queen, and the queen thing grew out of his personality. He was finding his feet. People sent him up about his persona, I thought they were insensitive. I thought the theatrical persona, the gayness, was an add-on. And I was drawn to his otherness.'

(Rosemary was wrong about one thing: Freddie's band at that time wasn't the Smile.)

Before he changed his style, his fellow students saw no sign of Freddie's gay tendencies.

This kind of strange, immature behaviour and his uncertain sexual identity and appearance made Freddie's friends feel something wasn't right, so they didn't take him seriously. In a sense, obsession can be positive, as it helps artists to express themselves. Freddie seemed to have been in a perfect hypnotic trance by then, and so didn't behave normally on the street either; he completely took on the role of a star, associated with the style and attitude that he felt he needed to show off.

His star-like behaviour and showing off was Freddie's way of announcing his decision: 'I don't care if people judge me. I'll decide who and what I'm going to be, whatever the cost.' Freddie's parents and childhood school had been too strict, which did not allow him any room to develop his personality, so the genie escaped from the bottle later and took control. When he decided to become a star, he resolved that nothing would stop him.

Even Freddie was astonished at how he looked during this period, as a mature man.

When he was still far from being a star; the style and behaviour of a star were one of the main reasons for this otherness, while the other main reason was the repression of his same-sex desires, and his emotional instability. The outlet for his repressed desires could be found in Freddie's dress sense and strange behaviour.

Endre Ady's painfully beautiful poem, *I want to be loved*, is ideally suited to Freddie's whole life; he had now reached a point when he wanted to show himself and be seen. It was a kind of silent prayer, 'love me, love me even like this; maybe I'm strange, but I am who I am. If you love me, love me like this too.' His whole life was about this.

His transition was a miracle, a transfiguration, the start of a transformation, the first stage in maturing as an artist, which later led to him writing the song, *'Killer Queen',* with the 'killer queen' being the essence of Freddie.

Two other precocious talents also came on the scene and were soon joined by a third. Together, they piled up one miracle after another, achieving unprecedented global success over the next 20 years.

They were all blessed, extremely talented, determined and strong enough to keep going even in difficult times. They kept going because of their great talent and a desire for success and later the unmatched success itself, and after a while, a sense of belonging gave them strengths.

8. 'Smile. Makes Sense For a Dental Student'

The phrase in the heading is taken from the film, *Bohemian Rhapsody,* and is the only reference in the movie that Freddie advised the band.

At the start of the Smile era, Tim and Brian began writing potential hits. The outstanding guitar playing and fantastic drum accompaniment foretold a promising future for the trio.

Freddie liked the style, the harmony and the strong lyrics, and that's why he stood by them, for the time being, as a fan, but he also wanted to go on stage. His first attempt was with the band, Ibex.

John Taylor was the band's bass guitarist. He talked about their first gig to Matt Richards and Mark Langthorne, let me quote him:

'It was clear to John that Freddie was desperate to get into a band. He wanted to sing. And Smile was a great band and had three singers: Tim,

Brian and Roger could both sing, so there wasn't a spot for Freddie. Having befriended Ibex, Freddie recognised an opportunity and told Ibex's members they needed a singer, proposing himself for the role. He started attending Ibex rehearsals, offering advice as he had with Smile, and assumed the lead vocalist position without any argument....The first gig he did, he got on stage, and everything was there, apart from the singing, he wasn't so good. It took him a little while to get the craft of the voice...but he certainly got that together. The show was all there from minute one, second one. There wasn't any doubt. Never any doubt. It was always going to be.'

Ken Testi opinion was similar to John Taylor's:

'Freddie was shy off-stage, but he knew how to front a show. He brought dynamics, freshness, and presentation to the band that had been completely lacking previously.' (Matt Richards & Mark Langthorne)

Around this time, Freddie moved away from home to Barnes, another district of London. Some members of Smile and Ibex also lived in this flat. Together, they managed to scrape up enough money to pay the rent. Freddie was the worst off financially; he hardly had any clothes, and his shoes had holes in them, so he took occasional jobs as an illustrator.

Even in this desperate financial situation, he thought of himself as a global star, when most people would have found it inconceivable behaving like that even on stage. Still, by then, Freddie had talked himself into being a star to such an extent that he couldn't have acted differently. Of course, it wouldn't have worked without his talent.

Freddie kept telling himself that he would be a star, with intensity and belief, and not just simply a star, but more of a legend, and he did this until the idea worked its way into his subconscious, and as a result, stardom began to emerge in reality. Once in the subconscious, an idea becomes a deep belief, it begins to control our behaviour.

Neville Goddard wrote the following words in his book, *The Power of Awareness* (1952):

'The power of our belief is an infinite power against which no earthly force is the slightest significance.'

His self-hypnosis enabled him to gather his courage and go on stage like a star, despite his fear and nervousness. The rest, the natural talent, was already in place: the rhythm and music were in his blood. Freddie could put all his emotions into the songs with his voice and performance style, so the audience inevitably fell under their influence.

Freddie's first gigs coincided with his relationship with Rosemary. At this time, the question of his sexual identity was increasingly occupying his thoughts. His performance style and choice of clothes were defined by this internal tension, which neither Freddie nor his audience were necessarily aware of, but it certainly created dramatic tension.

The band members of Ibex gave him the nickname 'old queen', that Freddie didn't like. Of course, everyone finds it painful to be ridiculed, especially for something we cannot change.

Freddie's otherness attracted Rosemary, and it attracted everyone else because people are essentially curious and like mysticism.

Without formal singing training, Freddie had to develop his singing technique at rehearsals and on stage, which was a big achievement. He dived in at the deep end almost immediately, and it was no coincidence that Rosemary said:

'Freddie was the only truly fearless person I ever met.' (Matt Richards & Mark Langthorne)

Rosemary reached this conclusion because Freddie bravely accepted himself and his otherness; I'm thinking of the theatrical costumes he wore on the streets or when he began singing on the road, as if it were the most natural thing in the world.

His intense social anxiety caused overcompensation, that is why he seemed 'truly fearless'. This overcompensation concealed Freddie's shyness, fear of strangers and lack of confidence.

His anxiety caused him to talk to Rosemary about his sexual fantasies and desires. He had to escape the tension somehow, hence often started crying.

On one occasion, he kept pestering Rosemary until she arranged for him to meet one of her openly gay friends. At first, she did not agree to his request, however, Freddie persevered until she organised the meeting, but he panicked and ran away when she was about to introduce them.

Although he craved the touch of someone of the same sex, he was also afraid to meet strangers, not knowing how he would be perceived and treated.

In the meantime, on Freddie's recommendation, the band changed its name from Ibex to Wreckage, hoping the new name would provide more opportunities to play gigs. However, the band broke up before Christmas, 1969. So, despite their name change, the band stayed together for only about another ten gigs.

And around this time, Rosemary split up with Freddie. The fact is, with a few exceptions, he and his friends barely mentioned her; it's as if she never existed. In Freddie's case, this makes sense. He has preferred to forget the unpleasant memories of their breaking up. Freddie only spoke about his private life with a few very close friends. Throughout his life, this subject was taboo as far as he was concerned.

Freddie was still waiting for an opportunity to make music, and so after some searching, he joined the band, Sour Milk Sea. Freddie could have been compared to many things, but not sour milk. The words sour milk in his later song, *'My Fairy King',* might well have come from this name, as one of the symbols of decay.

One of the band's members, Jeremy Gallop, remembered Freddie like this:

'He was so impressive. There was an immediate vibe. He had a great vocal range. He sang falsetto; nobody else had the bottle to do that.' (The Times, 20th August 2004)

'On-stage, Freddie became a different personality – he was as electric as he was in later life. Otherwise, he was quite calm. I'll always remember him being strangely quiet and very well-mannered. Extremely well-mannered, in fact. My mum liked him.' (John Stuart and Andy Davis)

Sour Milk Sea, also broke up in the spring of 1970, and surprise, surprise Tim Staffell, Freddie's friend, also left Smile, so Brian and Roger didn't have a singer.

9. Queen's Time Has Finally Come

'I have seen the future of pop music, and it is a band called Queen.' (Jack Holzman)

'To be honest, I don't think any of us realized it would take a full three years to get anywhere. It was certainly no fairy tale.' (Brian May)

'You've got to learn to push yourself, be there at the right time and learn how to deal with the business. These days I think it's got to be talent plus a very good business sense.' (Freddie Mercury)

'Between March 1974 and December 1992 Queen had forty-one UK Top hits and amassed nearly seven years' worth of Top 75 chart placings...Queen, of course, also sold albums, more than 80 million at the last count, and rising.

They were, on the surface at least, an unlikely force to acquire such widespread adoration. Fronted by a vainglorious bisexual, their music was schizophrenic: at different times absurd, choral, linear, funky, far-out inane, rocking, mawkish or pulsating. Critics and few had much regard for Queen save for a grudging acknowledgement of Freddie's stagecraft, claimed Brian May knew just one guitar solo, while Roger Taylor and John Deacon were supposedly nothing more, and nothing less, than rock journeymen. And yet few groups, if any, have honed so many styles of music into gilded hit singles.' (Mark Hodkinson)

The above Mark Hodkinson quotation summarizes how the critics viewed Queen. Behind many expressions of criticism, there are individuals who, like all individuals, were only able to write their criticisms through subjective filters, i.e., their perceptions arising from their personalities. A less diverse character, a conformist, let's say, won't like an extraordinary style of music and will reject anything in this category without further reflection. It is the most comfortable position, probably followed by condemnation of otherness.

British society was relatively conservative, and conformed to traditional norms dictated by religion, the royal family and aristocracy. The cultural revolution of the 1960s was about this, and it led to extremes, such as torn clothes, unkempt appearance, long hair for boys, miniskirts for girls, excessive smoking, drinking, the use of drugs, and sex orgies. It was precisely these excesses that made the protests conspicuous and influential. These extremes couldn't be ignored by society.

As a result, various progressive laws were adopted, such as allowing abortions and contraceptives, and legalizing homosexuality. It meant you could do what you wanted at home, it wasn't a crime, but if you did it on the street, you could still have gone to prison. Post-war immigrants now enjoyed more rights than before.

The global success of the Beatles perfectly conveyed the mass demand for change.

Freddie's flamboyant character, the diversity of the songs and their extraordinary nature, the band's unique music and performance style made Queen the favourite band of millions of people. The variety of the songs came from the four diverse personalities and diverse requirements. The band's style was defined by Freddie and equally by the other band members. All I can say about the guitar playing of Brian May and John Deacon, and Roger Taylor's drum solos, is that the wonderful and inimitable sound of Queen would never have materialised without them. And as for the exceptional and fascinating nature of this sound, the band's sensational success says it all. No doubt it needed all four of them to make this sound; Freddie's magical singing and his songs were just one element in the formula.

The sound of Queen filled stadiums all around the world, and made it possible for the band to have unparalleled success at the Live Aid concert held at Wembley Stadium in 1995.

But let's go back to the beginning for a bit to see how Freddie, Brian and Roger joined forces.

Brian and Roger attended one of the Wreckage's gigs and were shocked to notice that Freddie really had something as the band's frontman. They weren't especially impressed by the band, but noticed that Freddie attracted looks like a magnet. However, they could have had no idea that fans would talk about him even decades after his death, as the most fascinating and adorable singer ever. If anyone fails to use superlatives when mentioning him in the comments section on YouTube, they will immediately be admonished by other fans. Fans protect Freddie like they would their own brother or sister. There can be no better proof that they love the man in Freddie, not just the star, and with good reason.

Brian recalls how they formed the band:

'Freddie was always there, you know, Freddie was always saying: 'Well, I'll sing, we can do this, you know, put the band together like this, etcetera, etcetera, and we can do this, this, this and this' and we gradually went, well, okay.' (Matt Richards & Mark Langthorne)

This decision was probably based on the principle, 'it's easier to give in than to resist', but of course, they didn't have the faintest idea of how well it would work out.

Freddie remembered things slightly differently:

'The idea of Queen was conceived by me whilst studying at college. Brian, who was also at college, liked the idea and we joined forces.

One day their singer decided to leave, so Smile split up. I remember at the time we were actually sharing a flat together, and Roger and Brian were auditioning singers while I was right under their nose. It was so funny, it never actually occurred to them to ask me.

Eventually, we decided we'd form a band together. It's as simple as that. We thought our musical ideas would blend. Because I'm such a forceful character, I feel that everything's got to be new.' (Freddie Mercury)

I don't doubt for a minute that the idea of Queen, the band that Freddie finally joined, had been conceived in his mind much earlier. He noticed that the band's singer, Tim Staffell, wasn't a showman, so he started trying to convince them: 'If I were your singer, I would do this and this...' Of course, Tim didn't leave the band because of Freddie, but because he felt they were going nowhere.

I can imagine Brian and Roger were hesitant, I guess primarily because of Freddie's strange character. In addition, they weren't convinced that Freddie was a good singer, like many others who shared the same opinion, having heard his first gigs. Fortunately, they and others were discreet enough not to give an opposing view, and didn't destroy Freddie's self-confidence as a result, although it's unlikely anyone would have been capable of doing so.

They also had to digest Freddie's theatrical concepts, which was utterly new to them. Luckily, both were extremely smart and probably understood they had to stand out from the proliferation of new bands, and bring something new and sensational if they were going to be noticed. While playing in Smile, they had learned that good music was no guarantee of success; they also had to sell themselves. This became clear for them in April 1970. Having given up their academic careers, they decided there was no other path, just keep straight on, persevere at any cost and create something unique and special. None of them were willing to settle for second best. Their talent, experience and determination constituted a solid foundation, while Freddie's incredible and effective innovations gradually persuaded them they were on the right path.

Given that all three were strong-willed characters, not just Freddie, fierce disputes broke out, even at the start. Thank God Freddie's dominant personality, fantastic sense of diplomacy and solid conviction about the right direction steered Queen on the best possible course. As they were old friends, their relationship was able to cope with disputes, so they survived the storms and eventually found that the battle was worthwhile. They always managed to make sure everyone was satisfied with the outcome.

Jonathan Morris, who was Michael Jackson's publicist and confidante for 28 years, said of Freddie:

'Freddie was this flamboyant showman at a time when bands went on stage dressed in whatever they'd been wearing all day.

What Freddie knew intuitively was the golden rule of showbiz: you make a show. It was what Epstein did with the Beatles.

Freddie's genius was understanding not just the song he had written, the words and melody too, and how it all sounded, but how you deliver it in a contemporary fashion which the audience will comprehend and absorb.' (Lesley-Ann Jones)

This wasn't just instinctive, he also observed and studied the world of theatre, the world of Jimi Hendrix and other successful stars, and noticed how they were different. The difference was the show. When they played gigs, they weren't just concentrating on music, but also the presentation.

Watching Queen's first concert recordings, I think we could all agree that suggestive power radiates from Freddie's eyes and his facial features. His gaze is delightfully charming. With his eyes and nails highlighted in black, the well-proportioned, well-formed body, the explicitly erotic and seductive clothing convey femininity and masculinity simultaneously, he makes an exciting impression. Exotic features – in any case - lend mystery to Western eyes; with his repeated and seductive dynamic, unique moves, perfectly adjusted to the rhythm, Freddie attracts and holds the attention of the audience. Likewise, the unusual sound of the music enhances his accentuated, erotic vibe, making an impression on both genders. Some of the lyrics are verses written in surreal style, taking us into a dreamlike, fairytale world, touching the deepest layers of our souls.

Roger's drums are shaman drums behind Freddie. The exotic sound of Brian's and Joe's guitar playing is capable of evoking heaven and hell. Freddie is the magician captivating the audience. His changes of tone and rhythmic movements add to the rapture and magic.

Freddie planned this impression deliberately; he knew what people crave: they want to relax, to step out of the monotony of everyday life; they want to be given a boost, and so he designed the spectacle and sound to be entertaining and to transcend at every moment.

Conscious planning is driven by thoughts or fantasies that want to emerge from the subconscious.

Human beings are emotional; impulses from the subconscious define our choices. Whether or not we are aware of them, our dominant thoughts always determine our decisions and behaviour.

Freddie himself once declared:

'Of course, I'm outrageous, camp, theatrical and dramatic, but I haven't chosen that image. I am myself, and in fact, half the time, I let the wind take me.' (Freddie Mercury)

When naming the band, there were many suggestions, but 'Queen' was Freddie's idea. He kept insisting on it until he broke the resistance of the other band members. He managed to convince them the name should be short, impressive and majestic-sounding. He believed this was the only name that matched the band's glorious march towards global success. Freddie's choice of name was brilliant, like his music.

Freddie commented:

'I was certainly aware of the gay connotations, but that was just one facet of it. Anyway, we always preferred to think of Queen in the regal sense rather than in the queer one.' (Freddie Mercury)

Freddie named the band after himself, I think deliberately; he was already working on the song *'The March of The Black Queen'* in which Freddie himself is the black queen. He favoured both meanings: queen-like, namely especially high-ranking, the best band, and the possibility of a gay queen was also there. Freddie always knew what he was doing and why, and the reasons he didn't share his ideas are understandable.

One member of Freddie's previous band, John Taylor, claimed that he indirectly named the band Queen.

'The name was my name. We called him the old queen quite a lot, me and Mike Bersin. He didn't like it, but he bore with it. I said, "If you have a band, it should be called Queen".' (Phil Chapman)

During this period, Freddie still didn't know which gender he was more attracted to, or he just didn't want to accept his gay tendencies.

His gentle, delicate, caring nature indicated feminine traits, whereas his persistent, career-centred, determined, smart-planning, realistic mentality was more typical of men. A formula for success even for the most remarkable artists: don't just work by instinct, but also with your mind, and use both hemispheres of your brain; if possible, in harmony. Only very few people can do so.

Sexually, it is also possible that he subconsciously identified with a female role model, perhaps one of his female relatives or acquaintances (perhaps with his aunt with whom he often stayed in Bombay), because he needed a defence tactic. He constantly dreaded being humiliated or ridiculed, and somehow sensed that he could use feminine behaviour, tenderness, attentiveness and kindness to make his friends like him, and not to hurt him. It worked out, both at boarding school and college, and among the musicians, he worked with. In the same way, his boxing and other sporting achievements formed part of a defence strategy, obtaining and demonstrating power, apart from the fact that he loved to compete and win, I guess because he had a strong competitive spirit.

He tried to keep his private life as secret as possible, and didn't even speak to friends about it.

The secrecy was indeed intended to conceal his gay orientation, which he was ashamed of. It also put his whole career at risk.

Many of his close acquaintances suspected that his unusually stylish, clean-cut, hipster image also concealed a man with a sharp mind and good business sense.

Freddie learned to keep both feet firmly on the ground at boarding school; he could only rely on himself, and matured quite quickly. He was willing to take on responsibility and learned how to achieve his goals; if he couldn't do it gently, he would use force. His fighting ability and willpower were apparent in every situation.

Later, when he knew that he wanted to be a musician, he consciously prepared for the role, and left nothing to chance.

Changing his name was part of his plan, partly because he wanted to forget everything about Farrokh Bulsara, a very inconvenient part of his personality, as a lonely, shy boy, timid and reserved, and an immigrant.

Freddie, the future star, was already proud of himself because he had anticipated his global success and couldn't allow himself to have a name that evoked his immigrant status and humiliations. He was emotionally detached from his family, so this wasn't something that stopped him from changing his name.

He changed his name from Bulsara to Mercury. Brian and Roger couldn't believe it because they thought he had gone too far. In Roman mythology, Mercurius was the messenger of the gods, and the child of Zeus and Maia, a nymph.

To be the messenger was Mercurius's most crucial role, but he was also the God of shepherds, travellers, traders, eloquence, literature, athletics and thieves. He was also well-known among Olympians for his cunning and astuteness.

Mercurius, the messenger of the gods, carried his caduceus wand with two entwined snakes, ending in an angel's wing.

'As a symbolic object, it represents Hermes (or the Roman Mercury), and by extension trades, occupations, or undertakings associated with the god.' (Wikipedia)

Mercurius performed many heroic deeds during his life, and was treated with deference in both Greek and Roman mythology.

In his childhood, Freddie's father told him many fascinating mythological stories.

Freddie told the story of his childhood fantasy world in his song, *'My Fairy King'*.

When his parents left him on his own at the age of eight - or perhaps even earlier - he built a fantasy world for himself in the alien environment, where he was the just, all-knowing Fairy King.

Freddie overcame his fears more easily by identifying with one of the heroes he knew about, such as Mercurius, who was not just the messenger of the gods but was an all-powerful god himself. This feeling of omnipotence must have helped Freddie through the difficulties of everyday life. The wand on which the two snakes are entwined and adorned by the angel's wing, also appeared symbolically in Freddie's life when he was a young adult. He wore snake-like rings and bracelets, and fairies appeared in his songs and also on the Queen logo. The sawn-off microphone stand reminds us of his magic wand, and a phallic symbol.

Freddie talked to Ken Testi about the sawn-off mic, saying: *'It's my gimmick, dear. You must have a gimmick!'* (Mark Blake)

The sawn-off microphone stand gave Freddie something to hold on to. He realised this special microphone was perfect for continually having the viewer's attention as he moved it around incessantly. It's like a pen in the hands of a hypnotist when he says, 'Focus your attention on this pen, just concentrate on this!'

A good performer comes up with something new every 45 seconds during a performance; gesticulates, moves around, or uses voice modulation, knowing that the audience's attention will be lost otherwise. Freddie realised this instinctively.

Freddie often put the tube or the microphone itself in front of his groin, using it as a phallic symbol. This can be seen by watching the Live Aid concert. You get an excellent view of how well Freddie used this device.

'In astrological symbolism, the phallus is the arm of the Sun god. His phallus is Planet Mercury, equivalent to the 'magic tool' (ultimate weapon, divining rod, magic fire tool) in folk tales.' (Hoppál, Jankovics, Nagy, Szemadám)

I later read a witty description in Peter Hince's book of how Freddie viewed the 'stage prop':

'Fred's trademark silver Shure 565 SD microphone, as he wandered the stage with the famous "wand": a custom-made chrome-plated tube, like a section of a microphone stand, which Fred used together with the mic as his stage prop. It could be a sword, guitar, machine gun, golfclub, baseball bat or whatever Fred wanted to convey with it. Most commonly, it was "My c*ck, darling".'

The phoenix, a symbol of the sun, was the central figure on Queen's insignia; its return symbolised renewal, resurgence, transformation and gaining strength.

The phoenix burns obstacles, destroys outdated views and replaces them with new ideas.

This bird symbolises both Freddie's and the band's renaissance, the breakthrough from being unsuccessful to successful and Freddie's transformation from unknown to known, from a potential star to a legend.

The two lions on the insignia symbolise John and Roger, who were both born under the sign of Leo. Cancer is Brian's star sign, while Freddie's is Virgo, represented by the two fairies. A royal crown can be seen in the centre of the logo, referring to Queen's royal rank as a quality classification.

The choice of name was deliberate. He wanted to dominate the world of rock and roll as a king or queen, and craved recognition and respect. Freddie claimed that he chose the name Queen because it was unconventional and attention-grabbing. A king or a queen is a ruler and a symbol of power, and Freddie aspired to rule the music world.

Subconsciously this also symbolised Freddie's desire for control and related to his gay fantasies, as clearly shown by his later songs (*The 'March of the Black Queen'*, *'Seven Seas of Rhye'* or *'Killer Queen'*).

1970 was an especially significant year for Freddie. In April, he finally became the singer in Queen, and then, through Brian May, he got to know Mary Austin.

10. Mary Is My Best Friend In The World

Brian invited Mary Austin out on a date because he liked her, but since they didn't fall in love, Freddie insisted that Brian introduce him to Mary, as he liked her too. According to Brian, Mary was very reserved, which was confirmed by everyone else close to her.

Mary was a 19-year-old, beautiful, fragile young woman who worked at Biba, where Freddie bought his clothes.

Many of their friends said the young couple were very attracted to each other and genuinely loved one another.

Freddie visited the boutique to see Mary for months but being shy, he usually took Roger along for needed support. He just smiled and said hello to her.

After Brian introduced them, it appeared the attraction was immediate, and yet Mary didn't go on a date with Freddie for five or six months. They finally dated in September, and five months later, they moved in together. Her unwillingness to go out with him was due to Mary's reserved nature, and it's possible that the impression Freddie made caused her to be ambivalent. Subconsciously she must have sensed there was some kind of inexplicable, perplexing reason for Freddie's otherness and yet must have liked this, as did Rosemary.

We know that Freddie could be very friendly, kind, persuasive and persistent, and sooner or later, he swept her off her feet.

Like Freddie, Mary was also shy, and she too wanted to move away from home and live her own life.

Both Freddie and Mary were very reserved and didn't speak about their private lives to anyone.

Many people believe Mary was the love of Freddie's life. I am convinced that Freddie's emotions were genuine. The relationship was based on deep affection, friendship and absolute trust. Most people rely on their own family for these factors, and Freddie was capable of loving from his heart and was very caring and tender.

This was what he said about Mary:

'All my lovers asked me why they couldn't replace Mary, but it's simply impossible. For me, she was my common-law wife. For me, it was a marriage. We believe in each other, and that's enough for me.

I couldn't fall in love with a man the same way as I did with Mary.'

Both of Mary's parents were deaf and without speech. The family was relatively poor, as both her mother and father could only do simple tasks. Mary was probably loved as a child because she was caring, motherly, kind and gentle, and everyone considered her very likeable.

Mary believed that Freddie had a certain degree of paranoia and thought people laughed at him behind his back. His college nickname and the ridicule he received probably caused this. His London friends were also continually teasing him. Freddie only accepted this because he wanted to fit in at all costs. We are all social beings and can be terribly lonely without a warm family background and friends.

Freddie received tender loving care and physical love from Mary, and they developed a deep and trusting relationship, which Freddie must have missed very much after the relationship ended with Rosemary.

When Freddie said, 'we believed in each other', it could have meant that he didn't have to worry about Mary leaving him or that she would hurt him intentionally.

Mary replaced the lack of family warmth; he had found a trusting relationship. What's more, it was a heterosexual relationship. This was crucial to Freddie, as it wasn't possible in those days to be openly gay. This would have put his career at risk. Living with Mary, nobody could have doubted that Freddie was heterosexual.

In his relationship with Rosemary, Freddie had learned that he couldn't talk to his sweetheart about his gay fantasies without the danger of abandonment, so he kept quiet about it.

Ostensibly, everything was fine, especially in the early years while the romance was new and exciting. However, when this period finished, Freddie became restless again and was overtaken by a desire for same-sex relationships.

Was Freddie really bisexual? We will never know, but Freddie bought a ring for Mary, and even asked her to marry him, but they never got married because Freddie changed his mind. It took him a long time even to introduce her to his family.

Their relationship broke down after six years. In an interview recorded in 2000, Mary told Mark Blake that their relationship began to cool after the first Queen album was released in 1973. When Mary came home from work, Freddie was often not at home, and only returned late in the evenings. Freddie made up various excuses for coming home late. The couple were no longer as close as they had been.

In another statement, she claims that initially, she wasn't in love with Freddie:

'It took a long while for me to really fall in love with this man, but once there, I would never turn away from him. His pain became my pain. His joy became my joy.' (Freddie Mercury – The Untold Story, DoRo Prod. 2000.)

It seems rather strange that she would have moved in with Freddie without being in love after going out together for five months. And if this is true, then why? All their friends who frequently saw them together, including Brian, said they were obviously in love.

Shockingly, she refers to Freddie as 'this man'. At the very least, we would expect her to mention the name of her late friend, whom she loved very much, who left her a house worth millions, especially in a public interview. Mary was very embarrassed when she talked about Freddie confessing that he was bisexual, and claimed she was delighted about the confession because she could see Freddie was suffering. After the admission, Freddie was his old self again, happy and contented. She stressed that Freddie couldn't have been sure how she would react to the news. However, it seems that Mary had time to prepare and think about how to respond, because she had suspected for quite some time that Freddie had found someone else. But what could she have said in the interview? She probably had mixed emotions, as she loved Freddie and didn't want him to suffer; that was why she let him go, but no doubt she suffered too and understandably found it difficult to forgive him.

I believe Freddie really loved Mary, and he genuinely wanted to live in a heterosexual relationship so that his family and people, in general, wouldn't hold him in contempt. But he wasn't faithful to Mary, as he never was faithful to his boyfriends either.

David Minns was Freddie's first long-term boyfriend, who wrote:

'We had already discussed his past gay life in his early days at school in India, visiting gay bars on tour and anywhere he could sneak away to and have sex with someone. It was clear that I was not his first affair by a long shot.'

David Evans Freddie's close friend wrote something similar:

'For obvious reasons, I fear he was never faithful, although neither was promiscuous.'

When Freddie realised that he preferred men and wanted to live with David, he still kept Mary by his side to keep up appearances. There is no doubt that he still loved her, as she was the only person he could always rely on.

He fought with the same determination and persistence to stay in close contact with Mary as he had to join Smile to build his career.

Everyone close to them said that Mary was a maternal figure in Freddie's life. And this was probably Mary's later role, once Freddie had made her reliant on him. She was the only certainty in his life at the time; he was devoted to her and wouldn't let her go.

When the time came, and Freddie found a deep love in the person of David Minns, he began suffering more alongside Mary. In Freddie's eyes, it was as if he had seen the real thing in David. This meant he didn't need Mary as much; he got warmth, love and affection from David, and drifted away even better from Mary.

Later, when Freddie had made it as an artist and had enough money, he bought a flat for Mary, from where she could see his house and visit him and the cats. They had two cats; Freddie adored these warm, purring pets, who flattered him, and he even let them into his bed. They were like children to him. He could give them a hug when he wanted, and move them further away when he had something to do.

Freddie bragged to Roger in the film, *Bohemian Rapsody*: 'Mary just moved in next door and can visit the cats and me.'

Freddie looked after and maintained contact with her as if she were his mother, even though they had broken up. Ideally, our spouse is our main confidante, but Freddie didn't trust anyone else because of his emotional problems, so he needed Mary, as he could always turn to her. It seems Freddie regarded Mary as a family member.

Although unintentionally, he made it entirely impossible for Mary to live her own life. She gave birth to two children by another man, but he left her because of Freddie, who demanded Mary's company.

Freddie invited Mary and her boyfriend to the dinners he gave. Mary sat on one side of him and her latest partner on the other side. The hidden message of this seating arrangement was 'I'm getting between you.' No man would appreciate this, and even the father of her two children got fed up with it.

(Freddie loved the kids, which is a further indication of his willingness to care for and look after others if needed. It was an amiable and likeable trait.)

He later gave Mary a job too, trusting her to look after his personal affairs, and she became an employee of his record label.

With two children to care for, Mary became financially dependent on Freddie. Most likely, Mary also valued her friendship with Freddie because she needed a friend she could trust, and a father figure in her life, someone she could always rely on.

Mary appears to be a victim in this relationship, but according to her statements, she really loved Freddie, and the more she got to know him, the more she loved him, so this bond was not a burden on her.

In another later statement, she said it seemed her fate was to take care of men, first her father, then her children and Freddie during his illness. (In fact, she didn't take care of Freddie, as he was only compelled and willing to spend a few weeks in bed. Mary was seven months pregnant at the time when Freddie stopped his AIDS treatments. She visited him almost every day, to see how he was, which is not the same as caring for him. As a paid employee, she continued taking care of his financial affairs.)

As an indication of Freddie's commitment to Mary, he left her his adored Kensington house and half of his other properties and future income. This was not just an attempt to soothe his troubled conscience and make peace; he also wanted to take care of her, just as he looked after everyone else that he loved.

In his book, David Minns described how Freddie constantly suffered from a sense of guilt and didn't want to cause Mary any pain.

When Mary allegedly asked Freddie for a child, he replied by saying that he would like to have kids, but would have a cat before a child.

It's not clear when Freddie said this, but I strongly doubt it was during their relationship. Freddie was intelligent and had no intention of hurting Mary.

Freddie's cynical reply may have been to a provocative question from the press:

'If I wanted children, I'd just go to Harrods and buy one. They sell anything there. Buy two, and you get a nanny thrown in!' (Freddie Mercury)

Whatever prompted Freddie's reply, it was his way of telling us how he felt about what had happened to him and his sister. Freddie resented his parents for hiring a nanny, and his mother not caring for them in person and sending him and his sister to boarding school. This was how he revealed his long-held resentment towards his parents.

11. At Last, a Good Bass Guitarist

The band tried three bass guitarists before finding the real thing, John Deacon, on 2 July, 1971. He was worth waiting for.

Chris Chesney recalled his audition: *'Deacon didn't drop a single beat.'*

The great team had finally come together: Brian, Roger, John and Freddie. They worked in this line-up until Freddie tragically passed away.

John was an electrical engineer and had graduated with honours, while Freddie had graduated from art college as a graphic designer; he wrote his thesis on Jimi Hendrix.

The band of scientists and artists was ready for the challenge, given that Brian, Roger and John were masters of their instruments by the time Queen was founded, just as Freddie was outstanding at playing the piano.

Freddie's friend Chris Smith said: *'He had this staccato style. It was like Mozart gone mad.'* (Mark Blake)

Brian and John were still committed to their studies and teaching work to some extent in the first year, but both tried to attend rehearsals so the group could get in sync as soon as possible.

As it turned out, the group was made up of four forceful personalities; they had mature tastes and opinions on the band's direction, especially musical genre and style. Given that they were all perfectionists, they aspired to excellence right from the start. The band's decisions were democratic, but arguments weren't settled by voting, but hearty quarrels. The quarrel continued until everyone was happy and satisfied.

These battles were not just about whose song should feature on records. Ultimately, battles were fought to continually improve the music, including performance style, instrumentation and arrangements, among others. (Of course, financial matters were also important, as none of them had surplus capital.) Whoever wrote the lyrics received the royalties, which always caused tension. This solution was Freddie's idea. So everyone was forced to write songs, and from this compulsion, brilliant hits were born.

They were all exceptionally talented musicians. Brian and John sacrificed their careers on the altar of music – whereas Freddie and Roger had intended to dedicate their lives to music from the outset. As they were all perfectionists, they weren't easily satisfied, but strived for unrivalled sound and unrivalled success. It came at a cost, but it was worth it, resulting in a happy end, as far as making music together was concerned.

First, they had no idea how to get into the music industry, before realising they needed some good and well-rehearsed songs and a demo that would help introduce them to potential managers and record labels.

When the new De Lane Lea Studios were handed over in Wembley, the sound engineers wanted to test them out. Through one of their friends, Terry Yeadon, Queen was chosen to try out the new studio, and the band received a professional-quality demo in return.

Terry Yeadon recalls Queen at the studios during that period:

'They were a little rough at the edges, which was only to be expected, yet Queen were very much there and had already been there before Freddie joined them, with Brian's guitar playing and Roger's drumming being, to a large degree, responsible for the sound, but Freddie unquestionably, put the cream on it. He was just larger than life and with such a personality that he kind of instantly bowled you over. Even in the most sterile environment of the studio, Freddie was very much a showman. It was almost as if he literally couldn't sing a song if he didn't also do all the actions to go with it.' (Laura Jackson)

They approached almost every management agency with their demo, but received only one offer, a contract from Charisma worth 25,000 pounds. They didn't accept the offer, as the sum was too low to buy new equipment.

John Anthony and Roy Thomas Baker heard Queen recording at the De Lane Lea Studios. John Anthony already knew Brian and Roger because they had made a single for Smile in 1969. They liked what they saw and heard, and so they took the demo recording along to tell Trident's owners, Norman and Barry Sheffield, about Queen, though it took quite a while for the meeting to finally take place.

Roy Thomas Baker worked at Trident Studios.

John Anthony was a very talented and well-known record producer in London. Lesley-Ann Jones wrote in her book that Freddie got acquainted with him 'by chance' and got him to invite the band to his apartment to talk about Queen's career. It was one of Freddie's best 'by chance' encounters, and it paid off more than expected.

On the advice of John Anthony, they only gave free concerts to their friends in colleges, clubs or elsewhere in 1971; he believed the band needed some time to bond with each other and they needed to rehearse.

12. Queen and Trident

The band played a concert at King's College Medical School in Denmark Hill on 10 March, 1972. A lot of managers attended this concert. Not long after the show, Trident contacted Queen, wanting to see them in concert. Two weeks later, they played a gig at Forest Hill Hospital, London, where Berry Sheffield, one of the Trident's owners, offered them a contract.
It was John Anthony who convinced Berry Sheffield to attend the gig to see them in person.
A few weeks later, Queen got in touch with the Trident office to talk about the contract.

Freddie talked on the business aspect as follows:

'It's not just having a recording contract and that's it, it's not all going to be peaches and cream. You have to keep in check all of the things that are going on. Talent isn't just about being a good musician these days. It's being aware. It's vital to do the whole thing properly. Talent is not just writing good songs and performing them, it's having a business brain because that's a major part of it – to get the music across properly

and profit from it. You use all the tricks of the trade, and if you believe in yourself, you'll go all the way.' (Freddie Mercury)

Norman Sheffield remembered the first meeting with the band as follows:

'Roger Taylor was a really good-looking kid, with long blond hair and charm. Brian May was tall, with a mane of curls and a little introverted but clearly very intelligent. The bass player, John Deacon, was also quiet. I could tell right away that the fourth member was going to be high maintenance. He was charming, acted a bit shy and reserved at times and spoke in quite a posh, mannered voice. When he relaxed, he had a very sharp sense of humour and spoke at a hundred miles an hour. Freddie apparently had a girlfriend, but we were pretty certain he was gay. I agreed to offer the Queenies, as we christened them, a loose kind of arrangement. There were times when the studio was dark, usually at 2 am. So we said: 'We'll give you this downtime in the studio to see what you can do.' (Matt Richards & Mark Langthorne)

The Trident's studio was the best in the world at that time, so it was very busy, and Queen could record only at night.

Based on Trident's offer, they were able to begin studio recordings at night in March 1972. It took one year, from the first studio recording, for the first album to be finally released. During this period, they didn't play any concerts. They spent their nights in the studio, and during the day they racked their brains about the contract. Brian and Freddie put pressure on the managers every day to make something happen after the recordings had been completed; they didn't understand why the record had not yet been released. They were anxious about the tracks 'being obsolete', or out of fashion by the time the albums reached the shops.

Probably, the reason for the delay in releasing the album was that Trident couldn't find a record company in time. Queen was disappointed, with good reason, because Trident had agreed in the contract to negotiate with record labels on their behalf. Obviously, no one expected it to take that long to find the right company.

These difficulties in the early days didn't add to their self-confidence, but they sensed something special was taking shape. They had worked very hard on the tracks and knew that they had made something very special. They just had to persevere. Brian says it was a very frustrating time for them.

They already had a few melodic tracks and some hard rock songs; it was Freddie's idea to have melodic tracks and heavy rock elements, such as in the song, 'Liar'. To begin with, Freddie and Brian wrote most of the songs. As Brian recalls:

'Freddie wrote in strange keys. Most guitar bands play in A or E, and probably D and G, but beyond that, there's not much. Most of our stuff, particularly Freddie's songs, was in oddball keys that his fingers naturally seemed to go to E-flat, F, A-flat. They're the last things you want to be playing on a guitar, so as a guitarist, you're forced to find new chords. Freddie's songs were so rich in chord structures.' (Matt Richards & Mark Langthorne)

The Trident contract was related to the management of the band, studio recordings, and copyright handling. Trident also undertook to negotiate with record labels on their behalf.

Queen signed the contract on 1 November, 1972. They didn't rush into signing as they didn't want to get carried away. At the end of November, Queen finished recording their first album, but it was full of mixing errors and couldn't be completed before the end of January 1973.

Brian and Roger fought a constant battle with the sound engineer, Roy Thomas Baker, who initially didn't understand Queen's sound concept. They wanted the recording to sound like a live performance. At first, they didn't make much progress with Baker; Queen didn't like the recordings that Roy made. In the end, they were able to remix the recordings with John Anthony to get the right sound. Luckily, they met Mike Stone, who Brian believes had the best ear in the studio. They got on well with him because he understood what they wanted to record and how. After the initial difficulties, Roy T. Baker worked with the band while the recordings were made in England.

The contract was highly disadvantageous to the band. Trident didn't want to take on the management tasks, and the company claims this was at the band's insistence. Negotiating with the studio and representing the band would have been an independent manager's job. The company regarded this as a conflict of interest, which of course, it was.

The band's view was that Trident wanted total control, which unsettled the members of Queen, and was probably one of the reasons the contract was only concluded in November.

After Queen signed the contract, Trident bought new equipment and brought in Jack Nelson from America, who had worked in record publishing for a long time. He was amazed at Queen's talent, and did everything he could to find a record label for them.

Talking about Queen, he said:

'They were probably the smartest band in the industry, and totally diverse personalities….but it made a creative force…..Freddie was a very complex guy. Incredibly talented. Brian was a rock'n'roll guitarist, and he brought that influence. Incredibly talented. John was the bass player. He brought the solid bit. Grounded them. Roger, the drummer, had a double degree.'

When the first album was complete, Trident found a publicist, Feldman & Co., but they also needed a record label to make the records and deliver them to the stores.

In 1973, Feldman & Co. persuaded Roy Featherstone, one of the chief executive managers at the legendary UK record label, EMI, to listen to Queen's demo. He liked what he heard, so in March 1973, Queen entered into a contract with the company involved in record distribution in the United Kingdom and Europe.

EMI organised a particular show by Queen at the Marquee Club on 9 April of that year. The guests included Jac Holzman, the founder and managing director of the US company, Elektra Records. He liked Queen and agreed to distribute their records in America, Japan and Australia.

When Jac Holzman first heard Queen's demo, he said:

'I heard the first Queen album, and I absolutely loved it. It was like a beautifully cut jewel, landing in your lap ready to go.

I was knocked out.

'Keep Yourself Alive,' 'Liar', 'The Night Comes Down' - all great songs in a sumptuous production that feel like the purest ice-cream poured over a real rock and roll foundation.'

I was a believer. I wrote an internal memo to staff saying, 'I have seen the future of pop music, and it is a band called Queen.' And the group took the comments in my memos about staging and performance far beyond my expectations. By the time of their huge hit single, 'Bohemian Rhapsody' - another seven-and-a-half-minute wonder, by the way - their stage theatrics were phenomenal. Freddie was extraordinarily flamboyant, a great glam rocker. I have rarely seen a band work so hard, have such success, and remain so nice. They were very special people. And when they were in full flight, they sold millions and millions of records. All by itself, my signing of Queen more than compensated Steve Ross what he had paid for Elektra.'

(Follow The Music: The Life and High Times of Elektra Records in The Great Years of American Pop Culture by Jac Holzman and Gavan Daws)

They worked obsessively on the albums, day and night, driving their technicians mad with their perfectionist attitude. But, it was worth it, the superb Queen sound came together, which changed from time to time because they always wanted to create something new, a different sound, a different style, but the originality and versatility were always there. I think the main thing about Queen's sound is that it was original and couldn't be confused with any other band, and nobody could imitate it.

By the time they finished the albums, one of the technicians involved in the recordings pointed out, alluding to Freddie, that *'Working with a born star was quite nerve-wracking.'*

The members of Queen talk about the voices of Freddie, Brian and Roger in the documentary film, *These are the days of our lives*:

Brian: *'We had a gift. We had three voices blended instantly. Freddie had this wonderful crystal clear, sharp vocal sound.'*

Roger: *'Naturally, I have got the powerful high voice.'*

Freddie: *'He has got the dog whistle pitch, very high voice.'*

Freddie jokingly mentioned that Roger's voice was so high that only animals (pet dogs and cats) could hear it.

(This is what Roger (Ben Hardy) was referring to in the film when Freddie (Rami Malek) makes him sing *'Galileo'* in an ever higher voice. While recording 'Bohemian Rhapsody' he said: *'If I go any higher, only dogs will hear me.'*)

Brian: *'I have got the warm sound – I suppose. If you put the three voices together, it sounded like some kind of Panavision.'*

I guess that, by 'Panavision', he meant their three voices were magical together, making an incomparable sound. But, of course, being an extremely modest man, Brian would never say anything like that. Brian's voice was warm, as smooth as velvet, and, I should add, crystal-clear just like Freddie's.
Roger's voice was higher than the average vocal range, it's unique and sounds passionate, greatly enhancing their sound.

13. Queen and Queen II Albums (1973 and 1974)

The band's first two albums, Queen and Queen II, were released in 1973 and 1974.
Before the first album was released, Trident sent the single, 'Keep Yourself Alive', to Radio 1 and BBC TV. Radio 1 started playing the track, but people only really started noticing when the BBC played the single for the first time on 24th July 1973, with an interesting video put together by the channel. The video wasn't about Queen, but 'Keep Yourself Alive' formed the musical background.

First, 'Keep Yourself Alive' was released as a single that didn't make it to the charts. The debut album was released on 13 July.

The album received a variety of reviews, but Rolling Stone clearly recognized what the future held for the band:

'There is no doubt that this funky, energetic English quartet has all the tools they'll need to lay claim to the Zep's abdicated heavy-metal throne and beyond that to become a truly influential force in the rock world. Their debut album is superb.'

Queen couldn't be ignored. Thanks to Freddie's exuberant and sensual voice, their unique sound attracted attention. Brian's guitar playing generated an exceptional, synchronised sound; John's perfect bass and Roger's modern, powerful drum solos, all formed the basis for their unique sound. However, the most extraordinary part was the polyphonic singing technique recorded in many layers, produced by Freddie, Brian and Roger. It is most apparent in 'Bohemian Rhapsody', on the fourth album but was already terrific on the first two albums.

Queen first album arrived in the studio without a label. Fortunately, the producer, Mike Appleton, at BBC, truly liked the songs, so they were included in the show with an invitation to phone the studio if someone knew which band was on the album. The next day they got a phone call from EMI. Mike Appleton was amazed at the vast number of listeners who had enquired about the band behind the track.

The debut album, which included the song, 'Keep Yourself Alive', reached number 24 and stayed on the charts for 17 weeks. The band had now acquired their first gold disc. The song was written by Brian May. Although he had written the original with Tim Staffell, Brian had fundamentally reworked it. A little later, it also went gold in America due to the number of albums sold.

'This remarkable debut album stands out, in total, as a very bold move. ….here is a band with a very clear vision of what they wanted to say and how they wanted to be heard. The confidence shines out. Queen was ridiculous, catchy and a whole lot of fun.' (Andrew Wild)

One of the critics even called the band 'second-rate Led Zeppelin imitators.'

Freddie's answer for the critic was very witty: 'We resemble Liza Minnelli more than Led Zeppelin.' Not coincidentally, Liza Minnelli was one of Freddie's great favourites.

The sound of the first album was explicitly heavy rock, whereas *Queen II* had both rock and melodic tracks, a sensational innovation.

Roger said in an interview, *'When the album was finally released, it was a huge shock. There wasn't much of a response. When the recordings are made, you tend to think this will be the 8th wonder of the world, but of course, it wasn't. I think we had too much self-confidence. We were even arrogant. I don't know why?'* (YouTube: Queen – From Rags to Rhapsody)

After the album was released, Roger made this pessimistic statement but couldn't have known that there was no cause for concern. On the contrary, their later albums had almost immediate resonance in the form of gold and platinum records and massive hits on the charts.

It is no wonder that they were disappointed at the time. It took time for people to get to know and love them. If you have a favourite band - like Queen for Queen fans - you don't run into the record store and look for records by other musicians. This doesn't even occur to you unless you really like them, for this to happen, you have to see and hear them. So it was sensational and a great stride forward that they were finally audible on radio and visible on TV.

Anyway, I think it's almost a miracle that even in 2021, we still listen to their albums from 1973-74 with devotion and enrapture.

The albums of successful bands, such as Led Zeppelin, The Who and The Rolling Stones - and Queen's albums were incomparable. Queen's music was so unique and new; it was so different from the prevailing trend, both in terms of musical and performance style, that it must have been quite shocking, in a positive sense. As if a light had suddenly been turned on in a dark room, or Queen had come from another planet. The difference is pronounced by comparison with successful contemporary bands, so I'm not surprised that Roger was disappointed. I had to browse YouTube for a few hours to see why the press could not understand where to place Queen. They couldn't be pigeonholed. It also explained why the managers quoted above, and other music specialists raved about them and were astonished. I would advise anyone to listen to the albums of contemporary musicians in the early 70s, when the first Queen albums were released. You don't have to be a music specialist to notice the difference between Queen and their contemporaries. I'm not criticising, just observing the factual differences, the extent to which the songs, rhythm, harmony, sound, lyrics and vocals had been refined.

Roger said in an interview: *'The recording of the second album took about three and a half months, what those days were epic.*
That album was the first of a nervous breakdown to the producer. We worked around the clock for months. We've realized the easiest way to get a hit album is to have a hit single with some musical validity. That is what we thought, and that is what we set out to do. And it happened very smoothly there. When Queen II came out and had 'Seven Seas of Rhye' on it, which was a hit, and the album became a hit as well. That was great for us.' (YouTube: Queen – From Rags to Rhapsody)

From that time, they started releasing the songs they thought were their best, as singles, creating more interest in the latest album.

On Tuesday 19th February 1974, Ronnie Fowler, manager at EMI, arranged for the BBC's Top of the Pops editorial team to listen to the *Seven Seas of Rhye* single before the release date was known.

Fortunately, the editorial team liked the song and needed some material at that moment because David Bowie's publicity film was late. Queen was taken into a studio the same evening, where the recordings began and were completed the next day. The song was included in the broadcast on Friday. It forced EMI to make sure the record was in the shops by Saturday. The song became their first hit, reaching a prominent position at number 10 on the British charts.

Tony Brainsby, Queen's first publicist, recalled the event as follows:

'I remember Freddie running along Oxford Street to watch their appearance on a set in a shop window because he didn't own a telly.'

According to Matt Richards and Mark Langthorne's book, it wasn't only Freddie, but the whole band was standing in front of the television at the local electrical goods shop window to watch themselves, as none of them had a TV yet.

I can just imagine the situation. It may have looked painfully ridiculous, but they probably didn't mind. The future global stars had to watch their performance in a shop window. They were difficult times, but it was worth it to wait for better days.

Freddie wrote the lyrics for *Seven Seas of Rhye* and began working on it back in 1969, in the Wreckage era. It's not known how far he got with it then, but its first release was on this single.

The song is a very important confession about Freddie's dreams and desires. Freddie himself said it was an absolute fantasy and couldn't be linked to reality in any way. I agree that it is a fantasy, but how it was related to reality is another question.

I think it is time to interpret this magnificent song.

'Seven Seas of Rhye'

'Seven Seas of Rhye' is a short, compact melange of the irresistible ingredients of early Queen: hammered piano intro in an odd time signature, pounding drums, guitar harmonies, bouncing bassline, stopped riffs, echo on everything. Roger Taylor's falsetto backing vocals and an unusually low, growling double-tracked vocal from Freddie Mercury." (Andrew Wild)

*'Fear me your lords and lady preachers
I descend upon your earth from the skies
I command your very souls, you unbelievers
Bring before me what is mine
The seven seas of Rhye'*

In the verse cited above, Freddie appears like a god who comes down from the skies, generating fear of having such power over people on Earth.

The preachers are those religious people who condemn homosexuality, and homophobes who look at them with contempt and resentment.

The reference to unbelievers also indicates that Freddie has power over these people, like a god. He demands to have what is his, the seven seas of Rhye. The unbelievers are those people who don't believe in what Freddie says, that gay men are normal and have the right to live as they want.

Freddie's fantasy world appears again in this song. He is very powerful, just like the Fairy King. The seven seas of Rhye is an imaginary world ruled by him, and in his fantasy, he creates a fair and just world where homosexuality is no longer a sin. (The name he gave to this fantasy world is another matter. In his childhood, his father often told him about the glorious history of the Persian people, which at the peak of their power (Persian Empire, around 480 BC) had domain over at least seven seas. This is just conjecture on my part, however, it was probably no accident that Freddie emphasised he was not of Indian or Pakistani origin, but Persian. He was proud of his roots, and rightly so.)

He can prevail over anyone, and in his imagination, he faces up to the most potent forces to achieve the longed-for fair and just world, where everyone is equal.

The next verse continues:

'Can you hear me you peers and privy councillors
I stand before you naked to the eyes
I will destroy any man who dares abuse my trust
I swear that you'll be mine
The seven seas of Rhye'

If necessary, he will destroy anyone who doesn't let his dream come true, who cheats or deceives him. In his anger, caused by a deep frustration, he will destroy anyone who stands in the way of him living his life freely and from whom he has to hide and live a double life. The phrase 'I swear' shows Freddie's determination arising from his deep desire for change.

The words, 'you'll be mine' suggests that everyone will obey him, and he can satisfy his sexual desires with anyone. Nobody can get in his way. The seven seas of Rhye is his because this is his fantasy world, which can't be taken away from him.

The authorities are those who could do something about it, for example, the legislators who could change his predicament.

The next verse makes it clear what the song is about, why strength and power are needed:

'Sister I live and lie for you
Mister do and I'll die
You are mine I possess you
I belong to you forever'

He would like to achieve freedom through possession and sexual relations with men. When he wrote the song, he was still bisexual, though he already seems sure of his primary sexual identity; by that time, besides Mary, he had also had relationships with men, and realised he preferred their company. The 'sister' is probably Mary, who he lives with and lie for her, while asking a man to make love to him because he's dying for him. He declares that they belong to him forever. His strong sexual urges intensify his fantasies. He increasingly craves his sexual freedom, primarily because he had not yet broken the news to Mary and had to keep his gay relationships secret and had to lie to her.

Last verse:

'Storm the master marathon
I'll fly through
By flash and thunder, fire
And I'll survive (I'll survive, I'll survive)
Then I'll defy the laws of nature
And come out alive, then I'll get you
Be gone with you
You shod and shady senators
Give out the good
Leave out the bad evil cries
I challenge the mighty Titan
And his troubadours
And with a smile

I'll take you to the seven seas of Rhye'

It was the senators' job to give out the good; in other words, to change the law to permit sexual freedom for gay people.

He takes on any risks because, in his imagination, he can survive anything. (This verse perfectly illustrates that he is stuck in the role of survivor.)

He even seduces the great Titans and their troubadours with a smile, and takes them into his fantasy world where he is capable of ruling over them and doing anything with them.

His determination reminds me of how determined he was when he announced he would be a legend rather than a star. This song is about the same determination; he can beat anyone and cross any obstacle to reach his goal.

He sings the song with such suggestive force that we have to take every word seriously. Nevertheless, we believe he will make his desires come true.

Only a few years later, he went to bed with whoever he wanted; all he had to do was point to a person, and they jumped. (This happened in a gay bar in New York, where male prostitutes awaited the guests.)

So the time came when the imaginary world of the 'Seven Seas of Rhye' came true in his life, which he probably bitterly regretted.

Rosemary said that Freddie was outraged that the legislature wasn't on his side, and that it failed to protect the interests of gays. The enacted law only permitted gay relations in privacy for people over 21. It had no practical effect, as everybody did what they wanted in private in any case, as did Freddie.

Freddie carried through on his intent and reached his longed-for world of sexual freedom in the US, mainly in New York and Munich, where he could make all his fantasies come true in gay nightclubs. Unfortunately, however, his longer-term relationships made him both happy and sad, disappointed and desperately lonely from time to time.

The sad truth is that this great freedom cost him his life.

Tony Brainsby was Queen's first publicist at Trident, and was recruited at extravagant cost because he was so popular and successful in London. Tony was an eccentric figure, and maybe that was why Freddie also accepted him. This was what he said about Queen:

'What I thought was commendable was that at no time did they style themselves "Freddie Mercury and Queen". It was always a group image. Freddie never tried to project himself as the leader. As far as I could tell, relationships within the band were mostly harmonious. They were unusual for rock musicians in that they were so intelligent. One could feel quite inadequate in their presence.' (Lesley-Ann Jones)

Freddie commented on this as follows:

'I've never considered myself the leader of Queen. It's the four of us that makes the whole thing work. It's 25 per cent down the line. I'm the one out front, that's all.' (Freddie Mercury)

Even Tony was very taken with Freddie:

'Obviously, Freddie stuck out the most. He was such a raving poofter; I couldn't believe my eyes at our first meeting. He was dressed in red velvet skin-tight trousers, had black varnish on his fingernails, long hair and of course, all those teeth – he was extremely touchy about his teeth. He was strong-willed, nakedly ambitious, but also very charming. In those days, Freddie was an inwardly very aggressive and angry man in the sense that he knew he should be a star and wasn't yet. It's not a side of him that he allowed too many people to see, but it was definitely all the way through him. He felt that stardom was his by rights, and he was

extremely frustrated at that time it seemed to be taking for him to reach it. In my view, he was very much the fight in the band.' (Matt Richards & Mark Langthorne)

Later, as he got to know Freddie better, he described him as follows:

'He had many stylish little quirks that would stick in your mind. He'd paint the fingernails of just his right or just the left hand with black nail polish. Or he'd just varnish one little finger. He'd say 'Darling' or 'My dears' in every other sentence, and his camp delivery was highly amusing and very endearing. He was great to have around. Never a dull moment. The girls all loved it when he came into the office. ....At the time, of course, he was living with Mary. To start with, his sex life was a complete mystery to us all: we could never quite fathom it. He certainly never spoke about it.

I really admired him. Here was a man bursting with creative powers which were not simply in someone's imagination. They existed. He knew he had it in him, however old he was at the time...twenty-seven, I believe. I mean, they were quite old for a band, weren't they, to be starting out. He'd all this inside him forever. How frustrating it must have been, knowing that he had what it took, trying desperately to make it big-time, and not getting anywhere for so long.' (Lesley-Ann Jones)

As the other band members completed their studies, Freddie's creative resources couldn't be used for quite a while. He just had to wait, but it was worth waiting. He knew that Brian and Roger were the musicians with whom he could make his dreams come true. He had to wait two years to start working on Queen's first album. This included John, who was ideally suited to the band. He was more reserved than the others but was a very stable resource. As an electrical engineer, he understood all their equipment, and even made his own amplifier, famously known as the Deacy Amp. After the break with Trident, John mainly kept his eye on the finances.

There are twenty songs on Queen's first two albums; Freddie wrote eleven. This represents an outstanding achievement. I should add that both band members wrote extremely successful hits.

Freddie's 'Jesus' song doesn't need interpretation. He was concentrating on the music part, the lyrics don't contain any personal message.

'Liar'

When Freddie wrote this song, he had been living with Mary for two years and supposedly they still were in love.

However, from David Minns's book, we know that Freddie regularly cheated on Mary and lied to her because he feared losing her.

The song *'Liar'* is about this constant remorse, sense of guilt, and frustration.

Freddie claimed that generally, the songs were not about anyone, but about the kind of feelings that could affect anyone.
The lyrics of good songs are poems, confessions and visions from the depths of the soul, and can be combined with fantasy, but always contain personal experiences, and most of the times associated with raw emotions.

Music did a great service to Freddie; it helped him work through his traumatic experiences, and brought out his feelings of depression related to his sexuality, and it reduced the tension that this generated.

Sexuality plays a huge role in everyone's life. We are instinctively programmed to conceive and give birth to our offsprings. Intensified hormonal system functioning may lead to enhanced sexual urges.
Freddie was partly able to suppress this strong sexual urge by immersing himself in the creative process, but only partly because his private life wasn't ideal from this point of view. He couldn't tell Mary or anyone else about this secret.

The conflict that Hungarian writer, Frigyes Karinthy, also addressed in his poem, *Előszó* ['*Foreword*']: '*If I can't tell anybody, then I'll tell everyone*' is ideally suited to Freddie's situation. He couldn't tell Mary, but he told everyone in the songs.

Freddie himself said he wrote some of his songs very quickly, and agonised over others, which took a long time to come to fruition.

Songs in which Freddie tried to express his deepest, repressed feelings were harder to pen, whereas other songs, like 'Killer Queen', were about his playful fantasy and linked to positive feelings that gave Freddie a boost, he was capable of dreaming up a song in the bathroom and putting it all together in one night and one day.

'Liar', which was on Queen's first album, deals excellently with a substantial, unresolved problem in Freddie's life at the time.

The song lasts six minutes and 25 seconds, making it longer than *Bohemian Rhapsody*, and demonstrates that Freddie intends to cover a highly disturbing conflict, requiring a lot of time and effort to convey something weighing heavily on him.

The significant nature of the topic is also indicated by the length of the introduction (one minute 25 seconds). The drums and then the guitars create an almost insane tension in the uncommonly exciting introduction. When Freddie starts to sing, our hands are clenched, our legs are c, our hearts are pounding, and we can hardly wait for something to happen. Freddie finally begins to sing.

In a soft, childish voice, he confesses to his father, as if to a priest in a confessional, that he has committed a sin and asks for help in the most fallible possible way, like an innocent child.

'*I have sinned dear Father, Father I have sinned,*' Freddie repeats, and pleads, '*Try and help me, Father.*'

The father appears to the child as omnipotent, almost like a god, who is dear to him and is worth turning to for help. But this is just Freddie's wishful thinking. The fact is that he and his father don't have the kind of trusting relationship that would allow him to ask for advice in person. It is saddening. In reality, there is nobody to call 'dear father', so the conversation is taking place in Freddie's mind. He feels terrible about having to lie to his loved ones. He sings about his unbearable feelings and thoughts in this song and about what would happen if he were to come out as gay. He is talking to his parents and addressing everybody in truth.

He begins to raise his voice and asks, *'Won't you let me in?'* Freddie wished his father would open his heart, show love, and accept him with his homosexuality, but he knows the answer without asking, even without conversation. He knows his parents' opinions, as they have already shamed him once during his childhood by taking him out of school. His parents thought what he had done was wrong, and with their disapproval, they were declaring him guilty, even unintentionally, and thereby drove him away from them.

'Oh, nobody believes me' he complains in pain. Not even his parents believe him, and his girlfriend and everyone else think that his same-sex desire is a joke, but in reality, it involves considerable suffering and a painful sense of lack.

If the desire is satisfied, then the price is contempt, declared guilty, reprisals, and judgement.

Next, singing in chorus, they shout *'liar'*. The chorus is the people's voice, the voice of those who view homosexuality as a sin. In the song, he is the *'liar'* lying to Mary and the whole world; he is in a heterosexual relationship to meet expectations.

Again he repeats the word in agony: *'Liar!'* – the criticism comes again, and then he asks, *'Why don't you believe me?'* A painful question, but then apart from him who could understand what he was going through;

obviously only a gay partner who, for the time being, is only in the picture on an occasional basis.

The self-torment continues; he confesses another sin to a sire with higher social status, let's say a king, for example.

'Sire, I have stolen
Stolen many times
Raised my voice in anger
When I know, I never should'

This confession is in a quieter, child-like voice, and again he says he has stolen many times. This *"theft"* refers to the fact that, at the time, he was cheating on Mary by having casual relationships. His voice is raised when he sings, *'I raised my voice'*, and then he does raise his voice in anger.

He is angry, disappointed and frustrated that he has to have such dialogues and explain himself as if he were in court.

He shouts out in pain, *'Oh, everybody deceives me!'* He feels cheated, and nobody has empathy for him. Nobody wants to suffer with him or help him. So he is asking in vain.

'Liar' – the accusation can be heard again. He then asks, *'Why don't you leave me alone?'* – the voice of his conscience. Why does he continue to dwell on this, repeating it again and again? Why does he have to deal with this all the time? It would be good to escape these agonising thoughts and the sense of guilt finally.

By contrast, as Freddie finishes the verse, and the music starts again; the guitars and drums adding to the hardly bearable tension. But, oh, what else might come; isn't it enough already? When will the flood of the self-torment end?

His heart is aching and his soul is anxious, but the voice won't leave Freddie alone, and says again:

'*Liar!*'

Then comes high and mighty lecturing from the father or king, as they know everything better:

'I have sailed the seas
(Liar)
From Mars to Mercury
(Liar)
I have drunk the wine
(Liar)
Time after time
You are lying to me
You are lying to me'

This answer means there is no need for confessions. I don't even have to listen to you to know you are a liar, as I am more experienced and wiser.

Freddie then asks for forgiveness in agony. He is humble, and again in a child's voice continues:

'*Father, please forgive me*
You know you'll never leave me
Please, will you direct me in the right way?'

But the apology, humiliation and remorse are of no use.

'*Liar, liar, liar!*' the judges shout.

'*That is what they keep calling me!*' Freddie continues to sing ever louder and more angrily.

'*Liar, liar, liar*' the judgmental chorus is singing now, almost yelling.

The singing fades out. The music can barely get more intense, but continues.
In the next section, Freddie changes the tone of the song, mockingly asking and continuing to sing:

'Listen, are you gonna listen?
Mama I am gonna be your slave
All day long
Mama I am gonna try behave
All day long
Mama I am gonna be your slave
All day long
I am gonna serve you till your dying day
All day long
I am gonna keep you till your dying day
All day long
I am gonna kneel down by your side and pray
All day long
And pray
All day long
And pray
All day long
All day long'

Freddie doesn't take this section seriously because he knows the reaction. He would do anything in humility and even pray all day, and still wouldn't be able to reason with his parents or anybody else, which is why the tone is cynical.

He stops singing again.

The next musical part increases the pressure even further, as if we can hear sobbing and begging. Finally, we can feel the tension of waiting for a judgment, and then comes the cruel conclusion, shouting so everyone can hear it:

'All day long, all day long, all day long
Liar, liar, never ever let you win
Liar, liar everything you do is sin
Liar, nobody believes you
Liar, they bring you down before you begin'

And at the end, with vitriolic scorn in his voice:

'Ooh, let me tell you this
So now you know you could be dead before they let you'

Freddie's inner struggle comes to an end, but doesn't bring relief. The last line is the saddest of all – now that he's gone, we know he was right.

Many people are still homophobic today, despising, mocking and abusing gay men and lesbian women. In the summer of 2020, two young women were attacked on a bus one evening by young teenagers in London. They were beaten up for holding hands.

Soon afterwards, three gay men were stabbed by an assailant in a London park. It's frightening. When will this come to an end? Will it ever end? I don't know.

However, I'm confident that fans of Freddie and Queen, even if they were once homophobic, will have left this judgmental stance behind.

Brian told a lovely story about one memorable performance of the song, *Liar,* in the documentary, *From Rags To Rhapsody*:

'The Rainbow was almost like a pinnacle. Not long before, we'd seen David Bowie rise from obscurity to be able to play in Rainbow, and it seemed such a big deal. And I remember at that time how amazing it would be if we could do this. And I think it was only a year later when we actually did that gig. And live, of course, we very quickly became aware of the fact you get one shot, so you've got to deliver, we wanted to capture people, we wanted to move them, engage them, and we used to say deafen them and blind them and more. And we have so many mishaps on the stage, and power cuts were quite normal.'

So, when the theatre got dark because of the power cut, Freddie brilliantly solved the situation with humour:

Freddie: *'I tell you what, we just pose, and you look at us. Anyone who wants to pose with us is cordially invited. Come on.'*

Brian: *'It was nice really because the audience was so friendly to us. It didn't matter. They were very patient. It is a great feeling when you realize that.'*

When Freddie was finally able to start writing and singing his songs with Queen, he had an opportunity to release the tension built up in him over many years, caused by waiting, inertia due to lack of money, a feeling of loneliness and hyperactivity.

He improved his singing voice beautifully in the first few months, and in time it just got more beautiful and more expressive.

Freddie was full of musical ideas and melodies that had long been trying to get out, which he had heard perfectly in his mind; 'all' he had to do was record them and make them successful. They had plenty of work, and it required all their tenacity and perseverance.

How to surpass Love Story in one minute 18 seconds

'Nevermore'

'Nevermore, Queen's first piano/vocal ballad – there are no guitars. It sets up the album's central epic, The March of The Black Queen. It's pure Freddie, heartfelt, focussed, beautifully sung.' (Andrew Wild)

Freddie wrote his first-ever love song, and it was recorded on the first album. He sings so heartbreakingly about his disappointment that anyone who listens to it knows this is not just any old love song, but founded on real-life experience. The lyrics and Freddie's singing are breathtaking. What a gorgeous piece. I don't know who the song was written for; I wasn't able to find out from the biographical data.

Andrew Wild suggested that it may have been written for Mary.

Mary never wanted to leave Freddie. Perhaps it was about a short romance Freddie had with someone else.

'Where Do I Begin', the theme song from the film, Love Story, is a beautiful song, but Freddie squeezed more emotion into this short song than is in Love Story, the film and music combined.

The lyrics say everything, and is worth quoting:

'Nevermore'

'There's no living in my life anymore
The seas have gone dry
And the rain's stopped falling
Please don't you cry anymore
Can't you see
Listen to the breeze
Whisper to me please
Don't send me to the path of nevermore
Even the valleys below
Where the rays of the sun
Were so warm and tender
Now haven't anything to grow
Can't you see?
Why did you have to leave me? (nevermore)
Why did you deceive me? (nevermore)
You sent me to the path of nevermore
When you say you didn't love me anymore
Ah ah nevermore, nevermore.'

When he sings the line, *'When you said you didn't love me anymore'*, sensitive hearts will start to bleed for Freddie.

These and his other love songs show that love is always the same. Gay men feel a deep love towards their partners in precisely the same way as heterosexuals. They crave their partner's company, presence and embraces in the same way as anyone else.

Listening to this song, I started to wonder why he never wrote a love song for Mary. Freddie said he could never have fallen in love with a man in the same way that he loved Mary.

People fall in love differently, with different partners; the difference lies in intensity, depth and passion. Freddie loved David Minns with deep affection, as witnessed by the letters and songs he wrote. This love was genuine.

(YouTube: Queen – 'Nevermore' – official video)

Queen's first tour

The band's first long-awaited tour took place in the UK in 1973. The main attraction was Mott The Hoople, a successful British rock band. It was customary for a support band to play before the headline act, allowing new bands, such as Queen, to be introduced to the audience.

The tour was made up of 20 concerts at first-rate venues. The last gig was at London's Hammersmith Odeon, just before Christmas.

Queen's popularity began to take off during and after the tour, and people started buying their records.

Although the music press continuously subjected the band to harsh criticism, readers ranked Queen 3rd in a public opinion survey of the best new bands.

Queen's second tour

By the time they went on tour to publicise their second album, they were the lead act and no longer had to play second fiddle.

'When we had the opportunity of playing with Mott The Hoople (in 1973), that was great, but I knew damn well the moment we finished that tour, as far as Britain was concerned, we would soon be the ones headlining.' (Freddie Mercury)

The tour consisted of 22 gigs in the UK between March 1 and 29, 1974.

Freddie's idea for Zandra Rhodes was to design them special outfits for this tour. The tunic-style white tops were made of silk and had bat wings, so Freddie was free to raise his arms high; he looked like he had grown wings. The clothes remind me of a fairy's tunic and *'My Fairy King'*. He had also dressed in white at his earlier gigs, but didn't want to perform in the same clothes again. The new outfits were good for developing their image, and emphasised Queen's sound and their look. In addition, they wanted to put on exclusive the most fashionable designer's clothes. The idea was readily accepted by the other member of the band, though Trident was less happy when it received an invoice for 5,000 pounds, however, it was certainly worth it for them too.

Zandra Rhodes didn't come cheaply, as she designed clothes for many leading artists. Queen was sending a message to their contemporaries; we're just as cool as you are. And they were right. By taking care of their appearance, Queen was suggesting that 'we're valuable and worthy of respect.'

There were various scandals on tour, students fought with each other, two people were stabbed, and of course, the press made a meal of it.

Nevertheless, the audience celebrated in dramatic style at the next gig; while waiting for the band to appear, they sang the British national anthem – *God Save the Queen.*

There could not have been a more worthy way to celebrate Freddie's queenly, and the other band member's kingly nature. It then became customary for fans to greet the band at concerts by singing the national anthem. They must have found this dramatic and celebratory reception shocking and astonishing, but no doubt they deserved it. Few would have had any idea of the effort required to put the albums together. Originally it was Brian's idea to play a recorded version of the anthem at the end of concerts. Still, he couldn't have anticipated that fans would not only sing the anthem to celebrate Queen Elizabeth, but also the band. The fans' idea was astonishing. There was no better way they could have expressed their admiration.

Whenever I hear the British national anthem, I always see the faces of Queen and Elizabeth II. Lovely faces, lovely people.

Freddie's songs were on the black side of the Queen II album. Andrew Wild wrote about them in his book:

'These seventeen minutes established Mercury as a writer and musician of a rare talent – subsequent live shows confirmed his unparalleled skills as a frontman.'

'The March of The Black Queen'

'The majestic magnum opus.' (Andrew Wild)

'The grandiose, magnificent, valiant 'The March of The Black Queen' might be an utterly ludicrous song, but it's one of Queen's best. The innovation and invention almost pull the song apart. But, somehow, the band's skill holds it all together. The song is a favourite of progressive rock fans. It has many different non-repeating sections: almost a suite of separate songs.' (Andrew Wild)

Freddie wrote another beautiful, exciting song, on the Queen II album, 'The March of The Black Queen', also about his sexual fantasies.

The first verse goes as follows:

'Do you mean it, do you mean it, do you mean it?
Why don't you mean it?
Why do I follow you, and where do you go?'

These lines are indicative of Freddie's inner doubts. 'Is this what I really want? Why do I have to follow my desires, and where will they lead?' – he asks himself.

He then talks to someone and tries to convince them what a wonderful experience they would have making love. But, in reality, he is conducting an internal dialogue with himself, replying to the question in the first section on why he follows his desires:

*'You've never seen nothing like it, no, never in your life
Like, going up to heaven and then coming back alive'*

The two lines shown above refer to an orgasm; if you were to go up to heaven, you will lose yourself in pleasure, as if you were dying, and yet come back alive. (Has anyone ever read such a great comparison? I don't think so. Freddie was at least as great a poet as a musician and singer.)

He continues convincing himself in the next section:

*'Let me tell you all about it
And the world will so allow it
Give me a little time to choose'*

Freddie needed time to choose a gay partner to live with, or be with him without judgment. But the time wasn't right. He could only fantasize about it, hoping the world would, once and for all, allow him to live his life with whom he wanted.

Anyway, Freddie was right; later, the world would indeed allow gay men to choose a partner, live with them and get married, but sadly he didn't live to see it, and throughout his life, he had to conceal his desires.

*'Water babies singing in a lily pool delight
Blue powder monkeys praying in the dead of night'*

Water-loving bathers are singing in a pool overgrown with water lilies, generating excitement and anticipating pleasure. Freddie adored flowers and singing, and always took great pleasure in both. The praying of the guys procuring gunpowder (who delivered powder from the warehouse to the ship's cannons) in the middle of the night is a startling, slightly scary image, compared to the water lilies, preparing our mood for the pleasure and fear generated by the appearance of the mysterious black queen.

*'Here comes the black queen, poking in the pile
Fie-fo the black queen, marching single file
Take this, take that, bring them down to size'*

The black queen is Freddie himself, choosing between potential lovers at will (poking in the pile). These lovers will satisfy his hunger, meaning his physical desires will be satisfied. He instructs his servant to put the chosen ones in their place, i.e., letting them know they're not as important as they think. They should acknowledge that they are the queen's property, and she can do what she wants with them. He gives the servant further instructions on how the chosen ones should be prepared for the act in the next section:

'Put them in the cellar with the naughty boys
A little sugar then a rub-a-dub-a-baby oil'

The chosen ones must be locked up with the bad boys, those who already know what good sex is like. They must be made delicious and desirable with sugar, baby oil, a sweet taste, scented skin, anything to enhance the sense of erotica.

And then comes the confirmation that the black queen is Freddie himself:

'Black on, black on, every fingernail and toe'

The black varnished nails carry a certain weight. If that weren't enough, Freddie wears black, enigmatic clothing on stage when performing the song. It is adorned with a few sequins, with a silver-coloured ornament on his right arm, resembling the glove that partly concealed his hand. It means, *'I'll show you something of myself, but not everything.'* This is also the reason behind the songs with secretive lyrics.

The black clothes and sequins intensify the mystery under the sparkling lights on stage, and the playfully provocative stage presence creates an erotic impression.

The long, black hair and androgenous, sexy, indiscreetly skin-tight clothes, which emphasise every part of his figure, also aim to arouse desire.
The demonic look (eyes highlighted in black) and the sexy clothing emphasise his desirability. The dark colours and dark stage symbolise that he is in darkness, i.e., they conceal Freddie's secret about his sexuality.

The sequins sparkle under the lights from time to time, meaning *'I'll show you something, I'll flash something of myself, but I can't go out into the light (sadly).'* Freddie probably created this impression deliberately, although he claims this wasn't the case.

(A famous surrealist artist once painted a woman's face without any pupils and a mass of hair braided with snakes. The title of the painting is *In the gates of time*. During my analysis, it turned out that the artist had a green cataract and was afraid of going blind. He had no idea what the picture was about. He was convinced this was just a surrealist painting, which didn't tell us anything about him, and at most, revealed the depths of his imagination, which in any case was true, and the picture was beautiful. Irrespective of the painting, he was terrified of the cataract but had no idea he had painted this fear in the picture. This was the secret message of the painting.)

The lyrics continue:

*'We've only begun, begun
Make this, make that, keep making all that noise
Ooh, march to the black queen
Now I've got a belly full
You can be my sugar baby
You can be my honey chile'*

We have only just begun, and we're still at the foreplay stage. Freddie gives instructions, letting them know what his desires are. What kind of sounds he wants to hear, for example, moaning and groaning. Then, when his belly is full, i.e., he has been satisfied, he offers to be his long-term partner and love, and treat him like his own dear child.

He gives the commands while making love. It is partly a sexual fantasy about unconditional obedience, and partly that it's better than being afraid of a partner. At least in his imagination, he has control. He doesn't have to worry about being abandoned and lonely.

And now the very touching part:

*'A voice from behind me reminds me
Spread out your wings, you are an angel
Remember to deliver with the speed of light
A little bit of love and joy
Everything you do bears a will and a why and a wherefore
A little bit of love and joy'*

An inner voice warns him that the relationship is not just about sex and getting physical, but also about kindness, love and joy. Freddie was a kind, loving person who desired to live like that. In the psychology of colours, white represents cleanliness, light, innocence and tranquillity. This part of the song tells us Freddie wanted to have all of these attributes in his life. The white stage costumes represented this desire.

These lines suggest that he is good; he wants to give love and pleasure, which is very accurate of Freddie – physicality is just the consummation of love, which a relationship should be about.

Freddie is an angel who has been blessed, but only in part. Like everybody else, he has both angelic and devilish attributes. The question is whether or not he's able to control the devil. (Freddie had a stage costume, half white – half black, split vertically down the middle.)

But there is a big problem, as the next section explains:

*'In each and every soul lies a man
And very soon he'll deceive and discover
But even to the end of his life, he'll bring a little love'*

Due to the intense desire, he nor his partner couldn't managed to stay faithful but Freddie's love for his partner stayed with him. This was relevant to his longer-term relationships because his soul was full of love and gratitude, accompanied by a sense of guilt and remorse. The black queen symbolises Freddie's physical desires. The dark colour also indicates that the desire is on the dark side, something to be kept secret and be ashamed of. In the psychology of colours, the black symbolises inhibitory control, sadness, darkness, fear, loneliness, deep void, power and secrecy. Sadly, all these attributes were present in Freddie's life.

Freddie still wanted to *'bring a little love'*, even though the relationship had ended. This was what happened in his life; until the end of his life, he gathered those he loved around him and still loved them dearly, even if he was in love with someone else. He held onto Mary till the end of his life; called David Minns on the phone years after they had broken up and as if nothing had happened, started sweet-talking him again, and did the same with others until he had created a small 'family' around him.

The black queen takes the power back from the angel in the next section:

'I reign with my left hand, I rule with my right
I'm lord of all darkness, I'm queen of the night
I've got the power – now to do the march of the black queen'

Physical desire was stronger in Freddie than the desire to be faithful; desire controlled him and commanded him to behave like the black queen, be sexy, and conquer. His desires brought darkness into his life and defined what he would do and when. The angel was the light in Freddie, the kindness, love and faithfulness. In contrast, cheating and infidelity represented the dark side, resulting in shame, guilt, frustration and nasty behaviour.

The intensive physical desires dominated his life and determined his fate throughout life.

The 'March of the Black Queen' also remind us of Freddie's 'marching' up and down the stage; he is proud, self-confident and a conqueror. This is where the title comes from; the term black may refer to his hair and the colour of his clothes.

The lyrics show the extent to which his physicality makes him vulnerable. The lyrics continue:

'My life is in your hands, I'll fo and I'll fie
I'll be what you make me, I'll do what you like
I'll be a bad boy, I'll be your bad boy
I'll do the march of the black queen
Walking true to style
She's vulgar 'buse and vile
Fie-fo the black queen tattoos all her pies
She boils and she bakes and she never dots her I's'

Because of his uncontrollable physical desires, he even puts his life in the hands of the one he loves. This gives his partner complete control; Freddie would be willing to do anything. He would be happy to play the bad boy, the sensual role of a male or female who is highly erotic, vulgar, abusive and evil, and who knows every trick. The reference to baking and boiling is indicative of the fervour of the relationship. Effectively she has tattoos everywhere and is insatiable. She never finishes; this is what the phrase about not dotting i's refers to.

From here on he is talking to himself:

'Forget your sing-a-longs and your lullabies
Surrender to the city of the fireflies
Dance to the devil in beat with the band
To hell with all of you, hand in hand
But now it's time to be gone
La, la, la, la, forever, forever'

In other words, forget your childhood, grow up and give in to sensual pleasures – the city of fireflies (a city of fireflies represents a huge sensual desire). The fire symbolises the heat in love and passion.

'Dance to the devil' means that be a bad boy; according to the Zoroastrian religion, homosexuality is an alliance with the devil. Everyone can go to hell, and you don't have to care about anyone else's opinion; they can go to hell forever.

He'd like to send everyone to hell and not to be interested in anyone's opinion but, for the time being, he does care about it, which is precisely what is causing the anguish, internal conflicts and struggles that the song is about.

Freddie knew exactly how to say what he wanted to say in euphemisms, so only those who listen carefully would understand.

In any event, his stage performance showed that he enjoyed singing this song. He enjoyed the witty lyrics. Then, smiling to himself, he made sure we had our work cut out and we would have to think for a while about what we had heard.

In any case, the content is reproduced brilliantly, cheerfully and playfully; the band members probably guessed or knew what the song was about. It's performed in a very impressive performance style, with exciting music.

I haven't analysed songs that haven't got any personal content (such as *Ogre Battle*), or those with straightforward lyrics, like *Funny How Love Is*.

'Seven Seas of Rhye' reached number 10 in the charts. A few days later, on 8 March 1974, the album *Queen II* was released, which achieved a prominent 5th place. Following the success of the second album, the increased fan base also bought the first album in rising numbers.

Freddie 28th birthday present was the *Queen II* album going silver. At a press reception, the award was given to him by Jeanette Charles, the best impersonator of Queen Elizabeth, at Café Royal in London.

They didn't have to wait much longer for the breakthrough hit.

Mott The Hoople invited them on their four-week American tour, during which they played six concerts in New York's Uris Theatre on Broadway. After the last concert, poor Brian collapsed, having contracted hepatitis. As a result, Queen was only able to play 20 of the 40 shows initially planned. They abandoned the tour and flew home; Brian was taken to hospital, and they began recording the *Sheer Heart Attack* album without him. In despair, Brian even thought they would drop him from the band. What an impossible idea; how could they have managed without him? They couldn't.

14. *Sheer Heart Attack Album* (1974)

'The album is very varied, we took it to extremes, I suppose, but we are very interested in studio techniques and wanted to use what was available. We learnt a lot about technique while we were making the first two albums. Of course, there has been some criticism, and constructive criticism has been very good for us. But to be frank, I'm not that keen on the British music press, and they've been pretty unfair to us. I feel that up and coming journalists, by and large, put themselves above the artists. They've certainly been under a misconception about us. We've been called supermarket hype. But if you see us up on a stage, that's what we're all about. We are basically a rock band.'

(Queen interviews – Freddie Mercury - Melody Maker 1974)

The single, 'Killer Queen', was released on 11 October, 1974, and reached number two on the charts. This song was released to introduce the *Sheer Heart Attack* album, with the title track written by Roger. Although *Sheer Heart Attack* didn't make it onto the album in the end, we can only come across it on the 1977 album *News Of The World*.
The album was released on 8 November, 1974, and reached number two in the UK. It was a huge success.

'Killer Queen'

'*Killer Queen is about a high-class call girl*', said Freddie at the time. '*I was trying to say that classy people can be whores as well.*'

'*It was a turning point,*' Brian remarked later talking about Killer Queen. '*It was the song that best summed up our kind of music and a big hit, and we desperately needed it as a mark of something successful happening for us. We were penniless, you know, just like any other struggling rock'n'roll band. All were sitting around in London bedsitters, just like the rest.*'

'*A wonderfully commercial song, and yet effortlessly clever and complex in execution, 'Killer Queen' was surely a conscious move away from the pro-glam of Queen and Queen II. Mostly recorded without May, the song includes the first flowering of the multi-tracking and vocal harmonising methods that would go on to become big parts of Queen's signature sound. May's main contribution is a guitar solo that elaborates on the vocal melody of the verses.*' (Andrew Wild)

The song is connected to Freddie in many respects, and can be clearly linked to his sexual fantasies, and we can also find some of his personality traits in this elegant courtesan.

The analysis of 'The March of The Black Queen' revealed that it was about Freddie; he identified himself with the black queen in the song. The same thing happens in 'Killer Queen'; he's just playing the role of a courtesan. He, too, would like to have more sexual relationships.

Freddie enjoyed the relative luxury he had in Zanzibar; he said he liked the idea of affluence. This was why he worked so hard – to ensure he wouldn't have to go without anything. Similarly, this courtesan also had a lovely life, keeping French champagne, Moët and Chandon (which was Freddie's favourite) in a stylish cabinet, offering her guests cake as elegantly as Marie Antoinette had in her time. We know that all kinds of delicacies could be found in the French Royal Palace, not to mention luxury. (Garden Lodge, Freddie's house, later measured up to these conditions in every way. Luxury, elegance and an extravagant lifestyle were part of his dreams and fantasies.)

The Killer Queen was so illustrious that her guests could have included 'Khrushchev or Kennedy.' She was able to invite guests in a way that nobody could refuse, just like Freddie. She was irresistible and inimitable, just like Freddie. She had practised her etiquette well, just like Freddie did among the school's nuns in Zanzibar during his childhood and later at school in India and Britain. The girl was first-class at what she did and used every resource to achieve what she wanted. Freddie's humour is revealed by the varied resources he lists: *'gunpowder, gelatine, dynamite with a laser beam, guaranteed to blow your mind anytime'*.

And this is true of Freddie too, partly the humour and partly his attitude to success, which he sees as guaranteed in every moment.

To avoid complications, the girl uses several addresses and speaks like a baroness.

Freddie also liked to avoid complications – for example, his relationship with Mary Austin – and was the diplomat in the band. He was the one that smoothed over the band's arguments. He said this himself, and Brian confirmed it several times.

Everyone was very impressed with Freddie's politeness. Even though English people tend to be quite polite as a rule, even the most ordinary people – of course, there are exceptions, as in everything – but Freddie even managed to surpass this. His friends' parents praised his great politeness, and he surprised his friends with this attribute. It must have been very conspicuous among rebellious young people in the 1970s.

The lyrics added to the woman's demanding nature: her perfume was French, of course, her taste sophisticated, she was meticulous and precise.

Freddie looked after himself too. Even under the most challenging circumstances, his appearance was always immaculate. His taste was *'sophisticated'*; he wore velvet, silk, belts, jewellery, jackets and blazers, while the others were in torn jeans, t-shirts and cardigans. When he became rich, he bought dozens of top-brand perfumes.

Moreover, the woman will go to bed in an instant. She's as 'playful as a pussycat', she is temporarily exhausted, out of action, temporarily *'out of gas'*, like a machine, she's able to drive anyone wild and will go anywhere to get you, and has an insatiable appetite, she'll go to China or Japan if that's the price of getting what she wants. Finally, she asks if you're going to try.

Freddie's playful sexual fantasy was inexhaustible. The black queen put the chosen lovers among the bad boys and placed them in icing sugar, and oiled them, which reveals everything. Freddie had two cats at the time and adored them, so he know how playful they could be.

Freddie would go anywhere to get anyone. He used hundreds of different tricks to build his, and the band's, careers, starting with a sexy, elegant appearance, a theatrical performance style, smoke bombs, a sawn-off microphone, and charming conversations with managers. His sexual energy was inexhaustible, just like his creativity.

Just as Freddie sings on the 'Funny How Love Is' on the *Queen II* album, he effectively notices opportunities for love anywhere and in anything. He always goes wherever he has to, revealing he is focused on it, and that's why he notices anyone in the same boat.

Matt Richards and Mark Langthorne quote the late Eric Hall, one of EMI's promoters:

'He (Freddie) used to be infatuated with me, I don't know why. Was I his type? I assume I must have been. He told me that song ('Killer Queen') was about me. He said to me, "I am the queen, Eric, and you're killing me because I can't have you.
I used to keep champagne in my little fancy cabinet. I had monster permed hair, like Marie Antoinette."'

This is an exciting addition to the song's meaning. Eric had set Freddie's fantasy in motion, but the track is clearly about Freddie. Eric just inspired Freddie as a potential lover. Freddie didn't like rejection and didn't give up easily. We don't know what the end game might have been here, as Eric kept a discreet silence about that.

In any case, given that Freddie was very busy with rehearsals and recordings at that time, I suspect he didn't have much time left for adventures in love, and so he was forced to live them in his imagination. Some lovely songs were created from this compulsion, but Freddie's addiction to work was just as strong as his sexual fantasy, which enabled him to release his energy by working.

He was also conscientious and wasn't in the habit of letting the band or the audience down.

It's interesting to observe that while the song is about a woman who is exhausted after sex, which for biological reasons tends to be more typical of men, this is just a minor thing and doesn't mean much. Still, the fact that he compares the woman to a machine makes me think of a later song, *'Don't Stop Me Now'*, the lyrics of which refer to him as a sex-machine.

In the same way, the possibility of laser therapy also arose due to a regrettable situation. Nodules had grown on Freddie's vocal cords because of the highly intensive series of gigs, and he fought them throughout his life. He sought almost every specialist, and without exception, they urged him to stop singing, rest for a few months, or lose his voice completely.

Queen was forced to cancel half of their first independent US tour. Later in his career, these nodules kept Freddie in constant fear. During the 20 years the band spent together, there was only one occasion when he had to march off the stage because he had lost his voice completely, but they often had to cancel concerts, while at other times he kept on singing to the end at, any cost, by taking honey and lemonade. Interestingly and touchingly, Roger and Brian often helped Freddie out in concerts. When he had a problem with his voice, Freddie just mimed the high notes while Roger or Brian sang, and nobody noticed. That's what I call fantastic collaboration, and of course, it was much more than that. They had become like a family.

Given the song's success, they were invited back on the BBC's Top of The Pops show, further adding to their popularity.

The performance can be seen on YouTube. Freddie is singing in his favourite fox fur coat, his nails painted black, richly adorned with jewellery, just as seductively as a real Killer Queen. It's an unmissable experience.

(YouTube: Queen – 'Killer Queen' - Top Of The Pops, 1974).

'Lily of The Valley'

'*A beautiful, lyrical, almost-perfect song with much of the pomp held in check. The key hook is the leaping piano motif in the introduction, then a swoop to a gorgeous, rich, genuine Freddie vocal backed by layers and layers of backing vocals.*' (Andrew Wild)

Another of Freddie's songs with beautiful lyrics, '*Lily Of The Valley*', starts with the question of why he has no relative equilibrium in his life, why does he always have to be on a real high or very sad. Elsewhere, he describes himself as someone who falls in love too quickly, and when the relationship has reached a nicely balanced level, and things are going well, he destroys it. By ending the relationship first, he avoids the painful and humiliating feeling of rejection.

His questions are rhetorical: '*Why does everyone tell me not to do this?*' This question is about his inner voice. He is aware he is ruining his relationships, but is unable to stop. He would give his kingdom for a horse to find the answer. Maybe Freddie didn't realise that his school years hadn't just caused a lack of affection and a sense of insecurity, but also resulted in emotional instability. This song represents a dialogue with himself, and he is in a fantasy world again. A messenger came from the seven seas to tell the king he had lost his throne.

He is the king, and the *'messenger'* is Mercury in mythology, which shows he has an internal dialogue. The *'Serpent of the Nile'* provides a little relief, Freddie sings. He loved old films; he probably talked about a movie from the 1950s, a melodramatic story about Antony, Cleopatra and Ceasar. This calm doesn't last long because wars never cease.

This is the internal war. The lost throne probably refers to his ruined relationship with Mary, the fact that love had cooled down, so Freddie was looking for new adventures (as Mary and David Minns reported.)

The *Sheer Heart Attack album's* tour began with 19 venues in the United Kingdom and lasted for three weeks.

From then on, they used pyrotechnics to make the show even more spectacular.

The last concert was at Rainbow Theatre in London, where they were so successful that they played the same venue again the following evening, in front of a full house.

This concert was recorded and available on DVD under the title *Live at the Rainbow '74*. However, the video is on YouTube. It's worth searching for the 'full' version.

The show is exhilarating and spectacular. Freddie and Brian start in their angel tunics, and Freddie is in full make-up. At the end of the show, Freddie puts on the black queen 'costume', so we can witness what I've written about Freddie's stage appearance in this one-hour show.

They perform 21 songs; the fourth is *White Queen*, written by Brian, a wonderful, lyrical piece. Freddie sings emotionally and plays the piano wonderfully, and Brian's guitar playing is awe-inspiring.

'In The Lap of the Gods'

'It sounds like music from the end of the world. The verse resolves to a rich, melodic chorus ('leave it in the lap of the gods') with added acoustic guitar, a low, humming lead guitar and some more of those ball-busting

falsettos. Beautiful. Other than Taylor's falsetto, the vocals are just Freddie Mercury, overdubbed many times.' (Andrew Wild)

'In The Lap of the Gods' is another one of Freddie's songs on the album (Starts at 27:53 on the *Live at on the Rainbow '74* video). Unfortunately, the official version is so distorted, it's difficult to hear the lyrics. And there is no other version available on YouTube.
The recording begins with Roger's amazing scream. You might think it can't be a voice of a man, but you'd be wrong, as this pitch is within his natural vocal range.

Freddie accompanies on the piano during the live performance, and this in itself makes it worth watching. The lyrics, melody and music complement one another magnificently; Roger's scream raises the song to an ethereal level, as if two angels are singing.

Freddie is very much in love again and living only for his lover. All his thoughts are with him and only with him. He would do anything for his love, their lips come together, but in the end, he trusts the gods to decide how the story continues.

Freddie reworked the song completely; there are two versions on the same album.

'In the Lap of the Gods… Revisited'

'A dramatic, anthemic sing-along with a tightly arranged rhythm section: their first attempt at We Are the Champions. Other than re-using the track's title, there seems to be no musical or lyrical connection to In the Lap of the Gods.' (Andrew Wild)

The lyrics and the music on the later version are completely different. It's no longer a love song. In the revisited version, Freddie sings as a disillusioned lover. His love was only interested in Freddie's money, but he wasn't a fool and wouldn't let himself be exploited. I don't know what happened between the two versions, but I'm guessing the partner he loved deservedly lost his trust and love, or at least this was how Freddie saw things. We don't know who he wrote the song for. I don't think it was just a fantasy; it wouldn't have continued on the same album if it was. Composing a song is far more difficult than giving it a different title.

Regardless, music written with intense emotion is always exciting and conveys a special vibe. The lyrics of these songs are great, and both have a personal message in them.

Andrew Wild thought there was no connection. Knowing Freddie's way of thinking from his songs and his interviews, I beg to differ. I believe Freddie chose this title to allow someone to hear this message.

The audience sings along with the chorus at concerts, and it's enjoyable to listen to the nice new tune in the 'revisited' version on YouTube.

It's worth listening to because the live version is always different from the recording. It's much more exciting musically, due to Freddie's improvising, not to mention that seeing and hearing them simultaneously produces a more pleasant experience.

Let me write a bit about Brian here. The music in Brian's song 'Brighton Rock' would even wake the dead. The guitar and drums are terrific in the middle of the song, at around 2:55 on the *Queen – Brighton Rock (Official Lyrics Video)*. In addition, Freddie sings more than half of the song falsetto, making the witty lyrics even more uplifting.

Brian's solo is indescribable. His style is completely unique; Peter Freestone is right, after a while, we can recognise it's Brian playing. It's not just his virtuosity, but also the unexampled sound that makes him utterly great and unmistakable.

Not to mention that, with his father's help, he built the electric guitar himself, the 'Red Special', because the family didn't have enough money to buy one. The 'Red Special' made sounds so special that they couldn't be imitated even with the most expensive guitars. It was even referred to as the fifth member of the band.

'...Brian's guitar is specially built, so he can almost make it speak. It will talk on this track.' Freddie's thoughts about May's The Prophet's Song on A Night At The Opera album. (Freddie Mercury)

Freddie was perfectly correct, and this can be felt in every song. Brian could imitate the sound of various instruments with his guitar.

'Brian May is a nimble-fingered and technical player with a razor-sharp understanding of harmony, but his melodic, singable approach to both riffs and solos means any player can learn from his style.' (guitarworld.com)

'She Makes Me' is Brian's song from the same album, a dreamy love song with beautiful lyrics. It sounds wonderful. Brian's singing is emotional and very impressive. The fantastic interplay between drums and guitar is unparalleled. This is one of the most lyrical Queen songs ever written. Freddie wasn't involved in the collaboration.

The snow-white fairy tunic was perfectly suited to the song.

This song demonstrates the emotional depths Brian was capable of feeling.

The best way to get to know someone is through their songs or poems, which say everything about the person who wrote them.

Comparing it with 'Love of My Life', which Freddie wrote for the next album, we can sense that Freddie had the same depth of emotion as Brian. Freddie's song is a masterpiece and became an enormous hit, whereas Brian's song has almost been forgotten, even though it lacks nothing by comparison with Freddie's song.

Freddie wrote about the studio work related to the *Sheer Heart Attack* album as follows:

'I enjoy the studio (but) it's so exhausting physically and mentally. It drains you totally. I sometimes ask myself why I do it. After Sheer Heart Attack, we were insane and said never again. Then look at what happened! After that album, we realised we'd established ourselves. We felt that there were no barriers, no restrictions. Vocally we can outdo any band. We went a bit overboard on every album that's the way Queen is.' (Freddie Mercury)

Following their successful British concerts, Queen played at ten different venues in six European countries at the end of 1974, just before Christmas, which was their first European tour.

The last stop was Barcelona. Freddie fell in love with the city right away, but could not have known what would happen to him there in 1988. If anyone had told him in advance, Freddie would have said this was crazy and absolutely out of the question. Appearing alongside Montserrat Caballé, writing an anthem for the city for the opening ceremony of the Olympic Games?

He probably hadn't even heard of Montsi, as the famous opera singer called herself when they actually met.

The band flew to the USA for their first independent series of concerts in America at the end of January 1975. First, they played the Beacon Theatre on Broadway in New York.

This was when Freddie had to go for check-ups and treatment for his vocal cords. One of the doctors, who had also treated Tom Jones, prescribed two weeks' rest and antibiotics, which Freddie accepted. He took a rest and Queen cancelled a few concerts. Prior to this, they had already played in Washington, where he was fully committed to singing with nodules in his throat against strict doctor's orders.

Freddie just couldn't be stopped; his hyperactivity and commitment accompanied him throughout his life.

The Japanese Miracle

After the American concerts, Queen travelled to Japan in April, where an even bigger surprise awaited them. The *Sheer Heart Attack* album and the single, *Killer Queen* were at number one in the Japanese charts. A huge crowd welcomed them in celebration at the airport. When they entered the arrivals' hall, the loudspeakers fell silent and began to play a Queen song. No other band in the world could have earned such an honour.

They were received with the greatest love and respect everywhere on their Japanese tour. Every influential businessman in Tokyo was invited to a dinner in their honour to pay respects to the band.

A bunch of sumo wrestlers were hired to keep the crowd in check, but not even they were able to keep the fans away. At one point during the reception ceremony, Freddie had to interrupt and ask the fans to take a deep breath and calm down.

A total of 80,000 people attended their eight concerts, and each played in front of a full house.

The fans chased after them like fans of The Beatles used to do. They hid in lifts and behind curtains in hotels, and constantly needed bodyguards to stop the excessive enthusiasm of fans from harming the band.

Queen was received by the same kind of hysterical crowds in every city.

In the end, they were forced to use the laundry lift for the sake of their safety. All this happened when people in the UK were only just getting to know them. The Japanese showed the world how to treat stars. This love for Queen is still felt in Japan today. This explains why many of Queen's videos have Japanese subtitles and comments.

Freddie really loved Japan; he admired and collected Japanese works of art all his life, and took the last love of his life there for 'a holiday of a lifetime.'

In 2004 Brian played and sang 'Love of My Life' in Tokyo in memory of Freddie; the audience began to cry, especially when they saw Freddie on the screen, and he continued singing the song. It was very moving, not just for the older generation, but also for some very young people who were also in the audience.

Brian was 67 years old in 2014 and sang just as beautifully as he had in the glorious days.

(YouTube: Queen + Adam Lambert Love of My Life Live in Tokyo 2014)

15. Break-up with Trident

A new chapter and new horizons in the life of Queen

When Queen signed the contract with Trident, the band members were still quite inexperienced. In addition, at that point, Trident was their only option, so they fell into the kind of trap that brought them to the brink of disastrous financial ruin, despite their success. If they hadn't made the album *A Night At The Opera* (1975), it's doubtful whether they could have continued, Brian said in an interview.

(YouTube: Queen - From Rags to Rhapsody - Subtitulado al español)

When recording their debut album, they could only use the Trident studio when other successful artists didn't need it, usually during the night. Their salaries were ridiculously low. Brian May said they were paid 20 pounds a week, which was the same amount they got right at the start. By then, they had already finished three albums, and the third was a big success. Strikingly, at the same time, the band's managers started to drive around in Rolls Royce cars and had swimming pools built for themselves. Freddie and the other band members began to wonder where the money had gone.

Freddie would have loved a new piano, while John needed money to buy a flat because he had recently married, and Roger wanted a car.

Despite Freddie's strong stance (he even banged his fist in anger on the desk of a Trident executive), Trident failed to meet any of their requests, claiming the band was expensive to manage, and had not been profitable yet.

The band had had enough. They found a new manager in the person of John Reid in September 1975, and with the help of a lawyer, Jim Beach, they got out of the contract with Trident. Jim worked for several months trying to recover 200,000 pounds that Queen owed Trident. The negotiations eventually proved successful, but the split ended up costing a small fortune. In the end, they compromised on a sum of 100,000 pounds, which Queen had to pay, and Trident also claimed 1% of royalties on the next six albums. Thanks to John Reid and Jim Beach, EMI gave Queen an advance payment of 100,000 pounds to make the final break-up possible.

Norman Sheffield wrote in his memoirs that he regretted having neglected Queen, in favour of Trident's other clients. And he had good reason for this regret, as the later story of Queen revealed.

Freddie remembered Norman Sheffield in the song 'Death on Two' Legs, which sparkled with hatred like the hammering of red-hot, glowing iron. He didn't say to whom the song was dedicated, to avoid legal problems, but as soon as Norman heard it, he knew it was for him, like a secret message from Freddie. One of the lines in the song goes: *'Do you feel like suicide? (I think you should).'* Freddie's overt anger in this recording perfectly reflects his tough side, the times when he struck back cruelly.

Of course, Norman didn't kill himself and far outlived Freddie, dying at the age of 75. The title of his memoir was *Life On Two Legs*.

After the break-up with Trident, they took the material they had recorded straight to the record labels, and their salaries were increased to 30 pounds a week. However, it was only after their 3rd successful album that they found the right people, who sorted out their careers without exploiting them.

Fortunately, thanks to Freddie, they didn't have to wait much longer for global success.

16. Freddie's Relationship with David Minns

In the summer of 1975, destiny decided that Freddie would get to know his first real love, 25-year old David Minns. Freddie wrote his most beautiful love songs, 'Love of My Life' and 'You Take My Breath Away', for him.

Despite claims to the contrary, Mary Austin wasn't the love of Freddie's life. Freddie never publicly said this. He told his then manager, John Reid, that he had written the song for David. Mary also said in an interview that the song wasn't about her; she hadn't left Freddie, he had left her.

Freddie first met David in a gay bar in London in 1975. At first, David did not believe that Freddie was also gay. They began talking about Queen's new album and the band's management, because David had once worked for Paul McCartney, and had started managing Eddy Howell.

Freddie suddenly started telling David about his private life. When they left the bar, Freddie leaned over to David and kissed him on the cheek, and asked if they could meet again. Freddie then invited him to the studio. They exchanged phone numbers, started meeting up, and fell in love. This was the first time Freddie had wanted a long-term relationship with a man he loved and trusted.

Initially, it was difficult to find time for each other, because they both had busy lives. In August that year, Freddie let David listen to *Bohemian Rhapsody*, as one of the first people to hear it.

Freddie told him he lived with Mary Austin, who was only an old friend. And then they had this dialogue:

"Freddie then announced: 'Look, I've got to tell you, but, you see, I really fancy you, well, in fact, I'm totally going mad for you, can we just go back to your place now?'

'Is this a good idea, Freddie?' - I asked.

'Because I don't fancy you.'

'Don't be silly,' he said, 'of course you do. I'll make sure you do.'"

(David Evans and David Minns)

Freddie and his unshakable style made me smile. It seemed as if he really could control David, even though he wasn't David's type, they kept meeting and then had a relationship.

Freddie didn't like speaking to David about his childhood. However, he did say that he gave up his religion because it regarded homosexuality as a sin. He felt he would let his parents down by coming out. He went to David's flat in tears on one occasion because his mother had asked him if he was dating men again. Freddie felt guilty; he was hurt and felt his parents were constantly putting pressure on him.

I think Mary must have complained to them, because Freddie was almost completely ignoring her at the time.

David believed that Freddie was a possessive type. The desire for possession is entirely normal between lovers who are devoted to one another, however, if the desire for possession is associated with excessive jealousy, this can poison the relationship.

They met almost every day in the autumn of 1975. Neither of them was openly gay, so they kept their relationship secret.

David began to be suspicious when he visited Freddie in his flat and noticed there was only one bedroom.

As I have mentioned before, Freddie told David that, as a teenager, he'd already had relationships with boys at school in India, and even though he lived with Mary, he'd also had relationships with men before he met David, but David was the first man he wanted to live with.

They were very happy in the first three months of their relationship, but then started arguing. Freddie's sense of guilt continued to be a cloud that hung over him, in part because of Mary and partly due to his parents. As a result of the pressure, Freddie was tense and began to behave aggressively and nastily. He was frustrated and obviously very hurt that he couldn't live openly and freely with David, and took out his frustration on Mary and David.

Their arguments often turned physical, and they would sometimes deliberately do things to make each other jealous. According to David's book, Freddie was incapable of discussing things calmly. If he couldn't prove he was right, he became aggressive and even had tantrums.

David wanted a relationship based on equality, but was forced to realise this was impossible with a superstar. The question is, what role did Freddie being a star with an emotional imbalance, play in all this? Even Freddie didn't know the answer; he squirmed in the captivity of love, without ever having the chance to learn how an intimate relationship works. He expected David to tolerate his hysterics and aggressiveness.

David often noticed how Freddie lied to Mary and deceived her by saying he was working late, when he was actually spending time with David. This dishonesty made David very uncomfortable, so he asked Freddie to tell Mary about their relationship, otherwise, he would have to end it. Freddie didn't want to lose David, so he took a risk and told Mary he was bisexual.

Mary stated in an interview that Freddie changed a lot when John Reid became the band's new manager, and it was clear something was worrying him. She was relieved that Freddie was honest with her. Referring to their relationship in an interview, Mary said:

'He decided ultimately that he had to tell me that he was bisexual, and I knew that really, he was trying, I think to tell me that fundamentally he'd decided that he was gay.'

(YouTube: Is This The Real Life NL version Part 1)

Mary was pleased about this confession because it made her realise that Freddie trusted her. He'd told the truth, even though he couldn't be sure how Mary would react. After the confession, Freddie seemed happier and less stressed, just as he used to be. Mary couldn't deny him the chance to be happy.

She treated Freddie with patience and understanding, which makes me think she really did love him. She didn't take revenge or hurt him, and continued to love him as before. Although she didn't say it, it's clear from her behaviour that she was not happy with Freddie's decision to leave her.

Freddie once told his friend, Mick Rock, Queen's photographer, that Mary was the love of his life. The question is, when did he say this? Is it possible that Freddie ever really felt this way? I don't know, but the fact is he never wrote a love song for Mary. The two songs, *Love of My Life* and *You Take My Breath Away* were both written after he got to know David.

Freddie broke up with David at the beginning of 1978; the band's lawyer, Jim Beach, phoned David to tell him that Freddie no longer wished to maintain contact with him. Minns claimed that Freddie liked to get other people to do his dirty work.

David also wrote that he really regretted not standing by Freddie, and thought that he might have been able to prevent him from getting infected with HIV, but this was simply impossible. Nobody could have stopped Freddie. (He even cheated on David continually in New York and on other international tours because he always succumbed to his sexual appetite. After a while, he didn't even try to keep it in check; in fact, he took every opportunity to satisfy his desires.)

The way he was treated and the break-up itself upset David so much that he attempted suicide, but fortunately failed.

Freddie thought David was trying to blackmail him, so he wrote a very wicked, sarcastic song about David's suicide *(Don't Try Suicide)*. Part of it goes like this: *'Don't try suicide, nobody cares.'* Freddie was right about one thing when he sang *'Nobody's worth it'*. I don't know what made Freddie react like this; I can only assume that he continued to resent David, who had gone out of his life, despite Freddie's request. As far as David was concerned, this was equivalent to a knock-out punch. Freddie hated losing and couldn't stand anyone saying no to him.

According to their mutual friend, David Evans, as revealed in his book, David was a kind, intelligent man who really loved Freddie, and his later loves and lovers couldn't come close to David. David might have been the greatest of men, but at that point, he was merely the catalyst that had helped Freddie to leave Mary.

David may not have realised it, but he helped Freddie make one of his most important and painful decisions: to tell Mary the truth about his sexuality.

In any case, Freddie needed a different type of man, someone who was capable of calming him down, constantly reassuring him of his love, and alongside whom he could find emotional security. But he had to wait a long time for this man.

The moment had not yet arrived in Freddie's life when he could settle down; he was away too often and unable to settle in a stable relationship. His career and love were both important to him, but he was incapable of striking a balance between the two, and this was made more difficult by his emotionally unstable personality.

Freddie broke up because he fell in love with someone else.

17. A Night at the Opera album (1975)

1975 brought some enormous and dramatic changes in the lives of Queen and Freddie.

Brian and Roger had hesitated when deciding whether Freddie would be a suitable frontman. Despite all his strangeness, they sensed that he had something that magically attracted people's gaze, though they still doubted that he could sing. Roger was serious when he compared Freddie's singing to a goat bleating, when they first heard him sing.

Through divine inspiration, they decide to give Freddie a try. Ironically, Freddie's strangeness, his unusual but very attractive personality, and his God-given talent helped the band become an international success.

Freddie made the most difficult decision of his life in 1975. And it was this painful experience that inspired him to write or finish the song that is regarded as his most memorable and beautiful song ever, *Bohemian Rhapsody*, which became a huge international hit. There are quite possibly no regions in the world where music lovers aren't aware of this song; it is so distinctive and well-known that almost everyone recognises it after a few bars.

How to have global success in five minutes 55 seconds:

'Bohemian Rhapsody'

'A mark of great record production is that it stands the test of time. Every good record has to start with a good song. But you can't separate the song from the production. To an extent, it's that gargantuan (enormous) production which echoes in our heads, even if we hear the song played without all that.' (Steve Levin, record producer)

(YouTube: Inside The Rhapsody – Queen (Full Documentary)

Brian May: *'I don't think we ever will know what Bohemian Rhapsody is about. If I knew, I probably would not tell anyway because I wouldn't tell anyone what my songs are about. I hate doing that. I think it destroys it really because the great thing about a great song is that you relate it to your personal experience, and you feel it in your own life.*

There would be many theories because Freddie was wrestling a lot of things in his personal life, and he may have just chosen to put them into the song in that way. You know he was certainly looking at rediscovering himself, and I think at that time it was probably too scary a thing for him to do. He actually did it later. I think it's nice to leave a question mark in here.'

(YouTube: Inside The Rhapsody – Queen (Full Documentary)

I really appreciate Brian's attitude. He decided that even after Freddie's death, he would respect the agreement that members of the band don't talk about the content of songs written by each other. For his part, he's right. He couldn't do anything else, and anyway, as the documentary reveals, Freddie didn't tell them what the song was about either. This was why John naively asked what the title of the song would be, Mama?

This was what Freddie said about interpreting his songs:

'People say 'What does that lyric mean?' I don't like to explain what I thought when I wrote a song. 'Does it mean this? Does it mean that?' is all anybody wants to know. F*ck them, darlings! I would say no more than what any decent poet would tell you if you dared ask him to analyse his work. If you see it, then it's here. You interpret it how you want to. There's no great big message. I try to conjure up something and get that into a song, and then I hope that people will try to make up their minds about it – which is a good thing.' (Freddie Mercury)

Freddie's was correct, nobody can demand that an artist explain his lyrics, so he doesn't need to interpret them. In the film, Freddie tells EMI representative, Ray Foster, who wants to know what the song is about: *'True poetry is for the listener.'* It means we have to learn to read between the lines.

When an artist writes a song, there is always a message, something he wants to say. Music works through emotions, but the lyrics are also hugely significant for the true listener. Anyway, I think that is why songs have lyrics.

The swear words are for those demanding people who want to pry into his private life to create a sensation and seek glory based on their ego.

Freddie hoped that people would put their own interpretation on his songs, because – according to him – it is a good thing.

Queen's greatness wasn't just in their music. For instance, let's consider Brian. He didn't write songs with lyrics as mysterious as Freddie's, but if we listen to 'She Makes Me', the impact would be substantially reduced without the lyrics. I must have heard it a hundred times, and every time I admire the music at least as much as the wonderful poetry.

When Brian said he didn't like explaining lyrics, he was referring to the same thing that Freddie spoke about; he didn't want people prying into his private life. And rightly so.

Of course, musicians don't write songs to tell people everything about their private lives. However their songs are inspired mostly by their personal experiences, so they are exposed to the risk that their words will be correctly interpreted, because there will always be true listeners who understand the lyrics. People don't just connect to songs through their emotions, but also with their minds; they are looking for meaning. They are curious as to why songs generate such feelings.

A lot of people called Queen the most intelligent band, I suppose partly due to their songs' lyrics. Even in their simplest songs, they had something to say because they were written by talented artists who were able to put their emotions into words and condense them into a track.

Freddie was one of the world's greatest artists and wanted to be a legend, so naturally, many people are interested in what made him what he was.

Is it just a coincidence that more than 1 billion people have watched Bohemian Rhapsody on YouTube? Of course not. I'm convinced that if people understood the lyrics, the number of views would be much higher.

The emotional vibrations generated in those people, who listen to the song, could move quantities of energy that are so large they would be enough to demolish the Great Wall of China in anger. Listening to the song, we feel fear, pain, anxiety, and right at the end, anger. Without knowing the meaning of the song, all we understand is that this unfortunate and otherwise nice young man has just killed a man and now has to face the consequences. He bids farewell to his mother and everyone else. He has thrown everything away. We feel like this young man is an unfortunate victim, and something really frightening has happened to him, but we don't know what.

Freddie conveys the message of the song with a brilliant musical solution, but it is only possible to genuinely sympathise with him if we know what he's singing about; if we understand him, he is no longer just a young man, but Freddie himself, whether he's a star or not doesn't matter. He was hoping for sympathy back then and wanted to be free of shackles and judgement. Sooner or later, most of his fans realised he was gay, yet they still loved him, and those who didn't love him turned their backs on him, and won't read this book. And neither should they.

When Freddie decided to issue a statement revealing that he had AIDS, he did a lot for other people living with AIDS. At least the millions who loved him softened their attitudes. Similarly, many others who came out as gay made the same contribution. When someone close to us – like Freddie - is ostracised for any reason, we begin to realise how much suffering it causes, and we think more deeply about it. Otherwise, we simply walk on by.

The word 'Bohemian' is generally used to describe people who don't care much about tomorrow, don't think much of social conventions, and have an unconventional life, are warm and kind-hearted, and quickly get over problems. Artists who are slightly frivolous and generally very jovial are often described in this way.

Freddie was indeed usually warm, kind-hearted and generous, though he didn't get over problems easily. On the contrary, he agonised and suffered a lot, especially if someone had cheated on him or left him. On stage, however, he didn't give much thought to conventions. That alone didn't make him Bohemian, but the song itself was so innovative, if we don't understand what it's about, it may appear Bohemian.

A rhapsody is a classical music genre that is not tied to stricter rules, creating opportunities for whimsical moods and musical motifs to emphasise a loose adaptation.

In the 1970s, a Bohemian lifestyle was virtually an accessory of rock'n'roll music and musicians.

I can explain the song title starting from what I have outlined above.

Freddie said:

'The 'Bohemian Rhapsody was' something that I'd wanted to do for a long while, actually. It was really three songs, and I just put them together. I'd always wanted to do something operatic, something with a mood-setter at the start, going into a rock type of thing that completely breaks off into an opera section – a vicious twist – and returns to the theme.' (Freddie Mercury)

The way the three parts differ entirely in terms of style perfectly matches what he wanted to say. I'm convinced there were never three different songs precisely because of the closely related content, as Freddie's contradictory statement above confirms. Freddie might just have said this so that people wouldn't know what the song was about, and he managed to confuse everyone. They only suspected, but nobody knew for sure. Most people are and were convinced that this song was Freddie's 'coming out,' i.e. his public acceptance of his homosexuality.

When writing the song, Freddie had no intention whatsoever of going public and had already sung euphemistically about being gay in his earlier tracks.

Freddie enjoyed creating something extreme that nobody had ever done before, and what he wanted to say was also unusual. So there was an odd combination of parts, using different tones and instrumentation.

The song dealt with a central problem in Freddie's life, which was why he ascribed great importance to it and felt that it would be like winning a knock-out victory over Muhammad Ali if he got over this crisis.

He knew he was fighting the greatest battle of his life, so he planned the operation in the kind of detail with which Napoleon planned the Battle of Austerlitz.

Despite being outnumbered, Napoleon defeated the combined Russian and Austrian armies in one day on 2 December, 1805, and this was probably the most triumphant of all his battles.

It took Freddie many years to prepare for his own Austerlitz, and the fact it was worth suffering to get the song out is best demonstrated by the song's triumphant career. It was worth taking the risk, it helped Freddie to reach the freedom he wanted so desperately.

Freddie found recording the song was at least as complicated as writing it. The music was so unique and intricate that they only managed to record it in six different studios because of its extraordinary complexity. The opera part, i.e. the chorus section, sounds like a 160-200 member choir, though only Freddie, Brian and Roger sang. John wasn't confident in his singing, so he didn't participate in this part of the production.

The song was recorded in three segments. When Freddie first played the ballad part for the producer Roy Thomas Baker and told him this was where the operatic section came in, they burst out laughing. Roy had already worked on opera recordings, so he had an idea what was in store for him and Freddie.

The recordings began in Wales in August, 1975. First, they recorded the introduction Cappella and then the ballad, accompanied on the piano, leaving space on the tape for the opera part, and continued with the heavy rock-style ending. Initially, the opera section was relatively simple, but Freddie kept adding new parts until the tape had become transparent from the many overlapping recordings. Whenever he visited Baker in the next studio, he would go up to him and say: *'I brought you some more Galileos, dear.'* I guess Baker was delighted.

They recorded the chorus in more parts layering the recordings on the same tape over and over again to the point of exhaustion. This produced a sound similar to a single recording of the operatic section sung by a choir. First, the three of them sang together and then they separately recorded the very high-pitch parts, which only Roger was able to sing, such as 'Galileo', and then placed these separate recordings one on top of the other.

(It's worth knowing that back then, the layered recordings weren't edited with a computer, but the tape had to be cut with a razor blade, and then the consecutive parts were pieced together. This was very exciting because if they hadn't managed to overlay the pieces correctly on the first attempt, the entire work would have been ruined; there was no way to make corrections that today's computer technology provides.)

The last studio where the recording was finished, was SARM Studios in London, which had the latest technology and was able to produce 24-track recordings, i.e., soundtracks could be recorded in 24 layers on the same tape, allowing the creation of a unique sound.

This was where the guitar playing was recorded, and the chorus part was synchronised.

When the recordings were finally completed after three weeks, they first listened to the result in this studio. Everybody's jaw dropped. The result was an original and perfect production, the likes of which no one had ever heard before. They all sensed they had created something enormous. No rock band had ever produced anything like it back, and nor has anybody since.

The producer Roy Thomas Baker and two sound engineers, Mike Stone and Gary Langan worked on the recordings, and of course, Freddie continually gave instructions to everyone.

I've seen that A4 sheet of paper on which Freddie wrote the song, shown by Brian in the documentary *Inside The Rhapsody*. You can't see a single note, just some not particularly tidy handwriting, covering the sequence of recordings. This was what Freddie used to direct the work.

Roger says Freddie had an amazing sense of rhythm and always knew which instrument was coming next and also when to start singing the song. They both said he wasn't just an outstanding showman and singer, but at least as good a musician. Brian says it was as if Freddie had an in-built metronome. In many of Freddie's songs, his piano playing was reminiscent of classical pieces. The beginning of the song 'Love of My Life' sounds similar to Mozart. His playing style was as unique as Brian's guitar playing.

This is how Gary Langan recalls the first time he heard the finished recording from start to finish:

'I stood at the back of the room, and my jaw was on my chest. I just hadn't heard or felt or witnessed anything like this track. It was just amazing. You knew then it was destined for such greatness. It had this whole charisma about it.' (Matt Richards & Mark Langthorne)

Freddie had managed to bring his charismatic being and his innermost, painful emotions into the song.

Gary Langan says:

'This was the technology, and Fred went together because here was a medium he could use to further his greatness. When 24-track came along, it must have been like the sun coming out for him, the fact that he could use multi-tracking to do all these vocals.' (Matt Richards & Mark Langthorne)

This was what John Reid said about the experience:

'I kept dipping into the studio and hearing things, and I'd never been involved with a group at this stage of recording, and I was fascinated by the way that they layered and layered and layered, and when they'd finished it, they played it to me, and I was astonished.' (Matt Richards & Mark Langthorne)

The *'bloody masterpiece'* was ready, as Rami Malek, in the role of Freddie, calls the song in the film *Bohemian Rhapsody* when they are negotiating with EMI.

In the film, Ray Foster, who played the fictional character as the EMI representative, was puzzled and annoyed about the new track, because it didn't resemble anything familiar and, moreover, was 5 minutes 55 seconds long, which no radio station would play because the standard was three minutes; this was what they were geared up for. It should be mentioned that we're talking about the single format here.

Freddie and the guys didn't give up. They made fun of Foster, who wasn't responsive to anything new or art, and only looked at record releases from a business perspective. At the end of the argument, Freddie stubbed out his cigarette on Foster's papers and told him the song on the record would be *Bohemian Rhapsody*, adding: 'You will forever be known as the man who lost Queen.'

This only happened in the film. The track was presented in a completely different way. Still, the Queen philosophy was perfectly condensed into this scene: we won't let ourselves be pigeonholed, we are artists and write what we like, we won't compromise; we want to create; we're not here to please record publishers.

Freddie and the other members of Queen all sensed they had created something sensational, and they eventually found a way to release the record as a single prior to the album, *A Night at the Opera*.

Freddie's character in the film describes the track as follows: *'Bohemian Rhapsody is an epic poem, with the pathos of Greek tragedy, the wit of Shakespeare, the unbridled joy of a musical theatre.'*

The description is very apt, providing a nice and brilliant summary of everything that can be said about this work, and is typical of Freddie's self-confidence, as far as music is concerned. (However, he wasn't famed for his eloquence; this scene in the film is just fantasy.) But the song itself sounds eloquent.

The members of the band all agreed that this song would herald the album, but the problem with the length of the song was genuine. Because of its length, it really must have seemed to the publisher that it couldn't make the song a hit because radio was the fastest and most effective form of publicity.

Anyone who listened to the song, including John Reid and Elton John, expressed their doubts about the marketability of the record.

However, as with any difficulty, there was a potential solution. Freddie was close to Kenny Everett, who had a show on Capital Radio. Right from the start, Kenny loved Queen's music and believed in Freddie's talent. When Freddie told him of his concerns, Kenny, who was seen as a hothead on the radio and attracted a large number of permanent listeners with his sensational style, decided to help Queen. Brian says Kenny stole a copy of the song, and to begin with, only played parts of it to arouse the curiosity of the listeners, and annoy them slightly, and then he played the entire song 14 times in total at the weekend. David Minns claims Freddie gave the recording to Kenny, saying he couldn't play it until it was released while winking at him. What happened, in reality, doesn't matter, but this story about Freddie is entirely believable.

Capital Radio was only available to people living in London, but I found an interview with David Hamilton in Lesley-Ann Jones' book, in which Hamilton said the late Eric Hall provided him with a copy, convincing him that 'Bohemian Rhapsody' would be a huge hit. David Hamilton also played the song on his own BBC Radio 1 show. So it wasn't just well-known in London, but throughout the country, and this publicity made a large contribution to promoting record sales.

The same weekend Paul Drew, who ran the RKO station in the States, happened to be in London. He liked the song and acquired a copy, and began playing the track to the American audience.

Radio listeners inundated EMI and Electra in America with questions, so the two companies realised it was worth releasing it as a single.

The single was released on 31 October, 1975 in the UK and went to number one in the charts in the week before Christmas, five days after the album was released. Freddie adored Christmas celebrations. Knowing about his life, I'm confident this was the finest Christmas present he ever received.

More than 1 billion people have watched the official video of the song since 1 August 2008.

Five years later, following the first release of Bohemian Rhapsody, voters on the Greatest Hits Radio (@grateshitsuk) on Twitter awarded the crown to Freddie's song, declaring it the greatest British hit.

The film character Roy Foster was unable to interpret the song, and nor has anyone else so far, or if someone analysed it, they haven't published it. The lyrics were considered nonsense and absurd; people thought Freddie wanted to be eccentric. They didn't understand the song but accepted it because it sounded terrific, and in general, I believe 99% of people had the same relationship with the song:

In this vein, Lesley-Ann Jones interviewed the late Tommy Vance, one of the biggest names in rock music broadcasting.

Among other things, this was what he said about the song:

'I heard it and thought it was a lunatic asylum of a pop song. It was so magnificently obscure, it had to make it. Technically, the song's a mess. It follows no known conventional or commercial formula. It is just a string of dreams, flashbacks, flash-forwards, vignettes, completely disjointed ideas. It changes the sequence, colour, tone, tempo, all for no apparent reason – which is exactly what opera does. But the intent was remarkable. It was the ultimate optimism. It had an indefinable quality, some remarkable magic. It is brilliant. And it is still revered as an icon today. What other song stands up against it? Absolutely fuck all. But try to dissect 'Bohemian Rhapsody's' lyrics, and you'll find that it's meaningless.'

The song is dramatic, and the claim that it didn't have any meaning is definitely not right.

Many people got a bit closer to the solution than Lesley-Ann Jones and many others who believed Freddie was implicitly telling the world he was gay in this song. This was even the view of Oscar-winning songwriter Sir Tim Rice, whose name is synonymous with Jesus Christ Superstar and Evita's lyrics. Their view doesn't explain the lyrics, but it's still better than saying the lyrics were meaningless.

They started from the idea that Freddie was confessing to his mother that he had killed a man. They concluded that he had killed his old self, who had kept a secret that he was gay and wanted to express his sense of guilt, while others believe it was about society condemning homosexuality, or this was his coming-out song.

I think people who tried to explain the song have misunderstood it and haven't answered how the individual parts are related or their significance regarding the message of the whole song.

Why was the chorus needed, the operatic section, or the rock at the end?

People's decisions are never determined by one single factor, but - as the synchronicity principle shows - it is not what happens that is important, but what happens simultaneously.

To understand the song, you have to know about every critical moment, the events going on in Freddie's life at the time, and see the correlations between them.

Freddie had fallen in love with a man for the first time to such an extent that he wanted to live with him.

We know that Freddie began writing this song in 1969, back in his college days. It was the first song he tried to write. The same year he showed the first two lines to Chris Smith, his friend, and said the title was 'Cowboy song'.

So it took seven years for the song that had been conceived to see the light of day finally.

Freddie started to write the song when he was in a romantic relationship with Rosemary Pearson. We know From Rosemary' book that Freddie felt a strong desire to have a same-sex relationship and cried in agony because nobody understood how much he had suffered.

Freddie's relationship with Mary served as a good disguise. Freddie loved Mary, even though he kept cheating on her, and felt guilty about it. He didn't dare to tell her the truth about his sexuality because there was the risk that she would, if distressed, tell the world about his secret, which would have immediately ended Freddie's career just as it was starting to take off.

However, his conscience also made demands on him because he loved Mary and never wanted to hurt her in any way.

In the first three years after Queen was formed, they had an extremely difficult and stressful period in every respect, working and creating at such a high standard, made all of them very tired.

The constant tension and exhaustion associated with work, especially the lack of success, and issues with the Trident contract, placed a massive burden on Freddie's shoulders.

His relationship with David Minns must have been the final straw, and the moment had arrived when he had to let off steam somehow and relive the almost unbearable tension.

These events forced him to confess to Mary, but the song was born a year earlier before they had the conversation in reality.

Under the pressure from the constant tension, Freddie had continually worked on the song until it came together in his mind. Working on the song, he was already mentally preparing to confess to Mary. In itself, the music would have been suitable for Freddie to let off steam, although, he had doubts about how the operatic nature of the song would be received, this may have added to the pressure and could have caused him to worry as well. The recordings were associated with a tremendous workload. By the time the chorus part were recorded they had been singing 10-12 hours a day for three weeks; the other parts were recorded relatively quickly. And time was pressing because they were preparing for a sold-out tour at the same time, aimed at promoting the album. They didn't think the recordings would take so long.

At the same time, as a result of the break-up with Trident, the album's success was literally a matter of life and death in terms of surviving and carrying on.

By the time the recordings were made, the tension inside Freddie must have been close to exploding. However, we know that he was highly disciplined. When it came to his work, with his incredible self-control, it was the only thing he was concerned with; and it was with the kind of intensity that exhausted everyone around him. When the song was recorded, Freddie threw himself into it thoroughly to get the most out of himself and the other band members; he knew this song would save them or be a total failure. He wanted to exclude the possibility of failure by putting all his effort and talent into the creative work. We know that the song begins with the chorus, the three of them singing.

'What is this about anyway, bloody Bismillah?'

Now let see what the song is about.

'Is this the real life? Is this just fantasy?' – the choir asks, with a beautiful melody without any tension in their voices for the moment – we can understand the meaning of the question from the lines that follow, as the chorus continues: *'Caught in a landslide, No escape from reality.'* As an act of God, a landslide is an unavoidable event that we can't do anything about, like an accident. It just happens. There is no escape; the reality is I can't do anything about being gay.
The question at the start refers to the fact that Freddie fantasises a lot and sometimes can't be sure what is reality and what is fantasy. The whole situation seems unbelievable to him because he is forced to do what appears to be very dangerous.

The above section answers the question: Freddie is facing harsh-hard reality; this is no longer just a fantasy game. This is a reference to David, with whom he was deeply involved in a relationship; he's unable to get out of it and return to the world of illusion and deceit because he loved this man so much and was certain he wanted to live with him.

'Open your eyes look up to the skies and see' – the chorus continues.

When we look up to the skies as if praying for an answer, we already know we have a problem for which we want a solution. ('Oh heavens', as we say.)

Freddie then sings powerfully, alone:

*'I'm just a poor boy, I need no sympathy
Because I'm easy come, easy go
Little high, little low'*

These four lines give a short description of the 'boy' who the story is about. The statement that 'he needs no sympathy' is partly the result of his pride; in general, he does not need sympathy, but right now, he really does need it. With this first sentence, he is trying to ensure that he will win the hearts of those touched by the conflict. Anyone would answer: 'Oh, you do need sympathy; everyone needs sympathy.'

The next phrase serves the same purpose: *'Anyway the wind blows, doesn't really matter to me, to me'.* In other words, *I've given up on everything; nothing really matters now because I've become insensitive.*

His traumas and tension didn't make him insensitive, but rather oversensitive; he needs understanding, sympathy and help. On hearing such a complaint, people's reaction would be generally: 'oh, how can you say that nothing matters to you, whatever you're like, whatever has happened, there is always a way out, we'll help you, you're not alone.'

The ballad part is just as mysterious:

*'Mama, just killed a man
Put a gun against his head
Pulled my trigger, now he's dead
Mama, life had just begun
But now I've gone and thrown it all away
Mama, oooh
Didn't mean to make you cry
If I'm not back again this time tomorrow
Carry on, carry on, as if nothing really matters'*

He confesses to Mama, who is Mary in this case, that he has committed a crime. *'I killed a man'* means two things. One, the person Mary moved in with no longer exists. Two: his crime is as serious as murder and unforgivable. This is how his religion and his parents viewed it, probably Mary and others as well, as it's punishable by imprisonment.

'*My life had just begun*, I'm still young, and my career is on an upward curve, but I've lost everything with what I've done. I guess you'll create a scandal, and everyone will know that I'm gay.'

When he talks about murder, he also says 'I am or have become gay, and there is no more heterosexual me. I have destroyed this part of me by getting involved in such relationships.' (This is not the same as coming out since the communication is private.)

And then: 'I didn't mean to hurt you, I *didn't mean to make you cry*, I love you, please try to carry on life without me, as if nothing has happened.'

So it's not a question of wanting to tell the world that he has changed, but instead, he only wanted to tell Mary.

The next verse goes:

'Too late, my time has come
Sends shivers down my spine
Body's aching all the time
Goodbye, everybody, I've got to go
Gotta leave you all behind and face the truth'

There is no way back, he can't carry on, he's shivering in fear, he feels the pain throughout his whole body. He says goodbye to everyone because he doesn't know what his decision will entail. Maybe everyone will reject him and break off contact, and he'll lose his friends, Mary, and his family. Still, he has to face this possibility, and there is no other way for him. His homosexuality and love leave him no choice, he's under enormous pressure.

This part means Freddie has to leave all his lies behind, however difficult and has to accept potential disdain because he must live his own life, yet he is terrified of what awaits him. He's afraid of losing a promising career, friends and love. This dread is genuine. As a young adult, it imprisoned Freddie. There is no pretence, sham or pity.

And then the most painful part comes when a mother's heart is broken. Freddie is very much afraid as if it were a death sentence. He is very attached to Mary, it's no accident that he kept his homosexuality secret for years as he sings this part:

'Mama, oooh - (anyway the wind blows)
I don't want to die
I sometimes wish I'd never been born at all'

What would a mother's reaction be if she heard this?

A mother would say: 'Oh, my dear son, you're not going to die, don't say you wish you'd never been born. I forgive you, of course, I forgive you, calm down, everything will be alright, don't be afraid. You know how much I love you and how important you are to me.'

But then again, Mary is not his mother, so Freddie has no idea how she would react. Based on his own personality, he would seek revenge and act wickedly after being deceived. That's what he was like. If he'd been cheated on, he would have been angry and unpredictable. He said Mama instead of Mary, which gave the whole story a completely different, dramatic hue. It was not a conversation between partners, he was talking to his mother, which indicates a deeper relationship. Not to mention that he was diverting attention from Mary by using the word 'Mama'. He didn't want anyone to understand the song.

And yet, since she is also a loving, motherly person, he tries to influence her, for a moment, in an imaginary dialogue during which he asked her to forgive him.

Brian's guitar solo leads into the operatic section, which starts with Freddie's rhythmic piano playing and the excitement increases.

They continue in chorus:

*'I see a little silhouetto of a man
Scaramouche, Scaramouche will you do the fandango?'*

Scaramouche was a typical character in 16th Century theatre comedies, who entertained the audience as a clown, while the fandango is a Spanish dance.

Scaramouche, here is Freddie. He is the one who clowns around playing a role while entertaining others as an artist, and now Freddie asks him whether he will dance the fandango, i.e. is he in the mood for fun?

'Thunderbolt and lightning, very, very frightening me' – they continue in chorus, decisively rejecting the request.

Freddie is not in the mood to entertain and is unable to dance because he's very scared.

In real life, Freddie generally tried to keep fear and fright away by joking, having fun or listening to opera, and he resorted to this here once again:

*'Galileo, Galileo,
Galileo, Galileo,
Galileo Figaro – magnifico'*

Probably, Brian's original profession was that what reminded Freddie of Galileo, the astronomer, whereas Figaro is an operatic figure from The Barber of Seville and The Marriage of Figaro. Figaro is a bohemian character. The magnificence and extravagance may refer to the choir itself, who are singing the opera part. This part in the song is especially suitable for giving Freddie a boost like an opera did in his younger days and adulthood. The words 'Galileo Figaro' convey a good atmosphere, not to mention the sound of the chorus in this part. This little bit of fun gives Freddie some light relief and relaxes him before judgment is passed.

Freddie sings the speech for the defence in the chorus:

'I'm just a poor boy, nobody loves me' - Freddie is alone, as he sings very emphatically.

Judgment is near now. Freddie strikes another emotional chord, no longer saying he does not need sympathy. On the contrary, he claims that nobody loves him, so he is deserving of pity.

This is why the enormous choir sound was needed as if a larger group of people was judging him; the group splits into two camps, as could happen in reality, those who stand up for and support him and those who condemn him:

And the chorus sings again, first the supportive group, confirming Freddie's claim and even adding to it:

'He's just a poor boy from a poor family
Spare him his life from this monstrosity'

The supporters ask the judge, who is Mary, not to expose him to this terrible humiliation, to forgive him and not condemn him.

'Easy come easy go - will you let me go?' - asks Freddie in the song, in other words, 'I have made mistakes, I was frivolous when I moved in with you and even promised to get married, but will you let me go?' asks Freddie.

And then the opposing camp of people who despise him and want to punish him:

'Bismillah! No - we will not let you go'

They refer to God because the holy books prohibit homosexual relationships. They consider it a sin and loathsome. (The meaning of Bismillah is 'The name of Allah'.)

The supportive members stand by Freddie:

'Let him go'

The debate continues; the matter isn't resolved so easily:

'Let him go'

The argument and dialogue are taking place in Freddie's mind. The huge chorus part symbolises how strong the voices are in Freddie's mind, both on the positive and the negative side: first he hears yes, she will let him go and forgive him, but the doubts are just as strong, the opposing camp in chorus sing, no we will not forgive you. This is the essence of the conflict.

The operatic sound, which is a major change compared to the ballad section, highlights the essential point, the inner tension, the argument, the doubts before the decision. This causes the most suffering (and explains why it was the most difficult to record as Freddie wants to emphasise this part. This was why he wrote the song because of the constant guilt and anguish he would like to escape from.)

He is talking to himself in the opera part. In contrast, the ballad part is intended for Mary and is beautiful and sad because their relationship was beautiful, and it makes Freddie sad to have to end it, and it expressed how much it hurt him to do this.

Adultery is not a minor matter; everyone openly condemns it, yet many people have done it. The feeling of having been cheated on is very painful, and Freddie is well aware of this.

His parents [also] 'cheated on him' in his childhood. Freddie was attached to them and loved them, and yet they sent him away from home to a boarding school. As a young child, he was evidently unable to process or understand the reason of the separation. He suffered terribly from loneliness. And now he had put Mary in this situation. The soul searching was no accident, not to mention the judgment and fear of losing his career. It's a huge, dramatic conflict, with significant internal forces creating tension.

'Will not let you go - let me go (never)
Never let you go - let me go
Never let me go - ooo
No, no, no, no, no, no, no'

In the end, Freddie even starts pleading:

'Oh mama mia, mama mia, mama mia let me go'

Mamma mia is an Italian expression, it means in Italian: Oh, Mum! In English, it means 'My Goodness!'.

The supportive members now change tactics, as persuasion hasn't been successful; they bring up a new, more compelling argument, blaming it all on Beelzebub:

'Beelzebub has a devil put aside for me
For me'

This argument is very witty and funny. Freddie knows very well this is no excuse. Everyone has devilish traits, sometimes we can push them into the background and not allow them to control us, and sometimes we can't.
At the end of the chorus, the music booms out with great force, preparing us for the shocking rock segment.

Freddie managed to pull himself together and find a solution, choosing the tactic of 'the best form of defence is attack'. And here is the evil scheme, the rock part, representing Freddie's aggressive, inner strength.

In a powerful, demanding and offensive voice, he asks:

'So you think you can stone me and spit in my eye
So you think you can love me and leave me to die'

The thought process behind the attack is that you can't want me to die of shame; you have to let me go if you really love me.

'Oh baby - can't do this to me baby'

The word 'baby' proves that Freddie is talking to Mary. The word 'baby' is used as a nickname for a lover or loved one. And it's also an ingenious solution: darling, you're not going to be so wicked as to do this to me. Freddie tries to curry favour, like always. In any case, where is the logic in saying you love me and would still leave me to die? Freddie knows that Mary loves him and is also a very reasonable woman.

'Just gotta get out - just gotta get right outta here' – that means, I have to escape the tension right now, or I'll explode!

Meanwhile, the thumping music continues, adding to the tension, and then it slowly gets softer.

And now Freddie's voice also gets softer, in a calm tempo, singing more quietly:

'Ooh yeah, ooh yeah
Nothing really matters
Anyone can see
Nothing really matters - nothing really matters to me'

Whatever will be will be, Freddie is tired of the inner struggle, surrenders to his fate: accepts that whatever has to happen will happen.

And the gong suggests this is the end. There's no more contemplation. He'll see what happens. Mary will decide, not he. In any case, the die has been cast. Freddie, like Ceasar, had crossed the Rubicon.

We know how the story continued, Mary forgave Freddie. David moved in with Freddie, but their relationship deteriorated, and they later broke up, though the 'bloody masterpiece' became a global hit, saving Queen from financial ruin. This was the best 'Fairy Fellers Master-Stroke' *in Queen's carrier.*

The album *A Night at the Opera* took its name from the film made in 1935 with the same title. The Marx Brothers played the main characters. The movie was a comedy, while Bohemian Rhapsody was a 'mock opera', as Freddie called it.

'Bohemian Rhapsody' was one of the first videos to get the kind of attention that videos get now, and it only cost about five thousand pounds. We decided we should put 'Rhapsody' on film, and let people see it. We didn't know how it was going to be looked upon or how they were going to receive it. To us, it was just another form of theatre. But it went crazy. We recognised that a video could get to a lot of people in a lot of countries without you actually being there, and you could release a record and a video simultaneously. It became very fast, and it helped record sales greatly.' (Freddie Mercury)

The video was directed by Bruce Gowers, who had already made several films about Queen's concerts. The recording took only 4 hours. The inspiration was the song itself and Mick Rock's earlier photo of the band, as seen on the Queen II album.

Gowers was ahead of his time, his video proved a great success. He made the film using prism lenses and without computers.

According to pop music magazine *Rolling Stone* in the USA:

'Its influence cannot be overstated, practically inventing the music video seven years before MTV went on air.'

The same magazine interviewed Brian on the 40th anniversary of the release of Bohemian Rhapsody. This is a quote from the article:

Interviewer: *'When you were recording 'Bohemian Rhapsody', did you have any idea what a big deal it was going to be?'*

Brian: *'I don't think anybody thought that. We were just thinking, 'This is fun, this is interesting, this will be something that people enjoy.' Freddie wrote it. Of course, we all interacted, we all contributed bits and pieces *and argued as we always did, but it was Freddie's baby and everyone respected that in the end.'*

'We had an unwritten law that whoever brought the song in would have the final say in how it turned out. But we weren't that shocked, because we were used to that way of working and we'd done things like 'My Fairy King' on the first album, and lots of complexity on Queen II, so it wasn't unusual for Freddie to come in and have this rather baroque-sounding backing track and wondering what was going to go on top. Probably the most unusual thing was, John [Deacon] said to him, 'What are you going to call it then, is it called 'Mama?'' And Freddie went, 'No, I think we'll call it 'Bohemian Rhapsody.'' And there was a little silence, everybody thought, 'Okaaay...' I don't think anybody said, 'Why?' but there it was. How strange to call a song 'Bohemian Rhapsody', but it just suits it down to the ground and it became a milestone. But nobody knew.'

If a song made it to the top 30, the rule at the BBC was that it had to be played on *Top Of The Pops*. The more often it was played, the higher it went in the charts until, in the end, it got to number one.

Television and, of course, the sensational video made a tremendous impact. The images and the music are closely related in people's minds.

Another big advert for the song was the American comedy *Wayne's World* (1992). In one scene, four teenagers are driving around the city. They were singing along Bohemian Rhapsody. The atmosphere gets better and better when they pick up a fifth guy who is visibly under the influence of drink or drugs. They put him in between them on the back seat and continue driving. Soon they begin to 'argue', start shaking their heads and sing, 'No, we won't let you go!', while the guy on drugs just sings: 'Let me go!' while trying to escape, but of course they don't let him, singing 'No we won't let you go'.

At the time of writing, eight million people have watched this video since October 2013. (YouTube: Bohemian Rhapsody Wayne's World HD)

Another exciting thing about the film is that the long, brown-haired guy in the video is Mike Myers. He portrayed EMI representative Roy Foster in the movie Bohemian Rhapsody (2018), who asked, *'What is that about anyway, bloody Bismillah'?*

Freddie's other songs on the *A Night at the Opera* album

Freddie wrote four other songs on the album, each in a different style, and all of them is genuine masterpiece.

It seems that Freddie's creative genie had escaped from the bottle. The mood of each song is different, and the lyrics are exciting and comical, like 'Seaside Rendezvous' and 'Lazing on a Sunday Afternoon'. I have mentioned before – in chapter 15 the song 'Death on Two Legs. (Dedicated to….)' written to Norman Sheffield one of the owners of Trident. As we know Freddie banged his fist on Norman Sheffield desk in vain, and eventually, Queen got out of the contract. Freddie felt he should write a song for him as a farewell. This farewell song wasn't a nice one, as they all thought Norman Sheffield didn't deserve one.

The lyrics are clear, no need to interpret them. These lyrics were the best examples to realize it wasn't worth making Freddie angry.

'Seaside Rendezvous'

'A fun up-tempo song, just piano, drums and vocals. The woodwind and brass arrangements are multi-tracked vocal performances by Freddie and Roger, respectively. Freddie gives a masterclass in vocal technique – bent notes, vibrato, falsetto – and Taylor's drumming has light touch.' (Andrew Wild)

This is what Freddie said jokingly about Seaside Rendezvous:

'Seaside Rendezvous has a 1920's feel to it, and Roger does a tuba and clarinet thing on there too, vocally, if you see what I mean. I'm going to make him step dance too. I'll have to buy him some Ginger Rogers step shoes.'

In reality, it wasn't just Roger, but both Roger and Freddie who very realistically imitated the tuba with their voices and the clarinet. I could hardly believe my ears. And they did the step part using thimbles on their fingers, drumming on the desk. They imitated the sound of the megaphone, and make it echo, placing a metal can on the microphone when Freddie was singing.

This is the first romantic song that Freddie wrote for David. It is about that time when they were courting. It's a very entertaining and seductive song due to the witty and charming lyrics and innovative music.

Freddie felt so happy with David and imagined all kinds of romantic situations in which they could be happy.

'Lazing on a Sunday Afternoon'

'Lazing on a Sunday Afternoon' is short, funny, joyful and surprisingly complex, in marked contrast to the preceding 'Death on Two Legs (Dedicated to)'. The backing vocals are lush, and the brief guitar solo is a harmonised variant of the vocal melody.' (Andrew Wild)

Freddie was so happy this time, he could come up with such funny lyrics and the music was also utterly entertaining. I love every second of it, no doubt Freddie was at the peak of his creativity when he wrote it.

'Love of My Life'

'Freddie Mercury's complex and beautiful classically-inspired piano part has echoes of Chopin and Beethoven, and his multiple harmony backing vocals are simply beautiful. Brian May contributes subtle guitar phrases in the tone and style of a cello.' (Andrew Wild)

In the end, it was a great hit known to almost everyone, 'Love of My Life', which Freddie wrote for David.

The lyrics are about Freddie and David's relationship. The lyrics start: *'Love of my life, you've hurt me/ You've broken my heart, and now you leave me'.*

Freddie wrote this song at the beginning of their relationship when David had no intention to leave Freddie. David was his love and his trusted friend, and I think he just wanted to tell him in a song how important he was for him. For Freddie, writing a song was the most authentic way to express the depth of his emotions.

The mere thought that David would leave him saddened Freddy. In the song, he sings about this sad thought and asks him not to desert him because David has no idea how much his love means to Freddie.

(I think Freddie was right. David Minns' didn't even mention that Freddie loved him dearly and the songs written to him in his revealing book about their relationship. Writing the book, he was focusing on mainly the events that happened to them, but he hardly talked about their feelings for each other, supposedly because when he wrote the book – after their break up - he was disillusioned and admittedly cynical. Anyway, we can thank him writing about Freddie's anguish caused by the pressure that his parents' and David expectations placed on him related to his sexuality.) The next line in the lyrics is most likely about one of their quarrel: *'When this is blown over/And everything's all by the way.'*

It sounds like an apology from Freddie, and in the second verse, he sings about his desired long term relationship with David: 'When I grow older/I will be there at your side to remind you/How I still love you (I still love you).

Freddie's letters written for David radiate love, care, and a sense of lack when they can't be together.

Love of My Life was one of the fans' favourites, and they often sang the lyrics along with Freddie. Freddie sings live on this video, with Brian accompanying him and the crowd singing along. Sixty-six million people have watched only this one video, despite many people having uploaded the song. (The number leapt from 66 million to 67 million in four months.)

(YouTube: Queen – 'Love of My Life' (Official Video))

Roger's song 'I'm in Love with My Car' was on the B side of Bohemian Rhapsody single, which was released on 31 October, 1975. It started out at number 47 in the charts and then crept upwards nicely until it entered the top 10 at number nine, and had to be scheduled to appear on BBC's *Top of The Pops*. The question was how to perform the operatic part on TV? This required Grovers' fantastic video that revolutionised publicity for rock music. As the video began to be played on TV, record sales rocketed, and the track made it to number one, where it stayed for nine weeks. It also got to number one in Canada, Belgium, Ireland and Australia. Sales broke every record, one million copies were sold by the end of January, and according to later data, over six million copies in total. The album was also released on 21 November and went to number one, selling 11 million copies. The way it was received abroad was also exceptional; it went to number 1 in Holland and New Zealand and made the top 10 in six other countries.

The breakthrough success of 'Bohemian Rhapsody' and the album, *A Night at the Opera*, made Queen world-famous; they became global stars within two years of publishing the first album in 1973, with the release of the fourth album. There was an enormous amount of hard work behind their outstanding success. The members of Queen were relieved. They were inundated with money from record sales, their financial hardship was over, they were free of debt, and they would not have to record the following album under nerve-wracking tension.

They deserved the success, and the question was where next?

You can get to the top but can never rest if you want to stay there.

This was what Freddie thought about the album after it was released:

'I'll never forget A Night at the Opera. Never. It took the longest time to do. We weren't really prepared for it. It was more important to get the album the way we wanted, especially after spending so long on it. I think we knew we had something special. We said: 'This can be our Sgt. Pepper.' It was the most important album for us, and it had the strongest songs ever. I knew it was going to be our best album.' (Freddie Mercury)

Yes, especially after almost 50 years, we can confidently say this album was Queen's Sgt. Pepper album. I should add, without LSD, if you aren't aware, Sgt. Pepper's Lonely Hearts Club Band was The Beatles' eighth studio album.

Part Three

Keep Yourself Alive

Freedom and love (Petőfi, Sándor)

Freedom and love my creed!
These are the two I need.
For love I'll freely sacrifice
My earthly spell,
For freedom, I will sacrifice
My love as well.

(Translated from Hungarian By Kery Leslie A.

18. 'Freddie never was the same again' (Mick Rock)

During the Night at the Opera album tour, Queen played 78 concerts, in the UK, USA, Europe, Japan and Australia. As usual, they played in Britain first, starting on 14 November, 1975. They played six gigs at the Hammersmith Odeon, the last one on 24 December. The concert was so spectacular that even the BBC recorded and officially released it on DVD as *A Night at the Odeon – Hammersmith 1975*. A lot of people have uploaded it on YouTube as well. Musically, it was one of the most exciting concerts Queen had performed, by which time they already had a brilliant repertoire.

Freddie's self-confidence had prominently grown. He sang more powerfully, improvised more and communicated confidently and impressively with the audience. His piano playing was effortless and masterful, and Brian's guitar playing was simply astonishing. And at last, we can also see Roger performing a fine drum solo in the middle of 'Keep Yourself Alive'. John was at his best as well.

'Keep Yourself Alive' was a crowd favourite and the first big Queen hit. This version was reworked by Brian, after having been written back in the Smile era. Shivers run right through me when I hear Freddie singing this part of the song:

'Keep yourself alive, wow
Keep yourself alive
Oh, it'll take you all your time and money
To keep me satisfied

Do you think you're better every day?
No, I just think I'm two steps nearer to my grave

Keep yourself alive, c'mon
Keep yourself alive.'

Showered with awards

Queen was given several awards during the album tour at the beginning of 1976, with US music paper, *New Musical Express,* awarding them the prize for *Best British Stage Band*. UK music magazine, *Record Mirror,* also awarded them *Best British Band,* and they pocketed further awards as a *Best Solo Album* and *Best Album*. Freddie received his second *Ivor Novello Award (Best Selling British Record for 'Bohemian Rhapsody')*.

Both the single and the album were top of the charts when they started the world tour for the album in the USA on 27 January, 1976. They had enormous success in America. Queen hosted parties after the successful concerts, paying tribute with an invitation to local dignitaries and artists. Freddie didn't like these parties and found the guests invited out of propriety, boring because of his hyperactivity and fear of strangers.

After the gigs, the band also held their parties, where eyewitnesses say the orgies were rather extravagant, with mountains of food and drink, naked and half-naked men and women, striptease dancers, anything that was exciting. Freddie's imagination alone would have been enough, but all four of them proved too much.

Freddie began to get a reputation as a crazy party animal involving drink, drugs and sex orgies. He wasn't overly bothered and was unable and unwilling to behave differently. His released pent-up and suppressed desires took control. Once the enormous stress that preceded the release of their most successful album had abated, he could start to relax. And he finally had money to live life as he wanted. He went from one extreme to the other with a huge thud.

Appearing in front of crowds of tens or hundreds of thousands brought great excitement before each gig. His blood would have been full of adrenaline and dopamine, which just added to his fever. When the concert began, the intoxicating effect of the music would have given him and the audience a boost.

Experiencing success generates serotonin, a hormone that produces a pleasant emotion and which would have encouraged Freddie to perform for the pleasure of his audience.

The hormone, oxytocin, is produced if we have physical contact with our fellow human beings. A substantial quantity is produced during sexual intercourse. Shaking hands, a way of showing togetherness with someone we accept, respect or love, also generates oxytocin. We need oxytocin because it strengthens our immune system and enhances our love of work and creativity.

As they left the stage after each concert, the hormones that had boosted Freddie began to subside within a few hours, slowly but surely, resulting in a sense of loss. Freddie especially needed the hormone replenishment, as he constantly craved love and physical contact to feel secure.

The concerts repeated almost daily, and the exhausting travel would have used a massive amount of energy, resulting in the need to recharge his batteries after shows. Given the lack of time, there was one fast way of doing this: sex. Freddie had an enormous sexual appetite and wanted his desires to be satisfied. Sexual satisfaction has a relaxing and stimulating effect on the body due to the surge in hormones.

In the same way, alcohol and drugs also provide a boost and have a relaxing effect. Understandably Freddie was restless and tried to get hold of some necessary energy replacement. The stage experience was better than an orgasm, Freddie joked, but he was right. Two hours in the loud music and singing, listening to the crowd roaring in the late evening provides the kind of stimulus that makes it impossible to just go to bed and quietly fall asleep afterwards. It was especially hard for Freddie, who was frightened of being alone.

Hypnosis is a natural phenomenon, as I wrote earlier, and can happen to us several times a day. And if we feel like we're on a high after a concert – even without drinking – we can be sure we've been in a hypnotic state due to the mental alertness and a physically relaxed condition.

(Freddie feels his stage persona, the 'monster', was alien to him, because it doesn't resemble his everyday self in any way. When he goes on stage, this status is triggered as a conditional reflex. When David Minns first saw Freddie perform, he was shocked and told himself this was not the man he knew.)

The same is true of the audience. People stared at Freddie with dilated pupils and hardly took their eyes off him, while feeling happy, relaxed, and excited.

A lot of people have written comments saying they became dependent on Freddie and Queen. The dependence is related to these feel-good hormones. Eating chocolate produces a similar effect in the brain but doesn't get close to Queen's music in intensity, which has a magical and mysterious effect. The superb sound, the snare-drum and the rhythm enhance these biological mechanisms. As a frontman, Freddie moved back and forth across the stage rhythmically. The frequent changes in his pleasant tone also produced a high, with positive, exciting emotions. Freddie drank and used cocaine before, during, and after concerts, which put him on a high, with positive emotions. These highs and excitement he felt, were, in a sense, 'contagious', and were taken on by the audience, resulting in Freddie and the audience becoming attuned to each other. Together, the excitement and the highs brought about a sense of pleasure before and after concerts, which very often increased to the point of frenzy and produced mass hysteria. (In these situations, their humorous approach was: let's take the money and run.) More than once, the band had to be rescued from concert venues by police escort or were forced to leave in style by helicopter.

In addition, Freddie was likely suffering from sex addiction, which would also explain his behaviour.

According to sexologist Susan Quilliam, there is hardly any difference between sex addiction and drug addiction. The person suffering from it acts obsessively often commits completely obvious, stupid mistakes, as he is incapable of anticipating the consequences. The manager of a British therapy clinic, Steve Pope, believes 75-80% of sex addicts were victims of physical or emotional abuse in childhood.

Freddie's life had completely turned around. He threw himself into the nightlife, and was willing only to give up this lifestyle when he realised he was infected and had become increasingly ill and weak.

Many of Queen's songs were feel-good songs. This is what makes them so irresistible, among other things, and then there is the spectacle, which can also generate ecstasy, as does the volume.

Freddie was exposed to this almost every night on tour, so it's no wonder he became dependent, and since he was incredibly lonely, he started looking for substitutes, like so many other people.

His hyperactivity made things worse as it could have caused unbearable restlessness and tension in itself. Those who suffer from it are continually buzzing, working, moving or fidgeting to relieve the pressure, at least to some extent. Unrelieved tension, especially if combined with high stress levels, causes frustration and irritation, which would have made Freddie argumentative and combative. In the worst cases, he behaved aggressively and arrogantly. This emotional rollercoaster and frequently being away from home, made it impossible for him to develop a deep, lasting and loving relationship.

Freddie's relationship with David Minns was a romantic, deeply loving relationship, but it couldn't last, as the circumstances weren't right at the time. The relationship was condemned to death from the start.

Poor David sensed this when he hesitated and asked Freddie whether he was serious about wanting a relationship with him. Of course, Freddie was serious, but he wasn't aware at the time of the enormous forces that would overwhelm him as he entered the gates of success.

At the beginning of February, 1976, Queen played four concerts at the Beacon Theatre in New York. After the concerts, they had dinner together with the other band members, but then Freddie disappeared to discover the gay scene. He enjoyed the opportunity of being on his own; he wasn't persecuted by the press and was happy to find that all earthly pleasures were available in the city; bars, pools and other clubs were spiced with sultry eroticism. This was a world in which Freddie could imagine himself. After a short stay, he would assess the terrain, and the same thing happened in all the big cities they visited. Freddie made reconnaissance trips everywhere, searching for gay clubs. Later, there was no longer a need to search; a guidebook on gay clubs in various cities became available. His later personal assistant, friend and carer, Peter Freestone, who also wrote a book about Freddie, claimed that Freddie never read a single book from cover to cover, except for that guidebook.

It seemed like he had finally found the world he fantasised about in *Seven Seas of Rhye*. The affluence, the adoration that goes with being a star, and the feeling that 'I can have anything and anyone, and I can do whatever I want', gave him a false sense of security. Yes, he could afford anything, but he didn't consider the side effects.

Freddie's dream of sexual freedom became a reality. His fantasy world was replaced by the 'real world' as Freddie called his company of gay friends.

While HIV had already been recognised in Europe, Independence Day celebrations in the United States on 4 July, 1976, commemorating the 200th anniversary, lasted a whole week. Ships arrived from all over the world to take part in the unique revelry. And the gay bars were also full; in particular, those places that Freddie had sought out became breeding grounds for the spread of the virus. But Freddie didn't know anything about it for the time being and was just enjoying his freedom.

'Boredom and dullness are the biggest diseases in the whole world. Excess is a part of my nature, and I really need danger and excitement. I was often warned to stay away from clubs because they are too dangerous. I love to surround myself with strange and interesting people because they make me feel more alive. Extremely straight people bore me stiff. I love freaky people. By nature, I'm restless and highly strung. I don't do things by halves. I can shift from one extreme to the other quite easily. I don't like anything in between.' (Freddie Mercury)

Nobody needs such a level of restlessness and excitement; this was partly due to his hyperactivity, though Freddie wasn't aware of it. People thought he was a workaholic, drank too much and took too many drugs, which were all true, just they didn't know the cause of these dangerous extremes.

Understandably, he felt good among people who were slightly out of the ordinary, just like him. He was easily bored, so to switch off from the creative world, he felt compelled to surround himself with extreme people who were good fun and unconventional, as he was. Risk and the excitement of performing raised his adrenaline level, and the highs that this produced would have caused him to be addicted to the concerts.

He'd had enough of conventions and thought that conventional people had shackled him up to the age of 30.

Sadly, he learned that boredom and dullness weren't the biggest diseases in the world.

The creative process itself is also associated with pleasant excitement and pumped-up feeling, as are recording sessions. The lives of global stars are not ordinary in any way, and Freddie, like other stars, must have felt this great success was unusual, as it intoxicated him like a drug.

After touring America, they performed in Japan again, where once again they were received by frenzied crowds. This was followed by an Australian tour, where the reception was friendly this time, not like on their first tour. Their concerts were practically sold out at every venue.

They were basking in glory, and plenty of money was flowing onto their accounts from the royalties. Freddie visited every elegant store in Tokyo and bought anything he desired; works of art, vases, paintings, whatever caught his eye. He admitted to never knowing how much money was on his account; all he knew was that money was for spending on anything that made his life beautiful and pleasant. Who wouldn't want that?

They returned home in April. Freddie was in a relationship with David but still living with Mary. David demanded to tell her the truth about their relationship since he had realized - in November 1975 - they weren't just old friends - he was jealous of her.

This was the summer when Freddie decided to tell Mary what had been weighing on his mind, and Mary's positive reaction was a huge relief to him. Finally, he escaped this stress.

Freddie bought a new apartment for himself, so he moved out of their rented flat to Stafford terrace, Holland Park, but the relationship was by no means over. Later on, Freddie bought a lovely apartment for Mary too in an attempt to compensate her.

Mary gave an interview to David Wigg from the Mail online newspaper in March 2013, in which she said:

'If he hadn't been such a decent human being and told me I wouldn't be here,' she says candidly. 'If he had gone along living a bisexual life without telling me, I would have contracted Aids and died.'

'The sad thing was that if he had been more careful in his lifestyle, later on, he would still be here now. With advances in modern medicine, things are different now.'

'I think Freddie reached a stage where he thought he was invincible,' she says. 'He convinced himself he was having a good time, and maybe, in part, he was. But I think in part he wasn't.'

'And then it was too late. The only person who could have made a difference was Freddie. But I think he'd stopped being honest with himself. Many of his so-called friends were there for the free tickets, the free booze, the free drugs, the free meal, the gossip and, of course, the expensive gifts.'

Freddie was famous for his generosity, which a lot of people exploited, but he was aware of this. He had reached a point in his life when he no longer knew whether someone was with him or around him only because he was a star and for his money or because of him as a person. From then on, he became more lonely. The mistrust he had brought with him from childhood intensified. These two terrible emotions must have led to him taking more and more drugs.

19. A Day at the Races Album (1976)

After arriving home, almost without any rest, they began recording the next great, exciting album, *A Day at the Races*. Freddie wrote for the album four very special songs. Each of them became very popular among Queen fans.

'You Take My Breath Away'

'You Take My Breath Away is one of Mercury's best ballads, sung without irony or pomp. Immaculate and atmospheric multi-layered backing vocals, all by Mercury, accompany a simple piano backing, with flashes of guitar and percussion.' (Andrew Wild)

Freddie sang *You Take My Breath Away* from the new album, A Day At The Races, at the Hyde Park (Live at Hyde Park, 1976) concert in front of around 150,000-200,000 people, accompanied only by the piano. He had also written this song for David Minns. In the softest possible voice, he sang magically, taking our breath away, and we're left open-mouthed.

This is one of Freddie's most heartbreaking songs. Such beautiful lyrics can only be written by someone who loves somebody from the bottom of their heart and with poignant passion. I dare say that these lyrics rival the most beautiful love poems in world literature.

Nathan Hodges wrote a nice article about the Hyde Park concert.

'It was a massive free concert organised with the help of entrepreneur Richard Branson (creator of Virgin Records) as a gesture for the British fans for their loyalty and support especially during the last year due to the massive success of "Bohemian Rhapsody" and *A Night at the Opera*.'

(QueenOnline: 'A Picnic by The Serpentine' – The Legacy of Queen's Concert at Hyde Park – Fan Feature by Nathan Hodges)

David Minns was at the concert. I suppose, he still loved Freddie very much at that time. Can you imagine just how he felt standing behind the stage, surrounded by more than a hundred thousand people, and the song was for him, sung by the world's most amazing voice? I am quite sure he choked back a few tears, just like most people who loved Freddie and loved David.

Maybe he never sang so wonderfully again. He had broken up with Mary, David was there, and Freddie loved him very much, according to the lyrics. At the end of the song, Freddie sang 'I love you' in a way that I have never heard in any other love song. It was so painfully beautiful. The emotions conveyed by Freddie in singing are so intense that anyone would have thought this was the world's most beautiful love story. No doubt, during the performance - he was thinking about those magical first three months, which – among other things - had made him confess to Mary.

A vocal teacher (for Vocal Splendor Studios) talked about Freddie singing 'You Take my Breath Away' live at Hyde Park.

'It's so incredibly beautiful and so intimate yet so universal and how he used his voice. I loved how the piano and the voice were really organic. It's like each one fed on the other.

He was so gifted in so many ways. It's a big, luscious voice.' (Valerie White Williams)

Freddie's voice touches the deepest layers of our souls. All his joy and suffering become our joy and suffering. It is particularly inspiring, and little wonder that many wannabe singers have tried to imitate him. Some are pretty good at imitating his voice. Still, the emotions don't come over since they're not founded on personal experience, and the singers haven't got that charismatic personality as Freddie had. Nobody can conjure up Freddie's virtuosity.

Fortunately, Queen's videos are excellent and complement the music very well, and they create the feeling that they are still together now, so we can still enjoy Queen exceptional music and Freddie's singing. All their songs, even the early ones, are timeless classics now. They'll never be out of date, like the great classical composers' works always offer something new, however often we listen to them.

The opinion-shaping singing teacher was visibly impressed when Freddie was singing; she got emotional and talked about him very happily and enthusiastically, though sadly in the past tense.

Anyone who watches and sees this recording and listens to him will be incapable of not loving Freddie as a man, if they have any feelings at all. His spiritual beauty and the depth of his emotions make 'You Take My Breath Away' a magnificent production, which can hardly be imitated.

A woman who attended the Hyde Park concert wrote in a comment under the video: *'everyone was in love with Freddie at the time, both men and women'.*

This performance by Freddie is like a dream world, where love's magical beauty lasts forever. I'm sorry it only lasted a short time for Freddie in reality, except for one partner, but this love was completely different to the others.

(YouTube: You Take My Breath Away (Live At Hyde Park 1976)

'The Millionaire Waltz'

'The baroque, tongue-in-cheek 'The Millionaire Waltz' borrows generously from 'Bohemian Rhapsody'. The classical piano playing, huge vocal overdubs, and rock breakdown are all present and correct, this time in waltz time.'

'May sounds like a one-man jazz band in places.' (Andrew Wild)

Freddie sings about romantic love again in 'The Millionaire Waltz'. The lyrics are entertaining and humorous. Freddie said he had written this song for their manager at the time, John Reid, who would have been honoured, but it's clear from the content that the song was also about David.

In this short section, Freddie condensed his lifelong philosophy.

'There is music and love everywhere
Give a little love to me
Take a little love from me
I want to share it with you'

'Brian orchestrated it fully with guitars like he'd never done before. He went from tubas to piccolos to cellos.' – Freddie said about the song. (Freddie Mercury)

Freddie was right: Brian's guitar playing is extraordinary in this song, what he's capable of is unbelievable, and the Red Special indeed talks in his hands. Freddie's piano skills are insane as well.

The song's lyrics are so clear, there is no need to interpret them.

'Somebody to Love'

'Broadway musical-meets-doowop-meets-Harlem-church-choir. The message of one of Queen's greatest singles is direct and universal.' (Andrew Wild)

The song is a worthy follow-up to 'Bohemian Rhapsody'. The sound of the chorus is phenomenal. The video brilliantly illustrates how the recordings are put together, which enabled the three singers to achieve the chorus sound. This perfect harmony can only be achieved with hard work, powers of concentration and extraordinary talents. Studio work was extremely tiring for Freddie because he strained every nerve and muscle and wouldn't tolerate any imperfections in his songs. The other band members were also perfectionists, which enabled another top-notch song to be born after 'Bohemian Rhapsody'. Roger's vocals and his drumming make this track more delightful. You can't listen enough. It is absolute perfection, with the backing vocals and the instrumentation beyond comparison, just like in *Bohemian Rhapsody*. The more you listen to it, the better it sounds – pure magic.

A video of this song uploaded in 2013, 'Queen – Somebody To Love (Official Video)', has been viewed more than 334 million times, which speaks for itself. Freddie believed this song was better than 'Bohemian Rhapsody' in some respects. Playing it and for him singing this song live was no easy task; Freddie referred to it as 'a killer'.

Aretha Franklin was a big favourite of Freddie's. He tried to harmonise her early style with his own and would have loved to have the gospel sound of the choir. I've heard many gospel songs, and I found this version by Freddie far more brilliant than others I have ever heard. The harmony between the three singers is superb.

The word 'gospel' refers to Christian themes, that is why Freddie starts to pray to the Lord: 'I go down (down) on my knees (knees), and I start to pray (praise the Lord)'.

In the song, Freddie summarizes his philosophy on life, this time in a completely different way. He articulates it very clearly, there are no more fabulous locations in his songs, Freddie's suffering comes to life.

The intensity of the music and drums conveys an overwhelming desire - this is what I crave. Freddie's was getting closer to confessing to Mary, but they still lived together when the song was written.

Freddie sings about the adversity in his life, which makes him cry, in these song lyrics. He never used to pray, but the beating of his lonely heart and the agony of his loneliness made him wished the Almighty would help, and in the next verse, he also prays to Him.

One of the sentences in the third verse, *'I got nobody left to believe in'*, is the most important message in the song, telling us why he was lonely, despite having a partner.

'I ain't gonna face no defeat (yeah yeah)
I just gotta get out of this prison cell
One day (someday) I'm gonna be free, Lord!'

By 'prison cell', he refers to hiding his homosexuality and living with Mary, thinking of a sense of limitation, of being locked up, which prevented him from living his life in England the same way as he did in America. He doesn't accept defeat, and he's not used to compromising, and one day he'll be free, he sings.

Now that Freddie was successful and had money, this became his most critical problem; he never knew why his lovers were with him, for money or his love. So, Freddie felt that nobody loved him, even though David was there, they didn't have much time for each other.

Anyway, he didn't love Freddie the way he would have wanted, so Freddie still suffered from such a sense of loss that he had to repeat 'Find me, somebody to love' many times.

Freddie needed a self-sacrificing type of man who would tolerate his jealousy, his excessive possessiveness, and his overwhelming need for closeness. In this song, he prays to the Lord for such a man.

The choir and drumming resemble an ancient African ritual. It sounds as if he wanted to make sure that his request wrapped up in a song and a prayer would be heard on Heaven and Earth as if chanted like a shaman.

His singing technique is unparalleled in power in this song, shouting his excruciating pain into the world.

'What I would like most of all is to be in a state of blissful love. Sometimes I wake up in cold sweat, in fear because I'm alone. That's

why I go out looking for someone who will love me, even if it's just for a one-night stand. ...What I really like is a lot of love.' (Freddie Mercury)

'Good Old-Fashion Lover Boy'

This is another atmospheric and cheerful romantic love song written for David on this album and is well-liked by the fans. The lyrics are again poetical: Freddie 'can serenade and gently play on your heartstrings', he 'can dim the lights and sing you songs full of sad things' and 'be your Valentino just for you'. Indisputable, he must have been a 'good old-fashioned loverboy', no wonder he could sweep anyone off his feet, only needed to turn his charm on and because he learned his passion in the good *'old-fashioned school of loverboys'*. However, it seems Freddie missed the lesson on how to be faithful in a long term relationship.

Despite the beautiful songs and box full of love letters written for David, Freddie started to play somebody else's heartstrings and went home from the American tour with his new love, Joe Fanelli, in January, 1977. This was a painful, agonising twist for David.

Let's quickly remind ourselves of 'The March of The Black Queen' for those with any doubts that the song is about Freddie and that he is the black queen.

'In each and every soul lies a man
And very soon he'll deceive and discover
But even to the end of his life, he'll bring a little love'

Freddie kept Joe Fanelli by his side, after their break up, right to the end of his life, by which time he had become Freddie's cook and carer. Freddie loved him like a family member, as if he were his older brother.

Freddie once said: *'The moment it gets too nice, I become bored. I spoil it for myself. I'm one of those people who doesn't want love to be harmonious all the time. I want a little bit of the ups and downs. I want a little bit of the shakedowns and dramas.'* (Freddie Mercury)

I think what Freddie wanted wasn't drama but constant affirmation. Lacking self-confidence and terrified of being abandoned and lonely, he directed scenes in such a way that his partner had to keep confirming his belief that somebody loves him. Freddie wanted to be cherished all the time as if he was a child because he felt unsafe. He needed permanent confirmation, as he couldn't trust anybody. Unfortunately, nobody could get this message, except one, but he came too late.

Freddie often deliberately made both David and all of his partners jealous, confessing that all he wanted was to finally hear that his partner was jealous; their jealousy would prove they loved him. Freddie suffered from a constant need for love and continuously craved hugs and cuddles to feel secure. And there was another important reason for Freddie's relationship failures. However much he wanted to belong to someone in a joyful, loving relationship, when he found a loving partner like David Minns, somewhere deep inside, ultimately, he didn't want to commit himself. He was afraid the relationship would be empty and dull in the long term, so he provoked arguments and, effectively, the relationship's failure. He created the kind of tension that meant his partner simply couldn't take any more.

Even he was convinced that no partner could live with him. When he felt the relationship was under threat, he immediately started looking for somebody else to make sure he wasn't left on his own. He also wanted to keep David by his side after he broke up, even though he had Joe Fanelli, so there would always be someone he could rely on. And this was one of the reasons where his intense desire for possession came from. Among other reasons, it was also why he needed Mary. He had to take out 'insurance' several times over.

Partners who had gone through a normal childhood couldn't understand the reason for Freddie's strange behaviour. Anyone who thinks it is nonsense to keep bringing up his difficult childhood is very much mistaken. Whatever happens in our childhood affects every moment of our lives.

When Freddie returned from the American tour with Joe, he told David he had fallen in love and tried to convince him to stay near him because he had enough love in him for the two of them, but David still loved Freddie and couldn't imagine being around and watch him in somebody else's arms.

The song Good Old-Fashioned Lover Boy was also released as an EP on 20 May, 1976.

This is what David thought about Freddie's inspirations:

'I gave him an escape from the world of rock music, which was, of course, his other great passion.

That passion went very deep. We would often sit at home when Freddie would become progressively very restless and fidgety. He always had to be doing something. Every waking moment.'

'It was fascinating to watch how he would soak up every atom of life, every particle of every person and situation he encountered to assist in the creative process of his songwriting.'

'I also hadn't quite realized how much Freddie drew from his relationships the ideas he needed for his work. He wrote many songs about the people he loved, not to mention songs about those he wasn't quite so fond of!'

'I would often accuse him of holding deeply old fashioned opinions. Perhaps it was this which inspired him to write Good Old Fashioned Lover Boy?' (David Evans and David Minns)

Freddie got David to arrange his 30th birthday party as Freddie insisted on maintaining their relationship right to the end, even if only as a friend, but David was less and less able to tolerate the large number of new visitors associated with Freddie being a star, especially those who exploited his generosity to abuse the hospitality. David finally broke up at the beginning of 1978, and the next time he received an unexpected invitation was to Freddie's 40th birthday in 1986. By then, the symptoms of Freddie's illness were visible on his face. Although Freddie denied it, David realised what was wrong.

David forgave Freddie after he had written 'Don't Try Suicide' for him in 1980. When Joe left Freddie after two years, he cried on David's shoulder.

David Evans, Freddie and David's mutual friend, wrote in his book in memory of David Minns:

'..one of the traits of his stardom was beginning to emerge. In order to survive and persevere, in order to maintain the momentum he and his career had now attracted, Freddie found it difficult to have people around him who were difficult. It happens around stars, some call it sycophancy, some call it arselicking. It's actually called making life easier both for the star and the satellite, and perhaps it's not just with stars, perhaps it happens to an extent in lots of outwardly devoted friendships.

But, whatever the reasons, the process begins to warp the perspectives of both the star and the satellite….. There comes a time when to see your star, you have to get through the asteroid belt.'

(The latter example of Paul Prenter, who arbitrarily kept everyone away from Freddie, is a clear illustration.)

Freddie took back his kingdom, the fairy ring, and began to exercise control over the audience and his employees and lovers, like a king over his subjects.

'Somebody to Love' single was released in November 1976, and its peak chart position was number 2 on the UK charts, while in America reached number 13 on the US Billboard hot 100.

The album was a huge international success, reaching number one position in the UK, Japan and Netherland, while in the US it was number five on the list.

20. Running amok

News of the World album (1977)

1977 began with the American tour, to support the previous year's album, *The Day at the Races.*

Queen held some sensational, raucous parties after the successful concerts and completely let off steam.

Around this time, Freddie started to run amok for night years, eventually leading to his illness and death.

The other Queen members overlooked Freddie's new lifestyle because they were busy with their own families. Even Roger, who was still a bachelor at the time, didn't go out partying with him but rather with the guitarist from the support band.

Freddie had broken up with Mary; David was far away, so he was free to enjoy the pleasures of the gay world, but now with men, he picked up in American clubs, some of whom could have been infected with HIV.

Péter Popper and his book *The Risk of Playing Chess With Gods* comes to mind, in which he writes: 'Don't play chess with the gods because they can always put a new piece on the board.' In Freddie's case, the new piece was the HIV, which check-mated him, even though he felt he was invincible. Péter Popper is effectively saying, don't tempt fate because you can quickly get into trouble.

The 20,000 tickets advertised for a New York's Madison Square Garden concert were sold out in minutes on 5 February. Freddie and Queen were superstars on the other side of the world. Freddie surrounded himself with an army of assistants, including Paul Prenter, introduced to him by John Reid. Prenter gained Freddie's trust, not just because he was gay but by fulfilling Freddie's every wish as his personal assistant. Prenter was another of the gods' new pieces on the chessboard.

'Paul Prenter wasn't my favourite person….and he could be quite a divisive person because he had Freddie's ear.' – said Peter Straker, one of Freddie's closest friends. (Matt Richards & Mark Langthorne)

And the band's manager John Reid felt the same, as did the band, which was why they left Freddie on his own at their customary joint dinner one night.

Freddie was furious about being left alone but didn't suspect that Paul could have been behind it.

John Reid's job would have been to get rid of Paul Prenter from the management, but he couldn't do anything since Paul was Freddie's favourite.

During the American tour, Queen played two nights at The Forum in Los Angeles, where Elvis Presley and The Jackson 5 had appeared back in the day. They then travelled to Canada and returned to Britain, with Joe Fanelli at their side.

Joe was a very sensitive young man, so he couldn't bear having to keep his relationship with Freddie secret, and he began drinking heavily as a result; their relationship lasted about two years and then Joe returned to America. Joe didn't want to stay in contact with Freddie between 1981 and 1983, but Freddie renewed Joe's British residence permit every year because he was very attached to him.

In the end, Freddie wouldn't let him leave. They remained very close friends, and Freddie employed him as cook and carer in his final home in Garden Lodge, which he bought in 1980.

Sadly, Joe too got infected with the virus and fell ill, but he cared for Freddie right up to his final minutes, though he died just over a year after Freddie.

They continued the album tour in Europe in July 1977 and then finished with 11 concerts in Britain. The crown-shaped lighting structure, which was 1.7 metres wide and 8.32 metres high and weighed two tons, appeared in the show for the first time at the Earls Court (London) concert.

This cost the band 50,000 pounds at the time. They let it down onto the stage before the show and pulled it up at the end. It couldn't be used on some stages because of its height.

Their blinding and deafening tactic can be seen at the start of the Earls Court concert, as well as the beautiful new lighting rig.

The entire concert is available on YouTube, where you can watch live as the crown is raised high. Songs were written before 1977 were played at this show.

(YouTube: Queen Live Earls Court 1977 Full concert (720 P 50FPS)

The 6th album was recorded after they finished the tour.

Freddie and Freddie sensationally successful songs, the 'We Are the Champions' and the 'We Will Rock You' was first released as a single on 7 October, 1977 with two A-sides. Both songs were colossal crowd favourites and were played at almost every concert. The single got to number two in the UK charts, where it held its position for three weeks, while in America it got to number four and was in the charts for 27 weeks. This was the first single to make it to the top 10 in America since 'Bohemian Rhapsody.'

The album was released on 18 October, but the band's disappointment 'only' reached number four in the UK, though it got to number three in America.

On 17 October, Queen was given the Britannia Award, Best British Single of the Past 25 Years, for *'Bohemian Rhapsody.'*

'We Are the Champions'

'Nothing less than a rock anthem, but with many nuances that other stadium-friendly songs don't have: a sophisticated arrangement with dramatic changes in dynamics; dissonance; many key changes; big choir-like harmonies; a wonderfully melodic bass line; the outstanding guitar arrangement in the second verse; and Freddie Mercury expressive voice.' (Andrew Wild)

'We Are the Champions' celebrates the success they achieved with 'Bohemian Rhapsody' and *A Night at the Opera.*

The song's lyrics focus primarily on Freddie's glory. As he said himself: 'I suppose it could also be construed as my version of *I Did It My Way.'*

Freddie very skilfully condensed the essence into two verses in the first person: he had paid whatever had to be paid to achieve success: finished his education, waited patiently to get into a band with Brian and Roger. In the following two lines, he summarizes what his homosexuality involved: *'I've served my sentence but committed no crime.'* As if he were in a prison cell, as he says in 'Somebody to Love'. He has made *'mistakes',* it's not clear what he's specifically thinking about here, but as we know, there were quite a few he could have chosen from (Mary, David, Joe) and who knows what else influenced his private life. He also received his *'share of sand'*, such as by the dirt unfairly thrown by the press, or when Fanelli left and cleared out Freddie's flat. So, Freddie was also hurt too, but he got over it.

It's true he was a champion of survival and had a good fighting ability, as he always managed to prove. A good example was how he stood up to being ridiculed. He didn't give up his dream of being a star and a legend, and that's what he became. He became a world champion. He must have felt like one, and rightfully so.

Even though he was a champion, maybe it would have been seen in a poor light if he had sung about him being the champion in the refrain, but instead, in a smart move, he calls everyone a champion, so we are the champions, the band, the fans who raised them high, and anyone who brings glory. Champions don't give up the fight as long as they're still alive, and if this was characteristic of anyone, it was Freddie. Even during his illness, he carried on working and fighting hard not to be treated like a victim, which his pride wouldn't have allowed, and nor would his fighting ability, or the fact that he loved extreme challenges. Not many people would have been capable of doing this; maybe nobody.

The verses are about what happened on stage until he reached the top. *'I ain't gonna lose'*, the song continues, and then the refrain comes: *'we are the champions my friend, and we'll keep on fighting till the end, we are the champions, no time for losers'*. The sense of glory penetrated his soul, which is completely natural, and who wouldn't want to reap the fruits of his labour or be delighted with the success he had achieved through such hard work and perseverance?

Freddie wrote a song about himself and Queen, of course, writing the lyrics so expertly that he also praised everyone else and even said thanks and thereby made another hit. It recognises his qualities as a businessman.

He had a fantastic ability to manipulate people, but I can't imagine he ever did so with bad intention. However, the tactic worked, people really love the song, and some of the leading football clubs regard it as their own anthem. The song is still played at sporting events today because it creates a fantastic atmosphere. Who wouldn't want to be a champion and bathe in glory?

The song lyrics are a masterpiece, especially those containing Freddie's confession, and the background music is perfect. The refrain section sells the song to the whole world because it includes everyone willing to fight like champions. The music for this part is melodious so anyone can sing it, even in monotone, and it has a perfect effect in groups.

Brian said in an interview that the song was about Queen, of course, and they would never have thought sports teams would sing it too.

A journalist asked Roger at the time:

'Only Queen could come up with the title 'We are the Champions'. I mean where has the modesty gone?'

Roger's answer was hilarious, with a slightly cheeky smile on his face: 'There wasn't any.' And then by way of explanation, he added: 'After what we have got from the English music press who cares?'

'The catchiest song of all time'

'Blending florid theatricality with arena-rock thunder 'We Are The Champions' is a power-ballad built around a cascading melody, multi-tracked vocals, Freddie's powerhouse main vocal, and Brian May's acrobatic guitar work. Thirty-four years later, scientists at Goldsmiths, University of London would declare 'We are the Champions' the catchiest song of all time following a scientific study. 'Every musical hit is reliant on maths, science, engineering, and technology; from the physics and frequencies of sound that determine pitch and harmony to the hi-tech digital processors and synthesizers which can add effects to make a song more catchy' – revealed music psychologist Dr Daniel Müllensiefen. 'Over the course of the study, the researchers found that catchiness was most influenced by four factors: long and detailed musical phrases, *multiple pitch changes in a song's hook, male vocalists, and higher male voices making a noticeable vocal effort'. And 'We are the Champions' had them all.'* (Matt Richards & Mark Langthorne)

(Dear Freddie, if he were still with us, would no doubt enjoy this video: David Armand miming 'We Are The Champions' on YouTube. It's great fun and worth watching if you haven't seen it already.)

Roger's hard rock track 'Sheer Heart Attack' was included on this album.

'..the energetic song 'Sheer Heart Attack' is a deliberately simple song. Roger Taylor plays everything except some liquid lead guitar lines from Brian May.' (Andrew Wild)

In an edited video of the recordings of live concerts, Freddie sang the song in two different outfits. Both of them were different phases of clothes that emphasized his homosexuality. We can see him in the ballet dress adorned with silver sequins and later in leather trousers, which were fashionable for a while among gay men in New York. Much later, around 1985, he took up a new style, wearing short, combed-back hair, jeans and a sleeveless T-shirt, which was compulsory in London's Heaven Bar. The change is also conspicuous among non-homosexuals, but it's not apparent why. This discriminating clothing allowed gay men to recognise each other more easily, without being evident to others.

(YouTube: Queen – Sheer Heart Attack (Live in Houston, Texas, '77)

Freddie is frenzied on stage while singing on the video, like the crazy, 17-year old, wild teenager the song is about: aggressive and not completely clear what he is saying. He feels paralysed. He reminds you of a guy who has taken drugs and doesn't know what to do; he knocks over one of the speakers, he is on his back and then, using mating gestures, he embraces one of the microphone stands. At the end of the video, he arrogantly shows his bum to the audience. Freddie played the role of this 17-year old perfectly.

Freddie once said:

'I feel like I'm the master of ceremonies, and that's as far as I like to go because they've come to enjoy themselves, and that's all. Entertainment is the key factor as far as I'm concerned, and no way would I like to feel that I'm a kind of political spokesman.'

He said this about the fact that he didn't want to send political messages in his songs. He certainly didn't send any with this performance, but he was a master of ceremonies, as he always wanted to be, and it seemed like the audience was also having fun.

(Looking back, sadly, he was right when he said: *'this thing about me living a life of excess is so blown out of proportion. I basically have a life of just above the norm.'*)

The mating gestures refer to the fact that even the microphone stand makes him think of sex. It seems everything makes him think of sex. When he bends down and shows his bum to the audience, this has several meanings, one being that anyone who doesn't like it can lump it (which reflected his behaviour in general, including on stage), and another showing off his gay nature. His clothing serves the same purpose.

By then, Freddie realised that most of the audience wasn't interested in his sexuality or was impressed by his coolness. They looked up to him because he dared to do anything, and others probably turned away from him or ignored this side of him and preferred to focus on his musical genius, which outweighed everything.

During this period, the glory often went to his head. To control the events he began to cause hysterical scenes if something didn't happen as he wished. He knew he was irreplaceable as far as the other members of the band were concerned. His self-aggression turned outwards towards others. The question is, why did he get angry then? Why the hysteria?

Hysterical scenes can be attributed to mental health issues; they arise from emotional tension and refer to life crises. A person behaving like this demands a greater level of concern from those around them.

Freddie had restrained himself for years and now as if he wanted to make up the years he missed; he behaved like a teenager trying to control his 'parents' with hysterical outbursts. This stage of progression had been missing from Freddie's life. As a result of the mockery, he developed a defensive persona, became a conformist, kind and caring guy to avoid being ridiculed or hurt. He never dared take on the role of boss. He withdrew into the background everywhere. Teenagers take on several different roles between the ages of 16 and 19 to develop a sense of identity, find out who they are and where their lives are heading.

Freddie was confused during this period. The success of his songs and the enthusiasm of the fans gave him a power he had not yet learned to deal with. Freddie moved from a star to a global superstar, which is a massive change for an emotionally unstable person.

I guess this new Freddie took the other band members by surprise; it couldn't have been easy to decide how to handle the new situation.

Freddie didn't have anybody by his side to look up to and listen to. There was one role model he looked up to in his life, Jimi Hendrix. Jimi might have been the best musician, yet he allegedly died of a drug overdose and was found in wine-filled vomit.

Freddie lived away from his parents and couldn't identify with either of them or follow their examples. As an adult, he behaved immaturely and became a champion, but not a champion of dealing with emotions.

Drugs and alcohol and such a level of success could have distorted Freddie's personality. Drugs and alcohol dissolve inner uncertainty, causing a lack of inhibition.

Two other songs on the 1977 album can be attributed to him: 'Get Down, Make Love' *and* 'My Melancholy Blues'.

'Get Down, Make Love'

'*A simple, tense, rocking, sexy song full of passion and heat. The chorus-verse-bridge structure is split by a 'Whole Lotta Love' style interlude with squealing harmoniser and pumping drums.*' (Andrew Wild)

The song 'Get Down, Make Love' is a powerful track with hard rock music. The lyrics are about Freddie sex life. Interestingly enough, Freddie was in love with Joe Fanelli when he wrote this song. Even so, it sounds as if he was primarily confined to one-night stands, which killed the emotions and romantic feelings in him, so they are absent from the song: he tells his partner to '*get down and make love, take my body I give you heat. You say you're hungry, I give you meat. I suck your mind, and you blow my head*' etc. It's not worth carrying on, this is what the whole song is about, raw sensual sex, but the audience still liked it. I saw them perform the song at a live concert in Montreal in 1980 on YouTube.

Some people believe Freddie also used drugs during gigs at the time, which might have been regular or occasional, but watching the live concert video above makes you wonder.

While Freddie was David Minns partner he wrote him beautiful love songs. It seems the relationship with Joe Fanelli didn't make Freddie satisfied and happy. Had it been like that he would have written some happy or lyrical love song instead of 'Get Down, Make Love' or 'My Melancholy Blues'.

After a while, Freddie's failed love affairs had caused him so much psychological pain that he decided it was better not to look for intimacy.

Still, he was incapable of doing so and fell in love again and again. He couldn't get enough of the emotionless, mechanical sexual acts. The one-night stands weren't just a matter of releasing tension; secretly, he always hoped he would find the real thing, although he was afraid of deep feelings by then.

Freddie didn't realise that a prerequisite for a deep, loving relationship is being faithful; falling in love is just a starting point, the school of love. Among other things, love involves making sacrifices for others.

This is what he said himself on the subject: *'I prefer my sex any involvement, and there were times when I was extremely promiscuous.'* He probably said this when he had already received the first positive HIV test in 1985.

Freddie talked about his love affairs in this quote:

'In terms of love, you're never in control, and I hate that feeling. I don't believe in half measures or compromise. ....I fall in love far too quickly and end up getting hurt all the time.' (Freddie Mercury)

In a video interview in 1977, Freddie talks about 'We Are The Champions' with a reporter. We can see a completely healthy, clear-thinking young man who answers questions modestly and firmly, with no sign of his stage persona. He is attractive and stylish, but his inner restlessness is apparent. He can hardly wait for the reporter to finish his questions, even though they are intelligent and only relate to music. He is vibrant, always moving and sipping on champagne. (YouTube: Freddie Mercury Interview 1977.)

Which one is the real Freddie? None of them and all of them. Freddie knew how to behave in an interview, like he knew how to design his stage clothes, to make the impression he wanted on stage. Freddie was a performing artist and a good actor and could make people believe what he wanted. I'm not saying he was a liar and a shallow deceiver.

Quite the opposite, he wanted to be open and honest, too honest, too open, which made him vulnerable. Extreme emotions, intense emotional storms, enormous love and enormous happiness on one side, while on the other hand, if someone left him, it was a huge disappointment, crazy pain, which produced frustration, anger and aggression, including self-aggression.

('Get Down Make Love' Queen - Rock Montreal 1981)

'My Melancholy Blues'

'More of a jazz torch than a twelve-bar, 'My Melancholy Blues is a shuffling late-night cabaret lament with no guitars, no backing vocals and an extremely rare Mercury piano solo.' (Andrew Wild)

It is a beautiful song, but Freddie wasn't in a good mood when he wrote it.

Someone had just left him, his heart was painfully empty, and he tried to alleviate his pain with drink. He was floundering in sadness because he knew he would soon face another storm, another love and another disappointment. Freddie fell in love quickly; he loved his partners passionately, so he suffered many disappointments. He hoped someone would come along and get him, but didn't believe it would happen. This request was a feeble attempt. He knew that due to his nature, he couldn't be taken or stopped.

The song's main message is an empty heart. He had asked in vain to be loved for by someone so many times in the song 'Somebody to Love.' He told the whole world, but nobody was listening, or anyone who did hear didn't know how to love Freddie.

As far as Freddie was concerned, it was a completely natural request for somebody to love him the way he was, no matter whether he was hysterical or kind and cute. If somebody could have finally accepted his extreme emotional imbalance, he would have been able to change for his own sake. He wanted acceptance because that's the benchmark of true love. It's easy to accept someone who always behaves lovably. Freddie was unable and even unwilling to always be loveable. He wanted to be himself and didn't want to appear different to how he was.

If Freddie had received acceptance, he would have escaped from the drugs and drink, the meaningless sex, AIDS, and anything with which he destroyed and finally unintentionally killed himself. His self-destruction is explained by this melancholy, depressed mood, which was accompanied by loneliness, a sense of emptiness, and pain. This was why he loved Mary and why nobody could replace her, because she was the only one who accepted him the way he was. There was only one problem with her: she was a woman. This was Freddie's tragedy. Partying, alcohol, drugs and sex are painkillers, and this is why he is attached to and bound by them. In his sober moments, he knew he's was doing something crazy, because he was too smart not to know. But his need for love was so great that he was incapable of settling for anything else.

As a child, there was no one he could rely on when he needed someone to listen to his every word and respond to his actions saying, "I love you and accept you the way you are. You are valuable and lovable".

In contrast, his parents and teachers were strict and demanding. They only 'loved' him if he could show results; this is related to his perfectionism and how he earned the love of his fans.

'My Melancholy Blues' has a sorrowful, resigned mood; Freddie's self-awareness is high, in line with his intellect, as is his willingness and ability to examine himself. The book titled: *A Life, In His Own Words*, testifies to this.

Musically the song seems simple, yet it made them all work hard because of its unusual style. Freddie is enjoying singing and playing the piano in a completely new style. John's bass can be heard more clearly, though we can hardly hear Roger's drums, yet they are there as a pleasant background.

There was no place for the electric guitar in this song. However, Brian had plenty of things to keep him busy with 'We Will Rock You', a fantastic hit. The song's video - made by Queen - has been viewed more than 436 million times and not by accident. Brian is an extraordinary composer; his songs are magnificent, just like Freddie's.

Watching the crowd of 72000 at the Live Aid concert and the extent to which people felt as one was uplifting. Unity is very uncommon in most people's lives, which is why fans feel so good at concerts - they sense that something links them together there. This feeling of togetherness can also be observed in the comments under the YouTube videos of Queen.

The new album tour began in North America in November 1977; every concert was sold out, and the band completely won the audience's hearts.

Queen had grown into a huge business due to the enormous level of interest. So Brian, Roger and John, voting Freddie down, decided to move on and replace their manager, John Reid, thinking he could not manage both Elton John and Queen. By this time, they had a lot of staff. They were able to travel on private aircraft.

Britain had a punitive tax regime at the time. One had to pay higher taxes on higher incomes, so Queen decided to work in Europe. Roger said in some cases, the tax rate was 90%.

This meant they had to spend 300 days a year outside Britain. They began managing themselves with the help of a tax specialist and an accountant. Jim Beach stayed on as their lawyer and became Queen's main business manager, while Paul Prenter and Pete Brown performed other management duties.

On returning home - at the end of 1977 – it seemed Freddie was using more and more cocaine and offered plenty more to his guests. This was confirmed by Paul Gambaccini in an interview with Matt Richards and Mark Langthorne, whom Freddie had invited to a party. Gambaccini was a close friend of Freddie's and a radio and TV presenter.

Irrespective of the cocaine and parties, Queen and Freddie gave their best performance at every concert. The tickets were sold out everywhere, and the audience seemed to be happy. If attention diminished for a moment, Freddie always came up with something to add to the atmosphere. By then, he was a real magician on stage, not to mention his voice, which was increasingly powerful. He even uplifts songs that were less successful and can sing the most difficult songs. Freddie's songs, almost without exception, are timeless masterpieces.

Queen played 22 venues in North America in November 1977. In his book, *Queen Unseen,* Peter Hince graphically described how Queen's crew worked. As the Queen's head of road crew, he was continuously on stage to support Freddie and John. He gave them the microphone at the right time, handed over messages from Freddie to the others, and served them drinks. This book is an exciting and witty description of life on tour with Queen.

'The stage manager, having checked that all was definitely ready, would call the dressing room by crackling walkie-talkie to bring the band up.

Having emptied their bladders, Queen, flanked by minders, wardrobe 'mistress' and assistants, were now bouncing on the balls of their feet in their hidden position and itching to get up on stage. A message was conveyed by headset to the house electrician to 'kill the house lights', and as the venue plunged into darkness, it created a huge adrenaline rush for both crew and audience. Queen would be swept by a combination of this energy and torchlight onto the stage and into the Dolls House: a free-standing frame covered in black drapes, located in the back corner of stage right. This was where the band would rest or hide from view when not active on stage.

Not even Access All Areas gained access into here.

The intro tape pumped through the PA and monitors, battling for level with the audience noise – as smoke machines hissed out an atmosphere for the lights to cut through as they came pulsing to life. No going back now. The hundreds of lamps in the rig flashed and flickered but remained tethered, not yet releasing their full power until the dormant metal monster slowly began to rise in the air, spitting light beams of multi-coloured fire. Awesome, but also quite scary...' (Peter Hince)

When the excitement reached a peak when Freddie marched on stage and announced, 'I'd like to f**k you all', and then the sensational show could begin - Freddie and his insatiable sexual appetite, and of course, his lack of inhibitions.

It seems the audience enjoyed the obscene remarks and his erotic movements because they threw everything on stage, from women's panties to penis ring. On one occasion, when someone in the first row put this particular ring at Freddie's feet, Freddie showed it to the audience and said: 'Thanks, darling.'

The crew were aware that Freddie was gay. When he was hysterical, Peter Hince tried to calm him down by saying a 'hardware store' near the concert venue was open at night and a gay phone box. I suspect these phrases were cryptic, humorous names for gay bars.

The band members also noticed the change when Freddie started taking men to his hotel room instead of girls. In any case, it seemed, or they pretended, they weren't especially bothered. They were also happy to see naked or half-naked female dancers or even wilder, crazy stunts beyond all fantasy.

'Most nights Queen were very good, and on occasion absolutely magnificent – or not quite so good. However, they were undoubtedly a great live band that were exciting to watch. The secret to this was

simple: they could play. Musicians who had mastered and applied their instruments firmly believing in quality in all they did. When Queen took to the road after a new album was released, they always strived to give their best to the paying public as these four guys unashamedly wanted to be The Biggest Band in the World.' (Peter Hince)

Freddie always had some good ideas; he could cope in any situation and knew how to make the audience love him.

Queen played New York's Madison Square Garden on 1 and 2 December, 1977. Before that, the New York Yankees had recently won the Baseball World Series. Freddie acquired a Yankees jacket and cap. At the concert, he sang *We Are The Champions* wearing this gear. The audience understandably went wild in delight, as they were also wild Yankees supporters.

Their last gig in Los Angeles was on 22 December, when Freddie was brought on stage for the final encore in a large backpack by a security guard dressed as Santa. As he got up out of the big backpack, he and Brian began to sing White Christmas, the Irving Berlin song. The choir behind them was made up of the stylishly dressed crew. Freddie and his fantastic ideas were unsurpassable.

21. Jazz Album (1978)

'We Will Rock You' got to number one in the French charts in January 1978 and stayed there for 12 weeks, and to celebrate this, Queen was given an award from a radio station as the band with the greatest potential. They stole their way into French hearts as well with this song.

The European tour began in Stockholm, and then returning to Britain, they gave the first concert at the Bristol Hippodrome in May.

The studio recordings for the new album lasted four months, partly in southern France and partly in Montreux, Switzerland.

After recording the album, Freddie made an album in his studio (Goose Productions) at his own expense for his best friend, Peter Straker. Freddie got to know the singer with Jamaican heritage in 1975, and they soon became devoted friends. They went to ballet performances and the theatre together and were like two brothers. Peter was a positive influence on Freddie. With his excellent sense of humour, he could ease Freddie's tension. Both of them loved the opera and the classics. In effect – according to Peter Freestone, Freddie's later friend and personal assistant – they taught each other to sing. Freddie believed many classical pieces have African origins, and they have something of Africa's unique sense of rhythm in them. This friendship pretty much stood the test of time, and there were times when wherever Freddie was in the world, he would call Peter almost every day.

Five of Freddie's songs are on the album, two of which went on to become smash hits, 'Bicycle Race' and 'Don't Stop Me Now'.

'Mustapha'

'Arabic chants and scales are not your standard rock fare. But then, Queen were not your average rock band.' (Andrew Wild)

The song Mustafa has no specific message for us. At most, people from the Middle East could enjoy its lyrics. It has not been translated for us, and it also indicates that the music is the essential part of the song, while the text – I suppose - is just a set of nice-sounding, rhyming Arabic words. Freddie had heard original Arabic songs sung in India and Zanzibar. Obviously, he liked the sound and enjoyed being able to imitate them. The music is also in Arabic style, which is a pleasant surprise for us. As we know it, variety delights us.

'Bicycle Race'

'Bicycle Race' is power pop-progressive in feel with a five-part harmony a chorus, a tense fun touch in the verses, anthemic rock in the bridge and multiple bicycle bells before the hard-rocking guitar solo. What should sound disjointed and confusing is uplifting, joyous and racing success.' (Andrew Wild)

The song's lyrics are easy to understand, so no interpretation is needed. They are hilarious and fun, praising Freddie's humour and imagination.

The only 'secret' message of the song: I'm relaxing now, don't expect world-shattering songs from me. There would have been nothing wrong with the relaxation, it was not surprising that he was thoroughly tired, but the ease, unfortunately, lasted too long and cost him too much.

It was inspired by the sight of competitors in the Tour de France passing through Montreux. Freddie imagined how much more exciting the spectacle would be if muscular naked men were to ride the bikes. This idea inspired him to write the song.

Drawing on this idea, a video was shot of sixty-five naked women were cycling at Wimbledon Stadium. No doubt Freddie and the other guys were delighted, but not everyone shared their enthusiasm. In America, the album included a poster of the naked girls on bicycles. Some parts of America banned the album because they regarded the poster as pornography.

I'm not so prudish as to share the American's opinion, but one thing is certain, no one but Freddie would have thought of making a video of this idea and no one else at the time would have dared to do it. I guess he didn't want to shape the public taste but to surprise Queen's fans. I guess the fans loved it, but they were not the only ones who saw it but also those who felt responsible for public morality. I can imagine Freddie was terribly disappointed and outraged at how misunderstood his intentions were. He must have thought it was an innocent joke and great fun.

Just imagine what would happen today if someone has been biking naked in Hyde Park.

'Jealousy'

'A beautiful overlooked piano-driven mid-placed ballad with a skipping, melodic bass line. The sound and arrangement hark back to Sheer Heart Attack. Such was Queen's strength in depth that this song could have been a big hit for anyone else.' (Andrew Wild)

Freddie quietly lamented in this beautiful-sounding ballad about his own jealousy that had brought so much sadness and pain into his life. He was not prepared that feelings of jealousy to poison love.

Modern psychological research suggests that although the genesis of love cannot be understood scientifically, it has been proven our love life can be understood a certain way. John Alan Lee, a Canadian psychologist, has proven through research that there are six types of love. One is mania, which has nothing to do with manic depression or bipolar disorder. There is a lot of negativity and ambivalence in this type of love, even though the partner receives a very intense, deep love. It is characterized by strong jealousy and desire to possess. It develops on a neurotic background. These compensatory traits put a heavy strain on the relationship. The research also has shown that this type of love is related to an unhappy childhood, living with many deficiencies, neurotic needs, as a lonely adult. They have a great desire for love, but they are also afraid of it, and their fears are often justified because most of the time, their love leaves them, or they break with their love being fearful of being left alone. It is tough for them to break up.

Freddie's love can be classifiable into this type of love. All of this was due to Freddie's traumatic childhood experiences.

Lee's research also shows a type of love called agape, which corresponds to mania. It is the love where a partner is a self-sacrificing person. When Freddie needed love the most, he found that type of love, but it came pretty late; Freddie was already infected and ill.

'Don't Stop Me Now'

'Don't Stop Me Now' must surely be one of Queen's greatest songs. This Freddie Mercury through and through - the lines 'Don't stop me now/Cause I'm having such a good time' could easily be his epitaph.'. Andrew Wild

Freddie's other hit song was the *'best feel-good song'* of all time. Freddie was really on a high when he wrote it. Unfortunately, Andrew Wild is right about the epitaph.

This song lyric is absolute proof that Freddie incorporated all of his experiences into a song, both good and bad, and rarely wrote any gibberish. This was about his lifestyle, what he utterly enjoyed and what made him happy.

According to the lyrics, Freddie is going to have a real good time tonight. He feels so alive that he thinks he can turn the world inside out while floating around in ecstasy. He compares himself to a sex machine, an atom bomb about to explode. He's travelling at the speed of light and burning at 200 degrees. That's why he feels like Mr Fahrenheit. The lyrics reflect his lifestyle and his plans for the future. Freddie enjoyed his freedom and the pleasures that his lifestyle could provide him.

This song is seen as one of the best feel-good songs of all time. But it doesn't create good feelings in me; I don't even like listening to it as I know where his ecstasy led – it's as if Freddie crashed into the stone wall surrounding his home at the speed of light, leaving a gaping hole behind him, leaving his 'family', love, band, and fans as orphans. The vacancy he left behind can never be filled.

The song is still excellent; Freddie's enthusiasm gives the song and listeners a boost, if it is possible at all after he has gone forever.

Regardless of what happened, I feel I owe him this quote.

'Queen's Don't Stop Me Now Is The Most Feel-Good Song Of All Time

Dr Jacob Jolij says the 1970s rock hit has all the elements of a feel-good record.

Music, even at the worst of times, has the ability to lift spirits as nothing else can.

But one song, in particular, has more power than the rest to help us find our mojo when we're feeling a little low.

According to cognitive neuroscientist Dr Jacob Jolij, Queen's 1970s hit Don't Stop Me Now has all the ingredients of a feel-good song.

Jolij analysed data from a survey conducted by electronics company Alba, which asked 2,000 people to reveal their favourite uplifting songs.

From his study, he drew this conclusion: a fast tempo (roughly 150 beats per minute), a major key, and happy lyrics are the key common elements of a feel-good song. Songwriters take note.

'My analysis confirmed very nicely what we already knew from the literature: Songs written in a major key with fast tempo are best at inducing positive emotions,' Jolij, an assistant professor of psychology at the University of Groningen, told HuffPost.

Virtually all 'feel good' songs were in a major key (save one or two), and all of them were at least 10 BPM faster than the average pop song.

In second place was Abba's Dancing Queen, followed by Good Vibrations by The Beach Boys and then Billy Joel's Uptown Girl.

Surprisingly, Pharrell Williams' Happy didn't make the top 10.

However, Jolij explained that our own associations with songs often determine the emotions they stir in us.'

When Freddie sings 'Don't Stop Me Now' it is not known exactly which party he is singing about; an imaginary one or one held that year, one on Roger's birthday, one on Freddie's, or a party they gave for Halloween. The latter was the most extraordinary party anyone ever staged. Four hundred guests were invited, and it cost £ 200,000. Even Brian May said they deliberately exaggerated everything at their parties. They just wanted to have fun. I have no doubts they had fun, however, the world's press reported the Halloween orgy in the headlines. The press called it the most depraved party, which it probably was, as far as the 'man in taste in the street' was concerned.

Evidently, they felt nobody and nothing could stop them. They could do anything they wanted without consequences, and it seemed they were right.

Freddie had such a good time on Roger's birthday that he swung on the hotel chandelier, at least according to the gossip, but then who could blame him when he had secretly always wanted to do this. Maybe he felt himself that night, like Superman. The rumours don't say anything about where and how he landed. It would have been great fun. I'm sure the guests even applauded the attraction, and deservedly so, he didn't get injured, and the chandelier wasn't torn off either. No one else would have dared to imitate him.

This was the first year they managed their own affairs and didn't stay in any country long enough to pay tax, so they had no problem funding the parties.

Because of the song's lyrics, the band members began to worry about Freddie, fearing he was or would become a drug addict. It was true that Freddie was on a high, and he could do whatever he wanted. He could live his own life freely. No one stood in his way.

The band members' concerns were not unfounded; clearly, the drugs and alcohol obviously had made a considerable contribution to Freddie's promiscuity. Under the influence of alcohol and drugs, we can all lose our heads. Freddie knew this very well and trusted that it would not happen to him.

'Let me entertain you'

Another of Freddie's tracks on the album, 'Let Me Entertain You', is pretty aggressive in terms of performance style and lyrics in contrast to the 'feel-good' track. Freddie wore leather pants, a jacket and a cap, and his torso was naked at the concert, which matched the Castro clone look, which was the style in gay bars in America.

The lyrics of the song are funny, to some extent, even though he offers his body for sale and other sexual pleasures to the audience. Freddie wrote about the male version of killer queen in this song. After accepting his homosexuality and started to visit gay bars, his offers are less sophisticated in this song and not so romantic than in 'Killer Queen'. The only message is that he had a good time in the gay bars. These experiences inspired him to write the song.

The music for the song is heavy rock, which Freddie sings well as always. Naturally, he greets the Japanese audience in Japanese in the video.

(YouTube: 'Let Me Entertain You' – Live in Tokyo 1979)

The fact he was sexually overloaded was nothing new. His sex addiction didn't subside, and nor did he give up cocaine. The next few years passed in this intoxicating mood in Europe, as if he were celebrating their incredible global success of the 1980s in advance.

Freddie was extravagant and no doubt often went too far without restraint, but the American audience loved him, as did his Japanese and European fans. Before Christmas of 1978, they held sold-out concerts at

35 venues in the US. Even the critics couldn't prevent Queen from having 20 naked women cycling up and down the stage in Madison Square Garden during their performance of 'Fat Bottomed Girls'.

They might have regretted their bravery later because their popularity in North America declined in the next few years, though not enough to stop the album from going platinum in the US, and gold in the UK. Freddie's song 'Don't Stop Me Now' *got to number 9*, while 'Bicycle Race'/'Fat Bottomed girl' single reached number 11 in the UK Singles Chart.

They spent Christmas at home but went on another huge European tour in the middle of January and prepared to record the next album, ominously in Munich, where Freddie was free to enjoy the pleasures offered by sex clubs, drugs and alcohol in the *Bermuda Triangle*. The name was very appropriate - it could also have been called the deadly zone.

22. Live Killers album (1979)

The European tour of the last year album – Jazz - began in Hamburg, and then in March, the band retreated to the Montreux studio, on the banks of Lake Geneva. This studio offered an unparalleled view of the lake and was suited to rest, as well as work. They worked a hell of a lot during the stay, and in April, they travelled to Japan for the Live Killers tour.

They played in 44 venues in Europe and Japan between January and the beginning of August. They were resting only in March during this time.

Twenty-one of the most successful concert recordings were included on the *Live Killers* album. Freddie wrote nine of them. The album was released in June and reached number three on the UK hit list.

The new album only got to number 16 in America, and this was the first time they hadn't made the top 10. Over the years, however, they twice had platinum records in America and gold in Britain.

Rolling Stone magazine published some harsh criticisms of Queen, however, the American criticisms didn't bother the British as the single 'Don't Stop Me Now' - released in the meantime - also made it to the top 10 in the UK.

'Crazy Little Thing Called Love'

'The bulk of the backing track was completed in a single session: a testament to the simplicity of the arrangement, necessitated by Mercury's self-confessed lack of ability on guitar, and as a tribute to the rock and roll sound of the 1950s.' (Andrew Wild)

Another of Freddie's songs, 'Crazy Little Thing Called Love', was released as a single and went to number 2 in the UK and number 1 in the US. This was the first single to top the charts in the US. I guess it happened because the song is reminiscent of Elvis Presley's style. The song lyrics are about Freddie's love life. He sings about having difficulty handling his love life, so he has to learn how to succeed in this, but he's not ready for it yet.

The lyrics are unequivocal and cheerful. The message is in this short part:

'Take a back seat, hitchhike
And take a long ride on my motorbike
Until I'm ready (ready Freddie)
Crazy little thing called love'

Freddie got the inspiration while having a bath and immediately shouted for a guitar. The next day the entire song was complete. Freddie had no intention of imitating Elvis, yet managed to do so. This might be the song in which he has to sing quickest, and he is capable of singing amazingly fast; it's worth watching.

(YouTube: Queen – Crazy Little Thing Called Love (Official Video)

Of the singles released until 1979, nine found their way into the top 10, seven of which were written by Freddie; one by John ('You're My Best Friend') and 'We Will Rock You' written by Brian, and 'We Are The Champions' were released together. It seems the band increasingly needed Freddie, and evidently, he knew this. It was no surprise that he would have felt as if he was walking two metres above the earth, and probably felt like Superman. He can be seen in a Superman T-shirt on many recordings. Freddie's superstar status was due to the super band, and of course, Freddie's mind-blowing performances and musical talent, but he wouldn't have succeeded without Roger, Brian and Joe. Queen helped him to rise out of the unknown. Freddie said, there is no Queen sound without one of them.

They spent the summer months in Munich, working in Musicland Studios and living in the same building.

They worked in the studio with Reinhold Mack, an experienced studio technician and director with excellent knowledge having previously worked with Deep Purple and The Rolling Stones. As far as he was concerned, Queen was not the easiest band he had ever collaborated with.

The first song he worked together with Freddie on was 'Crazy Little Thing Called Love'. Freddie played the acoustic guitar himself. He only knew a few chords, so the song was relatively simple musically, but still has a great sound. Brian later 'naturally' improved the recording with his guitar playing. This track first appeared as a single, before *The Game* album.

This is what Mack said about Freddie:

'Fred was easy. We thought along similar lines, and it took him fifteen to twenty minutes to come up with something absolutely brilliant.

Mack continued to rave about Freddie's studio technique, his spontaneous inventiveness, his commitment, his enthusiasm, the speed and dexterity with which he worked.

I got on exceptionally well with Freddie. I liked the fact that he was a genius. He really was, in terms of the perception of music and seeing the focal point of where the song should be.' (Leslie-Ann Jones)

Freddie was a frequent visitor to Mack's family; he got on very well with Mack's wife and middle son and told him a lot about his childhood. He enjoyed the family environment very much.

Mack overheard Freddie talking to his son, and his impression was that Freddie must have been painfully lonely in his childhood.

Mack said: 'Freddie told me a number of times, 'Perhaps I'll give up the whole gay thing one of these days'…..I do think he could have given up being gay because he loved women. I saw what he was like in their presence, and he wasn't the kind of gay man who didn't like them in his life. He was the opposite.' (Leslie-Ann Jones)

It seemed to Mack that Freddie had started to get bored of his lifestyle, the promiscuity, and the pleasures to be found in bars.

I think Freddie missed the intimacy of a family, the peace he saw in the family, but this was just a thought for him. It wasn't the first time when he said that he would have children some time. Freddie told this probably because he loved children yet loved his lifestyle and freedom more.

Mack sensed that Freddie missed the calm and emotional sense of security that a long-term relationship would have provided, and he sang about this in 'Somebody To Love'.

The same gay environment awaited Freddie in Munich that he had discovered in New York.

The atmosphere of permissive bars, with striptease dancers and live sex on stage, in stark contrast with what they were familiar with in London, didn't just 'bother' Freddie but also the other band members. They were no longer able or willing to work at the previously tight pace and style, recordings were now interrupted for food and drink, or a little distraction late at night the night until morning, and then carried on working - tired and grouchy - the following afternoon.

They got tired of the lifestyle of recording, tour; recording, tour; recording, tour; and needed to relax.

Brian says there was an increase in tension and heated arguments in the band during recordings, especially between him and Roger.

Brian felt this new lifestyle had taken its toll on him emotionally, and perhaps on Freddie too.

They would have liked to appear at Wembley Stadium after the European tour but weren't given the opportunity, presumably because of the previous year's 'naked women on bicycles show'.

Freddie had always enjoyed the ballet and loved Nureyev and Baryshnikov in particular, but I don't believe he ever thought he would perform with the most prestigious London ballet company. In October, he received an invitation from London's Coliseum Theatre for a short show. Freddie practised with the company for a few days. Members of the company had some fun when Freddie marched into rehearsals in a ballet outfit; he couldn't dance but was very enthusiastic. Freddie sang and danced with great passion and, in the end, was hanging upside down in the air. He performed in the show as a surprise guest. He sang 'Bohemian Rhapsody', and 'Crazy Little Thing Called Love'.

(YouTube: Freddie Mercury live performance with Royal Ballet Bohemian Rhapsody London Coliseum 07/10/79)

The choreography was beautiful, Freddie of course, didn't dance quite like Baryshnikov would have done, but the audience enthusiastically applauded the surprise show.

This appearance brought him an unexpected gift in Peter Freestone, who soon became his personal assistant and butler and a friend for life, and even his carer in his final last days. Peter was responsible for the ballet company's cloakroom at the time, which was how he came across Freddie in the changing rooms. They only spoke briefly at the time, but Paul Prenter asked him shortly after the show whether there was any chance of him accompanying the band on *The Crazy* tour that year.

The same year Queen received an invitation to write the music accompanying the film *Flash Gordon* and produced a major hit, 'Flash'. The film, made in 1980, was directed by Mike Hodges and the legendary Italian director Dino de Laurentiis and was made in 1980. *Flash* was also the title of Queen's 1981 album.

This one is the first version of the Flash Gordon video. It's exciting to watch how the original recording was made.

Listen to Freddie singing this part in electrifying falsetto: *'he saves with the mighty hand every man, every woman, every child with a mighty flash'.*

(YouTube: Queen – Flash (Rare Original Version of Music Video (1980))

Queen worked with composer Howard Blake and director Mike Hodges, who spoke about Freddie as follows:

'Interestingly, I found Freddie the antithesis of his stage persona: quiet, sensitive, almost shy. His musical talent was obviously prodigious and totally instinctual. It struck me that his surname has a certain ironic ring

to it as he was, just that, mercurial.' (Matt Richards and Mark Langthorne)

How is it possible that Freddie's stage persona was fundamentally different to who he was in private? The frontman role he took on can be understood most simply by thinking about an actor going on stage. The only difference is that Freddie always played the same role; he sang and created a show.

The Crazy Tour was the first occasion when Peter Freestone was responsible for Queen's wardrobe, and this was the tour where Freddie got to know Tony Bastin, with whom he had his next long-term relationship, as they were together for around two years.

Freddie broke up with him because he realised Tony had cheated on him while he himself was carrying on his drug-taking, drinking, sex-crazy lifestyle in Munich, which he kept secret from Tony. Freddie inundated Tony with gifts and kept sending him first-class airline tickets, but this didn't particularly impressed Tony. Freddie suffered another disappointment and tried to stifle the pain in drugs, alcohol and revelry.

The Crazy Tour featured 20 concerts in England in just over a month. At the end of the concert series, they played at the Hammersmith Odeon, which was one of their most successful gigs.

No official video was made of the concert, but someone has put it together pretty well. This time, the tricky lighting can be very well observed with the lighting structure known as 'the pizza oven' over the musicians' heads, with red, white and green lights and enormous heat. We can sense the dramatic tension that the mysterious lighting would have created, with changes from darkness to intensely bright.

By this time, Freddie's improvisational technique was breathtaking on every song, especially, 'Now I am here'.

He was very relaxed on stage. Similarly, it's interesting to see how beautifully he sings Brian's 'Save Me' and John's 'You're My Best

Friend'. It was typical of Freddie that he did his very best to sing as the songwriters would have wanted, even though these songs weren't written in Freddie's style. Their performance is frenetic, and the audience is roaring by the end of the show.

(YouTube – Queen Live at Hammersmith Odeon 1979 (2021 DEFINITIVE SOURCE MERGE/MATRIX)

23. The Game and Flash Gordon albums (1980)

Queen, the best band in the world

Freddie, the superstar

The year 1980 started well as 'Save Me' got to number 11 in the UK. This was Queen's 15th single, and was written by Brian.

Queen returned to Munich to continue recording *The Game* album in February. The single, 'Play The Game' was released on 30 May and got to number 14 in Britain. Many fans were shocked when watching the video and didn't like the fact Freddie had grown a moustache, so they sent disposable razors and black nail varnish to Queen's offices. Freddie wasn't bothered about the protests and kept the moustache. His appearance was unusual, but so was the fact that he now looked masculine, his feminine traits had disappeared, and the seductive movements were now decidedly manly.

Other fans were outraged by the significant changes as far as the music was concerned. What had happened to the principle of not using synthesizers, which they had talked about a lot? What's this about not using two sounds when one is enough?

They thought the Queen sound, which was so unique and attractive, had gone.

'Play the Game'

'Play the Game' *is a powerful ballad in the classic Queen style. Brian May's powerful guitar flourishes, and John's Deacon's contrapuntal bass patterns provide the dynamics. But it's Freddie's percussive piano and splendid vocal that are at the heart of this wonderful song.'* (Andrew Wild)

'Play the Game' is a love song without any mystique, with simple but good lyrics, which Freddie quite probably wrote for his latest lover, Tony Bastin, who was later undeserving of this honour.

The performance, the lyrics and the music are not passionate or emotional. The focus is on play and playfulness. Freddie feels he doesn't have to fight hard for love. He just has to let his heart decide. Supposedly, Freddie's past failures are starting to harden him, or it wasn't that deep love in the first place.

The music, which was introduced with a synthesizer, is slightly grating compared to the usually agreeable or exciting intro. Fortunately, Freddie's falsettos, Roger's drumming and Brian's guitar playing eventually rectify the unusual sound live. For the sake of comparison, it's worth watching a live concert to hear the sound.

(YouTube - Queen - Play The Game - Live Montreal)

(YouTube: Queen – Play The Game - Official Video)

'Don't Try Suicide'

Freddie wrote this song for David Minns thinking he was blackmailing him when he had become suicidal. The song lyrics sound as if Freddie wanted to take revenge with these vitriolic words. I wonder how could David forgive him after all this, but he did. He must have been a great soul. Obviously, he was overwhelmed with pain and couldn't think clearly.

The lyrics of the song is clear, no need to interpret it, but it is interesting to read the fans' reactions to the song under Queen official lyrics video. Let me quote some:

'plant mom!!!: that awkward moment when Queen literally saves your life'

'Cigarettes after Die: When a song speaks directly to you'

'Sevinç Aydoğan: Oh my dear Freddie, I am pretty suicidal, but I will absolutely not try suicide. Your wish is my command!'

'Craze961: I would have never expected this song to be so upbeat due to the seriousness of the topic'

'Charlee Lean: This hits different knowing that Brian became suicidal after Freddie died.'

and the last one:

'Miss Egg: I hate how much negative attention this song gets, it's literally saved lives.'

I hope Miss Egg was right because the song's lyrics caused David another heartache.

Luckily Brian May only contemplated suicide after Freddie's death. He said to Daily Mail in 2011:

'I regarded myself as completely sick. I was wounded and very much in pieces. I went into a serious depression – I was subsumed by feelings of loss. Being in a touring band puts your friends and family on hold. You're focused on one thing: the band. When that finishes you're out on a limb. The band finished, so there was a terrible feeling of loss. The band was my family. We lost Freddie and my dad died at almost the same time. I didn't want to love – I'd lost myself completely.' Thank God, Brian could come over his pain and depression and recovered.

David Must have been similarly desperate as Brian was when he took the overdose after losing Freddie.

John's song 'Another One Bites The Dust' was a fantastic success. He plays the bass guitar, piano, rhythm and lead guitar on the single. There is no synthesizer. Roger later added a few drums and Brian some guitar and harmonised it all. It saw the light in August, going to number one in America and stayed there for five weeks, selling three million copies in America alone. (Funnily enough, the American radio DJ thought it was a black band playing. Lol.) It went to number five in the UK and also topped the charts in many other countries.

When *The Game* album was released, it surpassed all expectations and went to number 1 in the UK and America. This was the first Queen album to top the charts in the USA.

Queen performed 45 sold-out concerts in America, four of them in New York's Madison Square Garden.

During his stay in New York, Freddie met Thor Arnold one night, and through him, he met John Murphy, who worked as a flight attendant. John was one of the lovers of another flight attendant Gaëtan Dugas, in whom the symptoms of AIDS first appeared in the form of Kaposi's sarcoma in Canada. (Hungarian Dr Mór Kaposi first described Kaposi's sarcoma in 1872 as a malignant connective tissue tumour.)

Freddie had a one-night stand with John Murphy, maybe this was the night when he first exposed himself to HIV, but it wasn't the encounter that sealed his fate. (Later on, they became good friends.)

There is one shocking thing that bothers me. What are the chances of fate bringing Freddie together with the lover of the man regarded as 'patient number 1' when hundreds of gay men fell ill in those years? This reminds me of when Freddie told his friend he would die at the age of 45, which I mentioned earlier when I wrote about self-hypnosis.

In the summer of 1980, Freddie achieved his life's dream. He had always wanted a luxurious, palatial home, the kind he had seen in Hollywood movies, so he asked Mary to try and find one for him. Mary soon came across Garden Lodge in Kensington. Freddie fell in love with it at once. It was an eight-bedroom Edwardian house, with mahogany staircases and marble tiles and a lovely, big garden. The building needed renovating, so Freddie could only move in a few years later, but he was delighted to boast about it to anyone.

He finally had a home, where he could surround himself with all kinds of opulence and luxury, just as he had dreamt about. Now he 'only' had to make sure he had a family to avoid loneliness.

However, when he finally moved into his long-awaited renovated home in 1985, he was already carrying the virus, and his AIDS tests were positive.

The European tour for The Game album began in September, with 17 venues. In the meantime, the single 'Flash', written by Brian, was released. It made it to the top 10 in Britain.

Queen played the first of three consecutive concerts at Wembley Stadium on 8 December, when *Flash Gordon* was released as an album; it got to the top 10 in Britain and number 23 in the US.

Flash Gordon, the film had premiered three days earlier, and was also a box office hit in the UK, though it wasn't such a big hit elsewhere. The success in the UK was probably due to Queen's fans.

John Lennon was murdered on 8 December, and his death was a big blow for Freddie and the other Queen members. Freddie considered him the best ever songwriter and was shocked by the news. He couldn't imagine this happening to anyone. He must have been as shocked as his fans were by the news of his own death.

Freddie wrote a song for John Lennon entitled *Life is Real*, which appeared on the next album.

24. The Greatest Hits album (1981)

No new music album was released in 1981, but the *Greatest Hits* album, a compilation of their biggest hits to date, was a great success. It was released in October, topping the charts in Britain and some other European countries, and reached number eight in America.

Queen played five concerts in Tokyo, and another seven were planned in South America, which began in the final days of February.

Their stay in South America was a fantastic experience for Queen, but it wasn't completely cloudless.

The first stop on tour was Buenos Aires (Argentina). Queen was the first western rock band to perform in Argentina, where military dictator, Jorge Rafael Videla, ruled the country. The concert attracted huge crowds; tens of thousands also flooded in from neighbouring countries. People stood in a queue for a whole day to buy the tickets, even though the concerts could only start at 10 p.m. because the heat was unbearable.

In Buenos Aires, Queen played five nights in front of 459,000 people, and 30 million saw them on TV - huge numbers!

The first concert was at Estadio José Amalfitani de Velez Sarsfield with a crowd of more than 54,000. This was when the audience started singing *Love of My Life* in perfect English to the sound of Brian's guitar intro, as they did all the other songs. Freddie was so amazed that he just stood and let the crowd sing and then joined in too. The singing was so deafening that the band couldn't hear anything until the audience calmed down to hear Freddie sing.

The audience sang along with Queen all five nights, and it was a fantastic, emotional experience for all four of them.

The crowd was amazed at the fantastic spectacle of the show, which surpassed anything they had imagined.

Queen felt the same way and was astonished to see that the same thing that happened in Japan was happening again, just on a larger scale. Information about flights was suspended at the airport, and they played Queen's music instead. One month before Queen arrival, the media talked only about them all they long. The fans did the same, prompted by the extensive media coverage.

Freddie was pursued everywhere by fans and journalists, so he was forced to hide and escape constantly but somehow managed to pay homage to his shopping passion, though he only had peace in the hotel.

A governmental dinner was held in their honour, which was rather unusual at a reception for a rock band.

The next concert in Argentina was held in the seaside city of Mar del Plata.

At the time, Freddie had a new lover, Peter Morgan, a bouncer from London. Freddie didn't have much luck with him either; on the day of the concert he accidentally noticed Peter walking with another man from his hotel balcony, so he sent him back to London straight away and broke up with him.

They travelled to Rosario next for another concert, where 35,000 people were waiting for them.

In March, they performed in Brazil. The first concert was cancelled, while the next one was in the second-largest stadium in São Paulo. The concert broke the record with a crowd of 131,000, the largest ever paying audience in rock history. The next night another 120,000 people saw the show.

'Love Of My Life' had been top of the Argentinian and Brazilian charts since 1979, so the audience here also knew the song word for word and sang it at the concerts. The band had no idea they were so popular.

David Wigg, Freddie's journalist friend, said:

'Not only did he cast a spell on his audience. He cast a spell on himself'.

Freddie and the team of gay men in his entourage separated themselves from the band's other members and their staff on this tour. They continued to do this during their time in Munich too. Freddie preferred the company of gay men to others.

Back to Munich: recordings of the Hot Space album begin, *Under Pressure* single with David Bowie

Munich was too distracting for Freddie and the other band members, and they began to relax at the expense of work. The *Hot Space* album was released in 1982 and wasn't as successful as the previous albums, largely due to the change of style, which Brian says was initiated by Freddie. Both Roger and Brian hated the album.

They played disco-style music with a synthesizer. In one of Freddie's favourite discos, he realised their music wasn't suited to that forum and thought they should change their style. I suppose his 'nice' manager, Paul Prenter was with him, as always.

The 'Under Pressure' was quite literally recorded under pressure, interspersed with a lot of arguments and frustration. The musical foundation was John's idea. Released at the end of October, it went to number one and was the second Queen single to reach this prominent position since 'Bohemian Rhapsody'. David Bowie and Freddie wrote the lyrics, but not in the greatest consensus. It was included on the album as a Queen and Bowie song.

They spent the summer recording the *Hot Space* album in Montreux, Switzerland, but Freddie celebrated his 35th birthday in New York. The celebrations lasted five days. He invited 100 friends from Britain, all expenses paid by Freddie.

Freddie heard on the radio and must have read in the newspapers at the time that more than 100 people had fallen ill in New York, and more than half of those had died before Freddie arrived.

After his birthday, they held three concerts in Venezuela, and the other two were cancelled due to the death of the Venezuelan President.

The next concert was in Mexico, but before then, Queen travelled to Miami for a week's rest, during which time the disease began to spread there too.

There were 50,000 people at the first concert in Mexico. The next day's show was cancelled because when the staff unpacked the equipment, a ramp collapsed, causing a few minor injuries and one broken leg. According to Phil Chapman's book, Queen had to pay compensation, and they were only allowed to unpack their belongings from the building after the concert once the payment had been made.

At the next venue, the ungrateful audience threw small stones, shoes and batteries at the band, yet the concert went ahead, as did the next day's too. Freddie bade farewell with the following words: 'Adios amigos, take your shoes, motherf**kers'. They resolved never to set foot in the country again.

Gaëtan Dugas reappears in Freddie's life

Freddie returned to New York to finalise the contract for the apartment he had bought there. Once again, he visited his favourite places, where he met a man from Montreal called Charles, who quite by accident also introduced Freddie to Gaëtan Dugas.

Charles and another friend of Freddie's, who he knew from a bar in London, spent the night together. Charles was one of Gaëtan Dugas' lovers. What are the chances of Freddie meeting another of Gaëtan

Dugas' lovers? I'm not a mathematician and can't work out statistical probability, but the coincidence is quite bizarre.

Freddie got involved in another relationship, but it soon ended. The man was called Bill Reid, and Freddie brought him to Europe. Their relationship was very stormy; they were constantly arguing and quarrelling, and their arguments often degenerated into violence.

He was the reason Freddie finally left New York and went to Munich, where he lived more freely than ever before, deciding to settle for one-night stands from then on.

Peter Freestone thought Freddie needed to quarrel before concerts and believed these emotional storms enhanced his creativity.

One reason for the arguments could have been Freddie's nerves before concerts, but even without shows, they continually argued. It wasn't just up to Freddie, who was evidently frustrated that the relationship wasn't working and relieved his tension in arguments.

Freddie didn't need this kind of stimulus before he stepped on stage. Being on stage meant that he had to perform like a top-class star, whatever had happened before the gig. First, he went into a 'trance', and this put the crowd in a 'trance' too. This was the spell that David Rigg had very clearly noticed.

Emotional tension doesn't enhance creativity; actually, it's rather debilitating. The quarrels were only good for one thing, helping to relieve the pressure before performances.

After the South American tour, they played three concerts in Montreal, Canada, where they filmed the concert for the first time in Queen's history. Video of parts of the concert can be found on YouTube.

They were in a good mood at the end of the year and continued recording the new album, while in October, their *Greatest Hits* album was released.

Freddie was increasingly concerned about the news coming from the US: by now, 270 people had AIDS in the US, and 121 had died from it.

In October 1981, the disease was declared an epidemic in the US. And within a year, the epidemic had raised its head in 14 other countries.

Before Christmas, *Time Out* magazine in London reported a rare and dangerous disease primarily affecting gay and bisexual men and reported on the first death from the disease in Britain.

In America, an increasing number of people were diagnosed with symptoms similar to Kaposi's sarcoma, a low white blood cell count, cytomegalovirus (a kind of herpes), and PCP (pneumocystis pneumonia), which today is seen as the result of a fungal infection causing pneumonia. All the patients were gay.

With the cooperation of doctors, they realised they were facing a new disease, which always ended in the patient's death.

Several patients were found to have had a personal relationship with Gaëtan Dugas or one of his lovers.

God must have loved Freddie because He had sent him several warnings. He met Gaëtan Dugas twice but didn't go to bed with him, 'only' with his lovers (Charles and John Murphy). The newspapers published news about AIDS, it was spoken about in clubs, and he heard the news about it on the radio.

According to one of his gay friends, Freddie had a dream in which everyone had died.

After a while, Freddie deliberately stopped watching the news, turned the radio off and didn't think about the possible meaning of his dream. He buried his head in the sand. What had happened to Freddie's intelligence? Why wasn't he more careful?

When he found out he had AIDS, he was able to give up smoking and drinking and stopped changing his sexual partners. Why didn't he face up to the real danger in time? Why did he believe he was invincible? We might think the drugs and drink had made it impossible for him to think sensibly, but I'm convinced this wasn't the case. Freddie had incredible willpower and would have been capable of giving up anything anytime. He knew he was at risk. He said he scrubbed himself clean after every sexual contact, and wondered whether or not he had caught the virus. Despite this, he continued with his dangerous lifestyle. Surely, he was afraid of catching the virus, which was why he had the dream in which everyone died. Why did he behave like a robot? Why did he bang his head against the wall? He acted as if he were hypnotised and relentlessly obeying a vague command coming from inside, which he could not resist.

Freddie claimed he could manage with just a few hours' sleep, which is one of the side effects of taking cocaine. This could also have been the cause of his hypersensitivity, excitability and irritability. However, he could control his use of cocaine and wasn't addicted to it. People close to him reported that Freddie preferred to get high by drinking vodka.

25. Hot Space album (1982)

Freddie on another 'Death Row'

In 1982 Queen worked on the *Hot Space* album in Munich until the end of February.

The album had a disco-funk sound, which both Freddie and John liked, so Roger's drums and Brian's wonderful guitar playing were squeezed into the background. The customary multi-layered harmonies disappeared.

Paul Prenter started to play an increasingly large role in Freddie's life, becoming his assistant and even influencing Freddie about the sound the new album should have, as he too loved gay disco music. He tried to reduce the influence the others had on Freddie, to spoil their relationships, evidently with his own interest at heart rather than Freddie's.

'Body Language'

'Dominated by a terrific coiling synth-bass line later reuser for a 'Kind of Magic', 'Body Language' is hypnotic but a difficult song to like. It's effectively an empty disco rewrite of 'Get Down Make love' with minimal input from the other members of Queen.' (Andrew Wild)

The 'Body Language' single was released in April, 1982 and got to number 25 in Britain and number 11 in the USA. The video they made for the song was banned by Music TV. A scantily dressed woman is seen, then a man writhes, while Freddie sings lustfully about sex - *'give me your body'* - and tries to convince his partner: **'Look at me I got a case of body language'** - which requires no explanation – as this is what the song is about. The hidden message in the video says everything, even without lyrics.

Its secret message could be: That's what my life is about now, so I can't tell you anything else right now. Try to enjoy the video the way I do and the new style of music. New world, new life, new music. That's life, things change, and I'm fine, thank you. Freddie either wasn't aware of this message or he just didn't care.

(YouTube: Queen Body Language - Official Video)

'Staying Power'

'Staying Power' is a wonderful song – sharp, sassy, fun. Freddie Mercury is 100 % committed to this track. Listen to his strong vocals, his complex, syncopated keyboard arrangements, his fabulous backing vocals.' (Andrew Wild)

'Staying Power', Freddie's other song on the album, is similar to 'Body Language'. The music is very good on the concert recording (Milton Keynes Bowl) as Brian plays guitar and Roger drums. It's a hard rock song, but the lyrics are just about emotionless sex, interspersed with sensual moans, characteristic of this period in Freddie's life. *Staying power* simply means sex to the point of exhaustion, intoxicated and sultry eroticism. Freddie proudly boasts of his sexual stamina in the song. He doesn't sing about the role cocaine played in it.

He hadn't yet realised that raw, sensual sex only dragged him down. The more often he was satisfied physically, the more burnt-out and empty he became psychologically.

The goal of intimacy between two people is warmth and closeness, enhancing the feeling of accepting and loving each other, whereas sex without emotion just increases loneliness. This concert was in the same year when Freddie quite probably got infected.

(YouTube: Queen – 'Staying Power' (Live at Milton Keynes Bowl, 1982.)

This was the worst stage of his life. Freddie later wrote the following about this time:

'I used to live for sex, but now I've changed. I've stopped going out, stopped the night of wild partying. I've almost become a nun. It's amazing. I thought sex was a very important thing to me, but now I realise I went completely the other way. Once, I was extremely promiscuous, it was excess in every direction, but now I'm different.'

Freddie changed his lifestyle because life forced him to do so. Ha had changed only when he already had the positive HIV tests in his hands and would have been very unsure of what awaited him.

'Life is Real'

'This touching, lush tribute to John Lennon appropriates the descending bass runs, piano chordings and sharp drum sound from Lennon's own 'Mother' from John Lennon /Plastic Ono Band. As tributes go, it's very fine indeed.' (Andrew Wild)'

Freddie had written the song 'Life is Real' in memory of John Lennon. Lennon's sudden, violent death shocked Freddie. He was unable to ignore the shady side of life and came to his senses for a while. The lyrics are surreal and beautiful but very sad, bringing Freddie's dark moments to life. According to the lyrics he had guilt stains on his pillow; he saw blood on his terraces and torsos in his closet, shadows from his past. Sleep was the only pleasure in his life, dreams were his pleasure domes, but when he woke, he found himself in a minefield, while love was a roulette wheel to him. Success was the only thing he lived for, yet it had a price that he was willing to pay.

He seeks shelter in loneliness, trying to comfort himself and has no other choice. He has swallowed the bitter pill and can taste it in his mouth. Music is his mistress; he feels like a whore to music; he depends on it so much. Life has been cruel to him.

The guilt stains on his pillow refer to his one-night stand-style sexual relationships. His earlier failures in love are the bitter pills that made him lonely. That is why he had banished himself to the empty, insensitive world of drugs, alcohol and emotionless sex, but at the same time was aware of the reality of life in his lonely moments and felt he had woken up in a minefield.

The minefield refers to the fact that he was playing a dangerous game and yet continued his masochistic, self-destructive lifestyle, despite having found pleasure and reassurance only in music. It seems as if he tried to make sure he would die at the age of 45. This song is about his anxiety caused by the fear of HIV, but he's not willing to face up to it.

The concern sent a message to his brain; 'be sensible' –but Freddie ignored it.

He only devoted one line to Lennon: 'Lennon is a genius living in every pore.' He talked about him in the present tense. It meant Freddie hadn't yet processed the fact that he had gone.

He behaved obsessively and was still incapable of escaping his sex addiction; combined with drugs and alcohol, he became so intoxicated that he forgot about himself. His sensible nature and famous business sense let him down, not to mention that he let himself became distant from the other band members, on whom he could always rely.

This vacuous, disco-style music was unusual from Queen. Brian and Roger must have felt that Freddie's change of style was not good for the band's reputation; ominous omens were these content-empty songs, Freddie's lifestyle, and his indifference.

The European tour for the album lasted from April to May of 1982, and then they played two concerts in Edinburgh, Scotland, in a hall with a capacity of 8,000, but not all the tickets were sold, whereas a crowd of 65,000 awaited them in Milton Keynes on 5 June. Before the gig, Bill Reid got so angry with Freddie that he bit deep into his hand. Freddie was in agony but went on stage as if nothing had happened.

They began the album tour in Canada in July and then performed in the States. In the times between concerts, Freddie returned to his New York home to rest and, as usual, spent his nights in bars.

They played New York's Madison Square Garden on 27-28 July, where both concerts were sold out, and the last show was in Cincinnati on 7 August. Freddie only flew back to England on the 13th, after spending five more nights in various New York bars.

They appeared on TV in New York on 25 September, performing 'Crazy Little Thing Called Love' and 'Under Pressure' on the prestigious *Saturday Night Show*.

Freddie and Bill shouted at each other for hours in the hotel the night before, threw glasses against the wall and in the end, Freddie sought refuge with Peter Freestone. By the morning, he was so hoarse he could hardly speak. Efforts were made all day to restore his voice, but it proved impossible, so Roger helped out with the high notes.

There is a report in Matt Richards' and Mark Langthorne's book claiming that coincidentally, on the day of the TV show, Freddie was pale and exhausted because he was recovering from the most severe bout of influenza he had ever experienced, with strong headaches and white residue on his tongue.

The book suggests Freddie's symptoms were in line with those infected with HIV, which appeared within 2-6 weeks of the infection. 70% of infected patients displayed the same symptoms as Freddie's. Robert Lang, who knew Freddie, told the authors, Freddie had seen a doctor at the time. However, the cause of the symptoms was not confirmed. There could have been another cause, but it's striking that all the symptoms appeared together.

Death Row in the subheading was a reference to New York's gay bars, which were closed down in a few years, as they had proven to be centres of HIV infection. This Death Row wasn't nearly as funny as the one on Kensington market.

Queen finished the year with a Japanese tour, where they were received with the customary level of enthusiasm.

Freddie had done everything possible to pick up the virus, though unintentionally, just as he hadn't gone to the boarding school in Panchgani of his own free will.

In all probability, Freddie's flings in New York that year sealed his fate.

'I pray I'll never get AIDS,' said Freddie. 'So many friends have it. Some have died; others won't last much longer. I'm terrified that I'll be next. Immediately after each time I have sex, I think 'Suppose that was the

one? Suppose the virus is now in my body? I jump in the shower and scrub myself clean, although I know it's useless.' (Freddie Mercury)

He must have said this before he received the first positive test.

Despite the fact it was known in the US that most of the patients had been in direct or indirect contact with Gaëtan Dugas, there was still hardly any mention of safe sex.

Queen was frustrated by the lack of success of the *Hot Space* album in Australia and the US, despite eleven years of constant hard work, recordings and tours, so they decided to sever ties with Elektra, their record distributor in America and Japan.

Roger had already released a solo album, and Freddie was inspired to release his own album too.

Jim Beach was given the role of negotiating the legal details of contract termination and finding another record distributor. At the end of the negotiations with Capitol Records, Queen entered into a contract with the EMI subsidiary, which included a Freddie Mercury solo album.

26. A Year Without a New Queen Album (1983)

Freddie began working on his first solo album, *Mr Bad Guy,* in Munich in 1983 when he met Giorgio Moroder. Moroder asked him to write a song for the rework of the silent movie, *Metropolis*, originally made in 1927. The song was 'Love Kills', released as Freddie's single in 1984, despite every band member contributing to the work. The song got to number 10 in Britain but only made number 69 in America, which was seen as a bad omen concerning the future. Freddie's first solo album was only released in 1985.

Queen did not release any albums in 1983, which was the first year they hadn't released an album and or gone on tour, and they all started to go their own way. There were rumours that the band had decided to split up, which they all denied. After a while one way or another, they all came to realise, sooner or later – that none of them could manage without Queen.

Freddie was no longer a driving force in the band in this period because he was more attracted to the Munich sex arena than anything else.

Nevertheless, slowly but surely, they finally began recording the new album, *The Works*, in Los Angeles in August 1983.

Eddie DeLena sound engineer in the US studio was impressed by Queen and Freddie. De Lena had worked alongside Mack, Queen's Munich sound engineer.

Leslie-Ann Jones quotes Eddie in her book:

'Freddie Mercury, of course, was larger than life. He had a tremendous presence; it filled the room when he entered. His speech patterns were often very dramatic and colourful, with the intonations of a stage actor. Queen's rock opera style was actually an extension of Freddie's personality. He was an extremely gifted vocalist and a great composer. There were times when we were recording his vocals, and he would be singing his next part in a complex harmony arrangement as fast as you could change tracks on the multitrack recorder. He would have the entire arrangement in his head and sing every part perfectly in one take. It was a demanding task just to keep up with him.'

The other members of Queen weren't as impressed with Freddie as in previous years.

'In the studio, Freddie was full of ideas and lateral thinking', – explained May. *'But he didn't have the greatest attention span. He would always peak at a certain time. If you had Fred for an hour when he was peaking, he was absolute gold dust. But then you'd hear, 'Oh, look, dear! I've done this. I have to go now', and you knew you'd had your slice of Freddie.'*

'Freddie and I both played on Man on the Prowl – says Mandel now. 'But Fred said to me, 'Why don't you take over later and play that rock'n'roll stuff. You do that better than me. Besides, they will all think it's me, darling!' I didn't care. I was being paid.'' (Mark Blake)

Fred Mandel was employed as an extra member of the band, starting with the Hot Space American tours; he was especially good at playing the synthesizer and piano.

Working with Michael Jackson

Freddie also worked for a short time with Michael Jackson during this period, in the studio in Michael's house, where they worked on three songs, including 'There Must Be More To Life Than This'. Even though Freddie enjoyed working together, to begin with, nothing came of the project for various reasons, but the recording is available on YouTube.

I regret to say that Michael Jackson's voice is no comparison with Freddie's. Listening to the recording, I don't think it was really in Jackson's interests to collaborate with Freddie, regardless of the reasons for the duet's failure or of how many copies of Jackson's *Thriller* album were sold.

Freddie sang the song so beautifully that nobody could compete with him. It's simply a phenomenal, unmissable experience. This song appeared on Freddie's solo album.

(YouTube: Freddie Mercury and Michael Jackson – 'There Must Be More To Life Than This' (Video Clip) Golden Duet)

At the instigation of Peter Freestone, Freddie and Peter watched Freddie's favourite opera, Verdi's *A Masked Ball*, with Luciano Pavarotti and Montserrat Caballé at the Royal Opera House in May 1993. This was the first time Freddie had seen and heard Caballé sing. He was very impressed with the wonderful soprano and wanted to know everything about her. The event provided Freddie with unexpected and wonderful inspiration, resulting in the 1988 album, *Barcelona*.

Recording of *The Works* album continued in Munich during the year.

This was the year Freddie put an end, once and for all, to the loneliness he sang about in 'Life is Real'. He showed that he seriously believed what he once told David Minns, during their relationship, when he brought Joe Fanelli home from America. He told David not to leave; *'I have enough love for both of you'*. As we know, Freddie was unable to convince David Minns, but he could persuade Joe to be his cook and friend. It proved to be a great decision.

Freddie's life in Munich

In Munich, Freddie got to know Winfried Kirchberger, the owner of a Munich restaurant, a restaurateur by profession. He was a large man with a muscular physique, and Freddie fell in love with him, so much so that he moved in with him. As usual, he overwhelmed his latest love with generous gifts.

Winnie didn't speak English, and Freddie didn't speak German, so communications between them were minimal right from the start, yet Freddie was supposedly happy in this relationship. Freddie was so committed that he even exchanged rings with Winnie, despite Winnie having a rather brusque manner. They broke up a few times but then got back together again and again. Both of them flirted with other men to make each other jealous. In the end, Freddie benefitted greatly from this trick because he only took Jim Hutton to Munich the first time to make Winnie jealous. Still, this encounter later turned into a profoundly happy relationship. Freddie's relationship with Winnie lasted from 1983 to 1985, including break-ups, at which point Jim Hutton finally won over Freddie's heart. Freddie wasn't able to convince Winnie to move with him to London, which I guess was a spot of good luck for Freddie in light of his future. (According to Barbara Valentin, Winnie died later of AIDS. She found him alone, starving in his home.)

While Freddie was living with Winnie, Peter Freestone says Freddie lost consciousness and had seizures on more than one occasion. The doctor said he drank too much and had taken too many drugs.

He worked half-heartedly in the studio and lost his appetite for work, which was uncharacteristic of Freddie. Earlier, work had been the most important thing to him. The other band members would have been increasingly worried about his behaviour.

By now, Freddie's life was radically turned upside down in every respect. During his relationship with Winnie, in January 1984, he got to know the Austrian actress Barbara Valentin, seen as the German 'Jayne Mansfield'. She was more well-known in Munich than Freddie. Like Freddie, Barbara loved the atmosphere in the bars and didn't mind drinking either. From then on, Freddie loved both of them, sometimes Barbara, sometimes Winnie, and sometimes both, or other guys he met in the bars.

In an interview Barbara gave to Leslie-Ann Jones in 1996 she said that she and Freddie had an honest, deep, loving relationship, which meant a lot to Freddie because Barbara was the first woman who didn't mind if he had a male lover as well, usually Winnie. Barbara and Freddie even bought an apartment together, had a sexual relationship and even talked about getting married.

Freddie certainly loved to be with her because when he'd had enough of Winnie, he sought refuge in Barbara.

Whereas Barbara was the kind of confidante with whom Freddie could talk about anything, Winnie could only fulfil the role of a lover because of their communication problems.

Barbara said that Freddie and Winnie really loved one another, but Winnie never showed any admiration or recognition towards Freddie or his art, and loved to play the role of a macho man who wasn't especially interested in Freddie, disrespected him and hurt him. And yet, Freddie was not able to easily escape this bond. Thank God Jim came along at the best possible time.

The question was raised among Freddie's friends and acquaintances of why he chose Winnie and similarly aggressive, uneducated partners and had long-term relationships with them.

Firstly, the question of attraction is influenced by numerous factors we're not generally aware of, the scent and appearance of the other person, their style of speech and many other small things that come with falling in love. When love comes to an end, we often ask ourselves how we could have been so blind.

Similarly, in Freddie's case, many factors contributed to his selection of partners, and these would probably have been related to his childhood traumas. In my opinion, Freddie didn't trust anyone and was sure they would leave him sooner or later, however great their love was. He said he wasn't an ideal partner for anyone, and he chose one-night stands because he had been hurt and disappointed so often. He didn't trust his partners for a minute, so every little thing made him suspicious. This attitude was reflected in his behaviour. Sooner or later, the way he behaved would provoke a break-up. The other main reason for unconsciously always choosing the wrong partners was his survival instinct, which forced him to solve this problem. Ideally, he should have learned to trust his partners. If he could have behaved differently with them, he wouldn't have subjected them to 'jealousy tests' and other similar humiliations, such as those that awaited Jim, for example. Not to mention that, in the first place, Freddie should have been faithful to his partners.

Childhood experiences largely drive relationships. Modern psychological research proves that around 8-10 years of age, a relationship model develops that remains within our subconscious, and then we look for that model throughout our lives. The greater the fit of the current partner to this subconscious model, the more chemistry is created, and couples fall in love. It's important to understand where all this can come from. Subconscious childhood complexes significantly affect relationships, pushing the relationship in a very marked positive or negative direction.

Everyone has childhood injuries, so we have sensitive points, vulnerabilities to certain factors.

Let's remember Freddie's song, 'My Fairy King'. Freddie got into boarding school at the age of eight, and a traumatic experience occurred shortly after that. In the song, he sings about this experience.

Our instincts are constantly striving to work in balance; the survival instinct keeps other instinctive forms of behaviour in check as long as we have the will to live. During this period, Freddie's behaviour resembled a kamikaze pilot, alcohol and drugs had taken control.

On stage, he always did everything he could to be accepted and always succeeded. If someone made a harsh remark to him, he handled it expertly. Freddie developed a firm will and was in control on stage. He believed he could cope with, or even knock out anyone, if attacked, just like in the boxing ring in his childhood, when he was 50 kg or even less.

The situation in his private life was different. He loved Munich because he felt free there. He was able to relax because he didn't have to be constantly ready for a fight. Nobody bothered him. They knew who he was but left him alone, not like in England. He wasn't afraid of strangers attacking him, as he once said. People indeed left him alone, but the same can't be said of love, alcohol and drugs. Instead, they have a relaxing effect - but they also can knock you out. If this happens, you don't even know who you are, and you feel strong and invincible when under their influence.

If Winnie attacked him, he felt broken inside because he was in love and was hurt by Winnie's arrogant and patronising style, and yet he stood by him. Life with Winnie was certainly never boring.

Only Freddie thought of this as a long-term relationship, which was why he tried to tempt Winnie to London, but Winnie had different ideas. Only Barbara gave any details of their relationship, Freddie has never mentioned him, but wrote him some great songs.

Barbara also said that she and Freddie 'shamelessly and deliberately' went too far and were regular visitors to Munich's gay bars. She believed Freddie enjoyed this kind of licentious lifestyle.

She reported that Freddie kept in regular contact with his parents and his sister and her family. Naturally, he held the incredible adventures of his life, his great loves, the drinking and drugs secret from them. Freddie also told her a lot about Mary and the fact that he felt guilty. Barbara said Freddie was very dutiful and liked to keep his promises. He never got over having let Mary down.

Barbara even met Mary and believed Mary really did care about Freddie's fate. She was guarded in her behaviour towards Barbara but was always polite and friendly.

This was what Freddie said about his relationship with Barbara:

'Barbara Valentin fascinated me because she's got such great tits! Barbara and I have formed a bond which is stronger than anything I've had with a lover for the last six years. I can really talk to her be myself in a way that's very rare.' (Freddie Mercury)

Freddie had a lot of partner and lover, but only three of them was mentioned by him. One of them was Mary, then Barbara Valentin and later on Jim Hutton. It could have meant that Freddie really loved Barbara, and they became very close friends. I suppose these three people played the most important role in his private life, they all accepted him and loved him, and Freddie appreciated their support and love.

'It's is a Hard Life'

Freddie wrote this song about his relationship with Winnie, which appeared on Queen's next album. This song represents the most painful and saddest confession he ever wrote about love: *'I fell in love/But now you say it's over and I'm falling apart'.*

The song impressively conveyed how sad and hurt Freddie was when Winnie broke up with him. He felt like his life was very hard because he always fought to find his true, long-term love, who would give meaning to his life, but his heart had just been broken again. He sings about trust, caring and long-term love:

To be true lovers together/To love and live forever in each others hearts/It's a long hard fight/To learn to care for each other/To trust in one another right from the start/When you're in love.'

In reality, it was Freddie who eventually broke up with Winnie after finding Jim, but during their relationship, they broke up many times, so Freddie most likely wrote this song about one of their falling out.

The lyrics show that Freddie has decided at least to try to be together with someone for the long term, and that he did know how a beautiful, loving relationship should work. Unfortunately, in practice, he wasn't able to make it work.

How sad that Freddie felt he had tried and done everything, but the relationship didn't work. (Freddie didn't realize that it wasn't possible with Winnie, no matter how much he loved him.)

Winnie's behaviour was disappointing; he even belittled Freddie.

Freddie did deserve better. In the song, Freddie sang that he was waiting for a new love, for someone to fall from the skies because his life was tough all alone.

Fortunately, he didn't have to wait long to live with Jim for six years in a more balanced, happier relationship, but this was mainly due to Freddie's illness and Jim's persistence.

The video for 'It's a Hard Life' perfectly reflects Freddie's world at the time. First of all, he appears in the wildest, most extravagant costume he had ever worn. He looks like the strangest creature on the planet. Enormous peacock fathers adorn his back, he wore a ridiculous wig on his head, not to mention those artificial eyes on his costume.

While it isn't hard to work out what the other band members were wearing, Freddie's costume was bizarre.

Freddie's world had become confused, resulting in the strange, incoherent video in which Barbara and Freddie appear together, along with the band members, also dressed up and feeling uncomfortable in this alien world, but, as with everyone, Freddie 'forced' his will on them. The band members allowed themselves to be convinced based on the notion that it's easier to give in than to resist. It wasn't as if they hadn't already been vulnerable to Freddie's whims. (I mean, in the sense that, if they wanted to keep him and wanted to continue making music together as a band. Freddie was their trump card; he could sell the songs that they usually wrote together.)

In the video, it seems like we're at a masked ball. People are running around trying to find their place in this strange world, where everyone wears masks and disguises. This masked ball symbolizes Freddie's alienation from the ordinary world; it's not possible to know who anyone is, which means you can't trust anyone. There is no honesty and openness, only hiding behind a disguise.

The band members didn't like the video; Brian was disappointed in Freddie's choice of clothes. He thought Freddie looked like a giant shrimp in love, which was a very witty description.

Brian loved the song and felt the video had destroyed the message. It was unsuccessful in America, as anticipated.

People instinctively sense that anyone who makes a video like that and appears in this kind of weird costume, must have something wrong with them, as was the case.

The video director was Tim Pope, but that doesn't mean the set-up was his idea. Freddie always paid attention to every detail and liked to instruct the directors on what he wanted to see in the video.

Nobody else would have thought of advertising this beautiful song with a video like this, only Freddie. He was right when he sang: *'I'm falling apart.'*

(Queen – 'It's a Hard Life' - Official Video))

Freddie could hardly move when the video was recorded because the ligaments in his knee had been injured in a Munich bar. As he said at the press conference:

*'Some c*nt kicked me. It might mean I will have to cut down on some of my more elaborate gorgeous stage moves.'*

During this period, he had no interest in what people thought of him and lost all his inhibitions. He sounded arrogant. He was angry when he said this and maybe had a hangover. He was unable or unwilling to exercise self-control.

Judging from the contents of the song, Freddie wasn't happy at all at the time, as Barbara confirmed:

'We were both trying far too hard to be happy' – she admitted. *'Because we were not happy. You get drunk, you take a blow, you play the monkey, you lay as many people as you can, all as if you are daring your body to stay alive. It is a sort of death wish. In the end, it just makes you more lonely, more empty.'* (Leslie-Ann Jones)

Barbara clearly sensed that Freddie was behaving as if he was intentionally rushing towards self-destruction. It's just a shame she didn't realise the role she was playing in this. Although by then, it was far too late.

Barbara noticed that Freddie's health was starting to deteriorate. His behaviour had changed; he became irritated and made remarks about the band's members. This was something he had never done before. Later he broke off his longstanding friendship with Peter Straker. Barbara suspected Freddie might be infected with HIV when he found a growth in his throat, which disappeared for a while and then reappeared.

He once told Barbara he felt as if his body was rotting. Barbara said Freddie had dark purple patches on his face, which he tried to hide using liquid powder before the make-up artist got to his face before video recordings. These patches may have been symptoms of Kaposi's sarcoma.

In all probability, Freddie caught the HIV infection in 1982. According to his AIDS specialist, Dr Graeme Moyle, infected patients survived on average for 8-10 years after infection.

Freddie was first tested in 1985; this was the first year a rudimentary test was available. He probably took the test because of the blue patches and the strange, inexplicable symptoms.

Freddie didn't tell Barbara the test result, but he wouldn't allow her to help stop the bleeding when he cut his hand. Barbara was sure then that Freddie had tested positive. The two of them never talked about it, but Freddie made a remark when one of his American lovers died suggesting that he had infected him. Of course, he couldn't be certain when the infection occurred.

If he believed he'd been infected in the early years, when he started visiting the bars, he must have been quite terrified. In any event, he put an end to sexual relations with Barbara. Freddie knew Barbara had realised what the problem was. She might have been the only person, apart from the doctor, who knew about it.

At the end of 1985, Freddie left Munich without saying goodbye to his friends and broke up with Winnie.

On one occasion, he revisited Barbara unexpectedly, and both of them cried in each other's arms. By then, hundreds of their friends had died, but Freddie still wasn't willing to talk about it. In the end, Freddie told Barbara he wanted to give up drugs, and this was why he was finally breaking up with her and was going to leave Munich. The part about giving up drugs was true, but he didn't tell her about the positive HIV result, perhaps because he was afraid Barbara would tell someone.

It was evident that he already knew he was infected and was trying to cut his ties and returning to London. This must have been quite a scary time for him.

As far as Peter Freestone is aware, an increasing number of articles appeared about Freddie and Barbara in the German press, and Freddie thought Barbara might have leaked details of their relationship. Still, Peter says it could have been someone else, someone who wanted to get him out of Barbara's life.

The truth is neither Barbara nor Winnie were good influences on him, so it was time to break up with them and the lifestyle he'd had there.

This was the end of their relationship. Afterwards, talking about Barbara or Munich was banned in Freddie's house for a while, while Barbara felt shattered.

Barbara and Freddie met up quite a few times later as friends. She even had a bedroom in Garden Lodge. Maybe Freddie missed her after a while, as a genuine confidante, and he got in touch with her again as a friend. Fortunately, Barbara's AIDS test was negative, so she got off relatively lightly from her relationship with Freddie and others who were infected.

As far as he could, Freddie focused on staying positive and tried to ignore the test results. He was probably hoping to recover through some kind of miracle cure, or that the test was wrong, which was a real possibility as the doctors told him that the test wasn't 100% reliable. Freddie noticed that something wasn't right with his health, but he might have attributed it to the intensive drinking and drug-taking, even though he had purple patches and the growth in his throat.

Back to *The Works* album

Freddie meets with Jim

After his opera house experience in 1983, Freddie flew back to California to continue recording *The Works* album, which lasted all year due to frequent interruptions. The album was only completed in January the following year. In November and December, Freddie moved between London and New York, spending his nights in bars. During this time, he first met Jim Hutton, his later partner, in a London bar. The similarity between Winnie and Jim surprised Freddie, and he sprang into action straight away when Jim's partner left the bar. Jim rejected Freddie using vulgar language, although this may have been a normal style of rejection in bars.

Jim had no idea who Freddie was, but his lover later enlightened him about who he had been talking to.

In any event, both Freddie and Jim remembered their first meeting.

HIV keeps spreading

Public hatred towards gay people increased between 1980 and 1983. This time it wasn't known yet how HIV was spread, so there was widespread fear of it. Police officers, ambulance workers and everyone else avoided patients like the plague, so most of them died while suffering alone and abandoned. The Thatcher Government was unwilling to devote attention or sufficient funds to research. The disease reached its height in London in 1983, with a total of 6,000 new cases registered.

In that year, a French research virologist, Luc Montagnier, discovered that a retrovirus was behind the disease, but they had no idea how to treat it.

Despite many infections and deaths, Freddie rejected all forms of protection and recklessly entered into any adventure that presented itself, so he probably exposed himself to the virus several times. In contrast, those who were more careful stayed with one partner in a lasting relationship.

During this time in 1984, he met with Paul Gambaccini in a London bar and told him that he didn't take protective measures and did everything with everyone.

27. The Works album (1984)

Recording *The Works* album only began nine months after they completed the last tour, in August 1983, because they were all tired after ten years' hard work. They'd had enough of each other too and were increasingly tense, so they decided to take a 6-month break, which eventually became nine months.

Because of how the Hot Space album was received, the band decided to return to the heavy rock style simplified the instrumentation and used a synthesizer. The song lyrics were about more serious subjects.

They recorded Roger's fantastic hit song 'Radio Ga Ga' in LA, which appeared single in January 1984. The song made it to number 2 in the UK and performed very well in the US charts, reaching number 16 in the top 100.

Great, now Roger had written a Top 10 song. It meant every member of the band wrote a Top 10 song by now. As far as I know, Queen were the only band to have achieved this.

The publicity video for the song was incredibly successful; almost 212 million people have watched it on YouTube since 1 August 2008. This video inspired the crowd at Live Aid (1985) to clap in unison to the song's rhythm, which everyone clearly enjoyed tremendously.

There are several exciting things about the video. First, they borrowed scenes from the reworked film Metropolis in return for Love Kills, and secondly, the applauding crowd was filmed using Queen's fan club members. We can also see some original recordings of London's bombardment during the Second World War and cuttings from Queen's first concerts recordings.

Allegedly, the American radio stations took offence because the song was originally inspired by Roger's young son. Once, he said, 'Radio ca ca' while on the toilet. In French, this was equivalent to a 'number two' in children's toilet language. Roger liked the phrase. The radio stations found out the origin of the song title and assumed it was a criticism of modern radio by Queen, so they banned it from their playlists, which was the first sign of Queen's fall from grace in the US.

It would have been much better for everyone if they had applauded Roger and had a good laugh, but they didn't do that for some reason.

(YouTube: Queen 'Radio Ga Ga' Official Video)

The *Works* album was released on 1 February, 1984 and, following 'Radio Ga Ga's footsteps, went to number 2 in the UK charts thanks to the amazingly popular hits.

Four of the nine songs were released as singles. 'I Want to Break Free' became perhaps one of their best-known hits due to the entertaining video and the outstanding music. John wrote the song. It's possibly Queen's most famous, after 'Bohemian Rhapsody'.

Dressed as women, they mimicked the British TV soap opera, *Coronation Street* on the video. One of the viewers commenting under the video wrote that Freddie was sexier than any of his girlfriends so far. How true, Freddie was damned sexy, especially in his movements. His imitation of the woman was hilarious. Freddie's talent as an actor is wonderfully demonstrated in this video. The single went to number 3 in the UK charts, while it only reached number 45 in America. This video was the final straw in America. Queen didn't understand why it got such bad reception. The video was meant to be humorous, and it was, except for Freddie's ballet insert, which conveyed his ravenous sexual appetite and decadent, overheated eroticism, so the video was placed on the banned list in America. Queen never appeared in North America again. Freddie was angry and didn't understand what was happening. He probably understood but just didn't want to accept it.

EMI asked the band to make another video, which would be acceptable in America, but they were offended and rejected the request. This decision turned out badly for both America and Queen in the long term.

This was what Freddie said:

'There is a big risk element involved with most things we do, and I think our staunchest fans will know that we can come up with all sorts of ridiculous things. Some of them will work, and some don't, but I think the rest of the group will take my view on this... that we don't give a damn. We do what we want to do, and it's either accepted or not.' (Freddie Mercury)

Freddie was right in one respect. The band had played for a global stage almost right from the start. They had become popular abroad before they did at home, so it would have been impossible to satisfy the demands of every country. As such, any country where their records were sold could have asked them to make another video because the one they had wasn't acceptable. Since America was a vast sales market, Capitol wanted to help Queen, but the band resented because they always wanted to play by their own rules. (Of course, sometimes they reluctantly compromised, as they did when the Hot Space album got a poor reception, so they tried to adapt the music for The Game album to the supposed expectations.)

Queen made a living from the market, and in the most incredible luxury, they couldn't sustain the 'take it or leave it' attitude forever. Queen's response to the US requirement was born more out of defiance than common sense.

The uncompromising style was quite typical of Freddie, as he put it:

'I want to eat my cake and keep it.'

Wanting to eat your cake and keep it is impossible for an ordinary person, but Freddie didn't recognise the impossible. This caused many problems in his life, but he had no intention of changing this attitude.

It wasn't just the video that caused problems in America, but also the distinctly harmful behaviour of Paul Prenter, the great schemer.

There is a quote in Matt Richards and Mark Langthorne's book by Brian May about Paul Prenter:

'We had this guy who looked after Freddie, who was called Paul Prenter, and he got a little too big for his boots, I think. This guy, in the course of one tour, told every radio station to fuck off, but not just fuck off, but 'Freddie says fuck off, Freddie says he doesn't care about you', and so we sort of lost our relationship with the media at a stroke.'

I can imagine Freddie saying this, but Paul should have known not to pass this on to the radio stations.

However, Paul Prenter's crudest comment about Freddie was still to come.

As a result of the two incidents, record sales began to fall in America, so the band saw no point in touring North America, where they had previously invested an enormous amount of energy to become popular.

Despite being condemned in America, the video is very popular among the fans; more than 510 million have watched it on YouTube, which is more than the entire population of the USA (currently 333 million). This is one of their most popular videos among fans; it is so entertaining. Even watching it for the hundredth time, I still have to laugh when Roger first looks into the camera. He looks sensational, with a smile like a real schoolgirl.

(Queen –'I Want to Break Free' Official Video)

'Keep Passing the Open Windows'

'It is a straightforward, cleanly produced Freddie Mercury pop song, with thinking piano octave, thrumming bass (later reused and laud guitar with occasional changes in dynamics. Harmless if not particularly memorable. 'Keep Passing the Open Windows' is unlikely listed amongst anyone's favourite Queen songs, despite the skill in execution.' (Andrew Wild)

Freddie wrote three songs for the album. *Keep Passing the Open Windows* was originally intended as the music for the film, *The Hotel New Hampshire*. This is where the title comes from, which is an often repeated phrase in the movie. Queen had been working on it for eight weeks when the film director announced he didn't have enough money to pay them. So the song was included on the album.

The song's main message, which is in the title and repeated countless times, means: just go ahead, don't be afraid, pull yourself together no matter how hard it is. Because 'things are looking better every day'.

Freddie felt he had no choice but to escape into the fantasy world, as always, when he was hopeless and sad. One thought brought him comfort: *'Forget all the sadness' cause love is all you need.'*

Love enabled him to forget all his worries. At least, that's what he hoped, as if love was the only form of salvation. He sang about failure and depression; in addition, he is tormented by nightmares.

All of these thoughts reveal the anxiety and fear that has made his life bitter recently. He seemed to need confirmation that things were going to turn out okay.

What else could he do?

He was sucked in by the deceptive world of the Bermuda Triangle, which at first seemed so free and cheerful.

He didn't even think that there could have been another solution than a romantic affair.

He felt as miserable as he did in the days when he was still penniless and a stranger in London. *'Without a job and no money to spend / You're a stranger'.*

The possibility of HIV infection made him utterly dejected: *'All you think about is suicide / One of these days you're gonna lose the fight/You better keep out of danger '.*

He was aware that he had every chance of getting infected or was already infected. This thought made him devastated for years all the while there were constant reports of HIV and deaths: *'That same old feeling just keeps burning deep inside / You keep telling yourself it's gonna be the end'.*

He tried to convince himself that everything would be fine, he just had to remain hopeful, but deep down, he believed there was no hope. So, he was trying to get rid of his depression by escaping into a fantasy world.

He felt that there was no other way he could endure his loneliness, the failed year and the bad reception of the *Hot Space* album, not to mention the events in America.

Freddie felt trapped, but he had finally realized that his lifestyle could not only ruin his career, but had already put his life at risk.

Sadly, he couldn't see a way out. He hadn't found anyone to cling to, but he knew that a positive, strong relationship could lift him out of depression. He needs someone to pull him out of the pit, so he sings, *'Love is all you need.'*

But the love he found at Winnie hadn't helped; it just pushed him further into a dark place.

No wonder he felt awfully lonely; he couldn't even speak about his worries as he couldn't trust anyone at all, which made his life so tragic and at times, unbearable.

The disco style that replaced Queen's beautiful music covered very well Freddie's deepest fears. Among others, that's why I think it's important to understand the content of the songs. I wondered whether Brian and Roger had noticed or not the scary content of the lyrics and the fact that it was about Freddy's life and his scary thoughts. According to Andrew Wild, it was: *'Harmless if not particularly memorable.'* True, the music wasn't memorable, but Freddie's words were cries for help, which no one heard. Disco-style songs usually have shallow, meaningless lyrics.

The sophisticated musical style did not match drinking, drugs, and unbridled sex. Freddie's sense of reality diminished to such an extent that he either didn't notice it or didn't want to notice that his decline had inevitably led to the decline of the Queen's music. That's why Roger and Brian hated the *Hot Space* album, they knew it wasn't Queen's world. They didn't get into this world where everyone was feeling insanely good, at least until they weren't sober, if sober at all.

'Man on The Prowl'

Man On The Prowl is a song in the style of Elvis Presley about Freddie's life in Munich.

Listening to the lyrics, Freddie seems to have written this song when he was in a bad mood. His sweetheart mistreated him and left him alone. *'She do me dirty, and I'm feeling so lonely.'*

Freddie suffered, being afraid his sweetheart would break his heart. He had mixed feelings, was hurt and wanted revenge, as he did in life. In the song, he makes his way to the bar and refuels with drugs: *'I'm gonna take a little walk on the wild side /I'm gonna loosen up and get me some gas'*. He enlivens himself, *'Go crazy, driving in the fast lane'*, before he goes on the prowl. The prey is another man with whom he can make his sweetheart jealous, hoping his partner would return.

He warns the prospective partner: *'You better watch out/I'm on the loose, and I'm looking for trouble'*.

But that's not the point. Freddie just wants his sweetheart to come home to ease his loneliness, feel that he is loved by him, and make him feel safe. He is afraid his heart would be broken again and actually prefers to sit at home and wait for his darling to return: *'All I want to do is sit on my ass'*.

Freddie loved Winnie madly, and being afraid of HIV and AIDS, wanted him to be his long term partner.

Freddie sings like Elvis Presley; whether deliberately or not, it sounds as if he wanted to imitate him. The style of the music doesn't convey his real feelings.

Fans regard this song as the little brother to Crazy Little Thing Called Love, which is similar.

'Is This The World We Created?'

This is a beautiful, lyrical song, written jointly by Freddie and Brian. The lyrics are about misery in the world, the suffering caused by famine, and the world we have destroyed as human beings.

'Love Kills'

The song 'Love Kills', a rock disco track, was released as Freddie's solo record. The song is about love just 'killing' Freddie, drilling through his heart and scarring him, and worst of all, it won't leave him alone. It's ever-present and won't let him go, despite just playing with his emotions, giving him a hard time. The lyrics are beautiful, worthy of Freddie's creativity and genuinely came from the heart; its success was no accident. The song was probably inspired by his relationship with Winnie. The reason for the haunting title was Freddie's fear of AIDS.

It got to number 10 in Britain but was number one in Europe's gay bars. The song was originally written for the film *Metropolis* (the music written jointly with Giorgio Moroder), and it did better in the charts than Brian or Roger's solo records. (YouTube: Freddie Mercury – 'Love Kills')

The Works album's tour only began in August in Europe and finished in May 1985. Queen performed 48 concerts in Europe, South Africa, Brazil, New Zealand, Australia and Japan. It's hard even to imagine how Freddie managed to sing his way through 48 concerts despite the problem with his vocal cords.

Tickets for the 12 concerts scheduled in Sun City, South Africa, sold out within 24 hours, but the crowds were hugely disappointed because Freddie's voice let him down at the first concert. He struggled through three songs in agony, with the others' help, but had to march off stage in the end. Only half of all the concerts could be held. Freddie was forced to rest and have injections.

Even before the tour, there had been protests in the UK due to South Africa's apartheid policy and they were placed on the UN blacklist because of the concerts. After arriving home, they were also expelled from the British Musicians' Union and given a fine. They believed Queen's gigs had supported the policy of apartheid.

Bob Geldof and Midge Ure wrote a song called *Do They Know It's Christmas*, with the royalties used to support people starving in Ethiopia. Thirty-six rocks stars sang on the record. Queen wasn't invited to the recording as punishment for appearing in South Africa.

Freddie and the others were very offended to have been left out, partly because it meant they couldn't be present among some of the great artists and partly because it would have had publicity value for them. This wasn't just Queen's loss, but a loss to everyone involved.

Around the time of Freddie's birthday, they were in the middle of playing a series of four gigs at Wembley Stadium when *The Sun* newspaper published a story about Freddie, suggesting he spent 1,000 pounds a week on drink and drugs and that he had confessed to being gay.

After the concerts, Freddie responded to the article in a report given to *Melody Maker*:

'*Melody Maker: Freddie, I understand you were upset about a story in The Sun that claimed you had confessed to being homosexual.*

Freddie: I was completely misquoted. But from the beginning, the press has always written whatever they wanted about Queen, and they can get away with it. The woman who wrote that story wanted a total scoop from me and didn't get anything. I said: 'What do you want to hear? That I deal with cocaine? But for God's sake, if I want to make a big confession about my love life, would I go to The Sun, of all papers, to do it? There's no facking way I'd do that. I'm too intelligent.

Melody Maker: But it's a good time to be gay. It's good for business, isn't it?

Freddie: But it's wrong for me to be gay now because I've been in the business for 12 years. It's good to be gay or anything outrageous if you're new. But even if I tried that, people would start yawning 'Oh God, here's Freddie Mercury saying he's gay because it's trendy to be gay.' (Melody Maker, 1984)

The newspaper was tipped off by a driver who Freddie had fired. The news was probably accurate, and it's possible the driver himself also used them because Freddie generously supplied everyone with everything. He had never been selfish or small-time in this respect. He usually picked up the tab, as confirmed by Peter Freestone in his book.

Freddie did have a short fuse, and it's possible he fired the driver in anger; at least, this is what road crew manager, Peter Hince, suggests in his book.

The biggest event in the concert series was the Rock in Rio Festival in January 1985, lasting eight days. 250,000 people came together at a purpose-built venue for the event: at the time, it was the biggest rock concert ever held in the world, and Queen was the headliner, as they were the biggest stars in South America. Queen played two gigs, first on an opening day and then closing the festival. The Brazilian TV channel Globo, which was available throughout South America, broadcast the event. Naturally, the band asked for recordings of their performances. Both their gigs were played at 2 am. Fortunately, Queen was used to staying up late.

The first day's performance was tough for Freddie due to a massive misunderstanding because when they started playing, 'I Want to Break Free', Freddie appeared dressed as a woman with large breasts so he could clearly be seen a long way away from the stage. As he started to sing, the spectators began throwing anything that came to hand at the stage. Freddie didn't understand what was happening and didn't back down despite being hit by a large piece of cardboard. He got angry and began to make fun of the audience, but fortunately, he realised the problem was with his clothing, so he got changed and carried on with the concert as if nothing had happened.

The press blew the incident out of proportion. The headlines said that the star's large plastic breasts caused a scandal at the concert because the song was regarded as an anthem for people fighting for freedom from dictatorship in certain parts of South America. Freddie's style of dress wasn't appropriate for an anthem, obviously.

A British journalist - Dave - Hogan - who saw the events up close said to Leslie-Ann Jones that the audience in the front row didn't see the stage at all, as it was too high. As they tried to cling higher, the security guards stepped on their hands, that is why people were throwing at them little objects, they didn't aim at Freddie.

It's a pleasure to watch the crowd going crazy at the concert recording as they cheer Queen on. Freddie sang until he could no longer breathe. Queen played their old songs twice as fast, as usual, leaving Freddie, who in any case was struggling with his vocal cords, trying to catch his breath, although the audience didn't notice anything; or only those with sensitive ears could have heard it.

The most shocking thing was discovering that Freddie looks ten years younger on recording the Montreal concert made four years earlier. This was the effect of constantly staying up all night, drugs, drink and strenuous work. Queen had essentially taken on too much, especially Freddie, in every respect.

(YouTube: Queen – 'Somebody To Love' – HD Live – 1981 Montreal)

Freddie sings terrifically on the Montreal video. It's no wonder he's a global star and a global sensation. If anyone hadn't yet heard him sing, it would be enough just to watch this video to understand why he was and still is such a big star.

Some people thought he had superhuman abilities, but they were wrong. He believed he was a superstar and worked hard to get there. His fighting ability, on the other hand, really was superhuman. The audience adored him and always followed his cues, which included singing along, clapping with him, and continuously moving their arms around.

(YouTube - HQ Queen ao vivo no Rock in Rio – 1985 – COMPLETO (Descrição)

After the Rio Festival, Freddie returned to Munich to finish his solo album *Mr Bad Guy*, which was released in April 1985 in the UK and in May in the USA.

The next stop was New Zealand, where Freddie, unusually for him, arrived on stage late and drunk.

They finished the album tour with concerts in Australia and Japan. Freddie returned to Japan with Jim Hutton in 1986, but 1985 was the last year when the Japanese audience could see him perform, to their great regret.

28. *Mr Bad Guy* Album (1985)

Freddie dedicated his first solo album, *Mr Bad Guy*, to his cats that he adored, which make me think this album meant a lot to him. It was released on 29 April in the UK, getting to number 6 and went gold for Freddie.

Undoubtedly, Freddie sings as convincingly and beautifully as on any of the Queen albums, but the disco style didn't match his fantastic voice. As the Barcelona album later brilliantly demonstrated, he was destined for much more than this album.

The single heralding the album, 'I Was Born to Love You', got to number 11 in Britain but made the top 10 in Germany and South Africa. After Freddie's death, it was also included on Queen's 1995 album *Made in Heaven*.

'I Was Born to Love You'

Freddie may have written the song for Winnie, as it was created while he was in Munich and given that they had moved in together, the love must have been quite overwhelming, at least on Freddie'd part. The lyrics are beautiful, a beautiful description of Freddie's deep emotions and a summary of everything a genuinely intense lover can and willing to give. The song tells us a lot about Freddie. He was a sensitive soul, passionate lover and caring partner. I am sure Winnie didn't realise who he was involved with. Although Barbara translated for them, the presence of a third party disturbs the intimate proximity. There was no pillow talk. At most, Freddie could reassure Winnie how much he loved and admired him by some german words, kissing, caressing and smiling.

In the video, Freddie sings the lyrics a bit mechanically, even though his voice is still perfect. There is a beautiful young woman with him on stage, and while singing 'I Was Born to Love You', he twice shoves the poor woman off the platform, so the unfortunate woman plummets down to the floor twice. It's an interesting start. And then the woman appears in the arms of another man, who also shoves her away while Freddie is cheerfully singing and dancing. His figure can be seen reflected in several mirrors as if he were singing about himself and were in love with himself. We know that he was vain and considered himself good-looking, and he indeed was, but so far, he hadn't shown much love or at least mercy towards himself.

The performance style suggests love had already lost some of its original magic when he performed and recorded the song. It could have been only the initial intoxication that had inspired the fantastically beautiful lyrics.

He carries on singing, then starts to pursue the woman through several rooms (in Garden Lodge, according to Freddie) until she finally crashes into an armchair, where Freddie throws himself on her.

The performance style is happy, completely dispassionate and entertaining; it's a pleasure to watch a sexy, manly Freddie bursting with good health, yet I feel sympathy with the woman.

'Made in Heaven'

The song was also released as a single before Live Aid and was the second advertisement for the new album.

This song is also beautiful and is about Freddie's life.

'I'm taking my ride with destiny/Willing to play my part/Living with painful memories/Loving with all my heart/Made in heaven, made in heaven/That is what they say'.

Freddie taking his ride with destiny, means he is in love again, despite his painful memories. In all probability, love was made in heaven, but knowing Freddie, we can't rule out the possibility that the word 'heaven' made him think of his favourite gay bar, where he also met Jim. The song is not about Jim. It could be about anyone. Freddie's way of performance is dispassionate, doesn't convey real feelings behind it. Again, the lyrics are about him craving romantic love and just waiting for the opportunity for the kind of love made in heaven. It was written in the stars that he would find love.

(He did find the love he wrote about in 'Made in Heaven' when Jim Hutton fell in love with him in 1985.)

The video is very contradictory, just like Freddie's personality. He is standing on top of a mud ball that is 190 cm in height. The flames of hell are burning at its base, seemingly naked women try to climb up to Freddie, but he's surrounded by men, who keep pushing them back into hell. When he sings that stormy times are coming to his life, he jumps down among the women, who are pushing each other around in hell, but none of them throws themselves on him, and they start to dance instead, which doesn't make much sense but is quite theatrical. However, jumping into hell symbolizes the hellish times still to come. Luckily Freddie wasn't fully aware of it yet.

The best part is when the ball of mud opens up, Freddie is standing on a small platform on top of the rotating globe, like a god, until 'hell's angels' disappear from the scene.

The only thing that seems to have been made in heaven in the video is Freddie himself. He is wearing sexy, unashamedly skin-tight clothes; his face is beautifully made up, he's charming and good-looking, and he poses like a sex god. This is the look that drives Latino women crazy in South America. He looks like Clark Gable, star of *Gone with the Wind* and once known as the King of Hollywood. Clark Gable cuts an old-fashioned figure today, but anyone looking at Freddie will see his Superman-style clothes are still top-notch in the 21st century. Many of us wouldn't mind if something like this were trendy on the streets, too; the situation might change in the next few decades, but for the time being, everyone still goes out in jeans.

On the other hand, Freddie does look much more masculine with short hair than when he did with had long hair, not to mention that in the meantime, he had also worked on his upper body, in line with the trend. And it worked for him. He had never looked as good as he did in these videos. He made both male and female hearts flutter.

But when will Freddie's heart finally flutter with happiness?

(YouTube: Freddie Mercury – 'Made in Heaven' (Official Video – remastered)

'Let's Turn it On'

The song was written in disco style. Both the music and lyrics were significantly simplified, so there is no need for interpretation. All Freddie says is to focus on the party, dance and sing happily, supposedly in a disco bar.

Hopefully, Freddie was thrilled when he wrote it.

'Foolin' Around'

The music style of this song is also disco. Simple, easy-to-understand lyrics, which is not a problem at a disco, where people drink and dance. They pay attention to everything but the lyrics of the music. Freddie had no particular reason to put any message into the song, other than someone fooling around with him, not taking him seriously. It could have been Winnie; knowing his personality, it wouldn't be surprising if it was him.

'Your Kind of Lover'

It was highly likely Winnie who inspired the lyrics of this song. They often broke up and reconciled. Freddie's feelings were sincere, so he longed for Winnie to feel the same way about him.

Freddie would have been happy with even a little affection from Winnie, who often deliberately hurt and made him jealous.

He asks his lover to *'Make a brand new start'*. He sincerely hopes they can get over their quarrels. Freddie promises everything to get him to love him again.

Freddie wants to take care of Winnie: *'I wanna be your kind of mother'*. The desire to take care of a partner is a sign of deep love.

He'd like to be in an understanding, loving relationship with him, and for them to be together without quarrels. Freddie is longing for happiness, and is trying to win his heart back.

'Mr Bad Guy'

Freddie self-critically calls himself 'Mr Bad Guy' in the song.

He feels he is ruining the lives of his partners, so everyone is afraid of him. His self-criticism has a basis, but based on earlier events, Freddie couldn't trust anyone and wasn't capable of maintaining a long term relationship. He was unstable and restless, and when he was writing this song, it probably seemed to him that his destiny was to ruin even promising relationships.

The style of the music is indefinable, and it's unsettling to listen to, as Freddie must have felt uneasy when he composed it.

'Man Made Paradise'

Freddie's life could really have been a man-made paradise idyll. He achieved everything he had ever dreamed of, but the ripples of his emotional life and his love failures meant excruciating loneliness for him. This song is probably for Winnie too, but he rejected Freddie.

'History repeats itself/ I seem to be all myself again.' Winnie didn't care about Freddie's thoughts and feelings, which made him so sad that even

the thought of suicide crossed his mind: *'When you refuse me all the time I'm suicidal on my own'.*

While in Munich, Freddie's health gradually deteriorated. He was terrified of the possibility of HIV infection, and his relationship with Winnie was so frustrating for Freddy that he even thought of suicide. Luckily, his instinct for survival and Jim's appearance in his life made him forget this horrible thought.

This is one of Freddie's most beautifully written lyrics, but the music seems to deliberately destroy the song's charm. The song is performed in a very unusual way, and the style of singing is also not harmonious. This contradiction perfectly conveys Freddie's feelings. As I have already written, he would have done anything for Winnie; Freddie even wanted him to move into Garden Lodge. However, he was unable to change Winnie's feelings. Freddie showed the beauty and depth of his emotions with the song's lyrics, while the music and the way he sang the song symbolize Winnie's indifferent behaviour.

29. He Is the One, Jim Hutton

'I want to be loved by you, nobody else but you' (Freddie Mercury)

Freddie had already run into Jim Hutton in a London bar in 1983, but Jim hadn't accepted Freddie's offer of a drink. Freddie didn't forget Jim, and when he bumped into him again at his favourite club, Heaven, on 23 March, 1985, Freddie offered to buy Jim a drink again, but Jim decided that he was going to buy a drink for Freddie, even though he had only five pounds in his pocket. Jim was already drunk and single, so he didn't mind having a drink with Freddie.

They chatted and carried on drinking until dawn, and by the time they reached Freddie's home and went to bed, they just had enough strength left to grope in the dark.

After this, Freddie didn't get in touch with Jim for three months, and Jim didn't particularly mind, but he was pleased when Freddie called him again. He explained to Jim that he hadn't been in touch because he'd been on tour.

Their meeting in Heaven was no coincidence. Jim didn't usually go to Heaven or only went rarely, and he wasn't heading there this time either, but he changed his mind at the last moment, making it possible for them to bump into each other 'by chance'. I don't believe in coincidences. Freddie was praying for love, and Jim was desperately looking for 'a harmonious, loving relationship'. So, the meeting came about, which brought the change Freddie had coveted in vain for at least 15 years. It seemed his wish would finally be fulfilled as one of the most beautiful gifts in his life.

Jim didn't believe in one-night stands. He believed in long-term relationships and that was what he was looking for when he met Freddie.

Freddie invited him for dinner in his home. As he didn't have much money, Jim decided not to take a bottle of wine, but rather two bunches of slightly drooping freesias. He was embarrassed of the gesture, as he had never bought flowers for a man before, so he threw them in the bin. This was a mistake, freesias were Freddie's favourite, and he would have immediately hugged him in tears straight away because, even with a magnifying glass, you couldn't find a more romantic man in London than Freddie - regardless of leading a wild lifestyle. And, what's more, he really loved small presents that came from the heart. Nevertheless, Freddie and Jim hugged each other when he arrived.

Freddie's best friends, Joe Fanelli, Peter Freestone and Paul Prenter attended the dinner. Joe's nickname was Liza, after Liza Minnelli. Freddie gave all his friends a female nickname. His own nickname was Melina, after Melina Mercouri, whereas he just called Peter Freestone Phoebe, because he looked like a Phoebe. And Paul Prenter's nickname was Trixie. Jim disliked Paul, because of his inquisitive gaze, wanting to know and see everything. Jim knew Freestone well because they had worked together in an Oxford Street department store.

It seemed to Jim that the guests were competing for Freddie's attention, and he was right.

Freddie offered Jim cocaine, but he didn't accept. Freddie took a small dose on several occasions, which loosened his tongue.

Jim worked as a barber, and had a relatively simple way of thinking, but was blessed with common sense. He was also intuitive, of Irish origin. A proud man, who wasn't especially interested in stars, and the fact that Freddie was a star didn't impress him much, but he was in some way attracted to Freddie as a man, despite the fact he wasn't Jim's type. This was typical; all Freddie's lovers said this before he swept them off their feet. He was irresistible and relentless, like a Japanese ninja.

Freddie sat next to Jim at dinner, and they continually flirted with each other and chatted without regard for the other guests. Freddie told Jim broadly about his life. During the conversation, they both started to feel a mutual attraction.

Jim fell head over heels in love with Freddie. He liked Freddie's big brown eyes and was surprised at how childish and shy he was despite all he had achieved. However, he seemed completely honest, which Jim also found attractive.

Freddie invited Jim to Munich for the weekend, and they both enjoyed their time together. Another invitation arrived for the following weekend, but this time Freddie didn't go to the airport to pick Jim up. Instead, Joe drove Jim to Freddie's place, but Freddie wasn't home. Joe didn't know where Freddie was or when he would go home. Jim went to a bar, had a few drinks with someone and went home at dawn. Freddie asked Jim for an explanation of where he had been. They didn't quarrel, but didn't speak for quite a while until Freddie suddenly apologised. Jim sensed that Freddie had someone else in the city. His intuition was right. Freddie was still in a relationship with Winnie. Barbara pointed to a man in a bar one night and told Jim he was Freddie's lover. Fortunately, Jim sensed it was better not to ask Freddie about him, to avoid starting an argument. The following weekend Freddie began a new game. When Jim arrived, Freddie told him he was going out for the night with Winnie. He didn't go home all night. Jim hoped Freddie just wanted to break up with Winnie.

This time the game Freddie played with Winnie and Jim worked out very well. At some stage, Winnie became jealous of Jim, and got so angry that he sold the new car Freddie had given him. When Freddie heard this, he was outraged and broke up with the Munich heartthrob for good. Freddie was finally able to catch his breath again and was able to dream about a new love with greater promise, but Jim had to endure seven trials first, like the suitors in fairy tales asking for the hand of a princess in marriage. He had already completed three of the seven, but the four most arduous ordeals were still to come.

They spent the next weekend in London when Freddie took Jim and the other 'family members', Joe, Peter, Mary and her partner, to Garden Lodge, which was almost ready to move into. (It took five years for Freddie to dream up and arrange each little detail of the construction of his new home.) The result was astonishing.

30. Live Aid (13 July 1985)

Queen's concerts were triumphant all over the world; apart from one or two rare exceptions, hundreds of thousands of fans worshipped them while screaming, clapping, waving their arms, and singing. And they would still have had the US market and fans, either if they had wanted it.

But, 13 July, 1985, was different. At the time, this was the largest ever rock concert in the world, and was held at two venues at the same time. The capacity of Wembley Stadium in London was 72,000, whereas 89,484 witnessed the event at JFK Stadium in Philadelphia, US, and more than 1.9 billion people watched the concert on 150 TV stations.

Bob Geldof and Midge Ure initiated the concert. The most significant American and British stars appeared, including Phil Collins, Rod Stewart, Elton John, George Michael, The Who, Led Zeppelin, U2, Madonna, Duran Duran, Black Sabbath, Paul McCartney, Lionel Richie, Cher, Elvis Costello, Jimmy Page, Eric Clapton, Tina Turner, and many other huge stars. The purpose of these great gigs was to donate the income from the concert to help the starving people in Ethiopia.

Queen hesitated about whether to perform because, according to Brian, they weren't sure whether they wanted to tour again or even appear together after their last tour. However, one thing was certain - they had entered into a contract with EMI for six albums in 1982, and five of them were still to be completed.

They were hesitating because of the displeasing events from their gigs in South Africa meant they thought they had lost some popularity in the UK.

Geldof asked Jim Beach to persuade Queen to take part. If they had missed the show, they would have regretted it forever, and fortunately, they said yes in the end.

Once they had said yes, they prepared extensively and worked out how to turn the concert to their advantage so that everyone would benefit, the starving people, the audience, and the band.

They knew who their rivals were; all the most prominent names, and they decided to outdo them. This competitive spirit was ever-present in Freddie because he always wanted to be first at everything. And as always, Brian, Roger, and John wanted to get the absolute maximum out of themselves too. And in any case, they had always wanted to be the best in the world, so there was a great chance to prove it.

They thought the other artists wouldn't waste too much energy on preparation, as they all appearing for free. And Queen was right.

Queen only had 20 minutes to perform, so they had to find a way to squeeze in their most successful hits; those which were most popular among the global audience. So, they practised for around three hours a day - for three days - for a 20-minute gig.

They knew they would have to rely only on themselves as artists, because there would be no Queen lighting, there would be no smoke bombs or dry ice, just them. However, there was one opportunity they exploited. Their sound engineer, 'Trip' Khalaf sneaked on stage before the gig and turned the volume up to maximum, so they were the loudest of all the bands.

Naturally, since Freddie was at the front of the stage, he had most of the responsibility for the performance. All of them knew that.

And they also worked out when to perform - when British people were sitting in front of the TV, but when Americans would be gasping from the heat; there was a fierce heatwave in both countries. The different time zones meant the concert began at 7 am in America.

Queen arranged with Geldof to go on stage before David Bowie, at 6.40 p.m.

When Princess Diana and Prince Charles arrived, the bagpipes were replaced by Status Quo's popular hit; and the crowd began to rock to the rhythm of the music. The warm-up began.

I watched all the other Live Aid stars perform, just to see for myself why everyone felt Queen was the best of all the performers.

I listened to Elton John, George Michael, Led Zeppelin, Phil Collins, and quite a few others and found the answer quite easily.

The first essential factor was the songs. All the songs that the other stars performed seemed monotonous to my ears, which were attuned to Queen's music. They were simply dull. It sounded as if they repeated the same chords. The lyrics were trite and lacking intellectual depth. Other performers had at least six or seven people on stage, including musicians, vocalists, and backup singers.

The six or seven people were unable to create the kind of show that Freddie created alone. Roger - the daredevil on the drums - hit the drums as usual; Brian and surprisingly even the reserved John were buzzing, drumming with his feet or dancing to the rhythm, and really enjoying himself. Brian was light on his feet as he jumped around, strumming the guitar in his sensational way.

Some of the more prominent names, like Phil Collins, Elton John, and David Bowie, sang well and with a certain amount of passion, but the musical accompaniment was simply weak. And Led Zeppelin didn't produce their best form either.

Queen's other secret was that they were able to write and play exciting music. The third secret, and Queen's primary weapon was Freddie's glorious singing voice; even if the other singers had made a more intense effort, they still could not have produced anything similar, not even the best of them. Their voices sounded plain, feeble and monotonous compared to Freddie's, not to mention his vocal range.

I guess everyone performed their hits, but the hits Queen selected were of such a high standard compared to the others, in terms of the music and lyrics, that I simply couldn't believe my ears. The other performers weren't melodic, or rhythmical, or alive. They had no passion or spirit.

However, the main proof was the audience's reaction. The crowd wasn't just made up of Queen fans – because of Queen was not on the list of the performing artists before the show. But when they appeared on the stage you could sense they were was buzzing with excitement. The cheers showed that something big was about to happen on stage.

Freddie, Brian, John and Roger ran energetically onto the stage, and didn't want to lose a second.

Then Freddie happily did some shadow boxing and wave, raising his arms to the sky as usual. he bounced over to the piano with a broad smile.

Freddie seemed extremely happy when he heard the cheers, as were the other band members. They calmed down, now all they had to do was play music, which had never been a problem for them; Queen was on top of the world. As Freddie began the ballad part of 'Bohemian Rhapsody', the crowd screamed in delight, and when he started to sing: 'Mama I just killed the man', the audience sang along word for word. Everyone knew the song; there was no need for a choir, as they had the incomparably beautiful sound of the audience, consisting of 72,000 voices. Freddie sang with a renewed passion, possibly like never before. As the final guitar chords sounded, 'Radio Ga Ga' started up right away on Roger's drums. Freddie grabbed hold of the gimmick microphone and marched all around the stage with a broad smile. The smile came from within, from his heart. After the first few drum beats, the audience started cheering again, recognising the song straight away. The two guitars and the drums were so powerful; it was like they were being played by five or six musicians, not just three. As Freddie sang, the camera panned to the audience, and they can be seen following Freddie, word for word, singing and shaking their arms, their fists clenched, as if they were dancing in a disco. And then the refrain – Freddie shouts, 'Everybody!' They didn't need a second invitation: *Radio ga ga, radio goo goo*', and all 72,000 sing and clap above their heads to the rhythm, as they had learned exquisitely in videos and at other concerts. They are all together, all hands clapping to the same rhythm. Freddie, of course, is setting the example at the front of the stage; he's clapping as well, enthusiastically hitting the mic stand in his hand. And then along come the drums between the two verses; Freddie throws himself into it, striding around and jumping like a grasshopper. When singing standing up, he stamps his feet to the drums and shakes his arms to the rhythm, holding them up high, sometimes moving his hips and smiling seductively as he sings, straining every muscle. John is smiling as he sings and starts to dance as well. And finally, we can see Roger as he plays the final drumbeat, playing sensationally. You could listen to him alone for hours. Especially at the end of the songs when he is always mind-blowingly good, and then Freddie drops to the ground, bends over the microphone, as if he were doing yoga, and holds the pose, before jumping up energetically in a split second and signals to Roger like a conductor as the last drum beat is heard – it's the end. And the crowd cheers!

Freddie stands on the edge of the stage and starts a singing lesson: 'Eeeeoooooooooooooh! Eeeeoooooooooooooh!' echoes the audience, imitating Freddie perfectly. The second and third times, the 'eeeeoooooh's' are embellished. By the end – in an ever-higher voice and for a longer time – he gets the audience to improvise professionally; they're laughing as they listen to Freddie because what he expects of them is funny. Still, the audience can't be deterred. It was unbelievable how accurately they imitated Freddie's actions. 'All right' shouts Freddie, and the echo comes back from the audience: 'All right.'

Freddie is grinning from ear to ear, but there's no time to stop, and Roger starts the next song: 'Hey, hey, hey' Freddie shouts happily, 'Hammer to Fall'. The rhythm of the music and the guitars provide a sensational introduction to the song, and then comes the amazing lyrics, Brian's wonderful song.

While the intro continues, Freddie playfully chases the cameraman further and further back with the mic stand, and the cameraman retreats, not wanting to be trapped on a skewer. Fortunately, Freddie gives up because he has to sing and starts vigorously. *'Here we stand or here we fall, history won't care at all'*. He focuses on the song with every muscle, but seizes every opportunity to add a bit of fun. Freddie starts charging towards the cameraman again, but this time he goes closer and closer, puts his hand on the cameraman's shoulder and moves his head up and down in front of the camera, making it difficult to be filmed. Then, as he turns away, he winks conspiratorially at the audience, smiling as if to ask whether they agree it was a good joke, while mischievously pointing back at the cameraman. During Brian's next guitar solo, Freddie introduces an acrobatic, rhythmic gymnastics exercise, combined with one or two yoga poses, while passionately 'playing' the guitar with the microphone stand. He carries on singing, and then during the guitar solo, Brian is the next victim. Freddie stands as close to him as he can and raises the microphone stand, as if he wanted to hit Brian with it, but spares him in the end and just makes some mating movements at his side. Brian doesn't even look at him; Freddie can no longer surprise him, whatever he does, or so it seems. Freddie makes use of every moment, and when he doesn't have to sing, you can be sure he'll press the mic stand to his groin area, pointing here or there, while the mic itself is looming in front of his groin – all the while smiling very cheekily. And then, at the end, before the last drum beat can be heard, he turns his backside towards the audience and bends over, taking a kind of reverse bow. But this is about something else; as we know, there are no sexual connotations here. The whole thing is just a joke. He's in a good mood as he already knows Queen holds the trump card. He takes the guitar to strike up 'Crazy Little Thing Called Love', but first tells the audience: *'This song is dedicated only for beautiful people tonight, it means all of you! Thank you for coming along, making this a great occasion!'* As he hits the strings, the audience is clearly buzzing again, and the atmosphere is improving because the song is very melodic and rhythmical.

Freddie can sing at 100 miles an hour, if required by the music. All hands are in the air, clapping rhythmically, shaking themselves about and rocking, while perspiration is streaming off Freddie. Still, he doesn't even attempt to wipe his face, and nor can he as he's playing the guitar while singing, and the way he improvises makes people's jaws drop. One would think the audience couldn't sing along with this one, but Freddie passes the last refrain over to them, just clapping and signalling with his head – now it's your turn! They don't need a second invitation and sing the refrain flawlessly, word for word *'Take a back seat, hitch-*

hike, and take a long ride on my motorbike, until I'm ready, crazy little thing called love'. The crowd sings, clapping as Freddie shows them how. Roger shouts out: *'Ready, Freddie?'* It sounds like great fun. As they reach the end, people are roaring in an increasingly intoxicated manner, until Freddie strains to lift the guitar as if it weighed a ton, and then easily lowers it behind his back and runs across the stage with it, smiling. And then Roger hits the drums, there's no time to stop. After the first few bars, the crowd starts to cheer. They realise the best part is about to come, really going on a rampage! 'We will, we will rock you'. After a few lines, the refrain comes along. Freddie just points to the audience and shouts: *'Sing it'*, and the crowd of 72,000 sings the chorus as if it were something they do every day. Freddie gives another instruction, *'Sing it again'* and of course, they sing it. At the end, Freddie gives them a little encouragement in the world's sweetest voice: *'I like it'*. And then, one more time before the guitar solo with the great drums, this song has the best rhythm, and who was it written by? Brian, the greatest rock guitarist of all time. And of course, Roger added something extra, as he always did, and the result was sensational. This song couldn't be left out of the show. The audience enjoys it the most, and they are now in ecstasy. Somehow, they have to calm down, so Freddie jumps over to the piano while the audience is still roaring in appreciation, and starts the inimitable hit: 'We Are the Champions'. The audience sings from the start. Everyone knows the song word for word, as if it's the British national anthem. They join hands in the air and rock rhythmically like fans at a big football match. Freddie starts to blow kisses to the audience during the last beats of the song and waves, while the other guys run forward to take a bow, Roger arriving last of all from behind the drums, hugging Brian in joy, and they take a bow together. What a touching sight! While the crowd is screaming in celebration, and Freddie shouts out: *'So long, goodbye!'* He bows with his usual regal splendour, and they march off stage.

Backstage, all the big stars raised their heads at the first cheer, the previous bustle, constant chatting, eating and drinking came to a standstill, and they listened to Queen's performance intently. They knew and sensed they would lose the battle that day.

Queen was the world champion, as the last line of the song goes. And, of course, the way the crowd celebrated and came together with Queen showed unparalleled collaboration. It was an outstanding performance by Queen and by everyone.

The way they completed 15 years of hard work was exemplary. This is how a champion team works – a world champion team. Without a doubt, everyone bowed down to them. Everyone recognised they were the stars of the day. They stole the show and stood on the top level of the imaginary podium.

According to a BBC public opinion survey, Queen's 20 minutes constituted the greatest live rock performance in history, overtaking Jimi Hendrix (Woodstock Rock Festival) and the Rolling Stones (1976 Hyde Park Festival). It was referred to as *'20 minutes that changed music'*.

The hearts of Queen's fans were beating faster than ever at the concert, and they were proud of their favourite band. This event is still mentioned today under the YouTube *Live Aid* video. It really must have been the experience of a lifetime for people who were fortunate enough to be in the crowd, and also for those of us who can 'only' see Queen's triumphal entry into rock history on video. The first such memorable event was 'Bohemian Rhapsody' and then came the South American gigs with huge crowds, and now more than 2 billion people were able to watch their Live Aid performance and celebrate them.

Lady Diana's heart might also have secretly skipped a beat in delight, remembering the short time she had spent with Freddie in disguise one night in one of London's gay bars. Diana could also hold her own, if we're talking about adventures. Still, everyone adored her too. Whatever she did was fine, just like Freddie. She could cope with anything except the final tragedy, but I'm sure angels carried both of them up high and didn't stop until they reached seventh heaven.

(YouTube: Queen Full Concert Live Aid 1985 FullHD)

Some of the comments about the performance under the video:

'I turned 60 in November 2020. When I was a teenager, one of my black classmates gave me some soft rock albums, including Queen. I was about 17 years old when I fell in love with their music. And I'm sitting here today, watching Freddie Mercury and, as an artist and fellow singer, I am completely inspired by this man. He stood on that stage, feeling unwell, knowing he had been diagnosed with an incurable disease, and he did what his spirit was sent here for. HE PERFORMED. QUEEN gave every ounce of themselves in this performance. And when we realise they had been on hiatus for quite some time prior to this show - for them to get on stage and do THIS - for Freddie to sing down to his bones - for the whole band to sound so fat and full and INCREDIBLE - let this be a lesson to us ALL. Always give your all. Don't leave any damn thing on the table. Everything we do COUNTS!'

'Live Aid was a Queen concert with some really good support acts.'

'Those 505 people who disliked this video are going to hell for sure.'

'I can understand those 500 people who didn't like the video. Nobody likes it if their favourite football team is beaten to a pulp either.'

In his book, Mark Blake quotes BBC Radio 1 DJ Simon Bates, whom Freddie promised an interview before the Live Aid event. Freddie's excuse for not giving the interview was that he was very ill. When they eventually met, Freddie showed him his tongue, and Bates commented to the radio listeners, describing it as *'the worst sight I've ever seen, and it's obvious he (Freddie) is still ill'*.

Freddie's tongue was covered in duffel-like white fur, a thrush infection, which is one of the symptoms of HIV. If he had known that the thrush infection was caused by HIV, he definitely wouldn't have shown his tongue to a radio presenter.

(YouTube: Freddie Mercury with Simon Bates, BBC Radio 1, April, 1985)

In Mark Blake's book, he quotes a BBC Live Aid medical official, who says: *'Doctors had said he was too ill to perform. He wasn't well enough at all, but he absolutely insisted.'*

The author of the book also claims Freddie was still suffering from a sore throat.

'A type of leukoplakia called hairy leukoplakia, sometimes called oral hairy leukoplakia, primarily affects people whose immune systems have been weakened by disease, especially HIV/AIDS'. (mayoclinic.org)

Hairy leukoplakia can be mistaken with oral thrush, most likely that is why the doctor in New York and also in Live Aid didn't tell Freddie his immune system was weakened.

Learning all of this I didn't find it surprising that Jim Hutton didn't mention this in his book, even though he would undoubtedly have been very worried about Freddie had he known he was ill.

However, indeed, Freddie always denied being ill to his friends and acquaintances, but I can't see any point in denying a sore throat. It's not a fatal or infectious disease, and a 'thrush infection' of the tongue alone didn't prove Freddie was infected with HIV. Perhaps Jim knew about it but didn't attribute great significance to it because Freddie used to calm others, saying, for example: 'Don't worry darling, this isn't the first time and won't be the last. I've done it often before. It'll pass as the others have passed'.

When he sang 'Radio Ga Ga' and raised his right arm, a purple patch can be seen under his biceps below the leather belt with metal studs. It was noticed by a radio reporter, Gambaccini, who later talked about it to the two authors, Richards & Langthorne. He was surprised that nobody noticed that the virus had done its job and Freddie had developed AIDS.

Barbara also saw the blue patches on Freddie's face, I am wondering how come Jim didn't see them.

During the 20 minutes concert, Freddie hadn't makeup and there wasn't any blue patch visible on his face.

31. After Live Aid

A Kind of Magic album (1986)

Queen's fans have two ways of measuring time: before and after Live Aid, and the other, during and after Freddie's life. I don't particularly appreciate using the latter because I prefer to think of Freddie as still being with us. The thought of him no longer being here scared many people, in terms of what was to come. These days they worry about how they would survive if something were to happen to Brian or Roger. Freddie probably didn't realise how much he meant to people.

Live Aid was Jim's first-ever rock concert. It was quite an initiation! Freddie took him to the side wing of the stage, and in his book about their relationship, Jim wrote that Live Aid was *'the most magical twenty minutes in my life'*. That was when the penny must have dropped for the first time about who Freddie Mercury was.

After Live Aid, Queen returned to Munich and began working on the new album with renewed, feverish energy. Jim visited Freddie every other weekend. Their relationship grew deeper, and Jim says they were happy. Freddie invited him to the studio, where he saw how obsessively Freddie worked, as he had in the old days. If Freddie said let's drop into the studio for five or six minutes, it usually meant five or six hours. He worked so intensely that he completely forgot that Jim was even there.

'Living On My Own / My Love is Dangerous' was released from Freddie's solo album as a single on 2 September, 1985, three days before Freddie's 39th birthday.

'Living On My Own'

The song is about how lonely Freddie feels if he is left alone. Sometimes he feels he's going to break down and cry when he's on his own.

Sometimes he feels he's walking too fast, in other words, making rushed decisions, and everything is coming down on him, driving him crazy. And the feeling is intensified when he's on his own. He doesn't have time for 'monkey business', by which he is clearly referring to those ex-partners who hurt him and cheated on him, including Winnie, on whom he had just wasted his time.

But then he also feels lonely when he has a partner, because he doesn't really trust anyone. For example, he didn't even dare tell Barbara or Jim the result of his HIV test.

He feels that nobody warns him he is heading for danger, and finds his head is always in a dream world. However, the conclusion says it all – he hopes there will be some good times ahead, so he's not going to stop looking.

He sings this song sensationally, improvising in a good mood like someone who really is hopeful. There is no dramatic effect, doesn't convey any bad feelings. The video was put together from edited recordings of his 39th birthday party.

The song's lyrics don't have a party atmosphere, but the music does. This kind of contradiction can be attributed to the fact that Freddie wasn't on his own when he wrote the song; Barbara or Winnie could have been there. Still, it was vivid in his memory, as he didn't have a satisfying relationship with anyone. On tour, he was on his own at night and felt lonely, so he went to bars to look for someone for a one-night stand.

He clearly felt very well on his birthday video, and had no time to even think about being lonely, as he is surrounded by three hundred people having fun in funny costumes. Freddie was distinctly concerned about his guests, talking to everyone as he enjoyed the party-goers wild, amusing jokes. This was the kind of party that reached Freddie's stimulation threshold. Anything less imaginative would have been boring for him. Well, he certainly must have been absorbed here. He had plenty to see and to laugh and joke about.

The following words were possibly his most heart-wrenching:

'Success has brought me millions of pounds and worldwide adulation, but not the thing we all need – a loving relationship. And that is the most bitter type of loneliness. You can be loved by so many thousands of people yet still be the loneliest person. And the frustration of that makes it even worse because it's hard for people to understand that you can be lonely. Can you imagine how terrible it is when you've got everything, but you're still desperately lonely? That is awful beyond words.

You see, loneliness doesn't just mean shut off in a room by yourself, it can be that you're in a crowded area but still be the most lonely person, and that's the most hurtful thing.' (Freddie Mercury)

He said that he was capable of loving; he gave a lot and expected a lot. He was not talking primarily about material issues here, but devotion, attention, genuine concern and love. However, he acknowledged that he liked things to happen as he wanted them to. In a long-term intimate relationship between equal partners, both parties have to accommodate each other. This was a tough nut for Freddie to crack, and he only managed to do it in the last year of his life.

Freddie said his partners tried to compete with him, and kept getting their fingers burned, resulting in the relationship breaking down. But there is no competition in a relationship of equals. Freddie's dominant personality could have forced his partners to 'compete'. Whether he wanted to or not, he evidently stifled them and imposed his will.

A genuine connection between partners is only possible if both act honestly and naturally. If they are fortunate, there will be no unbridgeable gaps. Of course, the first requirement is a strong attraction; falling in love and a long-term love can then be built later. This was the type of relationship Freddie desired.

He needed the kind of partner he found in the other members of Queen: cooperative, intelligent and emotional. He never found anyone like that because it wasn't easy to find someone with his level of intelligence or that of the other members of Queen. It was Jim Hutton's particularly deep love and his eternal devotion that helped the relationship overcome all obstacles, as he was an ordinary but pure-minded, rational, honest and passionate man.

Jim Hutton proved to be the kind of man who could accept the 'problematic' Freddie, with all his baggage. As far as Freddie was concerned, Jim was like an unexpected, wonderful gift from God, but of course, this didn't exempt him from having to heroically endure Freddie's tests.

The thought might have already occurred to Freddie: 'Oh my God, this might be my last chance to have someone by my side if I have to take my final leave.'

(YouTube: Freddie Mercury – 'Living On My Own' (Official Video Remastered)

(YouTube: Freddie Mercury – Living On My Own (Freddie's 39th birthday) – Official Music Video (High Quality)

Queen worked on 'One Vision', written by Roger and released as a single in November, 1985. This was the opening track on the new album, *A Kind of Magic* and one of the songs accompanying the film titled *Iron Eagle*. Martin Luther King Junior's famous 'I have a dream' speech from 1963 inspired them to write the song, or to be precise, Roger 'drew inspiration' from the words. Roger originally wrote the song, but it appears on the album as a Queen song.

The song reached number seven on the UK charts as a purely heavy rock track. Freddie's performance style by then was incomparable, regardless of whether it was a rock or lyrical track. This song is also full of astonishing improvisations, and the music is very forceful, striking like a hammer. It's exceptional; you feel like they're about to explode during the performance. Roger is to be highly congratulated.

In the last line of the song, as if from nowhere, what does a man with a wonderful vision ask for? World peace? Racial equality? Freedom? No, fried chicken!

Queen would often let off steam after recordings with a light-hearted version of the song's lyrics, sometimes changing just one word. And this was what happened at the end of 'One Vision'.

Freddie was referring to this when he said that loyal Queen fans didn't mind if seriousness suddenly turned into parody because, this is more entertaining. We all need laughter and comedy. Life doesn't have to be full of drama. Of course, there are some dramatic moments, but joy and humour are best suited to helping us get through them.

Everyone regarded Freddie as a big clown, in the noblest sense of the word. If he was in a good mood, he was incomparable with his sharp remarks, just like Roger. They were capable of laughing at themselves, proving their greatness as human beings. They didn't believe they were on top of the world, yet artistically, they definitely were in terms of rock music. They knew this, but also knew that nothing lasts forever and that to stay at the top, they constantly had to come up with something new and different; otherwise, they would become boring to themselves and the audience.

And they needed change, to sing or make music differently. The human nervous system needs constant stimulation to function healthily. Freddie, the born genius, was full of creative force, not just when writing or recording songs. He also created a theatre from every minute of his life. Even when he was very ill, he even died in a different way to an ordinary mortal, and sadly we will look further into this at the end of the book.

Their use of video technology became increasingly stunning. The video for this serious song is very entertaining; it's about the band itself. We can see edited parts from recordings of live shows, and even band members relaxing, and a portrait of Queen. It's brilliant and not to be missed. It's nice to see them happy and relaxed during this recording.

(YouTube: Queen 'One Vision' (Official Video)

The video shows Freddie at work, directing the recording. He stands behind the mixing console and even tells Roger how to play the drums, and Roger accepts it because he knows Freddie has the perfect product somewhere in his mind, and will notice where the original idea can be improved. And the German sound engineer, Reinhold Mack, is also sitting next to Freddie. It's worth watching how much work goes into one single recording to reach the level where it can be finalised and when everyone is satisfied with it. This video alone allows us to understand the secret of Queen's greatness, the serious cooperation and the obsessive attention to every detail. We can see how they worked together and how they collaborated to work out what would improve the original idea. We can also observe how Freddie directed everything; he was the composing genius among them. The fact that the others recognised Freddie's genius and were capable of playing their instruments as Freddie envisaged also shows the brilliance of his musical partners. All four of them were incredibly talented. Having four astonishing talents in one band with full commitment is very rare and explains why they were so successful. (I should note they were under the spotlight of cameras, so they had to behave, but I'm sure that in the old days, in the beginning before Freddie went out of control, this was pretty much how things worked. This was why the band members, especially Brian and Roger, often said, 'We're the most democratic band'. Live Aid was a good lesson for all of them. Outstanding cooperation (such as rehearsals, planning, implementing the Live Aid schedule, etc.) produced exceptional results, just as it had in the days before Munich.

One musician they toured with said they were like the four musketeers. One for all and all for one!

This was generally fitting, except for the period when they went through the most frustrating time because of Freddie's extreme behaviour. Brian, Roger and John suffered profoundly from Freddie's whims, but eventually, they decided to stand by the band before Live Aid, which is why Roger and Brian are still together as Queen, though now without John.

When Freddie died, John said, *'There is no Queen without Freddie'*. I fully agree with him, but I don't think Roger and Brian should have to suffer forever for something they could not control.

Brian once said in pain: 'Freddie really fu**ed us up.' He was right, apart from one thing – Freddie was never completely fine, and they could see that too. They knew something wasn't right, and in the end, if they 'only' got 20 years out of him, that was still more than anyone could have expected from one life. Freddie was one in a million.

I should add that whatever Brian or any of them said at any time, what they did for Freddie when he was very ill was unprecedented. The fact is, they didn't crack psychologically when they saw Freddie's agony, but instead put on a good front even though they could have cried from grief. This raises them to the highest pedestal. They gave us a lesson in humanity, which we should all be grateful for, and we should follow their examples when it's our turn.

John now lives in retirement, and to the fans' great regret, doesn't say anything about himself, but we all sincerely hope that he is happy and healthy.

(YouTube: Queen – The Making Of 'One Vision' (High Quality)

This video shows the old, familiar Freddie and not the drug-taking, drinking version of him when he was incapable of working in a disciplined way. Fortunately, he took back control, and the fact that he was capable of giving up cocaine shows his exceptional willpower to survive at all costs. He was a great fighter.

'My Love is Dangerous'

This track on his solo album introduces Freddie's 'love' very honestly.

In this song, he is singing about the emotionally burnt-out, frustrated, selfish, hurtful Freddie, with whom it's not worth picking a fight or embarking on adventures, because he just repeats that his love is dangerous.

This was what he was like in his relationships. Jim is the best example; he wasn't the perfect partner either, but he loved Freddie like nobody else had; with all his heart, as we will soon see. Unfortunately, from the beginning of their love story, Freddie hurt Jim on many occasions.

The lyrics are Freddie's dramatic confession about his 'Bad Guy' side, but the music and the way of singing don't convey this tension that the lyrics have. It doesn't scare anyone.

Of course, in real life when it came to love, Freddie was sweet and kind, when he was in a good mood and his partner behaved as he expected.

But when his mood had changed or the partner made him upset the bubble would burst sooner or later. The word compromise only entered Freddie's vocabulary in the final phase of his life.

(YouTube: 'My Love is Dangerous' -Official lyric video)

Now, let's go back to Freddie and Jim to illustrate Freddie's 'bad guy' side. On one occasion, out of nowhere, he looked at Jim unexpectedly in a bar and just crudely said, *'F**k off'*. Jim got up and went home to Freddie's house, gathered his belongings, and went home. Later, just after dawn, Freddie kept calling at Jim's home until the landlord couldn't take it anymore and evicted Jim. Freddie then made his move and sweet-talked him into coming back. Fortunately, Jim forgave him, although Freddie had struck him below the belt. Freddie asked him to move to Munich with him, and Jim's answer was 'yes'. A quarter of an hour later, Freddie asked another question: 'And if I move back to London, will you come with me?' Jim replied that he would think about it, and Freddie left it there. Later, Freddie moved back to London, and Jim moved back with him, only to be told by Freddie to get lost. This was Jim's fourth test, which he didn't cope with well, but at the time, he was still an apprentice to the master, though he later learned how to get through the tests.

Freddie hated it if someone took advantage of him and wanted to scrounge off him, but when Jim wanted to work so that he didn't have to depend on Freddie, that was different. 'You and your f**king independence,' Freddie shouted angrily, whereas all he needed to say was 'Look, I love you, and I see you as my partner. I want you to be with me all the time. I've got enough money for both of us, more than enough.'

Not only would Jim have given up the idea of working, but he would also probably have hugged Freddie and been moved to tears. Freddie knew very well what he should have said, but he could not control his anger when he should have, and his excessive impulsiveness continually got him into trouble.

'Princes of The Universe'

One of Freddie's songs appears on the album, *A Kind of Magic*, with him as the sole writer. He also co-wrote two of the songs on this album with John.

Freddie wrote the song, 'Princes of The Universe', for the film, *Highlander*. The song could be heard in the movie and was also the theme tune for the TV series spin-off, so almost everyone knows it.

'The music backing this fanciful narrative is appropriately grand, matching swaggering mid-tempo verse melodies to a breathless, high-voltage chorus that builds to a bombastic peak. Queen's recording of 'Princes Of The Universe' is a stomping hard rock delight, layering, squalling guitars over a throbbing mid-tempo backbeat during the verses and speeding up to a furious blitz on the chorus. Freddie Mercury delivers the lyrics in an operatically powerful style, and the group supplies appropriately regal backing harmonies throughout.'

(Donald Guarisco, Allmusic)

On first reading, this expert description sounded to me like a foreign language, as I'm not a musician, just a music lover, but I wanted to quote the opinion of a music specialist. The description is worthy of attention. Donald Guarisco clarifies the kind of abilities Queen had, and shows how marvellously a genuine music specialist can describe in words what he has heard.

I think of his description while listening to the music; without even concentrating on the English lyrics, I can sense all that I've read in the quote. The chorus is breathtaking, the peak is climactic, and I notice the 'squalling' sound of the guitars even more.

This is why it's good to have a description from a music critic who evaluates the song realistically. Just listening to the music, the experience is different from concentrating on the lyrics, especially if English is not your native language. And in any case, words are more difficult to understand in a song. However, the language of music is universal, and the emotions come across even if we don't understand the words.

In a certain sense, the song's lyrics were adapted to the film's subject. The main character is immortal and has been fighting other immortals for decades because *'only one of them can survive'* at the end of the fight. The main character defeats his final opponent, and his reward was mortality. A real happy ending, wouldn't you say?

An extended TV series was also made from the film, so Queen made their way into millions of homes worldwide.

The final struggle takes place in New York's Madison Square Garden, where Queen had so many successful gigs. This must have evoked some pleasant memories for Freddie. Ironically, he was writing music based on the story of an immortal man at a time when he was probably aware he was living the final chapter of his life, or at least he didn't have much chance of survival.

Freddie's fighting ability and constant combat readiness resembles that of the Highlander, Duncan MacLeod. It's worth noting the eerie parallels with Freddie's life in the song's lyrics.

*'Here we are, born to be kings
We're the princes of the universe
Here we belong, fighting to survive
In a world with the darkest powers'*

When Freddie wrote these lyrics, HIV was seen as the darkest force because there was no hope of survival. Freddie also thought he was born to be king, the king of pop and rock music, and on their last tour, he put on a crown and a regal robe.

'People say you've had your day' – the lyrics continue – *'Fly to the moon and reach for the stars, with my sword and head held high, got to pass the test first time'*. Freddie had indeed had his day. He had become successful and had reached all the heights he had desired. He could hold his head up high in pride, like a star, but the question was, would he pass his next test with a more reliable testing method?

The song's lyrics continue: *'I know that people talk about me. I hear it every day, but I can prove them wrong'*.

The rumours about Freddie's health started circulating at the time of Live Aid in 1985. One day, a reporter called one of Queen's offices and asked John, who happened to be available, whether the rumours that Freddie had caught the virus were true. John replied that it wasn't true, and he expected the press to report that the rumours had been denied. At the time, John didn't know for certain, because Freddie hadn't told them he was infected.

In the last line of the song, Freddie declares: *'I'm here for your love, and I'll make my stand'*. He may have thought he wouldn't give in to the rumours and HIV. I assume he was thinking of Jim's love.

From the lyrics, it seems Freddie had developed a strong belief that even if he was infected, he would recover. His hope came in part from his natural desire for life. He was young and wanted to carry on living, and also because Freddie's doctor had said that, in rare cases, an HIV infection could be overcome with a very strong immune system. Freddie must have taken hope from this. The problem was that his lifestyle and his constant fear of being abandoned and alone had dragged his immune system down, and importantly, Freddie had kept the HIV infection secret and had put off going to a specialist, who could have given him hope.

Freddie finally got unconditional love from Jim, even though he didn't survive the dreaded disease. Life is the best playwright. Freddie's story is more dramatic than the story of any immortal man, and although he shaped reality more or less consciously, he certainly didn't want his life's story to end like this. Freddie's hit became immortal through the film, just as he did through this and all his other songs.

The other outstanding song in the film was 'Who Wants To Live Forever', written by Brian. This was not Freddie's song, so I don't want to interpret it, but this is one of the most heartbreaking songs written during Freddie's terrible time. Of course, Brian didn't know what would happen, but I can imagine the pain Freddie felt when he sang it.

In Queen's video clip, Brian sang the first verse softly and almost painfully. Then Freddie sang the next part in his own theatrical, star-like manner, as if he was in an opera, but just as sadly and resignedly as Brian. It's very traumatic. The interplay of these two sounds and the more powerful, passionate song enhances the dramatic effect. Roger's drums stand out from the interplay like giant heartbeats. The masterful interaction of Brian's guitar and the symphonic orchestra also provides an unparalleled sound. The instrumentation raises the song to a phenomenal masterpiece, one of the most beautiful pieces of film music ever written. We all must be very grateful to Brian for this song.

(YouTube - Queen – 'Who Wants To Live Forever' Official Video)

The main character in the film certainly didn't want to live forever, but nor did he want to die such a cruel death by being beheaded. It's a shocking idea that there is only one way of taking his life, by cutting off his head. It sounds terrible, but this is what gives the film its dramatic twist. Immortality has a high price, eternally fighting for his life, as Freddie too had to fight until the end of his life.

'There's no chance for us, it's all decided for us' – the song continues – 'as if this world has only one sweet moment set aside for us, who wants, and who dares to live forever, when love must die?' These lyrics are moving, condensing the tragedy of the film's main character, Freddie's life, and the tragedy of people's lives into a few sentences. Freddie no longer had a chance; everything had been decided when he sang this song. His beautiful love was also condemned to death. Both he and Jim had tears in their eyes when they talked about what Jim would do after Freddie passed.

Jim probably also died inside for a while after Freddie had gone, just like Brian, John and Roger.

'Love Me Like There Is No Tomorrow'

Freddie's last song on the *Mr Bad Guy* album,'Love Me Like There Is No Tomorrow', is dedicated to Barbara, as a farewell song to her and Munich. However, their friendship did not end in 1985 because they met again several times. In 1991 she even visited Freddie in Montreux, in his new flat.

The song is about Freddie's life in Munich and his permanent departure. The first verse is evidently about Winnie, who always killed conversations because he always had to be right. When Freddie got caught in love, it was like he had stepped into quicksand, because Winnie always ruined their plans.

The next verse is about Freddie's departure; he was finally ready to leave Munich permanently for his own sake; he had packed his bags and felt as if he was leaving home, but he only had a one-way ticket; there would be no return.

Before leaving, he turned to Barbara, his best friend, and asked her to love him as if it was their last chance to love each other, because they had no future together.

They drifted apart – suggesting that they hadn't had sexual relations since Freddie's test. Given that they were both on the wrong track, it was better not to continue the sex-drugs-alcohol-sex-drugs-alcohol lifestyle, because there are limits that must be recognised. This song reveals that Freddie's test was positive, even if he hoped the result might be a mistake. He sang that he had never felt so low in all his life. At the time, a relationship with Jim was still just a possibility. For the time being, Freddie didn't attach much hope to their future because of his earlier failures in love, and in any case, he was terminally ill, at least according to the prognosis for HIV. His future was uncertain, so he asked Barbara again to love him one last time. Freddie knew that Barbara loved him dearly, but she was a woman. Anyway, Freddie didn't want to commit himself. It was Jim he was attracted to at that time.

Barbara and Freddie didn't actually say goodbye to one another. One day they were together, the next Freddie suddenly decided to leave everything behind. He had to force himself, knowing it wouldn't be easy for him to kick his drug habit, lose Barbara, and renounce his 'free' lifestyle, but he was also aware that he couldn't carry on if he wanted to survive. Freddie went through a dramatic conflict because of the frightening end game. He had to end the life he had conducted at supersonic speed, and he couldn't live the life of Mr Fahrenheit any longer.

In October 1985, Rock Hudson, the good-looking American actor and a real ladies' man, died of AIDS under very unfortunate circumstances. As a final hope, he decided to travel to France for treatment, but collapsed at the airport and was taken to hospital. In the end, he received the wanted treatment, but it didn't save his life. He was a good friend of President Reagan, but Nancy Reagan refused to help him.

The Reagan administration, like the Thatcher government, allocated minimal funds to research. When it turned out that nothing could help the actor, for some inexplicable reason the hospital 'forced' the actor to announce he was suffering from AIDS in a press release. At the time, apart from his lover, no one knew he was gay.

Paul Prenter noticed that Freddie was especially interested in Rock Hudson's death and the subsequent events. 'Courtesy' of the press, Rock Hudson's artistic achievements were destroyed, or at least the press did everything possible to generate contempt, rather than pity for him.

Freddie was probably horrified at the impact it would have on his image and his fellow artists' lives if it were revealed that he also had AIDS.

According to the book written by Matt Richards & Mark Langthorne, Freddie repeated the test at the end of 1985 with the latest, more reliable test, which also showed a positive result.

This is probably just an assumption, because nobody has confirmed it as being factual but at the end of 1985, ELISA was a more reliable test, so it's natural to assume that Freddie would have wanted to know whether the previous positive test was correct. Given that he left Munich suddenly, this was probably what happened.

Even before Christmas, Freddie subjected Jim to another test. Whenever they ended up in a bar, Freddie began flirting with someone else. Two weeks before Christmas, Jim decided he'd had enough of the games and demanded that Freddie decide whether he wanted to be with him or not. To add weight to his words, Jim packed a few things and left Freddie. A few days later, Freddie called Jim and lured him back with an apology, something he never did before.

They spent Christmas together in Freddie' new house, with quite a few guests, celebrating in style. Freddie generously handed out cheques in large amounts together with gifts. He gave Jim 1,000 pounds, as he did the others, to buy something they wanted.

From this gesture, it seems Freddie wasn't aware how insulting it could be for a partner to give money as a gift, but interestingly, Jim wasn't offended. Through this gesture, Freddie devalued Jim to the level of his other employees, his subordinates. This could mean that Freddie had difficulty making a distinction between a partner and an employee.

They spent New Year's Eve in a bar again, where Freddie took another man onto the dance floor. Jim got angry, pinned Freddie to the wall, and again demanded that he decide what he wanted.

Freddie and his friends, who had arrived together, responded by leaving Jim in the bar without a coat or wallet. This was Freddie's answer. Typically, nobody told Jim they were leaving. It seems that Freddie's friends hadn't yet accepted the fact that he could have someone more important than them. Maybe they were hoping Freddie would dump him impulsively too, or that sooner or later Jim would get fed up.

Jim walked home wearing next to nothing in the freezing weather. When he finally reached the house, Freddie was waiting for him at the door; he knew he was to blame. Jim started shouting at him, and Freddie dragged him to the bedroom, waited for Jim to calm down, and then said he only wanted to find out whether Jim was jealous.

Freddie didn't even consider that he could simply have just asked Jim. He was probably jealous of Jim's old friend, who Jim had invited to the Christmas party. It seems Jim believed 'what's good for the goose is good for the gander', but he was mistaken.

Freddie was cruel to him again and again, so Jim had to learn his lesson. After the New Year's Eve party, Freddie announced that Jim and his friends had stolen a vase that had disappeared. By now, Jim had had enough of the accusations and told Freddie that he would go and visit all his friends, but if he didn't find the vase, he would never return.

Freddie replied, 'It's okay, it was only a vase'. It turned out later that Joe had broken the vase before the celebrations and had thrown it in the bin, but didn't dare tell Freddie. I wouldn't rule out the possibility that Joe had also been playing the game, as he was also jealous of Freddie.

Fortunately, Jim was so much in love that these 'minor' inconveniences didn't prevent him from staying with Freddie. I don't think it's very likely that financial considerations were involved, but of course, it can't be ruled out. Being dropped into a land of milk and honey must have been no small matter for someone who had previously worked for 70 pounds a week and lived in a rented room.

I imagine many people would have been upset when hearing statements like: 'You and your friends'. Freddie denigrated Jim and had effectively insulted him because of a vase, which he could have replaced with a thousand others, but instead, he attacked Jim without any solid evidence.

Freddie poisoned the honeymoon period for Jim, but somehow Jim always put the hurt and insults behind him.

In addition, Mary was still Freddie's official partner, so Jim trailed behind them at every major event, which he 'understood', because he hadn't come out as gay either.

It's astonishing that Jim continually tolerated this level of humiliation to maintain the deception. Freddie was a generous, caring and emotional man, but he had to play these terrible games with Jim and everyone else before Jim to keep up appearances because of the general hatred of gay people.

32. *Magic Tour* (1986)

Queen started the tour of the album in Stockholm, in July and finished in August in Stevenage, in the UK. They gave 26 concerts throughout Europe. During the tour, Freddie made two remarks about touring, saying it was very tiring for him, and he wouldn't be doing it forever.

Freddie might have already considered giving up touring, given that insurance companies in America had begun to examine whether artists were infected with HIV as grounds for exclusion, before issuing an insurance policy.

Freddie's declaration that he wasn't HIV-positive was enough in Britain and Europe, but they wouldn't have settled for this in America. Freddie probably hated the US by then for placing their videos on the blacklist due to their 'homosexual' content ('I Want To Break Free'). When he told the other band members that he wouldn't tour there again, he was serious.

Queen recorded the new album with an unusual approach. While John and Freddie worked with Mack in Munich, Brian and Roger worked with David Richards in the Montreux studio. In any case, the band's members had earlier started working on solo albums or performed alongside other bands even before Freddie's first solo record. These solo performances began at the end of the 1982 tour when Brian said they'd had enough of each other to such an extent that they almost hated each other. So, they decided to have a short break and didn't release an album in 1983. Instead, they began working on the following year's album.

The other band members may have suspected something was wrong with Freddie from his comments and the rumours, but they didn't ask why he didn't want to perform any more concerts, even more so because he had previously made such statements when he was tired, and they thought he just needed a rest.

I guess that, because of their friendship and 15 years' working together and their additional commitments, they didn't even consider the possibility that Freddie wouldn't tell them such important news.

Freddie didn't tell Jim either, and I don't think Jim considered the possibility that a star like Freddie, who visited bars regularly, could already be infected, as there were no apparent signs, and in any case, love makes fools of even the wisest men.

However, Freddie knew that Jim wasn't a believer in one-night stands, and so there was a chance he wasn't infected. However, he couldn't have been sure because lovers don't always tell each other every detail of who they have been with, where and when, and in particular, they don't talk about their casual adventures.

Whatever was on Freddie's mind when he got to know Jim, which was before his final test, he probably still believed he would recover. By the time the second HIV test was completed at the end of 1985, he must have thought it didn't matter anymore; Jim was probably already infected, so Freddie probably felt it was better, in his own interests, not to talk about it. He must have had legitimate fears that Jim would leave him for good after their next argument, and would shout from the rooftops that Freddie was HIV positive.

The opening track on the album, 'A Kind Of Magic', was released as a single in March and reached number three on the UK charts, and the top 10 in several other European countries.

Apart from the five songs on the album that were written for the film, Highlander, they wrote three other songs not related to the film. Freddie collaborated on two of them, which were originally written by John.

The single, 'A Kind Of Magic', was Roger's idea, but Freddie reworked the song. When they finished the album, the four of them again went off in four different directions. In May, however, they had to start rehearsals for the huge tour to promote the new album.

The tour included Budapest, which was seen as a sensation in the West, because Queen was the first rock group to play behind the Iron Curtain. Lesley-Ann Jones devotes an entire chapter of her book to the Budapest gig. The concert recording can be seen on YouTube.

Most of us who lived in Hungary at the time did not see ourselves as living behind the Iron Curtain. Nevertheless, it was a big thing for Queen to perform in Budapest, not because they were from the West, but because it was Queen.

There's a big difference. In the 70s and 80s, Hungary could boast the kind of pop and rock musicians who could have competed with any Western band, apart from Queen. Omega, LGT, Illés, Piramis and Bergendi are just some of the biggest names. I regard Gábor Presser as the Hungarian Elton John.

There was genuine peace in Hungary during the time of the Iron Curtain. There were no starving masses, and nobody lived on the street. Everybody had work, even the few people who were illiterate. There were no shootings or knifing incidents on the streets, and we felt safe. All our food was bio, grown in the gardens of village farmers, where the sun ripened the fruit and vegetables.

Even the smallest villages had a school, nursery, two or three churches, grocery stores, pubs, a pharmacy, doctor's surgery, dentist, community centre, library and police station.

The most serious crime was theft, which was committed disproportionately by a specific ethnic group.

There were no super-rich and no billionaires, but then nobody really missed them. Nor were there any drugs, and nobody missed them either, there was no organised crime, and we managed fine without that too.

We could attend university for free. Medicines were almost free. Apartments were cheap. One of the fundamental principles of socialist culture, perhaps Lenin's only smart phrase, was: 'Learn, learn and learn.' One of my workplaces at the time was in a factory's office. 'Work has become a matter of honour and glory' was written on the factory building. This reminds me of Japan. People set up cooperatives in the villages, which meant the community had farming machinery, and everyone who took part in the cooperative's work was given animal fodder and wages. The fodder was enough for a family to supply its own requirements for meat. Everyone had a garden, and there was plenty of bio-fruit and vegetables. Hungary was in an exceptionally favourable situation compared to many other socialist countries because its leaders weren't corrupt.

The Soviet army was there, but they didn't bother anyone. The soldiers lived in the barracks or camped in the forests and were invited to events as guests of honour.

The one-party political system was undoubtedly odd, but there wasn't a harsh dictatorship, apart from a relatively short period after the takeover of power in 1956 and for a while afterwards.

Freddie sang the Hungarian folk song, *'Tavaszi szél vizet áraszt' (The spring wind makes the waters rise)* nicely, which is known to almost every Hungarian because we all learned it in primary school. Of course, the audience appreciated the effort. It's not easy for native English speakers to speak Hungarian, but Freddie even learned Japanese words by heart to please the crowds there, and yet Japanese is even more difficult than Hungarian. Hungarians loved Queen as much as Westerners, and so did people in other socialist countries.

But no doubt, people are more interested in Freddie than life in Hungary back then. Maybe I am just feeling nostalgic, like most of my peers.

So, Queen arrived in Hungary in July, 1986. Unfortunately, I was not aware at that time how big a deal it was, so I didn't go to the concert. At that time I was a fan of Pink Floyd, and the best Hungarian bands.

Queen prepared for this tour with extra lighting on the largest stages and at concert venues with the capacity for the largest crowds. There was a crowd of 82,000 at Budapest's Népstadion, and it was a full house. Tickets were sold out in advance, like all the other venues. One of Hungarian television's most intelligent reporters, Endre Acél, interviewed Freddie in Budapest. Acél asked him whether this tour was the start of a long-term relationship with Hungary. Freddie simply replied, 'I'll come back if I'm still alive.' It was a shocking comment from a young man aged 40. Acél Endre was stunned, as Freddie didn't say anything else, but turned around and walked away. Acél Endre probably wasn't aware how much Freddie hated the press. He couldn't have known that the Hungarian press didn't write cruel, unsubstantiated comments about valued guests, at least not at that time. Things have changed since then.

Freddie first wore the royal robe and crown, embellished with ermine, in Paris when he said goodbye to the crowd, crowning himself king while a recording of the British national anthem, God Save The Queen, recorded version was played as the band marched off stage.

Royalty typically wore their crowns and robes on special occasions. And Freddie did the same. The occasion really was special.

Freddie intended these concerts to be a farewell, and wanted to make them memorable for everyone. This resulted in large-scale events, with bigger stages, more lighting, and royal robes for the royal frontman, and a royal band!

There was no bigger band in the world at the time, in terms of the show, the music, or the performance, and there hasn't been one since. Nobody has managed to fill their shoes. Queen built this far-reaching career so methodically that it was impossible to imitate them. It took 15 years' hard work and cost an enormous amount of money to build the giant stages, and it reached the point where nine 15-metre-long trucks were needed to transport materials from one location to the next to build the stages on time.

They were already building a stage on one site while dismantling the stage at another location, and playing a gig at a third venue. According to Brian, the logistics, the technical equipment, lighting, projectors, transport, and the workers' wages were so expensive that 1986 was the first year that Queen earned money on their concerts. Until then, they had continually reinvested all the money into making the show bigger, including more extras, and making it more special every time.

Freddie played a very active role in everything and he always wanted to know about everything. The ideas came from him and the band, while the implementation was the task of their extremely experienced lighting technicians, sound technicians, and logistical managers. It was a fantastic achievement. Careful work was required by a large number of people for the giant stage, which was potentially hazardous, and for the technology to work perfectly and without any accidents.

The legacy they left behind is still alive after more than three decades, so much so that the live recording of their final Wembley concert had 4 million views on YouTube between June 2019 and November 2020, just this one concert recording alone.

Freddie wanted to make sure people remembered him as a fit and healthy star, as he didn't know what the next few years had in store for him.

The Magic tour was a huge success, with more than one million people seeing them live. The Wembley and Budapest concerts can be seen on YouTube. They really are magical. **Freddie is considered one of the best vocalists of all time.** He sang everything exceptionally well at these concerts. Listening to them is an unforgettable experience.

And even on video, the experience is sensational because the cameras often show Roger, Brian and John too. Banging the drums for almost two hours non-stop was an astonishing physical performance. Roger's voice is incredibly exotic, with an exciting sound, and perfectly complements Freddie's voice. The vocals are exceptional. The composition of the songs they played was also fantastic; the audience received the new songs very well.

Peter Freestone wrote in his book:

'Freddie always used to say that although drum-machines are supposed to be infallible, Roger could be guaranteed never to miss even one single beat'.

Brian's guitar solo in the concert was awesome; I thought it was three guitars playing simultaneously and at times couldn't believe my ears, or that this really was just one guitar, producing astonishing sounds in wonderful harmony.

Brian was voted the best guitarist in 2020 by Guitar Magazine.

According to Peter Freestone's book: *'Freddie never knew anyone better at working out harmonies than Brian and always relied on him for the end result where musical harmony was concerned. John is John. Freddie knew John was like the proverbial rock and could always be relied on'.*

These final gigs in the UK were especially memorable for British fans; two nights at Wembley and one night at the huge open-air stage in Knebworth Park near London, Freddie's final live show on 9 August, 1986. A significant date in rock history.

This was the venue for Queen's largest paying audience in Britain, with a total crowd of 120,000.

This was a worthy farewell at the end of a long series of concerts, befitting Queen's greatness, if only the final act in 1990-91 hadn't been so horrendous.

Looking back on their Wembley Stadium gigs, this was what Brian May said:

'1986 was a great pinnacle for us, I think we were damn good at that point. Freddie was stunning and had developed this amazing way of dealing with a whole stadium. We all contributed to that, but Freddie was the great connecting point.

Wembley stadium is special because it's a home town, and it's a legend. We played it as part of Live Aid, which was a terrific blast, a terrific buzz, and come back and play it ourselves and sold out for two nights and even still have more tickets on demand. It could have been 4-5 nights for us, so it was a big, big occasion for us.

I think it was somewhere in Spain when a little argument broke out and John got quite iffy about something, and Freddie just turned around and said, we are not going to do this forever, maybe it will be the last time, and that was a bit of a jolt.

I didn't know whether that was an instant response or overreaction, or there was something else in his mind, and I think he already knew what he was going to be dealing with.

The great thing was on tour, you could put aside things to a point and get on with the consuming business of touring because it was great fun, but I think he knew at the end of this tour, he has to look into this, and he already told us in a way - you know - this may not happen again.

We knew each other very well, and we just glued together; it was a wonderful feeling, really, and it is quite a shock to look back to those moments'.

(YouTube: Queen - The Road To Wembley Full Documentary)

At one point during the Wembley concert, Freddie announced to the audience the rumours weren't true, Queen wasn't going to break up and would work together until they died. He was telling the truth, even though wasn't very precise. He meant until one of them died, but the two phrases had the same meaning. As John said, there was no Queen without Freddie, just as there would have been no Queen without Brian, John or Roger.

Freddie fought to the end to make sure they finished the contractually required albums. He couldn't even stand up, but kept working as long as he could sing, as long as a sound came out of his throat, and not because he had to, but to have a reason to get out of bed.

Freddie's announcement was received by happy cheering from the audience.

Knowing he was already ill, this statement was quite macabre. As I listened to him, it seemed he was completely confident and optimistic about Queen's future. He was very convincing, laughing and joking. What a character!

He arranged for a special bus to take his closest friends, and even his doctor, to this concert. And he invited the 'New York Daughters', as Freddie called his closest friends from New York.

It's not hard to imagine why; Freddie knew and sensed that this was his final appearance.

He sang as beautifully as he could, knowing he didn't want to perform anymore. He wanted to make sure that his fans never ever forget his last performance.

His heart was probably breaking as he did his comedy routine. Maybe it was just the businessman in him, encouraging people to buy the records and stand by Queen. If his announcement was intended to serve a business purpose, it worked. Their last three albums all got to number one, bringing Queen platinum and gold records. Live At Wembley (the concert recording) got to number two in sales and charts. Naturally, this wasn't all a result of his announcement, but also reflected the outstanding quality of the albums and these wonderful gigs in 1986.

Perspiration was dripping off Freddie at the concerts, and his voice broke from time to time as he performed at a crazy pace; the tempo was faster than on the records, as if they wanted to play all concerts for the next five years, for the rest of Freddie's life, on their final tour. Freddie raged incessantly around the giant stage. 26 two-hour concerts after an 18-month hiatus represented a superhuman effort and required tremendous stamina.

I tried to imagine Brian, Roger and John's reaction when they found out the truth, and I wondered how they viewed Freddie's announcement about the band's future.

At the end of the Knebworth Park show Freddie also remarked to Brian:

'Oh, I can't f**king do this anymore, my whole body's wracked with pain!'

He could have told his mates politely and firmly, 'Sorry guys, I'm tired and don't feel I can do this anymore. Let's think about what else we can do together'. The 15 years of working together and the sense of belonging, which was always apparent one way or another, was enough reason for any of them to communicate as diplomatically as possible that they wanted some kind of radical change. Freddie was usually the diplomat in the band, but this time, unfortunately, his sense of diplomacy abandoned him, though it was no wonder in his terrible situation.

I guess he must have been terrified of the disease and didn't want to give anyone the chance of finding out that he was infected. So, he preferred to say he was tired. In any case, they were all very tired at the end of the tour and had had enough of everything.

So, he employed his tried and tested tactic again; attack is the best form of defence, and made these statements in a tone that didn't allow any questions from the others about the problem. This was generally how he resolved delicate issues.

They all knew they depended on each other musically, because their solo careers never really took off. Queen was better than any of them as solo artists, including Freddie.

If they'd had enough of each other, the main reason was they had to spend together too much time and all of them were tired. In addition, they usually worked through all the songs together, and the one who came up with the idea got the royalties. Of course, given that Freddie delivered the most songs, he earned much more than the other band members. Originally, it was his idea to pay the royalties to the person whose idea the song was. Fairness is the basis for a good working relationship regarding financial matters. We can't really see any other examples of album songs not being written by the band but by its individual members.

Freddie probably kept his spirits up with cocaine and vodka, enabling him to see the tour through to the end.

He hadn't yet given up drugs and drinking, as testified by one of his earlier friends Chris Chesney, who had played music with Freddie in the band, Sour Milk Sea for a short time in 1970. They met by chance during recordings for 'The Great Pretender'. Freddie received Chris as a friend, offering him champagne while drinking vodka, as if 'it was going out of fashion'. He also offered Chris some cocaine, as reported by Mark Blake.

The album was released before the tour and reached number one in the UK. They went on tour with this positive feeling, huge self-confidence and satisfaction.

Freddie no longer visited nightclubs while on tour, gave up the one-night stands and looked after his voice. Everyone noticed the change. Roger asked Jim what he had done to Freddie. Jim must have been very proud that Roger attributed the change to him, but I'm convinced this wasn't the case.

Freddie had been in love with partners before, but this never stopped him from being unfaithful. It was his fear of AIDS that caused the change, and he didn't want any scandals on Queen's final tour. All he wanted was for it to be memorable, both for him and the audience, and he likely felt tired and unwell.

The extent of the change can best be measured by the clothes he wore on stage. There were no more tight-fitting jeans, no cut-off, sleeveless vests like he'd worn at Live Aid a year earlier. Sexuality was no longer evident. On the contrary, he wore a loose T-shirt with a fantasy character on it, distinctly asexual loose pants and bright yellow jacket. Freddie loved bright yellow colours, which usually symbolises happiness, pleasure and satisfaction, but can have a completely different meaning on an individual level.

Even before the tour, Freddie started to stay out late at night when he was living with Jim in Garden Lodge, but his friends had warned Jim that Freddie regularly appeared in bars at night, hunting for other men.

Jim wanted to be sure about what was going on. It turned out that Freddie had spent a night in his former apartment with a young guy. Jim knew this because he was secretly following Joe, who went for Freddie in the morning.

Jim didn't say anything to Freddie, choosing to avoid a scene. Instead, he decided to go out one night and have some fun, and didn't go home at all that night.

Freddie angrily kicked Jim out of his house, and Jim moved out, thinking it was high time to break up because Freddie wasn't willing to be faithful to him.

A few days later, Freddie calmed down and begged Jim to return, and Jim acquiesced relatively easily. Just the two of them went to Dave Clark's rock musical opening, which featured Freddie's song, *Time*. This makes me think this change wasn't down to Jim, or at least not just to him. Freddie might rightly have been afraid that Jim would just leave him one day because, despite being in love with Freddie, Jim's pride wouldn't allow Freddie to constantly make a fool out of him, or at least not to the extent that Freddie did to his other partners.

Freddie did not understand the concept of loyalty, which can be attributed to the fact that he didn't spend his teenage years, when he began to be interested in sexuality, in a family environment where he could have learned about generally accepted social norms, such as being faithful, intimacy and the importance of these norms. In contrast, he lived in a house with eight boys. I imagine that back then they had no rules about who they played sexual games with, since they were all children and didn't recognise adult rules. By the time he left the institution at the age of 16, he would have thought it was normal behaviour for boys, and as an adult, for men to form a family, as they did Ashleigh House, Panchgani. In one of his letters quoted earlier, Freddie wrote to his parents: 'Here in Ashleigh House, we are like a second family'.

This was the family model he developed in his adult life when he surrounded himself with gay men at home and looked on everyone as family members, where he was the head of the family, holding the reins. The role of 'wife' was destined for Jim and, to a certain extent, constituted a subordinate position in Freddie's own family, similar to the role his mother had in Zanzibar. She was a homemaker and was financially dependent on his father. Similarly, Jim depended on Freddie financially once Freddie had employed him as a gardener. (This is true, even though Freddie talked about Jim as his husband.) It's a well-known fact that women wear trousers in some families and other families, this is the men's role, or they are considered the primary decision-makers.

This was the model Freddie learned, which worked in his childhood and adulthood when he shared an apartment with the band members and other friends. Though, at that time, he hadn't yet had physical relationships with other men, at least not with his flatmates, because he kept his homosexuality secret from everyone.

If Jim hadn't accepted the position of a gardener, his uncertain situation meant he would have had to ask Freddie for an allowance sooner or later, which Freddie also knew. In any case, Jim loved to keep the garden tidy and would have done so even if he hadn't been paid. But Freddie paid Jim such a high salary that it wasn't worth him changing 'jobs'. Freddie wanted to make sure Jim stayed with him.

At that time, he often told Jim he loved him and asked Jim whether he felt the same. Jim loved him and always reassured Freddie of this, but he wasn't as romantic as Freddie, and neither was he a man of many words.

Freddie and Jim didn't talk about the future of their relationship until just before Freddie's positive AIDS test in 1987, however, Jim had decided to commit himself when he bought Freddie a ring for his 40th birthday. Freddie wore the ring, but only at home, as he was afraid of the press.

During their last tour, Freddie was asked in a TV interview in Barcelona who his favourite singer was. Freddie's reply must have surprised the reporter and the viewers because he mentioned Montserrat Caballé as the singer he most admired at the time. Caballé was born in Barcelona, so some may have thought he was just being polite, but he wasn't. He had really been impressed by the opera singer's stunning and powerful soprano voice.

After the interview, Caballé's older brother, who was also her manager, called Jim Beach to say the artist would like to meet Freddie, and asked if he would write a song for her to sing at the opening ceremony of the Olympics. Freddie hesitated because he considered the world of opera so sublime that he wasn't sure he could write a song for an opera singer, but in the end, he agreed to meet Montserrat in the spring of 1987.

33. A Holiday for Life

After a worthy celebration of Freddie's 40th birthday, Freddie, Jim and Joe travelled to Japan. He promised Jim this holiday would be the experience of a lifetime for them.

The holiday cost over 1 million pounds, which ensured that Freddie's promise would be fulfilled, at least in part, but Freddie made this holiday memorable in every respect.

The first surprise for Jim was that they didn't go straight to the hotel after the 12-hour flight, but to the giant Seibu department store that had been kept open for Freddie, and where Freddie went shopping for four hours. Freddie's battle cry was 'shop until you drop'.

Naturally, they stayed in the hotel's most exclusive Imperial Suite, where Joe even had a kitchen, his own separate room, and a small living room.

Jim hardly slept that night due to jet lag, and after breakfast, Freddie was ready for another adventure: 'Let's go shopping!'

Jim was up to the task, and they went from store to store and spent two hours just shopping for silk ties, which Freddie had never worn before. When they finally returned to the hotel, they had difficulty entering the lobby because Seibu had delivered the items Freddie had bought the previous evening, so there were mountains of boxes on both sides of the entrance; he had managed to spend 250,000 pounds in one evening. No wonder, as one pair of chopsticks cost 75 pounds. Poor Joe had the job of drawing up a list of the purchased items, so they would know what to expect back home when the goods arrived in London.

Freddie's escort was their Japanese event organiser, a nice, pretty young lady called Misa, who invited them to her own birthday party where Freddie met a Japanese painter. Freddie persuaded him to paint a picture for him, explaining in detail what he should draw, which was fine, but he even stipulated what kind of brush strokes to use. Freddie had painted as a child and had a huge collection of French impressionist and Japanese paintings, so he knew exactly what he wanted.

Misa took them to the opening show of *Cats* (by Andrew Lloyd Webber) at a theatre. After they had taken their seats, it turned out Freddie was the guest of honour. To Freddie's great surprise, the audience gave them a standing ovation. Freddie hated these kinds of surprises, so Misa was reproached.

They visited the Golden Pavilion in Kyoto and the ancient city district. Freddie was captivated by the wonderful garden in the temple and the few million boutiques in the city district. He bought an old, portable terracotta barbecue in an antique shop, even though they didn't have the exact shade of colour he wanted. I can imagine how much this annoyed Freddie.

He dragged Jim through every square centimetre of a huge department store in Osaka, but didn't buy anything and just showed him his favourite fish, the koi, swimming around in a pool.

These fish really are beautiful. It's no wonder Freddie wanted a few of them. The pool in his garden was almost ready for them.

Day in and day out, they went from store to store until Freddie and Jim came across an exhibition room where masterpieces by the most prominent Japanese artists were on show. Given that these objects were seen as a national treasure, they had to be exhibited before being sold. Of course, Freddie would have loved to have bought some of them, but didn't understand that it was simply impossible. He kept murmuring in Misa's ear until eventually, the exhibition was given a new title: *'With the kind permission of Mr Freddie Mercury, from his private collection'.* Freddie spent half a million pounds buying a few items from the collection of wood and metal lacquer works, as he adored these Japanese works of art.

Poor Jim had an upset stomach, and was confined to bed for a few days. Freddie took good care of him and didn't want to leave his side. He arranged for a doctor to be called and a phone call to be made to Jim's workplace to say he would be returning late. Then, Jim still was working as a barber. They postponed their return journey to ensure that Jim enjoyed the holiday. As soon as he was better, they were back shopping! Freddie bought a red kimono for himself, but there was one problem – he couldn't find an antique kimono holder anywhere, the kind he had seen in a museum. Eventually, somebody found one for him, and Freddie was relieved that his kimono would have a stand.

Jim wrote the following in the book about their trip to Japan:

'It had been a very romantic trip. Freddie didn't need to ask if I had enjoyed it all, the happy expressions I'd worn on my face for three weeks had said it all'.

It seems he really wanted to please Freddie or really liked shopping too; he showed admirable endurance to keep up with Freddie, in part because of his energy and partly due to his hyperactivity. In any event, Freddie held a master's course for him on the astonishingly beautiful world of Japan.

Jim also enjoyed the pantomime theatre and the musical *Cats*, even though it was performed in Japanese, of course.

They arrived back at Heathrow dead tired because their flight was significantly delayed, and an unpleasant surprise awaited Freddie.

In his absence, the *News of the World* had published an article claiming that Freddie had secretly taken an AIDS test in London under the name, Freddie Bulsara. The headline read, *'Queen Star Freddie in AIDS shock'*.

A journalist from *The Sun* newspaper was waiting at the airport to ask Freddie whether the news was true.

Freddie got very angry. *'Do I look like I'm dying from AIDS?'* he asked. The article also claimed Freddie was still living with Mary.

If the news had been false, Freddie wouldn't have got mad and would have just brushed off the unwelcome journalist, one way or another.

In his book, Jim wrote that the article made false claims; the whole thing was a bare-faced lie.

This was what he initially thought, but he later realised Freddie had become unusually restless and seemed absent-minded, at times for days, denying he had taken an AIDS test when Jim asked.

Freddie didn't look like someone who was dying of AIDS. Queen had finished the huge tour to promote their last album. After that Freddie and Jim travelled non-stop all over Japan for three weeks, touring and shopping, but it was Jim rather than Freddie who had to stay in bed. He looks happy and content in the photos that were taken.

Jim attended Freddie's concerts in England and Budapest and was also there at Live Aid. He was very proud of Freddie and noticed the admiration and enthusiasm of his fans wherever they went. Jim also attended the birthday party and the end-of-tour revelries in London, which he also really enjoyed.

But the newspaper article and Freddie's reaction to it made Jim think about the kind of lifestyle he must have led as a star before they met, not to mention that during their time together, Freddie had gone to bed with others, so Jim concluded that Freddie was probably worried about his health.

Jim was right; sadly, Freddie had cause for concern. And the special holiday in Japan also was no accident. Freddie adored Japan and loved Jim, and probably thought they should go while he still felt fine. During this period, he either didn't have any symptoms or didn't talk to Jim about them, which was understandable, as he didn't want Jim to end their relationship due to fear.

John Murphy and Tony Bastin had died before Christmas 1986. Tony had been Freddie's lover for almost two years, but he'd only had two one-night stands with John. One of John's lovers died at this time, so Freddie was increasingly concerned about his diagnosis, especially as he hadn't yet told Jim about his earlier tests.

Freddie didn't visit any clubs for the remainder of the year; instead, they stayed at home in the evenings, watching TV on the sofa.

Freddie often asked Jim whether he loved him. Jim always answered yes.

He wasn't the only one who really loved Freddie, but they had already been living together for a year without Jim being rude or aggressive to Freddie, even though Freddie was often in the wrong, especially in the first six months of their relationship, until he was convinced Jim was a faithful, devoted lover, on whom he could rely.

34. *Live Magic* Album (1986)

Queen's *Live Magic* album, a selection of 15 hits performed live, was released on 1 December, 1986. The recordings were made on the Magic tour. The album got to number three on the UK charts, bringing Queen two gold and two platinum records. Freddie didn't want to tour anymore after the album was released.

This was what Brian told Discoveries Magazine in September, 1993 (Brian May and the Queen story):

'I want to break the cycle of album, world tour, album, world tour,' he (Freddie) said.

'We didn't know actually what was wrong (with Freddie) for a very long time,' May relates. *'We never talked about it, and it was a sort of unwritten law that we didn't because Freddie didn't want to. He just told us that he wasn't up to doing tours, and that's as far as it went. Gradually, I suppose in the last year and a bit, it became obvious what the problem was, or at least fairly obvious. We didn't know for sure.'*

They decided to only work on solo projects in 1987, and not another new Queen album, which was probably why they released the *Live Magic* album before the end of the year.

Some fans believed Queen was only interested in the money by that stage, because they noticed with disappointment that the recordings had been significantly edited. For example, on this album, the operatic part was left out of 'Bohemian Rhapsody'.

The disappointment was understandable, but the strong criticisms were unfair. These songs had been on earlier Queen albums for a long time.

Money was always important to Queen because they couldn't have held extravagant concerts, as they did in 1986, for example, without it. In any case, people who couldn't attend the concerts were probably pleased about the album, or they wouldn't have bought it.

Queen was never famous for trying to please the record labels, but they genuinely did care about their fans, partly because they made a living from them and partly because they were perfectionists and always wanted to get as much out of themselves as possible.

Queen was the world's best group with the best singer. They deserved to have a good lifestyle and had worked hard to achieve it.

In the film, *Bohemian Rhapsody*, Freddie (played by Rami Malek) is seen vocalising in front of a mirror before Live Aid when he looked at his cats and saw they were staring at him uncomprehendingly. He said to them: *'Do you think you could do better? Everyone is a critic.'*

Now, in the internet age, anyone can see Queen for free. So, fans are compensated day after day. The fan base is increasing rather than decreasing in Great Britain and Europe, and they still miss Freddie decades later.

They celebrated Christmas at home, and Freddie hardly left the house for the rest of the year. They invited his closest friends to visit, including Paul Prenter.

After 1985, Queen, as a band, no longer employed Paul, and Freddie, who liked him, immediately took him on as his own manager.

However, by 1987, given that Freddie only worked on his solo album after Queen stopped touring, he no longer needed Paul Prenter as manager.

By now, Paul was a massive drug addict and was constantly in financial trouble.

35. 'The Great Pretender'

1987 began with fireworks in Garden Lodge, to the great delight of the residents and neighbours.

Jim and Freddie spent Valentine's Day evening together in a romantic atmosphere.

At the end of February, Freddie's next solo single, 'The Great Pretender', got to number five in the UK. The record was made with the collaboration of Mike Moran, who Freddie got to know during recordings of the musical *Time*. Mike and Freddie didn't just work together, but also forged a deep friendship.

'The Great Pretender' wasn't Freddie's song, but a cover of *The Platters* highly successful hit from 1955. Mike had a flair for reworking music tracks, with new rhythms, instruments and musical arrangements, so he was an outstanding assistant to Freddie.

Freddie sings very well and tries to outdo the original singer, Omar Ross.

The song was originally a love song in which the abandoned lover pretends to be fine, but was lonely and felt rejected.

Freddie had chosen this song as he pretended too he was fine, while he was restless about his positive HIV tests and the deaths of his lovers. I guess the fact that Jim didn't know anything about it bothered him. The song lyrics go:

'Oh yes I'm the great pretender (ooh ooh)
Pretending I'm doing well (ooh ooh)
My need is such I pretend too much
I'm lonely but no one can tell'

Freddie must have believed that he was forced to play the game, if he didn't want to be left alone. He couldn't be sure how Jim would react when he would realise the truth. The only question was, how long could he continue playing under the radar?

The video was a success, befitting of Freddie's personality. He loved to perform and loved to show his talent. He revived his old successes with edited parts of old video clips. The 100 life-size cardboard cut-outs of Freddie suggest that 100 Freddies wouldn't have been too many. How true!

The video is very upbeat and great fun, with the three 'ladies', Freddie in a red dress and wig, Roger as Tina Turner, and Peter Straker's 'vocals'. All three are very pretty and feminine. Freddie's movement when he licks his finger is simply phenomenal, even the sexiest actress couldn't have done it better. Roger and Peter also gave great performances, and their hip movements are hilarious.

Freddie completely forgot all about his problems during the recordings and was full of laughter while preparing for it. This can be seen in another video.

Freddie was an amazing showman; his performance style in this video was exceptional. This is one of the best videos of him; it shows Freddie, the vain, good-looking, breathtaking heartthrob, and the sexiest 'woman'. Of course, the video wouldn't be half as good without the two other 'women', and it is a perfect production with them. Freddie is stunning in his elegant silk suit and is barely recognisable without his moustache; his face has been nicely made-up. Some writers have claimed that the signs of Kaposi's sarcoma could already be seen on his face at that time. Jim's book was very honest and factual, but doesn't mention this. Freddie was trying to push depressing thoughts from his mind, so he kept himself as busy as possible.

(YouTube: Freddie Mercury – 'The Great Pretender' - Official Video Remastered)

(YouTube: Freddie Mercury 1987 Behind The Scenes of The Great Pretender)

Peter Freestone thought Jim idealized their relationship to a certain extent. I don't know for sure, but Freddie loved him dearly. He had a framed photo of Jim as a child and put it on his bedside table, so it would be the first thing he saw when he woke up. Only a man in love would do such a thing. Freddie didn't treat Jim as he should have that is true, but it wasn't only Jim's fault.

 Anyway, nobody could hear or see them when just the two of them were together, not even Peter. Freddie wasn't famous for talking about his private life.

I should point out that living with Freddie was not easy, even for Jim in his position as a gardener, but there were good reasons for this. Jim insisted on his independence, which he had long since lost by falling in love with Freddie. Freddie didn't know the meaning of the word 'no'.

Barbara told Lesley-Ann Jones that Freddie had called Jim stupid several times and had trampled angrily all over the tulips that Jim had cultivated. Freddie probably did do and say such things, and by comparison to Freddie, everyone in the 'family' probably was 'stupid' at the time when Freddie was angry. He was quite good at noticing the imperfections of others. His brain was razor-sharp, and he had his own ideas about everything. He even supervised how Peter and Jim decorated the house with flowers for his birthday, as he didn't trust anything to chance; everything had to be perfect, and he knew he had good taste.

This was precisely the problem with Queen's other members: they had their own opinions and voiced them, but in the 'family', Freddie probably allowed only his cats to do this. Even if Jim had an opinion, he usually kept it to himself because he was wise enough to avoid deliberately upsetting Freddie and would do anything he could to please him. Jim really loved Freddie, and didn't just say it, not like those who had exploited him, such as Paul Prenter.

36. Montserrat Caballé

'When I was planning to do my second solo project, I really didn't want it to be just another bunch of songs.'

'So I was looking for ideas in that direction, and suddenly those two wonderful names came up like a tidal wave, and they were Montserrat Caballé. It was really a shot in the arm and all those clichés. It was something that wasn't calculated; it came rocketing out of the sky and just fell upon me. It virtually enveloped me, and I could think of nothing else. It was fabulous. There was so much scope, so much life and energy in it, and as far I am concerned, it wasn't just a work thing. I was totally in awe.' (Freddie Mercury)

Freddie, Mike Moran, Jim Beach and Peter Freestone travelled to Barcelona to meet Montserrat Caballé at the Ritz Hotel in March, 1977. Freddie was so nervous that he wanted to turn back on the way to the restaurant. Fortunately, his 'bodyguards' stopped him from doing so.

Freddie was the king of rock'n'roll in Europe and Japan, while Montserrat Caballé was the queen of opera worldwide, especially in Catalonia.

At the start, the lunch was embarrassingly polite, but the two superstars soon got the measure of each other, and Montserrat saved the day by putting Freddie at ease. After five minutes, they got talking to each other, and it turned out they both had a wicked sense of humour, and both of them loved the champagne that had been served. They talked fast and said a lot, because Montserrat only had three hours free.

Freddie brought along the recordings of three songs on which he sang Montserrat's part; one was 'Exercises In Free Love', which later appeared on the *Barcelona* album as 'Ensueño', and two other songs that were still in raw form. The music originally requested for the Olympic song was one, and the title of the other one was 'The Fallen Priest', but Freddie just regarded these as ideas at that stage.

They listened to the recordings several times, and then the conversation turned to an album, which was Montserrat's idea, after Freddie explained to her that it meant at least eight or nine songs on a record.

'Fine,' Montserrat replied, 'let's have an album then'. Learning and singing eight or nine songs must have been child's play for her, but composing them required tremendous hard work on Freddie and Mike's part. Freddie was cautious of the idea and wondered whether he would have enough ideas for eight or nine songs, but he didn't dare or didn't want to disagree with Montserrat.

Caballé listened to 'Exercises in Free Love' and announced that she would sing it three weeks later at her Covent Garden Opera House concert. And then she patted Mike on the shoulder, gave him the role of pianist and 'invited' him to write the sheet music for the song, and said she would come back to the hotel that evening to try and sing it. When she came back, thoroughly exhausted Mike before finally bidding farewell.

Naturally, Freddie was invited to London's Royal Opera House to listen to the song performed by Caballé. Montserrat announced she would be singing a song by someone the audience would definitely know and who happened to be sitting in the audience, and then pointed to Freddie.

Freddie was made to stand up and take a bow, so everyone could see him under the spotlight. Peter says Freddie just wanted the Earth to swallow him up, he was so nervous. Montserrat had thoroughly rehearsed the song, and the audience was ecstatic and captivated after the show, so Freddie could calm down.

(In a 1988 report – given to Spanish TV – Freddie told how Caballé had blown kisses to him in the theatre, which he returned, but he was terribly embarrassed. Caballé had a good laugh during this report.)

Freddie hardly dared to dream that one day a prima donna, whom he most admired and who was celebrated halfway around the world, would make his song successful in such a magnificent venue as the Royal Opera House.

I can just imagine how proud Londoners were of Freddie, and they were right to be proud. Not many contemporary British composers had ever written a song for Montserrat Caballé! Freddie and Mike were probably the first and only ones, given that the artist naturally sang classical pieces. In this context, Freddie and Mike joined the ranks of the classics that evening and stayed there forever with the *Barcelona* album. I suppose some music critics wouldn't agree with me, but I am sure that all of Freddie's fans share my opinion.

We only had to wait a year for the album to be released.

The music for the song, 'Exercises In Free Love', which was performed in the theatre, is wonderful. I believe the way Freddie sings on this recording will amaze everyone.

The song is on YouTube. It's not an official Freddie Mercury video, but it's worth listening to because Freddie can't be heard singing soprano anywhere else.

(YouTube: Freddie Mercury Opera Voice)

'Ensueño' (Dream) or how Freddie called it earlier 'Exercise in Free Love', was added to the album. Freddie's voice is wonderfully suited to Caballé's coloratura soprano, as if they had always sung together. The duet, sung in Spanish, is incomparably beautiful and an experience not to be missed. It must be exciting to opera lovers, while it's almost compulsory for Freddie's fans who want to know all about his amazing abilities.

We can witness the meeting of two wonderful souls, which has great value in itself. I'm convinced that if Freddie had ever studied singing, he would have been an outstanding opera singer as well. The unparalleled inspiration that Montserrat Caballé gave Freddie cannot be overestimated. These songs raised Freddie's creative genius to an even higher level.

(YouTube: Freddie Mercury Montserrat Caballé – 'Ensueño' Con Letra.mp4)

The song isn't performed live on the video, but it's still exceptionally beautiful. One of Freddie's Spanish fans thanked him in a comment under the video for introducing him to Montserrat Caballé. Nobody could have paid him a greater compliment. A Spaniard, who knew about Freddie, but wasn't aware of Montserrat Caballé: I guess she hadn't been a great opera fan.

After the show, Montserrat visited Freddie in Garden Lodge, where Freddie welcomed her with a dinner, a champagne dinner, of course.

After dinner, Montserrat was in the mood for singing. Freddie kept asking her whether it was time to leave for the airport, but Montserrat just kept asking for another cigarette in reply. Mike played the song fragments they had composed the previous week. The singing often turned to laughter, and the fun lasted five hours before Montserrat decided it was time to leave. She was the first person to top Freddie, in terms of energy. The sad thing was, it was no longer difficult to outdo him during that period.

At the time, Freddie's face already was filled with Dermafill to disguise the weight loss, as much as possible. The filler gave him some additional self-confidence.

Montserrat and Freddie began recording one week later. Freddie surprised her with his unusual method of working. She thought all she had to do was to sing from sheet music, but Freddie got her to use her voice in ways that she was not used to, to get the most out of it, naturally, as Freddie imagined it.

'He told her: Puccini and all these other composers are dead. I'm alive, dear' – this was how he explained why he was giving her instructions.

'Later she admitted that in those sessions Freddie got more out of her voice than she knew she was capable of.' (Jim Hutton and Tim Wapshott)

It must have been similar to when he got Brian to play unconventional chords that were unfamiliar to guitarists.

37. Jim's Final Test

Jim and Freddie had a terrible fight on that fine day when Queen received another Ivor Novello Prize for their outstanding contribution to British music. Jim didn't provide details of the cause of the argument. Nevertheless, Jim accompanied Freddie to the celebrations. When they returned home, Freddie apologised to Jim, hugged him, and the argument was followed by sweet reconciliation.

Jim travelled home to Ireland for Easter to visit his family. Freddie's voice was anxious when he phoned Jim, and he told him he'd had a large lump surgically removed that day, but didn't want to say more over the phone.

The next day, Jim returned to London. Freddie told him the biopsy had revealed he had AIDS. Jim couldn't believe his ears and suggested he visit another doctor.

Freddie told him he had already seen the best doctor, and offered Jim the option of moving out if he wanted, saying he would understand. Jim replied that he loved Freddie and wouldn't trample over him now or any time in the future.

God sent this man to Freddie to console him. Jim didn't know what to do with the shocking news and suggested not talking about it anymore. Jim tried to push the fatal diagnosis out of his mind. He did the same as Freddie; tried to pretend that a miraculous medicine would be found, or that the diagnosis was wrong.

Freddie suggested that Jim get tested. Jim refused because he didn't want Freddie to feel guilty. Jim knew he couldn't have been infected by anyone else, if he was infected.

It was a brave approach on his part, and testimony to his wonderful spirit. He behaved like a husband, despite Mary continually trying to push him into the background. Jim passed the test of love and honour with flying colours and had withstood the final test. He knew he belonged to Freddie and wasn't interested in anything else. If only there were more people like him on Earth.

(Freddie's fans are very grateful to Jim for standing by Freddie and loving him, and they express their gratitude under every related video. Sadly, he can no longer read them.)

With Jim's consent, Freddie let Mary, John Reid and his old friend, Dominique, Roger's partner, in on the secret.

They also agreed to tell Joe Fanelli, who had been Freddie's lover for almost two years, as it affected him just as much as Jim.

Peter Freestone wrote in his book that the 'family' noticed something wasn't right with Freddie, but they couldn't be sure what the problem was and only suspected it was HIV.

38. The Treacherous Paul Prenter

Apart from Freddie, nobody ever liked Paul Prenter because he tried to tear Freddie away from Queen, telling him he would be much better off alone and should do solo albums. He was employed for eight years and was constantly at Freddie's side. He was Freddie's main sycophant, as can be seen in the videos, where he is always lurking and watching Freddie, looking at him as if he was a god. A lot of people claim they were lovers, but there has never been any proof of this, and in terms of their outcomes, it doesn't matter.

Freddie indeed wanted to help him before Christmas 1986, so he gave him the keys to his old apartment and some money, allowing him to spend the festive period in at least some comfort. One day, without Freddie's knowledge or consent, he had a party in the flat, leaving filth and rubbish behind. Freddie was angry because he felt this was insolent behaviour, so he fired him immediately. Prenter threatened to get even with Freddie but didn't say how.

A three-page article was published in *The Sun* newspaper on 4 May, 1987, with photos of Freddie's former lovers who had died from AIDS, and Prenter told the paper that Freddie had been involved in countless one-night stands. Then another two articles appeared with photos, even naming Jim as Freddie's current partner. Prenter also claimed that Freddie had called him one night to complain about how afraid he was that he'd contracted HIV. Prenter also spoke about drug use, even framing Rod Stewart and Kenny Everett as regular drug users.

Freddie and Jim were both devastated by the newspaper article. Freddie never spoke to Prenter again and could only tell the press that Prenter had done the same as he had.

Freddie didn't want to invite press attention, because, at the time, he had the greatest need for calm. He learned that Prenter had received 32,000 pounds from the newspaper for the article. Prenter's brother defended him, saying his younger brother was suffering from AIDS and needed the money for treatment.

His betrayal struck Freddie below the belt and hurt him very much because, at one time, they had been very close friends. Freddie could hardly believe Prenter was capable of such a wicked act.

39. The Ibiza '92 Festival

Freddie, Jim and the other 'family' members travelled to Ibiza for a week to try and put Prenter, the photographers and journalists behind them, but as it turned out, they even followed them to Ibiza like vultures.

In his book, Jim says a painful and deteriorating wound appeared on the sole of Freddie's right foot, and he found it increasingly difficult to walk.

They attended a festival organised to celebrate the Olympic Committee's decision to select Barcelona as the venue for the 1992 Olympics.

The festival was held in San Antonio. Duran Duran, Marillion, Spandau Ballet and Chris Rea were among the performers.

By way of a surprise, Freddie and Montserrat Caballé closed the event with 'Barcelona', which they had recently recorded and which was very popular with the Olympic Committee. Unfortunately, the song was on playback, but this didn't bother the audience, who showed their gratitude for the captivating production with thunderous applause at the end of the show.

Freddie told Mike Moran: 'I think I should hold back slightly; after all, she is an opera singer'. But when Caballé began to sing, it was like a volcano had erupted. Freddie looked at Mike as if to say, 'Oh my God! I'd better pull myself together.'

Well, he did pull himself together, and the recording proves he managed to do so amazingly.

(YouTube: Freddie Mercury & Montserrat Caballé – 'Barcelona' (Live at Ku Club Ibiza, 1987)

Most of the comments on the video are written in Spanish, Japanese, English and Russian. Just one of the many:

'If this doesn't give you goosebumps you're probably dead' (Blackbird Singing).

How right Blackbird Singing is! She or he would have made good music critics.

Montserrat Caballé remembered their time together as follows:

'Here is the room where we first met. When I entered the room, his hands were so cold. I was very cold too. So I could feel his cold hands, so I thought, he is cooler than me, he is nervous too. That is good because when people are nervous, it means they are expecting something from the other one. A piano was in the corner prepared. So we went to the corner, and he was playing, and I was beginning to sing. We could have gone on for hours and hours, so when we were finished, we looked at each other, and I knew he had conquered me.'

'Musicians understand each other very well. They are married in music. He loved me a lot, and I loved him, too.

For the opera world, it was a real revolution. Many, many people, young people come today to the opera, and they say we wanted so much to find out who is that woman, who screams so much with Freddie. And we are very thankful to him because this way we made two worlds come together, for the first time.'

'One day, he said, in front of many friends together, I love music, and she is the music.'

(YouTube: Freddie Mercury – The Untold History – parte 8 (legendas pt)

The two artists, from different worlds, were global sensations; Freddie and Montserrat Caballé encapsulated the story of their 'love' in an album for the big, wide world.

Caballé was among the select few who were allowed to attend Freddie's funeral in the company of his closest friends and family. I can just imagine how grief-stricken she was by the news of Freddie's death, and would have preferred to hear herself singing anywhere other than at his memorial service.

She always spoke about Freddie with great love and respect. Her statements are very moving. She was proud to have him as her close friend.

Jim was sitting in the audience at the festival. Everyone thought the concert was over when the music for 'Barcelona' sounded. The audience immediately fell silent and watched intently, some of them wiping away tears. Jim overheard some young Spaniards excitedly discussing the song, saying: 'This will be the new Spanish national anthem.'

As the song finished, the longest and most spectacular fireworks Jim had ever seen began, and he said that Freddie was delighted with the public acclaim, as if he had won every first prize in the world.

Jim adored this album, and later listened to it a lot when he was mourning Freddie.

Freddie and Montserrat Caballé's relationship was also like fireworks, really beautiful, sparklingly passionate and as exhilarating as love.

Freddie was in love with Montserrat Caballé as a person and with her incredible voice, while Montserrat found Freddie was the most passionate admirer in her life.

'Barcelona' tells the story of Freddie and Montserrat's meeting and everything Freddie felt about her.

Freddie had loved the opera since childhood and often sang opera arias at home to see what he was capable of. He was very proud of himself when he managed to sing his favourites perfectly. Montserrat suggested that Freddie sing baritone and thought they were going to sing real opera. Freddie replied: 'That's impossible. What will my fans say if they don't hear my rock voice?' So, this was how the songs were created, as the first rock-opera crossover. The new style proved successful and is much more exciting, making the album magical and unforgettable.

Freddie conquered the hearts of opera lovers with this song, just as Freddie's fans took Montserrat Caballé, and, if not opera, then at least this album, into their hearts.

Jim couldn't have been prouder of Freddie, not even if he had climbed the Himalayas in a pair of shorts and sandals, like Wim Hoff, the extraordinary Dutch 'Iceman'.

The single, 'Barcelona', was released a year earlier than the album in the UK in October, 1987, and got to number eight on the charts.

I am going to interpret 'Barcelona' in a later chapter on the *Barcelona* album.

'Freddie's collaboration with Montserrat Caballé was such an enormous success in charts all over the world that it caused her to be mobbed by Freddie's fans. She told Freddie she was absolutely astounded by how well the record had done and said that for the first time in her career, she had been mobbed by screaming teenagers when she went through an airport.' (Jim Hutton and Tim Wapshott)

40. Freddie's Heroic Efforts

During 1987, Freddie started to show symptoms of Kaposi's sarcoma, which he covered with make-up on his face. Another open wound appeared on his right calf muscle, which didn't improve despite careful treatment.

At other times his white blood cell count fell dramatically, but despite strict medical instructions, Freddie worked obsessively on the *Barcelona* album, which was a real challenge for him and gave him enormous strength.

However, as he got weaker, he needed Jim more than ever, who took advantage of the situation. One night he angrily attacked Freddie for always taking off the ring he had given him when he went out. Freddie wore the ring all the time from then on wherever he went. Poor Jim felt like a part-time husband.

When he moved in with Freddie, Jim didn't realise he was getting someone who was male, female and a young child, and all three liked to cause hysterical scenes.

And the cats, which Freddie treated like his children, also contributed to these scenes. One of his cats that he had named Goliath, strayed from home one night. Someone found it and brought it home after midnight. Like a good father, Freddie was relieved and hugged the small animal. Then he put it on the floor told it off, even shouting at it for wandering off.

Jim left his job that year because he'd had enough of it. He called Freddie in despair, who was pleased with Jim's decision and immediately took him on as a gardener with a decent salary. To Jim's credit, he didn't just look after the garden but also Freddie's favourite fish as if they were his own children. (If only Freddie had allowed Jim to be continuously by his side while he could, instead, he was mowing the lawn on the day Freddie died.)

Freddie was very grateful for his love and care; when Jim passed his driving test, Freddie bombarded him with tiny, funny gifts all night long, and bought him a brand-new Volvo the next day.

'He knew I loved him, but he needed to hear me say it. Even though thousands of fans around the world loved him without ever having met him, the only person he seemed to want to know really did love him was me. His fondness for me made me feel very special. I'd never known anyone want my affection so much, and I was deeply flattered. And I loved him dearly in return.' (Jim Hutton and Tim Wapshott)

Jim and Freddie often got involved in terrible arguments but always forgave each other. Slowly they became something like a real married couple.

As time passed, Jim began to realise that Freddie's tolerance levels were continually declining, and he had to adapt if he didn't want his love to suffer.

Freddie wasn't just kind and attentive towards Jim when he was in a good mood, but to every member of the family. No birthday was allowed to pass without a special, customised birthday cake and generous gifts, not to mention Christmas festivities when, in addition to the gifts, he also gave everyone cheques in large amounts. They slowly became a real family, as if they were brothers. They all loved Freddie from the heart and would have done anything for him right to the end. They were Freddie's main support pillars, along with his doctors. Regardless of how often he produced hysterics, they knew deep down he was kind, loving and caring, and so they didn't take it to heart, especially when Freddie needed love and attention the most. Freddie was blessed to have found a real, loving, caring family in Mary and these men. Moreover, his parents and sister regularly visited him, but later, when his condition took a real turn for the worse, he tried to keep them away to spare them any distress. He stopped resenting his elderly parents because they were very proud of his success, especially his mother.

In addition, he had a few true friends, like Peter Straker, with whom he often stayed up all night laughing hysterically because Peter could always make Freddie laugh. Peter hadn't been let in on the secret, but knew full well what the problem was, however, others, such as the other members of Queen, could only guess at what was happening to Freddie. In 1987 he wasn't even willing to talk to Jim about what his doctors had told him. He had to forget about the anticipated tragedy at any cost, so that he could continue working, because he still had so many creative ideas, and the *Barcelona* album wasn't finished yet. Mike Moran and the Oscar-winning songwriter, Sir Tim Rice, were also there as good friends and outstanding assistants when they worked together on the *Barcelona* album.

41. Queen Back Together Again, 1988

Queen began working again on *The Miracle* album in January, 1988, which was completed and released in 1989.

Prior to this, given that Freddie no longer wanted to tour, Roger, John and Brian were looking for opportunities to play live. Roger even set up a band, but it turned out again that their fans preferred to see the members of Queen, in Queen the band, rather than as solo artists, and were passionate about the music Queen had produced.

Freddie wanted to keep himself busy at all costs, so he didn't have time to deal with his disease.

Influenced by newspaper articles and rumours going around, the other members of Queen began to suspect that Freddie might have AIDS. However, they dismissed the idea because it was too unpleasant to contemplate; they were all still young and felt they had a lot of energy and creativity left in them.

On the other hand, it was clear to them that Freddie was very ill, even if they didn't talk about it openly, because Freddie wasn't willing to do so. They sincerely hoped that Freddie would recover by some miracle. Indeed, only a miracle could have helped. Nobody knew better than Brian that a guitar string will break if it's too highly-strung, but if it's too loose, it doesn't make a good sound. Freddie always overstretched the string, constantly overloading himself.

During the course of the year, they continually worked on the album, moving from one studio to the next, but returned to the original creative method and were working together again, at last. No longer avoiding each other, but working as a team again gave them all huge momentum.

One interesting and significant change, which started from 1988, was that all songs were Queen songs. It no longer mattered who had the idea for the song. They shared the royalties equally.

The question was whether it was Freddie or the others that initiated the change. As they were no longer touring, they may have been afraid of selling fewer records. Fortunately, they were wrong on this front, but sadly right that Freddie didn't need the huge incoming royalties much longer. Freddie was probably thinking the same thing, and he needed Queen more than ever.

In any event, to the great delight of Queen's fans, the team was back together again and enjoying working together.

They could only record the album in segments; Freddie had to travel from one studio to the next to complete the *Barcelona* album that year.

Freddie, Jim, Joe and Peter travelled to Ibiza again for a quiet holiday so Freddie could rest at the start of the summer. This time they stayed in Roger's house so that nobody could bother them. Everything was fine, but Freddie had to manage without his beloved cats, which wasn't easy for him. When they arrived home from the holiday, the cats were waiting excitedly for their owner and all lined up in the hall to welcome him. Smart cats!

Freddie's doctors put him on AZT therapy. At the time, AZT was a very promising drug, which helped keep him fit for a while, but it had such negative long-term side effects that he had to stop the treatment for a while. However, he continually tried to extend his life with any available new drugs.

Jim noticed that Freddie was getting weaker during the year, and others acknowledged that he soon got exhausted during recordings. He just said he didn't feel well when he left, so that he could rest, but he didn't give up. Gathering all his strength, he strived to get the best out of himself. His doctors at the time said he had around three years left if he was lucky.

Under time pressure, Freddie pushed himself even harder. He began to lose weight and needed to put ever more liquid powder on his face to conceal the patches, which they tried to remove with laser treatment, with a certain level of success.

42. Festival 'La Nit', Barcelona Album (1988)

'With the Barcelona album, I had a little bit more freedom and a bit of scope to actually try out some of my crazy ideas. Montserrat kept telling me she also found a new lease of life and newfound freedom. Those were her own words, and I was very taken by them. She told me on the phone that she loves the way our voices sound together...and I was smiling from my ass to my elbow. I sat at home like I'd just swallowed the canary, thinking, 'Ooh! There is a lot of people who'd like to be in my shoes right now'.

A Montserrat Caballé performance is sensational. She has that same kind of emotion as Aretha Franklin. The way she delivers a song is so very natural, and it's a very different gift. It was fantastic singing on stage with her. What an experience! It was really a dream come true. And just before we went on stage, I couldn't help wondering if all this was happening to me. And though I knew I was taking a big chance doing something like that, it gave me such a fantastic rush. I was a wreck, and so was she. I was bringing her into my rock'n'roll world, and so she was shaking like a leaf, and saying 'Will they accept me?' She asked me how we should do it, and I said: 'Oh, we should just stand there and deliver the song.', which is how operatic recitals are done. I had to sort of restrain myself too. I had to keep in mind that I couldn't do my usual balletic stuff; none of those prancy poses and all that. No, I had to just deliver it- in a fucking tuxedo – which I'd never done in front of an audience before - and just go for it. The atmosphere was amazing'. (Freddie Mercury)

Preparing for the Barcelona performance on 8 October, Freddie was trying to regain his strength. He and Jim travelled to Montreux, rented a villa and devoted time exclusively to rest. He loved the quiet and the lake, and could relax and recharge his batteries slightly, spending a lot of time in the fresh air walking around the lake.

Dr Gordon Atkinson, Freddie's doctor, was explicitly opposed to the Barcelona trip because Freddie's red blood cell count had fallen to half the normal level.

Freddie was unstoppable, as always, and in any case, Montserrat and the Spanish royal family were waiting for him, so he had no option but to travel.

As if this wasn't enough, his vocal cords also got infected before the concert, and he was in terrible pain; he decided not to let Montserrat down, preferring to mime than to cause disappointment.

He was very nervous before the show, which can be seen on his face as they marched onto the stage, though it's only obvious to those who saw how he flew onto the stage at Live Aid. He had a throat infection then too, and was also very nervous, but he was in his element straight away when he saw the crowd.

However, this event was very different to the world's largest rock concert.

This was the world premiere of three sensational songs from the *Barcelona* album, but the usual line-up wasn't there. He didn't have the backup behind him, and it's a shame they weren't sitting in the audience; at least, it would have meant a lot to Freddie. I'm curious as to whether he invited them; probably not, because at least one of them would have gone to see Freddie on stage for the last time. But unfortunately, they didn't know what was going on. If they had known the truth, I'm certain all three of them would have been there in suits and ties.

Freddie and Montserrat's duet was the main attraction at the festival, so they closed the event with Freddie's three songs. The audience included the Spanish King Juan Carlos, Queen Sofia and their daughter, Princess Christina.

The event was held on Castle Square in front of the Son et Lumière Fountains, celebrating the arrival of the Olympic flame.

The square was magically lit with beautiful evening lights. The Barcelona Opera House Orchestra and Choir provided the music and backup vocals. The vocals and musical accompaniment were sensational, and the songs were absolute masterpieces. Each song is like Mont Everest in the Himalayas.

Freddie seemed slightly awkward, possibly because he was nervous, and he had to restrain himself not to do his usual seductive, big movements as in a rock concert. Still, he resolved the problem skilfully in the end, sometimes leaping away from Montserrat and came near to punch the air. His movements were very animated, and he used even more energy to control himself. This made him even more attractive.

That evening was one of the highest points of Freddie's life. It was the icing on the cake, and what a way to do it! It was a shame he could not sing, but you have to admit he had never mouthed the words more touchingly and beautifully in his life or at such a wonderful venue and in such distinguished company.

'I dress to kill', Freddie once said. That is to say, he dressed to make everyone's jaw drop when he appeared. He looked very elegant, even though he hated the tuxedo he wore.

Montserrat smiled proudly as she marched onto the stage next to Freddie. The two of them would have deserved the triumphal march from Aida. They looked stunning together.

'Golden Boy' was the first song they performed, followed by 'How Can I Go On', and they left 'Barcelona' to the end as the climax.

Even mimed, Freddie and Montserrat's production was extraordinary. I admired how well they imitated singing; their movement was in perfect harmony with the song's lyrics. It's hard to believe they were not singing on the recording. In any case, their spectacular performance and the exceptional sound of the music diverted attention from their miming.

Freddie taught the world how to write a classical crossover, and on the album cover we can read: 'Genre: Opera, Classical crossover'.

When they sing the lines, *'I love you for your passion, I love you for your silence'* from 'The Golden Boy', nobody would doubt these emotions were real. Freddie sang so passionately as if his life depended on the success of the song.

During the recordings, he realised with childish pleasure that he had his own recording of Montserrat. He was as happy as an orphan who had received a toy train from Santa! In the 1988 Spanish TV report mentioned earlier, Freddie said that, before their first audio recording, he found it hard to believe he was actually working with Montserrat. Until then, he had to keep reminding himself he wasn't just dreaming.

In the course of their work, he was increasingly self-conscious when he heard Montserrat's voice. He often listened to the recording, unable to get enough of the fantastic performance. When they appeared proudly in front of the Spanish royal family and their Spanish fans, the joy of this acceptance was evident on his face.

I'm sure that when preparing for the festival, he was intent on delivering the most outstanding production of his life. The presentation was perfect just the way it was, breathtaking. Not only did the attire 'kill' but so did the performance and the music.

Fireworks flashed and sparkled in the background during the performance. The most moving moment was when the music for 'Barcelona' started. The audience stood up, as if they had heard the music for the Spanish national anthem! Not to mention the rapturous cries and thunderous applause at the end of the song, as more and more fireworks flashed in the background.

(YouTube: Festival "La Nit' Barcelona 8 De Ocubre De 1988 Font Mágica)

'Barcelona'

Freddie sang about Montserrat and the experience of meeting her in person for the first time. He was incredibly happy. When he first heard her sing in the theatre, he jumped up from his seat, forgetting himself, and excitedly grilled Peter Freestone about who the singer was, wanting to know everything about her right away. The whole album can be attributed to this experience, which captivated Freddie.

The song was released as a single in October, 1987, a year earlier than the album itself.

At the beginning of the song, Barcelona is cheered by the choir in a large-scale overture, expressing their joy that the city would be hosting the Olympic Games.

After the overture, Freddie and Montserrat take turns singing the first verse – Freddie in English, Montserrat in Spanish. The Spanish lyrics try to convey what Freddie sings in English. Freddie sings about a dream that wasn't a dream, but reality. *'I had this perfect dream, this dream was me and you'*. Montserrat sings about a dream, too, in which she meets with Freddie. Her instincts guided her to Freddie to convince him to write a song for the opening ceremony. Freddie is very proud of their relationship, so he sings, *'I want all the world to see'*. He thinks so highly of Montserrat that the world needs to hear and see who inspired him to write the song: *'A miracle sensation, my guide and inspiration'*. Writing the music, Freddie realises that his dream will come true. The theme continues: *'The bells are ringing out, they are calling us together, guiding us forever'*.

The bell and the peaceful gathering of the people hinted at the celebration in Barcelona, where he and Montserrat would meet again and perform duets. He wished his dream would never go away. The Spanish lyrics are also lovely, in English, it reads: *'For you, I will be a seagull of your beautiful sea, Barcelona, open your doors to the world'*.

Freddy is less interested in the Olympics itself, so he stays on the topic:

'Barcelona!
It was the first time that we met
Barcelona!
How can I forget
The moment that you stepped into the room
You took my breath away'

Freddie continued to sing about his admiration of Caballé, as if this song wasn't an anthem of the Olympic Games. We know this time Freddie is not in love, but it sounds like it, nonetheless.

The Spaniards at the ceremony understood only Montserrat's lyrics, so they weren't bothered by it. Anyway, the city's name is often mentioned in the song, and the music is so uplifting that the lyrics were less significant, especially not on the first hearing. The Olympic Committee also considered the song's lyrics before their decision, so Freddie could have rightly felt very proud.

'Barcelona!
Such a beautiful horizon
Like a jewel in the sun'

With the quoted last two poetic lines, Freddie certainly won the hearts of the Spaniards.

(YouTube: Freddie Mercury & Montserrat Caballé – Barcelona Live at La Nit, 1988 Remastered)

The Olympic Committee liked the song's beautiful, romantic lyrics and its great music.

'There were two main musical themes for the 1992 Games. One was 'Barcelona', composed five years earlier by Freddie Mercury and sung as a duet with Montserrat Caballé. Due to Mercury's death eight months earlier, the duo was unable to perform the song during the opening ceremony. A recording of the song instead played over a travelogue of the city at the start of the opening ceremony.' (Wikipedia)

(YouTube: Barcelona 92 Opening Ceremony)

At the very beginning of the Ceremony, only a short part of *Barcelona* can be heard. Too bad, Montserrat and Freddie weren't visible for a second while they sang Freddie's song.

I can imagine Montserrat Caballé was heartbroken listening to it in 1992. However, Freddie was happy to perform duets with his adored soprano; that was the big thing for him – he knew he wasn't going to make it.

At the opening ceremony, Montserrat Caballé was singing opera arias with other popular opera singers.

'The Golden Boy'

The lyrics of this song were written by Sir Tim Rice. The first verse is clearly about Freddie, drawing a perfect picture of how he became a performer. The description is so accurate, it even could have been

Freddie who wrote it. Tim Rice must have known Freddy very well, or Freddie provided the ideas for the lyrics.

Tim Rice's style is different, less lyrical in wording, but it sounds excellent. The girl in the song is a fictional figure who loves Freddie only for his fame and *'Wanted him for luxury for limelight and his name'*. As we already know, Freddie had a constant fear of being used by people who weren't real friends, or by lovers who just wanted to take advantage of him, knowing how generous he was.

Due to Freddie's determination and persistence, there was no doubt that he would become an outstanding musician. These traits and his talent made it possible for him to become a *'master of his fate'*.

Ultimately, that song is about Freddie's success and his relationships, and how he became a famous and wealthy celebrity. Montserrat's sweet-sounding voice and Freddie's forceful rock voice provided an exciting combination, while the choir echoed their words. Montserrat's impressive soprano could prevail, as she sang the second verse and the refrain alone. They both sounded sincere as their positive emotions permeated their hearts and souls. That is why their singing is so captivating.

This warm emotional charge radiates from Montserrat's face, and she is smiling happily when Freddie sings about the *'boy'*.

The next verse is again about the *'boy'* who *'grew into the part'*, just like Freddie, but there was no doubt that he would be successful.

The *'boy'* was not interested in anything. He just wanted *'his work'* to be *'noticed'* and *'adored'*. Sounds good, and that's all that matters.

The lyrics and the beautiful harmony of the rhythmic, melodic music are uplifting; Montserrat's soprano and Freddie's voice fit perfectly.

The music is powerful and wonderfully highlights the song's message, which is, in a nutshell: 'I know who I am; a very passionate, successful, loving man and sometimes I am exploited when I am in love.'

I listen to this song very often because I admire Montserrat's and Freddie's voices, their singing style, the instrumentation and the unparalleled harmony between the singers, the choir and the symphony orchestra. Freddie and Mike created a mesmerising masterpiece.

(YouTube: Freddie Mercury & Montserrat Caballé – 'The Golden Boy' Live at La Nit, 1988 Remastered)

'How Can I Go On?'

The song was written and recorded in the spring of 1987. Unfortunately, Freddie received confirmation of his AIDS diagnosis at the beginning of April.

It was at this time that he had to accept what awaited him. At that time, there was no hope, as there was no cure available. In addition, he didn't feel well, so he had every reason to feel desperate.

That makes this song one of the most tragic songs he has ever written.

Jim, Joe, Peter and others were close to him, so even though he would have known they would all support him, this would have been only a slight consolation when he got the terrible news. He felt the need to compose a song about it, to alleviate his excruciating pain and the pressure he was under. He had fame, fortune, a fabulous home, and he had found Jim; he had everything, but had lost the most important thing – hope that he could be healed. He never talked about it in his everyday life, except with Jim on rare occasions. From this time on, he lived in *'this great big world of sadness'*. Luckily, the work and the music gave him exceptional strength, and it seems that he somehow came to terms with his fate.

There is a very sad thought in the lyrics: *'I'm naked, and I bleed, but when your finger points so savagely, is anybody there to believe in me?'* As if being in this terrible state of mind wasn't enough torture for him, this cruel thought allowed him no peace of mind. He must have been afraid that some would blame him, amongst them Jim and Joe, who were living with him. Not only might Jim blame him, but there was the thought that Jim and Joe were going to share his fate as well. These experiences and thoughts made him sometimes *'tremble in the dark'* and want to be away from people. The only way to forget about his depressing sadness was to write songs for the *Barcelona* album, making himself extremely busy as this task was totally different and more complicated than working on pop or rock songs. So, Montserrat couldn't have come into Freddie's life at a better time.

The song is about Freddie's desperate sadness, uncertainty and fears. Will there be someone to take care of him? Will he have the strength to face his destiny? *'All the salt is taken from the sea'*, and he feels *'dethroned'* (the terrible childhood memories come back); he feels as lonely as he did when he was separated from his family. Even his beautiful dreams (about his future) are lost and nowhere to be found. Is anybody there to comfort him? Finally, at the end of the song, he turns to God to take care of him.

The performance is a dramatic, poignant experience. The fact is that only Jim and Montserrat knew, and Mike Moran must have guessed what the song was about – the audience would have had no idea.

'Montserrat became very emotional at the first playback of 'How Can I Go On?' because of the sentiment and the sound of Freddie's voice talking the lines that she sings after her. Tears flowed down her cheeks and almost brought tears to Freddie's eyes as he was the depth of her emotion. Perhaps he too was actually listening to the words for the first time rather than living inside them.' (Peter Freestone)

Freddie didn't write it deliberately, the words came out instinctively, driven by his pent-up emotions.

Freddie's amazing talent is expressed in this section, which made Montserrat burst into tears. Who would have thought he would repeat the song's lyrics in a talking voice in an operatic piece?

Under the circumstances, it's difficult to understand how they were capable of singing these tragic lines. When the show took place, Montserrat already knew exactly what the song was about, as Freddie had told her at the final recording that he had AIDS, explaining why he didn't hug her at that time.

No doubt they weren't concentrating on the words, but just on performing the song well, and were preoccupied with the miming and theatrical movements, as if the song wasn't even about Freddie.

In this beautiful song, Freddie is praying for confirmation from his 'family', from Jim and his friends, asking for their support, not to leave him alone because he needs them now more than ever. And he couldn't have asked them more nicely.

They listened to his poignant prayer, loved him to the end, and took care of him; they stood by him until the last beat of his heart.

(YouTube: Freddie Mercury & Montserrat Caballé 'How Can I Go On' Festival 'La Nit' Barcelona 8 DE Octubre de 1988)

'Guide Me Home'

This song is the last one on the album, and Freddie wrote the lyrics sometime at the beginning of 1988.

A year before, Freddie wrote *How can I go on?* A year later, it seems Freddie had begun to accept his fate: *'Now the wind has lost my sail, now the scent has left my trial, who will find me, take care and side with me'*.

He has started to think about who would '*guide*' him '*safely*' home, who could '*save*' him and '*lead*' him to his destiny.'

In reality, he didn't let anybody '*guide*' or '*lead*' him, even though this song proves that he craved for someone's continual encouragement, and to be loved as much as possible, to feel safe when he embarked on his final journey. Everybody in the house had to pretend as if everything would be just fine. Even Jim had to continue to work in the garden.

As Jim mentioned in his book, Freddie didn't want to be a burden to anyone.

For Jim to be in the garden all day long was a bit easier than being with Freddie all the time, thinking about what would happen, when and how.

The last two lines in the lyrics are: '*But how can I go on? How can I go on this way...*', which indicate that Freddie wasn't ready to go yet, but couldn't help thinking about it, as he did in this song, to somehow prepare himself for the inevitable.

The music is similar to a classical piece and sounds divine. Their singing on this album is simply magnificent.

(YouTube: Freddie Mercury & Monserrat Caballé – 'Guide Me Home')

'The Fallen Priest'

Sir Tim Rice wrote the lyrics for this song. He very wisely wrapped Freddie's life story in the lyrics. The story is about forbidden love, as the man is a priest who sins with this passionate love.

In the first verse, Rice wrote '*a life of sacrifice controlled me*'. It is about Mary, who sacrificed her life for Freddie, at least this is what Freddie thought.

'Those promises I made/ no longer hold me' – he sang – and *'the shackles fall away"*.

His love and desire are so strong that he can't and doesn't want to resist, and is *'searching for an earthly paradise'*. Yet, at the same time, he wants to resist because he knows he *'should be a rock against depravity and sin'*.

The story is about Freddie's struggle with drugs, alcohol and promiscuity. He feels he is a *'victim'* of his *'weaknesses and passion'* – which he was. He always knew he wasn't on the right track, but couldn't resist. He was searching for the *'heights'*, while he was *'in the hands of God who rolls the dice'*. He took the risk, and he fell from the *'heights'*. He wasn't lucky. Even God couldn't help him, and sadly he sacrificed his life on the altar of one-night stands in the name of love.

'Why do I believe in you
You're destroying my world
Hold nothing back
Give me all there is
I want it all'

Freddie believed in love even though he was afraid of it, as he knew it controlled him. Even after when he already had known about HIV infection and its danger, he didn't stop looking for 'love' in the night bars, because as he said: *'I want to eat my cake and keep it.'*

Knowing the history of his life, we can see that he really was a victim who deserves our sympathy.

(YouTube: Freddie Mercury & Montserrat Caballé 'The Golden Boy')

'Ensueño'

The song's lyrics were written by Montserrat Caballé, as Freddie did not have the time to write it. It is a song about a beautiful love story.

The lyrics are beautiful, but you can notice from the style that it was not written by Freddie. No hidden messages at all. They recorded it in Spanish to the delight of the Spanish audience.

The song's lyrics are about romantic love, and are a bit melodramatic, which is what we'd expect. The music is so delicate, and what makes it really gorgeous is that Freddie sang it in his natural baritone voice. The only musical accompaniment is Mike playing the piano throughout the song, so we can focus on the singing.

I suppose they intended to write the lyrics in Spanish so that the Spaniards would feel they were part of the album. I think it was an admirable gesture from Montserrat, and I was amazed she undertook to write the lyrics.

(YouTube: Freddie Mercury Montserrat Caballé 'Ensueño' Con Letra mp4)

'La Japonaise'

Freddie wanted to pay his respects to the Japanese people with this song. Some of the lyrics are in Japanese. The music is very engaging, part of it was written in Japanese style, and Freddie imitates their style exceptionally well. Montserrat uses her voice in different ways to sing subtle, dynamic variations and use a bunch of pitches, vibrato and bent notes in one short word. This song would have been much harder to sing than the other songs.

This lyrical song, written by Freddie, is about his and Montserrat's beautiful friendship. He likens their relationship to the natural beauty of Japan. *'A wonderful morning open, the dawn calls me, a pound pours into my heart, like a dream'*.

This relationship made Freddy very happy and so liberated that he was able to think of the beauty of nature that Montserrat reminded him of.

'My guardian angel in the sky, you've served me well all these years, greeting with both hands, trusting with no fears, till the end'. The keyword is trust, which was of great value to him. He called her a *'guardian angel'* who served him well by allowing him to write duets for them to sing together. Freddie is singing happily; it's clear that Freddie enjoyed this recording and loved this song. Montserrat's mere presence and working together with her made him forget his disease. Montserrat herself was a gift to Freddie, beautifying his most difficult years.

Both the lyrics and the music are wonderfully in line with the rest of the songs on the album.

(YouTube: 'La Japonaise' Freddie Mercury & Montserrat Caballé (translated Lyrics)

According to Montserrat, Freddie's eyes were glistening with tears during the show in Barcelona. The knowledge that this was almost certainly his last live appearance, his last live show must have been exceedingly painful. When Montserrat noticed that Freddie had tears in his eyes, she grabbed his hand, and Freddie kissed her hand.

The album was released two days later in the UK and got to number 15 on the charts. Many people think 15th place is respectable, and maybe it is, but not for this album. I think fans of Freddie and Queen were probably not opera fans, and so were unable to appreciate the album, and didn't pay attention to the lyrics. This was Freddie's finest album; its beauty can be compared to songs on Queen's first albums, such as 'You Take My Breath Away', 'Nevermore', 'Lily of the Valley' and 'Love of My Life.'

Freddie prepared for the recordings brilliantly, as Montserrat had very little time for studio work. Freddie recorded everything in advance, including Montserrat's part. The sheet music and recordings were sent to her, as Freddie wanted to be certain Montserrat could learn the song by the time of the recordings.

Freddie's creative genius raised him to dizzy heights, causing him to think he couldn't surpass this performance.

'What else is there left for me to do?' Freddie asked after completing the album.

No wonder he forgot for a moment who Freddie Mercury was, forgetting that he was always able to draw inspiration from anything and his imagination never let him down.

By 1988 however, his disease began to weigh him down to such an extent that he could not have known what else he was capable of doing. All he knew was that he wanted to sing until he dropped down dead. If only he'd known the next three albums of Queen would make it to number one on the UK charts, but sadly he was unable to enjoy their final success.

I listened to the songs with very mixed feelings, because I knew they were Freddie's honest confessions about his life and himself. According to Peter Freestone, these songs are Freddie's memoirs – and they really could be. He said a worthy farewell to the Spanish, Japanese fans and Montserrat.

Here is a quote from Peter Freestone and David Evans book about Freddie:

'A lot of the material can and must be looked at as autobiographical as this album mirrored exactly the real Freddie Mercury' – (Peter Freestone and David Evans)

I hope I have proven above that he was right.

43. *The Miracle* Album (1989)

AIDS was still seen as a stigma in the UK in 1989, so it was understandable Freddie didn't want to talk about his disease.

Princess Diana was the first prominent personality to show the world how to treat people who have AIDS. She opened the first AIDS centre in London, where she shook hands with Jonathan Grimshaw, who had lived with AIDS for five years. Until then, the commonly believed myth was that HIV could be spread by shaking hands.

Freddie's solo career ended with the *Barcelona* album, so he was happy he could work with Queen again to devote the rest of his life to music. The disappointment of not being able to sing discouraged him from appearing in public, not to mention his appearance after losing so much weight.

The band considered the new Queen album one of their best. 'I Want It All' was the first single of the ten songs, which made it to number three. Judging from the style of the song, it was probably written by Brian, as was 'Scandal'. This was Peter Freestone's claim, based on the guitar playing.

Similarly, Peter Freestone said that 'Khashoggi's Ship' and 'Rain Must Fall' were Freddie's songs, and 'Party' could be attributed to Roger, whereas 'Miracle' was a joint effort with John. According to other sources, 'Miracle was Freddie's song as well. The last song on the album, 'Was It All Worth It?' was certainly also written by Freddie, which is clear from the style and content of the lyrics.

Five singles were released from the album, all of which made it to the top 25, whereas the album itself, released in November, took the coveted number one spot in the UK.

Publicising the album was Brian and Roger's job, given that they weren't touring and Freddie no longer wanted to appear in front of the cameras.

Reporters increasingly bombarded them with questions about Freddie's health. Both of them denied Freddie had any problems. Freddie knew he wasn't just keeping the band members in limbo, but also the employees. After a long silence, as it was no longer possible to hide his condition; he had to let Brian, Roger and John in on the terrible secret.

This was effectively only confirmation of what they already suspected, but didn't want to believe it. The announcement affected them all deeply; acknowledging the inevitable was a shock for them. What would happen to them?

How would they get through it? This question hung in the air, but nobody raised it. Instead, they all embraced and defended Freddie. Nobody spoke about it because they understood why confidentiality was so important. They knew exactly what was at stake and stood by him like partners, in good times and bad.

The following quote is from the book written by Matt Richards & Mark Langthorne. It appeared in *The Times* magazine in September, 1992.

'He never asked for sympathy from anyone else,' recalled (Brian) May. 'He was a very strong person and always liked to be in control of his own destiny. He knew that if he did announce it, his life would become a circus, and he would be prevented from going about his business, which was making music. He wanted it to be business as usual until the end. There was no drama, no tears in his eyes. He was incredibly self-contained. We didn't feel we could speak about it to anyone. It was particularly hard lying barefacedly to our friends. And, of course, we had to stand by and watch this incredibly talented, strong man, in the prime of his life, gradually wasting away. There was a terrible feeling of helplessness.'

'Khashoggi's Ship'

Freddie still denied having any problem with his health in the lyrics of 'Khashoggi's Ship'.

'Who said my party was all over, I'm in pretty good shape' the song begins, remembering the parties he gave.

The journey on *Khashoggi's ship* addresses the crazy, dangerous period when he attended and gave parties non-stop, and his visits to nightclubs. The only thing Khashoggi had to do with the story was that he was also rich and pursued a dangerous business, like Freddie. He could afford anything, and it didn't matter that he had acquired his wealth.

'This big bad sucker with a fist as big as your head' was almost certainly the HIV, which wanted to get him, but he *'said kiss my ass honey.'* Of course, HIV doesn't give up so easily: *'He pulled out a gun, wanted to arrest me'*, but Freddie doesn't give up: *'Now listen, no one stops my party.'*

He performed the song by almost shouting all the way through, angrily fighting demons, frustrated and miserable. Deep in his soul, he knew there was little hope, but he still didn't want to give up, and he fought every moment to get the most out of what remained of his life.

This is the first video on which Freddie can be seen with a beard. Jim suggested he grow a beard, so he didn't have to spend as much time putting on make-up. His movement was still spirited, and he tried to produce his old form. Three years had elapsed since their last live concert, but he was hardly recognisable, his hair was thinning, and he had lost a lot of weight.

'Rain Must Fall'

Freddie talks to himself in 'Rain Must Fall'. He continues to try and dismiss dark thoughts and console himself; *'life is so exciting'*, *'your world so inviting'*, and yet for some reason, *'you're acting so bizarre'*, because he's trying to pretend everything is fine: *'Your world is so inviting/Playing really cool/And looking so mysterious, honey/Your every day is full of sunshine.'* Freddie wished his life was full of sunshine but it wasn't, he just pretended as if was everything just fine for the sake of himself and everybody else around him.

The word *'mysterious'* referred to the fact that nobody understood why Freddie had stopped touring, but rumours were going around about his health and the possibility that he had AIDS.

Nobody was allowed to talk about AIDS at home, as if it didn't even exist; not even Jim wanted to talk about it, *'but into every life, a little rain must fall'*. The bad news arrived like lightning from a clear sky in late April, 1987, and two years have passed since then, but *'no problem'*, just *'be cool'* as if everything were fine. Freddie truly was a great pretender, just as he had been in his childhood; he didn't complain to his parents about his loneliness or traumas. Maybe if he did, they would have considered bringing him home from boarding school.

In the next verse, he sings, *'They can blind you with science, bully you all over, with property or finance'* and *'you call the shots and name the price'*. Freddie was trying to say that whatever happens in life, we make our decisions, so we are the only ones to blame if *'rain must fall'*; we have to endure the consequences. It's possible to find success and recognition, as he did, but even the most successful person can be plagued with problems. Freddie had finally achieved a fairy tale existence, with success, fortune, a beautiful home and a *'family'*, but now this was all about to be ruined. Despite all of this, he sings *'Be cool, ha, kiss, kiss!'*.

He tried his best to entertain, make good music and write meaningful lyrics, but there was no way to hide the sadness he must have felt. He tried his hardest to be cool and suppress his inner torment, as he thought his illness was only his business. Even though he had positive, loving relationships, they couldn't provide emotional support, as he was unable to talk about his condition.

The *'problems at work'* refer to the fact that anyone can be in a situation where they are unable to alter the opinions of others. At the time, people who had AIDS were unable to get the same level of assistance and support as those suffering other diseases, because AIDS sufferers were looked down on and despised.

It also means he can't work the same way before the infection.

'You want a clean reputation
But now you're facing complications
'Cause into every life, a little rain must fall'

This was what Freddie dreaded most, losing his reputation. He now faced serious complications. Something had happened to him which now placed everything he had built in his adult life at risk; malicious people could destroy him.

'Play it nice and cool' he sings, reminding himself not to lose his self-control. He didn't want to lose his head and live in dread every day, so he chose to work and be creative instead. But he needed to deal with his anguished thoughts, and since he couldn't speak to anyone about them, he expressed them in the two songs above.

The instrumentation and tone are more cheerful than 'Khashoggi's Ship', and the song is more melodic. Fans disagreed on who wrote the song, with some believing that Deacon wrote it. Someone commented below the YouTube video: *'How do you know this is Deacon's track?'* A fan replied, *'From the fact that it's good to dance to.'* Another fan said, *'It's no accident he's called Disco Deacy.'*

Sadly, the time for discos had passed, both for Freddie and the other Queen members.

Brian said that Freddie was much more humorous than people generally thought.

He surely had a great sense of humour, and this was how he tried to alleviate tension whenever possible, but his humour wasn't the same in this phase of his life. There is no humour in these songs, even though they tried to smuggle some humour into the video. At least they tried, and no doubt laughed when lying on top of each other on the shelves during the recording. We just have to look at Freddie's face as the video starts, with the band members sitting on a train, which says it all. The image at 3:43 is very moving, Freddie's face is careworn, and the others surround him and smile as if everything was just fine. They tried to look happy to cheer themselves and Freddie up. I admire all of them for making such a heroic effort to persevere for as long as possible.

(YouTube: Queen – 'Rain Must Fall' (Official Lyric Video)

The great miracle was how the band finally came together and collaborated, as they had done previously, but we know why it was possible at this stage.

There were no more fights; he had no energy for that now. The way they stood by Freddie and supported him, and the way they accepted that Freddie didn't want to be treated like a patient showed their greatness as human beings. They were greater than they had ever been at any time on any stage. Their life's work was this togetherness, which kept Freddie's spirits up and showed they respected, honoured and loved him. Whatever happened between them in the past was forgotten. They had always been partners and kept going in good times and bad, because Queen, as a band, turned out to be greater than any of them.

The album cover perfectly depicts this overriding sense of unity, as the brilliant artistic work merges their four faces into one. The faces of the four wonderful artists became one. They worked together as one on their last two albums, *The Miracle* and *Innuendo*.

'The Miracle'

Peter Freestone wrote that 'The Miracle' was a collaboration with John, and Brian spoke with wonder in the video, *Days Of Our Lives* about how Freddie was able to write such a beautiful song and see the wonders of life when he knew the prognosis for his disease.

Judging by the content of the song, Freddie probably wrote the beautiful lyrics, listing the beautiful things in life, the most important being peace on Earth, and promising *'one day you'll see, we can all be friends'* at the end of the song.

(YouTube: Queen Miracle Official Video)

'Was It Worth All It?'

The comments below the YouTube video of this song indicate that some people regard it as Freddie's way of saying goodbye. This could be correct, as there would not be further opportunity to make another album. Freddie wrote this heartbreaking song about Queen and their career. The lyrics have no mystical content, so there is no need for interpretation.

I am sure his answer would be yes to the question in the title, even though he wrote *'Living breathing rock 'n' roll, this Godforsaken life'* which could mean it was his way of saying this life wasn't easy for them, as they were always on the road, and worked like crazy to be the best band in the world.

Freddie wanted to be a legend, and he chose Brian and Roger to help him achieve his dream, and the same goes for John, who joined the band later. No doubt they were there behind him, and all of them became legends.

For those millions of fans who loved them, the answer, of course, is yes; but no one could imagine that Roger and Brian would go with Queen +. Without a doubt, this step and all of their efforts to keep Queen alive are astonishing, and we need to thank them.

Roger had said he intends to put Freddie's statue in his garden. This statue had previously stood for 12 years in front of the Dominion Theatre, while the We Will Rock You musical was played, after which it was removed.

I am so glad Roger wants to do this, and I think it was wrong to remove it in the first place.

The album was released in May, 1989, and went to number one in the UK and number four in other countries. Queen released five singles from this album, three of them got into the top 10.

44. Life in Garden Lodge (1988-1989)

At the end of 1988, according to Jim, Freddie felt ill and had influenza-like symptoms, so he didn't want to go out for a drink with others in a bar, but he offered Jim the option of going out without him. Jim returned home drunk. Freddie woke up and was very angry and hurt that Jim hadn't stayed with him.

Freddie just wanted to be nice when he offered Jim the opportunity to go out without him. Jim should have known it wasn't right to leave Freddie alone, just as Freddie hadn't left him on his own in Japan even though Jim only had an upset stomach.

Poor Freddie just wanted confirmation that he could rely on Jim, whatever happened. Jim and Freddie had a terrible argument and insulted each other. At the end of the argument, they were both crying.

Freddie asked Jim, *'What are you going to do when I die?'*

'I don't know', Jim replied, still crying. *'I can't handle it all.'*

'Well, how do you think I feel?' replied Freddie.

Jim looked over and saw that Freddie was also crying. Jim often cried in despair when nobody could see him.

And the same despair held Freddie captive, which was why he had to work hard if he didn't want to surrender to the agonizing thoughts.

Before this quarrel, Jim had travelled home to Ireland for two weeks, and when he returned, Freddie found fault with him, saying he had neglected the garden and hadn't raked the leaves. This was another signal from Freddie; his problem wasn't with the leaves; he was upset because Jim had left him on his own again.

Jim had a simple way of thinking; he didn't consider that Freddie would have found it difficult to tell him not to go away, even though he just had to say the words and Jim would have discarded the idea.

Freddie got used to looking after himself with the help of others, but he didn't expect Jim to even consider leaving him alone for two weeks, if he really loved him.

According to a psychological study, 75% of people have to be told what to do, and the remaining 25% are self-directing, so they know what to do themselves. Jim belonged to the 75% group and Freddie to the 25% group, which was why they often misunderstood each other's motives and often quarrelled as a result, usually started by Freddie because he was impatient and frustrated.

In 1989 Jim wanted to erect a small building for himself in his mother's garden. He couldn't get a loan, so Freddie offered to lend him the money.

But as the building work progressed, Freddie started talking about the house in Ireland as their joint home, in the same way, he spoke about Garden Lodge as *'our house'*. Freddie wanted to secure Jim's future, probably afraid that he might have caught the virus, but Jim didn't dare get tested for the time being.

Queen starts to work on the *Innuendo* Album (1989)

As soon as they finished *The Miracle* album, Freddie wanted to get started on the next one right away, which turned out to be the last album they made together. The other band members knew the reason for the hurry, so they didn't hesitate.

In 1990 Freddie suddenly lost a lot of weight and could hardly walk, but insisted on taking short walks on the shores of Lake Geneva in Montreux before they began working in the studio. He adored the swans on the lake and loved to feed them. Jim bought him a stick to help him walk more easily, but Freddie wasn't willing to use it.

Around this time, Mary gave birth to her second son, Richard. Freddie and Jim regularly visited her, both in hospital and at home. Freddie loved holding the baby for a few minutes. He overwhelmed Mary with a whole range of baby clothes and toys. Jim made a wooden cradle for the baby, and Peter Freestone bought some nice baby blankets. Who knows why, but Mary chose not to use the cradle, except to store the stuffed animal toys that Freddie had bought.

The 'family' really outdid itself. Freddie was determined to make sure every family member's birthday was celebrated in appropriate style, and they went out for dinner in elegant restaurants. A 3-D version of the twin-dome conservatory designed by Freddie and built at Garden Lodge was made in the form of a cake for Jim's 40th birthday, which he was given at the end of the evening as a surprise.

And Jim did a lot for Freddie too, making tables, shelves and similar objects, even though he had never done anything like that before. And he bought a lot of small gifts for Freddie too, to give him pleasure. Freddie was delighted with small gifts that came from the heart. When his guests came, he bragged about the tables Jim had made, saying: *'My husband did it for me.'*

Despite working non-stop in the studios, Freddie also kept an eye on everything at home. He tried to furnish and decorate all the rooms in the house that were still empty or bare, as he didn't want to leave anything untidy or unfinished.

At the end of 1989, Cilla's *Goodbye to the '80s* show was broadcast from the ITV studio, where outstanding sportspeople and artists of the past decade were rewarded. Queen was also given a prize as the best band of the decade, so all four appeared in the studio. Brian gave the acceptance speech, but everyone was curious about Freddie and wanted to see whether the rumours were true. This time nobody could have been in any doubt about the fact that Freddie was very ill, his lean physique revealed everything, not to mention the thick make-up covering his face.

In February, 1990, Queen received another award at the Dominion Theatre for their outstanding contribution to British music. Freddie was under scrutiny again. This was his last public appearance, and later he could only be seen on music videos.

On the same day, Queen celebrated the 20th anniversary of the band's formation one year early because of Freddie's disease, with 400 guests, including Freddie's dearest friends, Liza Minnelli, Rod Stewart, David Bowie and other stars.

After the celebration, as Freddie was getting into a waiting car, he was ambushed by photographers who managed to take a photo of him, clearly showing how frail and emaciated he was. The following day the photo appeared on the front page of the newspapers. Nice of them, wasn't it? Who doesn't love the paparazzi?

They flew to Montreux in March to continue recording right up to early summer.

Freddie gathered all his strength during the recordings and sang beautifully, though he could barely even walk or stand.

Barbara visited Freddie during their stay in Montreux. They stayed up all night and chatted. In the morning, when Jim got up Freddie told him he had written a song for his favourite cat, Delilah.

Freddie didn't neglect his 'family' because of his disease; he took care of and looked after everyone all year round, anticipating this might be the last year he could do so.

Freddie sent Jim out with 500 pounds to buy different coloured flowers for Joe's birthday, and then they spent two hours arranging them as a surprise. The dinner still went ahead, even though Freddie withdrew relatively early because he was tired. Joe came home with some bad news in the same month. Since he felt ill too, he had taken a test, and it turned out that not 'only' was he HIV positive, he had also developed the symptoms of AIDS.

The others couldn't find the right words and were devastated; Joe was five years younger than Freddie. This very ill young man cared for Freddie lovingly and devotedly to the end, as if he was not sick himself. He only outlived Freddie by a year, so he himself was likely weak at the time, but he just did his job heroically. Freddie bought him a house, so he would have somewhere to live after Freddie passed on.

Around that time, Jim also became very anxious and secretly got tested. The test result was HIV positive, but he didn't yet have AIDS. Nobody talked about the test in the house.

Freddie's condition deteriorated even more drastically. He didn't sleep well because of Jim's snoring, so Jim sometimes spent half the night with him, just lying next to him until Freddie fell asleep. Later he found it was better to move out of the joint bedroom altogether, because he didn't want to disturb Freddie.

Freddie gave another example of his unconditional love and devotion to Jim. One morning he woke up to find that Jim hadn't got up. When he went to his room, it turned out Jim had the flu. Without any further thought, he snuggled up to him, comforted and kissed him, and wasn't interested in the fact that a bout of influenza could be fatal for him. Jim should have frantically avoided any close contact with Freddie, but he didn't do that. Freddie's kindness and his love and devotion to Jim showed through, again and again. As soon as someone needed him, he jumped through hoops without hesitation, whether it was for people, animals, his cats or his fish.

Fortunately, he didn't catch the flu. He cared for Jim while he was ill, and as if that wasn't enough, he designed and ordered some new Biedermeier-style bedroom furniture for him.

He increased Jim's salary during the summer, and even though Mary was going to inherit the house, Freddie told him he could stay as long as he wanted after his death, and if he wanted to move out, he could take anything he wanted with him. Mary had agreed to this. Jim knew that ownership would be transferred to Mary, but he wasn't interested; he wasn't concerned with financial matters, he was only interested in Freddie. Nevertheless, he replied that Freddie should put it in writing to ensure Mary kept her word. Somehow, he sensed he couldn't trust Mary.

Mary, however, could always rely on Jim; from time to time, he would assure her that if she needed anything, anytime, she just had to ask.

Despite all this, Freddie and Jim had another big row during the summer and eventually, after a few days, Joe told him that Freddie thought it was better if he left.

Jim was shocked, but could see no other option but to look for a flat, so he rented one.

The next day Mary called and told him he could keep his job as a gardener, but couldn't take the Volvo with him.

When Jim started to pack his belongings, Freddie appeared and asked him to stay. Jim stayed, but was very hurt by the way he'd been treated and was troubled by depression. What hurt Jim most was that the 'family' seemed pleased at the thought of him leaving.

I'm convinced that, without exception, they were all jealous of him because they sensed how much Freddie loved Jim, and in contrast, they probably didn't think much of him because of his ordinariness. They thought nothing of his kind-heartedness and friendliness. Jim put up with this pain for Freddie.

In August, Freddie admitted to his sister, Kashmira, that he was dying. Kashmira suspected this was the case, but was still shocked by the news. Freddie wouldn't let her tell their parents the cruel truth. His mother gave an interview in 2000 in which she said they knew Freddie had AIDS, but didn't want to talk to him about it because they knew it would be very uncomfortable for him.

Freddie celebrated his birthday in September with a relatively small circle of friends at Garden Lodge. Freddie bought a small gift for every guest, which he probably intended as a farewell gift because he wasn't confident that he would make it to Christmas or his next birthday.

After his birthday, Freddie 'freed himself' of Peter Straker and Barbara, as well as one of his drivers and the driver's friend.

Jim says Freddie was afraid of information leaking from the house, as had happened a few times, and which he understandably resented. His frailty meant he didn't have patience for anyone or anything; work took up all his strength. Jim asked Freddie why he had argued with Peter, but Freddie just gave a short, evasive reply.

The album recordings progressed slowly because Freddie's condition was deteriorating; he was continually given medicine through a catheter, and the side effects caused constant nausea, headaches, feeling unwell and a high fever.

The area around Freddie's house was inundated with journalists and photographers, like vultures hunting for prey; they even observed the bathroom window and took photos from the boot of a car. Their behaviour was incredibly inconsiderate.

The press began to pursue the other members of Queen, and even though they denied that Freddie had AIDS, the photographers didn't give up.

On one occasion, when Freddie and his doctor, Dr Atkinson, were leaving the clinic, they managed to take another photo of him, which was published as a full-page, grainy image in *The Sun*. The journalist claimed, 'This photo is proof that rock superstar Freddie Mercury is battling a serious disease'. The photo was captioned 'Freddie Mercury's sad face'.

The photo scared fans, who began to fear for Freddie, and it made Roger, Brian and John angry. Even though they denied Freddie had the disease, these people were capable of doing anything for money.

Freddie's wonderful humour and strength gave those around him the strength to tolerate the intolerable, and even make the last moments they spent together magical.

On one occasion, Freddie asked jokingly: 'The reason we are successful, darlings? My overall charisma, of course.'

It sounds like a joke, but it wasn't a joke at all. Freddie sold all the songs, and it was he who captivated everyone with his personality.

According to Peter Freestone, Freddie never bragged about writing more hits than the other band members; he was proud of himself, but would never hurt or offend the other members of Queen.

Freddie was a survivor; the survival skills that he'd developed unwittingly in boarding school were now really useful to all of them.

According to Brian, Freddie never complained. They all admired his spirit and fighting ability, and a kind of marvellous harmony emerged between them like never before. Freddie had demolished the wall that had separated them.

45. Innuendo Album (1991)

Freddie once said:

'After all these years, you don't want it to be such a fight to get anything done. You've already done that thing, and I think most of it should be fun – like live recording should be done. I think we are four people that, in the end, need that kind of thing, even though we don't like it. If it were too easy, we would lose interest. So we think 'Oh my God' we'd better go back in and carry on fighting'. (Freddie Mercury)

This time there were no fights; Freddie's illness brought the team closer than ever, and they made light-hearted videos, such as 'I'm Going Slightly Mad', which was Freddie's song. Even though Freddie wore a wig and heavy make-up, the video is very cheerful and humorous. Freddie looked remarkably good in the video; his face looked good, and he was dressed smartly, just like the others. They seemingly enjoyed the recording. (Freddie's biographers don't share my opinion of Freddie's appearance. However, in the comments under the YouTube videos, it is clear the fans adore this video and like the fact that Freddie dressed up, though it's true we all watch this video with some bitterness, and it brings tears to the eyes even after so many years. When Jim appeared unexpectedly in the studio during the video recording, he didn't recognise Freddie!

Brian, the most sensitive person in the band, wrote a song with the well-known title 'The Show Must Go On'. Although the song supposedly wasn't about Freddie, it's astonishing how well some of the lines were suited to his situation.

To avoid creating negative emotions in Freddie, Brian suggested renaming the song, but Freddie wouldn't agree. I think, among others, Freddie's illness and approaching passing inspired Brian to write this song. The great sadness that affected Brian's life always brought the best songs out of him. I sense that he was saying farewell to Freddie with this song, which was why he offered to alter the title. He didn't want Freddie to think that life wouldn't and couldn't stop, not even if Freddie, the life and soul of the band, were to say a final goodbye. Brian was trying to give himself strength. This great song must have been part of his coping process.

One verse was especially suited to Freddie:

'Inside, my heart is breaking, my make-up may be flaking, but my smile still stays on.'

Freddie didn't want to change the title, and said he didn't have any problem with it at all. Brian says the way he sang it made it perhaps one of their best songs.

(YouTube – 'The Show Must Go On' Official Video))

Although every song is designated as a Queen song on the album, maybe the old fans recognise the songwriters' styles.

The title track, 'Innuendo', was Freddie's song on this album, the second one was 'I'm Going Slightly Mad', the third, 'All God's People', and the fourth were 'Bijou'.

'Innuendo'

The lyrics of 'Innuendo' convey a depth of content; Freddie put his heart and soul into it. One verse is especially beautiful:

'If there's a God or any kind of justice under the sky
If there's a point if there's a reason to live or die
If there's an answer to the questions, we feel bound to ask
Show yourself - destroy our fears - release your mask'

Freddie probably felt destiny, or God, if He existed, was unfair to him. He didn't understand the point of being born, of living or dying, and was waiting for someone to answer the question, why did he have to die?

Everyone can feel for him; his death was senseless, just like the other victims. There is no reasonable explanation. People are just as vulnerable as any other creature; being human is no guarantee, our lives often hang by a thread, and we'll clutch at anything just to stay alive.

This verse is about Freddie's fear of death, which he never showed to the 'family' members or even Jim, and especially not to outsiders.

In the middle of the song, the flamenco, a Spanish dance, starts (played in a virtuoso manner and improvised by Yes' guitarist Steve Howe) and is very reminiscent of the operatic part of 'Bohemian Rhapsody'. It gives a little bit of joy, like in 'Bohemian Rhapsody' the words: *'Galileo, Galileo, Galileo Figaro'*. Even though Freddie was very sad, he still pretended he had no reason to be sad, and continued the 'great pretender' role. If he could have taken off his mask, he wouldn't have been so lonely; he would have been able to share his sorrow with someone, but he couldn't. He had to be brave, just as he had been as a little boy. He lived his whole life like an abandoned child: struggling alone with life's difficulties as best he could. And he said proudly that he learned one thing early on, how to look after himself, so he didn't have to rely on anyone. He wore a suit of armour throughout his life to protect himself from emotional intrusion. He found some consolation in love affairs, but was unable to relax because he lived in constant dread, believing that any intimate relationship could end at any time, just as he had to break off from his family a long time ago. This was why he was so lonely. And this constant dread meant not even the love of everyone was enough.

(YouTube – Queen – 'Innuendo' (Official Video))

The video is innovative and memorable, but quite shocking, inspired by the lyrics. Since Freddie could no longer participate in live recordings, the DoRo Productions had to make this unusual video. We can only see the band members in flashes from old recordings or they appear as cartoon characters. Old recordings are flashed up on the screen, adapted to the content of the song, including scenes from the Second World War, Stonehenge, Hungarian folk dancers, Spanish flamenco dancers, locusts, marching Russian soldiers, and prayers at Mecca.

The video backs up my interpretation of Freddie's fear: first of all, we are only able to access the show through a lot of doors until Freddie starts to sing; we can see the audience, who are not humans but puppets, before the song starts. We see the same dead toy doll several times, lying under a broken window. The music itself is very depressing from the outset, the puppets are unusual, distorted or incongruous (piglets in front of the curtains) and, overall, are quite frightening. When Freddie starts singing about natural scenes, they don't appear in all their beauty (mountains, waves, wind), but as raging elements, which are indistinct, while incomprehensible Arabic captions appear, possibly from the Quran. The 'audience' stares in the direction of the stage during the show; there are no stamping of feet, clapping or anything that we are used to.

'While we live according to race, colour or creed
While we rule by blind madness and pure greed

Our lives dictated by tradition, superstition, false religion
Through the aeons, and on and on'

The above verse is about the unfairness and the crazy world we live in.

Traditions and binding religious teachings defined Freddie's whole life. But, in part, he rebelled and demolished every tradition in his life. He even abandoned his religion.

The fact that Freddie couldn't write joyous, enthusiastic, life-affirming songs in his condition is completely understandable. But, instead, they are very clear and honest and therefore to be treasured. He tells us what was hurting him and how he felt mentally and physically when the song was written; I'm thinking here of his appearance as a cartoon character.

'Oh yes, we'll keep on tryin'
We'll tread that fine line
Oh oh, we'll keep on tryin'
Till the end of time
Till the end of time'

Freddie and others who are facing severe hardship, whether suffering from injustice or disease, have no control. Their only option is to follow a narrow path that their circumstances and abilities allow. People have always done this since the beginning of time. Freddie showed an exceptional example of how to accept bad news and bear the unbearable. In the cheerful flamenco musical part in the middle of the song, the dolls come to life, and the lyrics become optimistic. Freddie sings:

'You can be anything you want to be
Just turn yourself into anything you think that you could ever be
Be free with your tempo be free, be free
Surrender your ego be free, be free to yourself'

This is reminiscent of his past when he could still freely do what he wanted and wasn't restricted by his disease. This is the reason for the cheerful part, and then he returns with the saddest part. In the words *'release your mask'*, the mask becomes a skull for a fleeting moment. This part confirms what Freddie was afraid of, what he had to face, and yet he had to keep going, trying, fighting to the last to live his life as he wanted (as far as his strength would allow). He didn't want the disease to control him.

DoRo Production won a prize for the video.

(YouTube – Queen –'Innuendo' (with lyrics))

Freddie wrote the lyrics for 'I'm Going Slightly Mad' with Peter Straker, who was still his friend at the time. What struck me about the lyrics is that they are not at all funny, if we take an in-depth look.

In the first verse, Freddie writes about the daffodils one of his favourite spring flowers:

'One thousand and one yellow daffodils
Begin to dance in front of you, oh, dear
Are they trying to tell you something?'

Freddie once said: *'I'm as gay as a daffodil.'* Daffodils often appeared in Freddie's photos. He was holding one single flower, and in this video, he appears in a field full of daffodils.

'You're missing that one final screw
You're simply not in the pink
My dear, to be honest, you haven't got a clue'

When Freddie sees a thousand and one daffodils in the field, he thinks of his many gay partners. He is not in the pink because of he is not in his best health condition. The missing screw, which didn't turn this one daffodil pink (as in nature), referred to the fact that Freddie had no idea who had infected him. Who was the only pink one in the field of yellow and white? When he sings that he's starting to go slightly mad, the whole thing turns into a drama, and the situation is really maddening, a young, strong, fit and healthy man defeated by a tiny virus.

'It finally happened' refer to what he had always feared, catching the virus and suffering from AIDS.

He tried to deal with this jovially in the song, and he was right; it must have been difficult to understand, with a sound mind, how a seemingly innocent adventure could have made him terminally ill. It made his destiny so dramatic and causes us to contemplate how much he suffered, simply to finally bid farewell to life.

'I'm one card short of a full deck' – this card is his health. With that card, his life would have been perfect. The lines that follow add to what he wants to say: *'I'm not quite the shilling'* – in other words, he's not complete; something is missing. *'One wave short of a shipwreck'* – the final blow will be when he can no longer work, and he thinks that is going to be the end. *'I'm not at my usual top billing'* – he can longer perform live. *'I'm coming down with a fever'* which was the side effect of his medication, and *'I'm out to sea'* the song continues, which would have been scary for Freddie, partly because he was afraid of the water and partly because on the open sea, help might come, or it might not. *'This kettle is boiling over'* – it's not working perfectly, referring to the fact that something was wrong with him; he couldn't produce his usual form because his health was rapidly deteriorating, work was too big a strain for him. *'I think I'm a banana tree'* – this feeling was so strange and confusing, as if he wasn't himself, but rather something completely different, no longer human, just vegetating like plants in general.

The imagery continues after the refrain, *'I'm knitting with only one needle'* – he can only work at half speed now.

'Unravelling fast, it's true' – what he is knitting is quickly falling apart, this is true – meaning his condition was deteriorating rapidly.

'I'm driving only three wheels these days' – I'm moving much slower than I'd like, I'm going so slow, it's like travelling on a three-wheel bicycle.

'But my dear, how about you?' – preferring as always to deflect attention from himself and onto others, Freddie asks, how are you? Just so that he doesn't have to talk about himself.

He adds a small phrase to the refrain at the end of the song *'I'm going slightly mad, and there you have it'* – and there you have it, you've caught the virus that you dreaded so much, he tells himself.

As I mentioned, Peter Straker helped Freddie write the lyrics, and they laughed all night as the comparisons became 'funnier' even though they reflected Freddie's reality. And Jim liked the lyrics too; he thought they were humorous.

Peter probably didn't realise what it was about, or he wouldn't have been in the mood to laugh and nor would Jim. Freddie knew what the song was about and yet still laughed, though I fear in agony rather than pleasure. This was the kind of convulsive laughter that is usually followed by tears.

(YouTube - Queen – 'I'm Going Slightly Mad' Official Video))

'All God's People'

This is a wonderful, lyrical composition about how we're all equal and that people should treat everyone equally, including kings and ministers. Freddie is singing about his own pain in the song and not that of humanity in general. Why did homosexuals have to be so badly treated, patronised and pushed away, as if they weren't God's creations? Why would people turn their backs on God's laws? All men are equal before God, and we should all remember this and act accordingly. Just as Jesus taught Christians, we have no right to judge others. *'Do not judge, lest you be judged'*, he said. Freddie then called on rulers to rule with their hearts and observe the dictates of their conscience.

Freddie's song describes the eternal truth that any form of discrimination, judgement and stigma is harmful, and has dreadful consequences for the individual, given that everyone should respect our right to human dignity.

As the song is about God and His laws, it is performed in gospel style. The music is as perfect as the lyrics, with beautiful harmony, reflecting the unity of the members of Queen and the harmony, peace and love between them. It's a stunning piece of music, worthy of Queen's greatness and uplifting in every respect. The fans' comments below the YouTube video suggest this song should be played in church. I agree, in the hope that people attending church won't just listen to the Word of God but also try to live their life accordingly.

Freddie turned away from religion precisely because it condemned homosexuality. We know the words in the Bible were written by people and have been edited several times in synods; some parts were left out, but the teachings of Jesus are eternal truths, like the Ten Commandments.

The video was made after Freddie's death, and his statue on the shores of Lake Geneva flashes up for a moment near the end.

The video is a magnificent demonstration of the magical world in which Queen performed, with Freddie at the front.

(YouTube – Queen – 'All God's People' Official Lyric Video)

Bijou

Last, but not least, is the song 'Bijou', written for Jim. The lyrics are very short. In brief, the content is about Jim and Freddie being destined to spend the rest of their days together, like two lovers, forever. At the end of the song, Freddie calls Jim 'My bijou'. When Freddie wrote this song, he was already very ill and had lived with Jim for five years, meaning the lyrics were no longer fuelled by love hormones, yet he still saw Jim as his partner and lover. Around this time, he was incapable of physical love and could only hug and kiss, but Jim says this meant more than sex. This statement shows how true and deep his love for Freddie was, more so than anyone else in the world; in effect, Jim would have given his life for him. Hopefully, Freddie was aware of this. Words don't matter, and people can say anything. Actions measure real love; love isn't just an emotion but an active presence, doing everything you can for someone. Freddie and Jim did everything they could for each other.

This was not a usual love song for Freddie, but he could finally say that he now had what he had craved all his life; he'd found someone he could stay with forever, even if forever meant while Freddie was alive. The lyrics are short, but the music says it all.

A few comments about the album, which say more than anything I could ever say:

'Bed

Red Special really is crying silver tears'

'Eric_Dincher 15

Innuendo is one of their best albums because it's all for Freddie's life, heartbreaking'

'MARCO POLO

This was the requiem for Freddie'

(YouTube – Queen – Bijou (Official Lyric Video))

'These Are The Days Of Our Lives' is Roger's song and might have been inspired by his children. It's one of Roger's best songs; when he wrote it, he probably had no idea that Freddie's disease would put the song in a completely different context, though we can't be certain.

The song lyrics are about his carefree childhood and youth when there were still only good things in life. Those days are gone now, but one thing is true, *'I still love you'*. Roger was probably thinking of his children.

When Freddie sang on the video, the lyrics seemed to be about Queen's past, about those beautiful 20 years they had spent together. It sounds like he was bidding farewell to Queen, and since he looked directly at the camera when he sang, he also seemed to be bidding farewell to his fans, saying, *'I still love you'*.

This is the last video where we can see him still in relatively good condition. He is barely recognisable, only his smile is like the old one, he's very friendly but very sad, a heart-breaking sight. It's clear he was very ill, but seeing him like this is better than nothing at all. These videos seem like we were given an opportunity to say goodbye to him.

Peter Freestone's book reveals that Freddie was no longer able to move during the recording because the wound on his heel meant he couldn't put any weight on his right leg, or he would have been in agony. Walking was almost impossible for him at the time, but he didn't want to be remembered as a cartoon character.

(YouTube – 'These Are The Days Of Our Lives' Official Video))

The single, 'Innuendo', was released in January, 1991, whereas the album came out in February. Both records went straight to number one on the UK charts, where they deserved to be. Most fans say the album is 'pure gold'. More than a hundred thousand copies were sold in the first week of the album's release. I believe the fans also thought that this would be Queen's last album with Freddie.

Freddie's voice is not as powerful as when he was at full strength, but it's still stunning. It's painful to listen to, knowing how much he suffered during the recordings.

He put everything into it and worked as if his life depended on it, to avoid disappointing his fans. On the contrary, almost without exception, the fans are grateful for the final albums, because as they see it, our Freddie still sings better than anyone else, even when he was dying.

Queen became an epic band during the 20 years they spent together; musically, they were right at their peak. It's no wonder Freddie's tragic disease signified a total collapse of the band, not to mention the emotional ties.

When Freddie was still healthy and was asked about the band's future, he said:

'Underneath it all, we like each other, and we like the music we make. That's basically it. And if we didn't like the music, we'd say 'C'est la vie' and 'Goodbye' to each other.' (Freddie Mercury)

Nobody envisaged this would be how they said goodbye, neither Freddie nor the other band members. It wasn't the fate they deserved.

John said after Freddie's death: *'There is no Queen without Freddie.'* I think the absence of any of them would have been just as tragic for the band; all three of them had become masters of their instruments, just as Freddie had mastered his voice, and probably, despite all the arguments and 'hatred', they still liked each other. John and Freddie liked each other in particular, they were good friends, but John spent time with his family when Freddie threw himself into the nightlife back in the day.

Freddie recorded the video for 'I'm Going Slightly Mad' all day. That evening when Freddie got home, Jim heard excited whispering from outside the front door. Freddie entered, holding a large parcel. It was Valentine's Day.

Jim asked excitedly what was in the parcel. Freddie answered, 'Surprise'. And it really was; Freddie had bought Jim a painting entitled *Surprise*, which he had seen in a Sotheby's catalogue a few days earlier. On the painting, two cats were playing on a garden path with a snail.

After the recordings, Freddie decided to buy a flat in Montreux to enjoy the peace, the lake and the fantastic view of the Alps. He would have liked to have retired here because of the increasingly oppressive presence of the paparazzi.

Jim Beach found him an appropriate flat, which comfortably had enough room for Jim, Joe and Freddie. A fine view of the lake and town opened up from the balcony.

They also planned a trip to Ireland, so Freddie could finally see the house Jim had built, which was now complete, but he could not make such a long trip. Nevertheless, Jim sensed Freddie was present in every room there because the two of them had spent so much time planning it, and Freddie made Jim take so many photos that he had effectively seen everything, as if he too had been there.

The Queen single, 'Headlong', *Brian's song* was released in May, and the lyrics reminded Jim of what he had to face at Garden Lodge.

Jim was right. According to the lyrics: *'And you're rushing headlong, you've got a new goal, and you're rushing headlong out of control. And you think you're so strong, But there ain't no stopping, And there's nothing you can do about it, Nothing you can do, no, there's nothing you can do about it.'*

Freddie decided he wanted to make another album, and asked Brian and the other band members to write songs that he would sing, and then they would finish them later without him. Of course, they respected Freddie's request and got on with the job. Freddie started work and sang the first three verses of 'Sweet Mother Love', but could not sing the last verse and said he'd come back to it. This was on 22 May, 1991, but Freddie was never able to return to the studio. This was his last recording. But the other band members found enough material that had previously been recorded, and released the *Made in Heaven* album in 1995, which also featured 'Sweet Mother Love'. Brian sang the last verse.

46. Sweet Mother Love

Freddie and Brian wrote the song, and it's evident to me that it was for Jim. The lyrics clearly reveal this. I don't know whether Jim ever knew this, but it's one of the finest songs Freddie wrote. Jim was deserving of Freddie immortalizing this beautiful relationship, and it's no coincidence this was the last song he ever sang. It's his saddest and most painful song:

'I don't want to sleep with you
I don't need the passion too
I don't want a stormy affair
To make me feel my life is heading somewhere
All I want is the comfort and care
Just to know that my woman gives me sweet
Mother love ah ha'

Freddie felt helpless and vulnerable when he wrote the song because, he was very ill; he needed the kind of love mothers give to their sick children. However, Freddie knew Jim was there for him and loved Freddie as if he were his own sweet child. His heart was full of kindness and concern for Freddie.

*'I've walked too long in this lonely lane
I've had enough of this same old game
I'm a man of the world, and they say that I'm strong
But my heart is heavy, and my hope is gone
Out in the city, in the cold world outside
I don't want pity, just a safe place to hide
Mama, please, let me back inside
I don't want to make no waves
But you can give me all the love that I crave'*

Freddie admitted he had no strength to keep fighting alone and didn't want to stress his partner with continual arguments. Other people may have thought that he was strong, but his heart was heavy, and he had given up hope of staying alive. So, he asked Jim to let him into his heart and to look after him, as if he were his mother. It's a heartbreaking twist.

*'I can't take it if you see me cry
I long for peace before I die
All I want is to know that you're there
You're gonna give me all your sweet
Mother love ah ha (mother love)'*

He didn't want to be left alone, because he had been terrified all his life of being alone, and suffered from a lack of affection. He now craved constant hugs and caresses, like a child; he continually needed confirmation that he was loved, because this gave him a sense of security.

*'My body's aching, but I can't sleep
My dreams are all the company I keep
Got such a feeling as the sun goes down
I'm coming home to my sweet
Mother love
God works in mysterious ways
Eeeeh dop, de dop, dep dop
I think I'm goin' back to the things I learned so well in my youth'*

He couldn't sleep because of the pain, which was why he needed company. The *'feeling as the sun goes down'* and he finally returns *'home'* where he'll always be loved, and no longer has to suffer from lack of affection. He thinks of God, who arranged things in such a way that he could go back to what he had in his younger days. Freddie is thinking of the care he got at home before being sent to Panchgani.

As I read Jim's book, I sensed that Jim didn't realise what the lyrics meant, or perhaps he hadn't even heard this song when they were caring for Freddie, since the album was only released in 1995. It would have been good for him to know what Freddie wrote in this song and who the lyrics were for.

However, a few months passed before Freddie was finally confined to bed; he bought the flat in Montreux in May and was busy decorating it. Jim put some plants on the balcony a few hours after the first visit. Then Freddie engaged Montreux's most sought-after interior designers to complete the apartment by Christmas, based on his own designs because he wanted to spend Christmas quietly there.

Freddie bought a fine Tissot painting of the artist's love, a beautiful young woman. Despite being so young and beautiful at the time of the portrait, the woman was suffering a fatal disease and died soon after the painting was completed.

During the summer, Jim took photos of Freddie for the last time in their garden at home, and though he seemed very frail and ill, this didn't bother them at all, as these pictures were some of Jim's favourites.

Paul Prenter died of AIDS in August. Freddie was very shocked by the news; he hadn't expected Paul to pass away so quickly. Jim says his death probably reminded Freddie of what awaited him.

Freddie didn't have to be reminded because he had already sung about what he was expecting in 'Sweet Mother Love' in May, so they celebrated his birthday very quietly. All Freddie wanted was to enjoy his private life while this was still possible, without being disturbed, and he didn't even want his friends to see what a terrible condition he was in. The birthday cake was a copy of the new Montreux apartment building. Jim says the birthday party was a quiet and sad event, as they knew Freddie wouldn't have another birthday.

Despite his weakness, Freddie gathered all his strength and gave a farewell dinner to his doctors, Dr Atkinson and five other specialists. One of them suggested that Jim take an AIDS test. So, Jim went to Dr Atkinson's clinic and didn't dare admit he'd already been through it. He didn't believe the result would be any different, but this time Freddie knew about the test.

As Freddie was very ill, he decided to travel to Montreux one last time. During the ten days he spent there, he could no longer walk without assistance and knew he would never have the chance to see his favourite lake with the swans again. He spent most of his days asleep in bed. Joe, Jim and Tony King, Freddie's old friend, looked after him.

November 9th was the last time they flew home from Switzerland. Freddie knew they could never return and he would never have the chance to see his new home completed. While they were in Switzerland, he decided to stop the AIDS treatment. Naturally, his doctors were opposed, but Freddie liked to control his own destiny. He must have felt there was no point in prolonging his suffering. He wasn't capable of staying up, singing or writing music.

Music was the most important thing in Freddie's life. It wasn't just a job, but it gave meaning to his life. He felt that if he couldn't write music, it was all over because he had no other skills, not to mention that he didn't want to burden anyone.

When he was alone, poor Jim cried a lot and went for walks at night because he couldn't sleep. He dreaded and feared losing Freddie and was dispirited by his own health.

One day while they were in Montreux, he got the bad news – over the phone – from Dr Atkinson. Freddie was in the room at the time. Jim had to tell him he was HIV positive.

'Bastards! I'm sorry, darling, you are HIV positive,' Freddie said, going pale, although there was no doubt in his mind what the result would be.

The 'bastards' he referred to were the people he caught the infection from and those from who they caught it. He said this in agony and knew nobody was to blame; no one could have known they were playing with their lives.

The same afternoon Tony King asked Freddie what would happen to the guys. By the guys, he meant Jim. According to Tony King, Freddie said Jim could stay at Garden Lodge as long as he wanted. Tony asked how he thought this would work when he knew Mary didn't like Jim. 'They'll sort it out somehow', Freddie replied.

I'm convinced Freddie thought the house in Ireland was there for Jim, and in any case, he was sure Jim wouldn't be alive for long, so he didn't put the agreement in writing and didn't want to antagonise Mary, who didn't want Jim to stay.

Mary had given Freddie the best gift in his life, his freedom. She had accepted his decision to leave her, and she didn't take revenge, at least not in the way Paul Prenter did. Mary knew Freddie was generous and had promised he would always look after her. And Freddie liked to keep his promises.

47. Last Hugs and Kisses

One evening, a few days later, Freddie and Jim were watching a romantic film from the 30s together. The heroine asked her sweetheart: *'Will we stay together as long as we live?'* To Jim's surprise, Freddie asked him the same question.

'Of course, we will. Don't be silly!' Jim replied, with a huge lump in his throat.

Jim spent every day in the garden. Freddie could only see him from the window, but spent his evenings with him. Freddie would often ask Jim if he loved him. Jim always confirmed that he did, then hugged him and kissed his forehead while Freddie's head rested on his lap.

Freddie slept a lot during the day because he was still taking painkillers. He watched TV when he was awake.

If Jim had known the lyrics of 'Sweet Mother Love', he wouldn't have moved from Freddie's side for a minute; although Peter Freestone said that Freddie didn't want life in the house to stop, so they pretended everything was normal. Freddie was probably tired and didn't want the others to endure the sight and the knowledge that Freddie had to say goodbye to life, which he loved so much.

Concerning the future, Freddie said in an interview:

'I don't want to be a burden on anybody else. I would like to feel that I went without having to be a burden on anyone, and that is not condescending. I just don't want to. It's the honest truth. I'd love to go out while I'm still on top.' (Freddie Mercury)

Freddie's wishes were fulfilled. Even though he needed support and assistance, neither his friends nor his 'family' felt it was a burden. They all loved him with all their hearts and were pleased to do something for him, and to be able to alleviate his suffering, even if only slightly, but they were all crushed psychologically.

Freddie really went out on top; the 1986 tour was their most successful tour, and the last three albums reached number one on the charts.

While he still had the strength, they flew to Montreux several times for Freddie to find peace and to collect his thoughts.

Jim worked in the garden so Freddie would be pleased when he saw the nicely maintained garden. He often looked out onto the garden from the bedroom window and shouted to Jim, who ran up to him during the day to tell him how much he loved him.

As the days went by, an increasing number of journalists and photographers surrounded the house, hoping to take a photo of Freddie. As soon as anyone left the house, they were pursued and harassed with questions about Freddie's condition. Freddie's famous friends, like Elton John and others, fortunately, found a solution by entering the house unnoticed through the rear garage, so they could see Freddie for the last time and at least say goodbye in spirit.

Even though Jim was working in the garden, Peter or Joe or Dave Clark (Freddie's old musician friend) took turns being with Freddie, and he was never left on his own, even during the day.

They also took turns watching him at night and acquired an intercom system to communicate with one another when required. Everyone wanted to be with him when he finally passed away. He was only eating a small amount of fruit and drank fruit juice, and said there was no point eating.

By this time, Freddie spent most of his days in bed, but still had some pleasant conversations with Dave Clark, who spent hours with him just to help the others.

Mary was seven months pregnant and had her other young son to take care of, but she visited Freddie every day.

Joe and Peter looked after him during the day, and he spent his evenings with Jim. They all took turns to look after him at night. He was never left alone, and even the cats hung around.

After Freddie stopped taking medicine, there was no significant change in his condition in the first week, but the following week he suddenly became weaker and was unable and unwilling to eat.

Peter Freestone wrote in his book:

'I'd stay in the main house until about ten-thirty, eleven o'clock, checking on him one last time before I would go to bed.'

Very rarely would he call for either Joe or me during the night. Although he could be a tyrant, a demanding, unreasonable prima donna, underneath the façade, he had one of the softest, kindest hearts imaginable. He realised the need for our rest so that we would be able to take care of him as he knew we wanted to during the day.'

Elsewhere he wrote:

'I heard a clock everywhere in the house, ticking away, ticking away, each minute being part of a countdown whose length we didn't know. Each tick was counting away the moments of Freddie's life.'

One evening Peter was lying down on the bed next to Freddie when Freddie asked him whether everything was okay in the house, and then said:

'I feel so tired, wondering whether I will ever see any of it again. Trying to visualise what's going on. I'm so isolated up here. All of a sudden, it feels a huge house.'

Peter sensed he had to tell Freddie what he had learned from the doctor.

'I sensed this was the only chance I would carry out the doctor's advice. 'Everything is fine.' – I said. 'Just as you'd like it, like always. And we are *fine too. We're coping. Don't worry about us. If you feel it's time to go, we're behind you all the way. Don't worry about us. Don't feel you're leaving us. Everything is fine.'* (Peter Freestone)

In the final week, his parents and sister came to visit, and so did Roger with his two kids. Freddie made a superhuman effort and entertained them for over two hours, trying to pretend everything was just fine.

Brian and Anita Dobson (Brian's second wife) also paid a visit to see how he was. Brian looked out into the garden and made some comment about it, to which Freddie replied:

'Guys, don't feel like you need to make conversation, I'm just so happy that you are here, you know, even if we say nothing, it's just having these moments.'

(Days of our Lives, BBC TV (Globe Productions, 2011)

This was how Freddie said goodbye, he was happy to feel these exceptional people around him who he loved and valued so much. He knew how difficult it must be for them to say anything, when it might be the last time they saw him alive.

It was as if Freddie wanted to keep these final moments in his heart so they would stay with him on the journey forever, wherever he was going. All he wanted was to enjoy those moments with them while he still could.

In the last week of Freddie's life, November, Thursday 21st proved to be a very sad day for Jim. This was the last time Freddie appeared at the window to shout down to him.

Jim surrounded Freddie with special love and affection that night. Freddie fell asleep in Jim's arms, squeezing his hand, and when he woke up, his first question to Jim was whether he loved him. He often squeezed Jim's hand at night and wanted to know more than anything that Jim really loved him. Jim reassured Freddie that he did, and stroked his forehead.

When dawn broke, Freddie decided to go down to the ground floor one more time to look at his favourite paintings. Jim offered to take him down, but Freddie wanted to do it on his own; he was no longer able to even put his arm on someone's shoulder.

Freddie sat down to rest for five minutes, and then stood up and set off downstairs and slowly stumbled down the staircase, holding onto the banister. Jim lit up each of the paintings in turn; Freddie was delighted and enjoyed looking at the beautiful paintings. He got tired very quickly, and Jim had to take him back to bed.

Jim wrote about that morning as follows:

'I think that Friday morning was the last time I could honestly say Freddie was happy, the last time that Freddie Mercury was still there, the last time he radiated that Freddie Mercury excitement.'

Later that morning, Jim Beach visited Freddie, and they spent several hours together, just the two of them. They decided Freddie would release a press statement, telling the world he had AIDS.

The 'family', including Jim, were shocked. No one was aware that Freddie had wanted to publish such a statement, not even Jim. They didn't understand why he had to do it in his final moments, or if he really wanted to do it.

Jim doubted this was what Freddie really wanted.

Jim Beach explained to them that Freddie's honesty could be a great help to other people who had AIDS. He was accepted worldwide and as a popular star, he could direct attention to the disease, treatment and especially prevention.

I believe Freddie went along with the statement, even if it wasn't his idea, but nobody can be certain.

He still hadn't been diagnosed as an AIDS patient when he began talking about the importance of protection, and this was why he gave up the one-night stands and probably chose Jim as his long-term partner after his positive HIV tests. This was when he still hoped by some miracle he would recover.

They agreed with Jim Beach, and it was decided to release the statement to the press at midnight:

The statement is reproduced below:

'Following the enormous conjecture in the press over the last two weeks, I wish to confirm that I have been tested HIV positive and have AIDS. I felt it correct to keep this information private to date to protect the privacy of those around me. However, the time has come now for my friends and fans around the world to know the truth, and I hope that everyone will join with my doctors and all those worldwide in the fight against this terrible disease. My privacy has always been very special to me, and I am famous for my lack of interviews. Please understand this policy will continue.'

People who were suffering from AIDS appreciated Freddie's statement; it became obvious to everyone that anyone could fall victim to this terrible disease. Since most people loved Freddie, they began to support the cause, as Freddie did in his will.

In addition to this very positive aspect, it was a sensible thing to do because, sooner or later, the news would have come out, even if only from the release of the death certificate. So, Freddie prevented the press from writing unfavourable news reports that could have embarrassed his friends who had denied he had AIDS for his sake.

Otherwise, it wouldn't have been anyone else's business, but the fact is when more than two people know about something, it is no longer a secret, so Freddie was able to depart with the knowledge that he had 'cleared the air' and done something for those who were already ill, and importantly, highlighted the need for treatment and prevention.

Freddie also charged Jim Beach with enforcing his will.

Freddie slept for most of Friday and also Saturday. When Jim visited him in the evening, Freddie had told Jim that the statement would be released at midnight.

They chatted happily all night about trivial matters. They didn't watch TV. Sometimes Freddie had a snooze, and occasionally when Jim started snoring, Freddie gently nudged him with his elbow; and if Freddie wanted something, he nudged him more firmly in his side. He wanted some fruit, so Jim sliced some mango for him. After eating it, they both fell asleep again. Freddie woke Jim at 3 a.m. but couldn't speak and just pointed to his mouth in despair. Jim tried to work out what the problem was, but struggled in vain. Thankfully, Joe soon came home from a night out and realised straight away what the problem was. A piece of mango was stuck in Freddie's throat, which Joe was able to dislodge.

Freddie next woke at 6 a.m. and had to go to the toilet, but didn't have the strength, so Jim carried him in his arms. As he put Freddie back to bed, he heard a terrible crack, as if Freddie's bones had broken. Freddie screamed in agony and began to writhe around.

Jim shouted for Joe, who held Freddie still, trying to calm him. Freddie grabbed Joe and strongly squeezed his throat. Joe struggled for air and managed to escape from Freddie's grip, and then calmed him down. It appeared Freddie had gone through a severe panic attack, probably caused by the pain.

Freddie fell asleep after the struggle. They called Dr Atkinson, who gave Freddie a morphine injection and thought he might live a few more days.

Joe and Jim knew this was impossible; they sensed that Freddie had run out of strength, and there was no hope of him improving even slightly.

Mary came over again to talk to the doctor, but she didn't stay at Freddie's side.

Elton John sensed he had to come again. When he saw Freddie's desperate condition, his heart ached for him. It was very painful to see his beloved friend suffering.

Jim had to leave the house for a while; the emotional shock hit him hard. He came back within an hour and saw Freddie was worse than ever. He could no longer react; he couldn't even move his eyes and just looked firmly straight ahead.

Dave Clark picked up Freddie's favourite cat, Delilah, and started stroking her.

It seemed like Freddie knew what was going on around him.

Then, somehow, he let them know he needed to go to the toilet, but Jim didn't dare lift him on his own and rushed downstairs to ask for Peter's help. By the time he returned, it was too late. They talked about changing the sheets, and Jim changed Freddie's shorts. Freddie even helped a little by moving his legs and then suddenly stopped moving. Without even looking, Jim sensed that Freddie was no longer with them.

When Jim looked up, he saw that Freddie wasn't breathing. His eyes were open and his face radiant, as if he were already standing at the gates of Heaven in front of the shining Christ. Jim committed this sight to memory, and whenever he went to sleep, he could see Freddie's radiant face in front of him.

When the angels took Freddie to the judgement seat, God asked him what good and bad things he had done. Freddie told God briefly about his life on Earth, maybe leaving out a few details, but God knew everything, nothing was secret from Him.

Freddie probably also mentioned Beelzebub, but God just waved His hand dismissively and asked Freddie, 'Where do you think you belong, my son?'

'I don't know where I belong, but I know I always wanted to go to hell, because I could meet many interesting people there'.

'As you wish, my son, God answered, I hope you have reflected on the matter well,' and as God said this, Freddie found himself at the gates of Hell where Beelzebub himself was waiting.

'I heard your song, son, it wasn't very nice of you to blame me for your earthly sins.'

'I didn't want to hurt you, forgive me', said Freddie, 'I didn't mean it seriously, it was just some kind of pretext, you know?!'

'I'm not renowned for forgiveness', Beelzebub replied, and opened the gates of Hell, where Freddie could only hear shouting, screaming and groaning. And then he began to sing in agony, with increasing volume, as loudly as he could, to avoid listening to the cries of those pathetic figures.

He had only just started the third song when Beelzebub asked him to stop singing because souls don't go to Hell to sing.

'I'm no good at anything else, what else can I do?' Freddie asked and continued 'We will we will rock you'. He then started drumming with his feet and clapping to every third beat of the drum, but the 'audience' didn't join in the fun. Freddie began to feel strange and tried other songs, but everyone was just busy with their own grief.

Freddie got angry and shouted, 'Oh, well, f**k all of you!'

He decided to drop everything and head for the exit. Beelzebub asked what he wanted.

'Take me out of here immediately!' Freddie demanded. 'I won't stay a minute longer.'

'I knew this was how it would end', answered Beelzebub. 'You know, your problem is you that you get bored quickly. But go, if you really want to.'

'Two angels were waiting at the gates and accompanied him straight back to Heaven. When God saw Freddie, all He said was, 'I thought you'd come back. You did the right thing. You can make yourself useful here and join the choir of angels.' Freddie happily agreed. The singing soon began. Freddie had to accept that Heavenly angels only knew lyrical songs and were continually singing about life's beauty and God's glory, which wasn't bad, but nor was it good. The music sounded as if it had all been written in the same style.

Freddie wrote a few tracks for them, but no matter how hard the poor winged creatures tried, they didn't understand why they should change their style. They had only ever heard horror stories about rock music. Freddie showed them how to improvise and improve their singing techniques, but no matter how hard they tried, he had to acknowledge that they were simply unable to improve and always sang the same song for the glory of God.

Freddie sat on the edge of a beautiful cloud in boredom, and decided to have a look around and see what was happening down below. He went wherever the wind blew the cloud and he soon found himself over Garden Lodge.

He saw his fans – those who had inundated the mourning 'family', or to be more precise, him, with flowers. He screamed in delight and applauded and thought of the birthday flowers and the house decorated with flowers.

He saw that Peter was busy, making phone calls to organise the funeral.

He went through all the Garden Lodge rooms and was pleased to find that they were all tidy, and the cleaning lady hadn't broken anything since he'd gone.

Time had stopped for Jim, so he stopped the clock that he'd bought for Freddie when Freddie finally left him at 7:10 p.m. on 24 November, 1991, and never wound it up again.

Jim called his mother and burst out sobbing as he heard her voice. A few minutes passed before he was able to tell her, with a trembling voice, what had happened. His mother tried to comfort him, but Jim was desperate. He asked her to get the bishop to say Mass for Freddie's soul in line with Irish Catholic custom.

Joe went to the gym, as he did every day. He had friends there, but the training didn't help. Jim said he fell apart completely and was inconsolable.

Peter coped better with his grief, which was understandable, as they were 'only' friends, not lovers.

Mary also paid her last respects, and later, Freddie's parents came to bid a final farewell to their beloved son.

Roger, who was only 300 metres away from the house, went to see Freddie one more time when Peter called him to tell him the bad news.

Freddie's face radiated calm, and even though his heart was broken, Jim was relieved and pleased to see that Freddie, who he loved so much, was no longer suffering. As far as he was concerned, it wasn't just the clock that had stopped, but life itself. His last gift to Freddie was a small **teddy bear**, which he put next to him in the coffin before his body finally left his wonderful home.

The 'family' members stared straight ahead, in a daze; they couldn't believe it had all ended like this, in a single moment. They knew the inevitable would happen, and yet they watched on uncomprehendingly as Freddie was taken out of the house and effectively evacuated with police assistance to stop the press pursuing him, even on his final journey.

On the day of the funeral, Jim arranged for a white wreath to be tied in the shape of a swan, which he knew Freddie would have liked.

His final message to Freddie on the flowers was:

'Others were taken, yes I know
But you were mine, I loved you so.
A prayer, a tear till the end of time,
For a loving friend, I was proud to call mine.
To a beautiful life, a sad, sad end,
You died as you lived, everyone's friend.'

Five cars were needed to transport the fans' flowers to the site of the ceremony.

On the morning of the funeral, Mary told Jim he couldn't travel with her in the first car behind Freddie's coffin, and Dave Clark sat next to her instead.

Jim, Peter and Joe were only allowed to sit in the third car, which broke Jim's heart. Freddie had barely gone, and Mary was already pushing him aside. Even Jim Beach, Freddie's manager, was ahead of them.

Mary was the 'widow', and the 'family members', who had cared for and looked after Freddie like a real family, felt they had been cast aside. In reality, Mary wasn't Freddie's widow, but she was his closest friend.By then, everyone knew Freddie was gay, and Jim Hutton was his partner, not her. Maybe this was how Freddie wanted things to be, but if so, Jim, fortunately, didn't know anything about it. Maybe Freddie wished to spare his parents another 'scene', knowing the press would attend the ceremony. I think this is the most likely reason, although Mary's later behaviour provides food for thought, because this was just the first of their ordeals.

Songs by Aretha Franklin and Montserrat Caballé were played at the ceremony. Freddie was pleased to hear his favourites again, but saddened by the sight of his loved ones in mourning. He started crying silently, and just cried and cried, especially when he saw the wonderful flowers sent by his parents, Jim, Mary, Elton, the guys from Queen, the 'family' and fans all over the world. He listened to the Zoroastrian priests, but didn't understand a word they said.

After the ceremony, Freddie calmed down a little, but didn't really know what to do and sensed there was no room for him in Heaven or Hell, so he thought all he could do was to float between Heaven and Earth.

The reception after the ceremony was at Garden Lodge, but Brian, John and Roger preferred to go to a restaurant.

Jim heard noisy, irritating partying, bursting champagne bottles and laughter coming from the house, which he found distasteful. He expected quiet lamentation, memories and tears, not that kind of rejoicing.

Freddie peeked into the dining room, saw the partygoers and thought, 'Just like in the old days'.

I don't know what reason they had to be happy, as they were Freddie's closest friends and family members. Jim listened in diplomatic silence to those who attended the reception.

Poor Barbara suffered too, not just because of Freddie's death, but also because she was cruelly rejected. She had bought a flight ticket and mourning dress for the funeral, and was about to leave for the airport when she received a phone call saying she wasn't welcome at the funeral.

It probably wasn't Mary who called, but someone from Jim Beach's office, an outsider, though Mary soon got rid of everyone who had 'taken Freddie away' from her.

All of a sudden, Freddie caught sight of Jim, devastated and crying quietly at the number 27 bus stop near Garden Lodge. Freddie sat next to him, embraced him in spirit and quietly started crying too. Delilah and Goliath were there. The cats suddenly felt a strange sense of happiness, so they started purring louder than they had ever done. Jim thought they were trying to comfort him, so he began to stroke them. His soul was so numb that he couldn't sense Freddie's presence and could only see the empty bedroom in front of him. He was alone in the world, as if he had lost everything.

48. Freddie's Will

On the afternoon of the ceremony, Jim Beach told Jim, Peter and Joe that – in line with Freddie's wishes – they could stay in the house for as long as they wanted, and Freddie had left them 500,000 pounds each. They were all shocked and hadn't expected such a huge sum.

Jim spent a few more nights in their joint bedroom. He lay on top of the bed, but didn't dare go to sleep because he dreaded waking up to find Freddie wasn't by his side. His life had turned into a nightmare.

Originally, they had planned to spend Christmas together at Garden Lodge, with Mary and her family and Dave Clark, but one week after the ceremony, Jim Beach appeared again, this time striking a different tone, speaking as a lawyer and not as a friend of the 'family'.

He announced that, sadly, since Freddie hadn't put anything in writing about them staying in the house, this part of his will was not legally binding on Mary, the new owner, so they had to leave the house by March 1, within three months.

From then on, Mary behaved differently towards them, especially towards Jim. The friendship was over, they were no longer 'family' members. Jim decided to travel home to Ireland for a week. Before he left, he bumped into Mary. According to Jim, she said to him: **'Freddie's probably waiting for you already'**.

Jim wrote in his book:

'It was a very cruel remark to make to someone who would inevitably share Freddie's fate'.

This remark and the fact that she didn't respect Freddie's wishes makes you think, but the comment Mary made to John Reid (Queen's first manager) makes a lot of things clear:

'I saw Mary a couple of times. I bumped into her now and again. She said the strangest thing to me; she said as I was trying to comfort her because she'd been through a lot and seen a lot, and she said to me, 'Well, I won, didn't I? He was with me at the end.' That was a bit scary.'

(Matt Richards & Mark Langthorne)

We know why Freddie appeared with Mary at red carpet receptions, while Jim shuffled behind them like a small dog. Whether Freddie wanted to or not, he completely humiliated Jim. Like many other people, she knew their 'marriage' was just a show, especially once the newspaper articles made it clear Freddie was gay, which had already become obvious much earlier in musical circles, because Freddie didn't make any secret of it.

Jim suffered terribly when he lost Freddy, but he was glad he could stay in the house because every single item reminded him of Freddie.

If Mary had truly loved Freddie after they had broken up, she would have kept Jim at the house as a gardener. The house was a large building with separate sections, so Jim could have lived apart from Mary's family – but no, she wouldn't even allow that.

If anyone has doubts about what I'm saying, consider what Mary told *The Star* two days after Freddie's death:

'So few people really knew him. My strength came from knowing him. I feel very much for the people that are looking after people and love people that are going to die of this disease, because it is dreadful. I

would like to say to the fans that my heart goes out to them and they are not forgotten.'

(26-11-1991 - The Star - Fear Over Star's Legacy of AIDS)

queenarchives.com

Mary sympathised with anyone who was caring for, or loved someone who was going to die of AIDS. Jim cared for Freddie; he was HIV positive and Freddie's unofficial husband. Mary showed her feelings for Jim and Joe with some wicked remarks and then expelled them from the house. This was how she thanked them for what they had done for Freddie. They didn't expect any gratitude because they hadn't done it for Mary, but out of love for Freddie, though they certainly hadn't expected torment and humiliation.

In the last week of Freddie's life, Mary suggested to Jim that he should ask Freddie to take his ring off because when he died, his hand would swell, and it wouldn't be possible to remove it. 'The ring stays', Jim replied. 'It's staying with him forever.' The ring was the symbol of his love and fidelity, which was why he was proud that Freddie wore it. This gave Jim strength.

Mary took her strength from Freddie's existence and didn't lose it when Freddie left her behind forever, because fortunately, he was able to compensate her with a house worth more than 4 million pounds and other assets. So, she hadn't loved him in vain for all those years. In the end, she won, as she told John Reid, as if she had been competing for something all her life. She travelled in the first car, but this didn't make her Freddie's widow. She wasn't the one Freddie asked every day whether she loved him. Jim didn't want to be a widower, he would have loved to have seen Freddie alive, but this was his destiny. Freddie called Jim his husband, and was wearing his ring when he died.

When Freddie found out what had happened, he wasn't surprised; this wasn't the first disappointment in his life. Freddie loved to insure himself several times over, which was why he bought a house for Joe and left him money, so he wasn't exposed to Mary's whims. Freddie and Jim designed and built a house together, which they also furnished together and which Freddie called 'our house' so that Jim could feel their joint home was in Ireland, if Mary didn't keep her word. And he knew Peter would find his own solution. In any case, the money Freddie left them was more than enough to live on without having to work again for the rest of their lives.

So, what had Mary won? Why had she fought all those years? To be Freddie's widow? If so, it hadn't worked. In any case, what kind of loving wife wants to be a widow? None. By the time Jim returned from Ireland, all three of them had been moved out of the house to the courtyard apartments, where nobody lived, as they were intended for guests.

The security system was improved in the Garden Lodge building. Jim, Joe and Peter were allowed in the house until 6 p.m., if they had some business there. The doors were locked after that, and more of Queen's security guards were brought in to guard the house and make sure fans didn't rob it.

Finally, in a gallant gesture, Mary offered the guys the opportunity to gather up gifts they had once given to Freddie, which were still in the house.

Jim assumed Freddie would expect him to look after the cats, which he loved so much, but Mary even denied Jim this pleasure. And she didn't allow him to take the framed joint photos, saying he hadn't asked for them, and when he did finally ask, she still didn't allow Jim to take them.

Jim's misery was alleviated by a letter from Freddie's mother, who was very grateful for everything he had done for Freddie. This was how she expressed motherly love towards Jim, which he really appreciated and very much deserved.

Jim, Joe and Peter left Garden Lodge on the 1 March. Jim even left the bedroom furniture behind that Freddie had designed for him, as he had nowhere to take it. Before leaving, he walked around the outside of the house one last time and looked up at Freddie's bedroom window once again to evoke the sight of Freddie shouting down to him from the window.

A friend offered him a room, where he stayed for a while. Then, after he left and right up to the first anniversary of Freddie's death, he visited Garden Lodge three or four times a week and called out to the cats. One or the other would jump over the wall, and he would hug and stroke them as he cried and told them his troubles. He spent weeks and months in a bleak and mournful mood, mentally broken, in part by Mary's behaviour. Then, finally, the first anniversary of Freddie's death came around, and the cats no longer appeared when Jim called out to them.

When Jim received his inheritance, he bought himself a modest house in London, where he created a lovely garden and had a small pond built in which he put some koi fish, and he acquired two cats. So now he could finally place objects that reminded him of Freddie in his own house.

There is a video on YouTube that will convince anyone of how much Freddie loved Jim and how happy they were together. This video was recorded the first time Freddie tried out their new Jacuzzi, and put too much shower gel in the water. He plays in the foam bubbles like a child and sings to Jim: *'I want to be loved by you and nobody else but you'*, while laughing happily as Jim puts foam on top of his head.

(YouTube: Freddie Mercury House The life in GARDEN LODGE (7:55)

There is a similar YouTube video with an almost identical title in which Mary poses on her own in every room after Freddie's death.

Poor Jim bought a fine, life-like painting of Freddie at auction, painted by one of his fans, and took it to Garden Lodge on Freddie's birthday. Mary let him into the house and accepted the painting, instead of telling him: 'Please keep it, as he belonged to you and should always be with you.' On the first anniversary of his death, Jim took flowers to the house again, which Mary accepted, though after chatting for a few minutes, Jim thought it was better to leave.

Freddie often made Jim promise he would take care of Mary after his death. Jim tried, but Mary didn't feel the need for his care.

Two months after the first anniversary of Freddie's death, Jim was hit by another blow.

Peter called Jim on the phone and told him that Joe, with whom he had since become friends, had passed away.

Jim was shattered again and totally devastated. Joe's death evoked the terrible torment he had endured barely a year earlier.

Not long before Joe died, he visited Jim to ask him for forgiveness for having always treated him as if he were just the gardener.

At the end of his book Jim wrote:

'I'd give anything to spend my time over again with Freddie. If that could happen, I would take a much more active role in directing the way his life – and illness – would go.'

He really would have had to fight to do so, because Mary, Joe and Peter treated him with arrogance, and they only became friends when they were in the same boat, having been evicted from the house. But this wasn't about Jim. He humbly kept a low profile and let them hang him out to dry. But he could say that Freddie loved him deeply, and he was the only one able to give him the kind of love he had craved all his life.

This was what Freddie said about their relationship:

'I am very happy in my relationship at the moment, and I honestly couldn't ask for better. It's a kind of ... solace. Yes, that's a good word for it. There is this kind of solace I've got now. I don't have to try so hard. I've got a very understanding relationship. It sounds so boring, but it's wonderful. Piaf did it, and so did Streisand. Now I have a hairdresser

husband, dear! I've finally found that niche I was looking for all my life, and no fucker in this universe is going to upset it.'

Mary knew this very well, as did the others; Freddie had finally found the one he needed, and that's why they were all jealous. This was why Mary treated Jim so badly. His close relationship with Freddie had pushed her slightly into the background, but it was not deliberate. He just loved Freddie with a passion in his own kind, friendly and gentle manner.

Jim passed away in 2010; Brian May said he died from lung cancer, not AIDS. Thank goodness he didn't have to suffer as Freddie and Joe had done, although God only knows what he went through during his disease. Lung cancer is no joke either.

Queen fans think of him with great affection and gratitude for making Freddie happy. If I were a sculptor, I'd make a statue for him too and put it up next to Freddie's so they could gaze into the distance together on the shores of Lake Geneva.

I'm confident Freddie didn't dare entrust his ashes to Jim because he knew he would have kept them to himself and taken them with him everywhere he went. Freddie was too tired and wanted to be finally at rest.

Jim supposed that Freddie's ashes were scattered in the garden at Garden Lodge under the weeping cherry tree. The entire house and garden can be seen from under the tree.

Freddie died two months after his 45th birthday. At the age of 16, he believed he would die at the age of 45. Could it have been a coincidence?

No, it was no coincidence. He had no way of knowing, but he was the victim of unintentional self-hypnosis. If he hadn't died of AIDS, he would have died of something else, as this was what he subconsciously believed. Belief is the largest organising force in the world, stronger than all the world's weapons or the biggest army.

One of the main teachings of Hindu masters is that the best medicine against life's most painful blows is not to think about them. Freddie often did this. Another teaching, possibly more important, is that we should always choose our words and reflect on what would happen if we say something and what would happen if we don't. The magical effect of spoken words cannot be overestimated. Jesus healed with his words. He learned the science of healing from the Hindu and Nepali masters during the 12 years he spent in India and Nepal.

49. The Biggest Send-Off in History (20th April, 1992)

The Freddie Mercury Tribute Concert – Wembley Stadium

In the statement he made shortly before his death, Freddie asked those he left behind to support the cause of people with AIDS. Brian, Roger and John organised a huge concert, similar to Live Aid. 72,000 tickets were sold out in three hours. The members of Queen wanted to say goodbye to Freddie in a worthy way, and do something for the AIDS cause.

TV stations broadcast the program in 76 countries, and more than 500 million people saw it.

Most of the artists who appeared had a global reputation as solo performers or as members of a famous band. These artists included David Bowie, Gary Cherone, Roger Daltrey, Joe Elliott, James Hetfield, Ian Hunter, Tony Lommi, Elton John, Annie Lennox, George Michael, Liza Minnelli, Robert Plant, Mick Ronson, Axl Rose, Seal, Slash, Lisa Stansfield, Paul Young and Zucchero.

Brian, Roger and John introduced the event and the audience welcomed them ecstatically. It was very difficult for them to be heard above the noise of the ecstatic fans. Brian shouted at the top of his voice: *'We are here to celebrate the life and work and dreams of one Freddie Mercury'*.

Roger said: *'We are here today for Freddie and the AIDS that affects us all. You can cry as much as you like'*.

All three of them spoke emotionally. John was close to tears, and his voice trembled, but he thanked the artists for accepting the invitation and introduced Metallica.

Most of the artists played Queen's songs at the concert, which lasted three and a half hours. As the first two or three bars sounded, the audience immediately recognised the music, and in many cases, easily drowned out the artists, most of whom were painful to listen to. These singers, who were excellent at performing their own songs, really struggled to produce anything comparable to Freddie, but a few of them managed to do so. Some artists completely ruined the production and the song itself, but the audience still applauded them gratefully, simply for trying, even if they were off-key. As always, Queen delivered their music again.

Extreme, with frontman Gary Cherone, stood out with their passionate performance style. Seal managed to sing *Who Wants To Live Forever* flawlessly and with unparalleled beauty, and George Michael sang *Somebody To Love* pretty well. The most exciting part was at the end of the concert when Axl Rose burst on stage for just a few minutes in a nice little skirt to help Elton John out in the rock part at the end of *Bohemian Rhapsody*. Resembling Freddie, he was very original and sang well. His performance was dynamic, captivating, honest, no-frills and loveable. His performance of *We Will Rock You* was also special.

Don't misunderstand me: I don't want to take anything away from the value of the artists who took part. They have their own fans who love them too. There was only one problem with the whole thing – it wasn't Freddie singing Queen's songs.

Jim was sitting in the audience. He was very surprised that Queen hadn't invited Freddie's favourites, which would have included Aretha Franklin, Montserrat Caballé, Cliff Richard, Peter Straker and Dionne Warwick. Each to his own, as the saying goes.

Montserrat Caballé was invited, but she was too busy to participate in the concert. In a later statement not related to the tribute concert, when asked whether she would sing a duet with anyone else, she said she didn't think so because anyone she sang with would have to be very special, after the duet she had done with Freddie. She couldn't allow her standards to drop.

Montserrat Caballé said in the *Magic Remixed* video on YouTube:

'The difference between Freddie and almost all the other rockstars is he was having a voice.'

Who was better to judge a singer's voice than Montserrat Caballé?

Just trying to imagine which rock or pop singer would be able to perform any of the songs Freddie composed for the two of them is impossible on any level. It would have been an absolute disaster.

However, the concert audience was very grateful; they chanted Brian and Roger's names and screamed in delight when one of their favourite Queen songs began. Ultimately the concert was intended to make the audience feel like they were at a Queen concert, and they could at least see Brian, Roger and John playing live. Hats off to the audience; they bravely put up with some very weak productions. Maybe the concert was a positive experience for them, but I don't think so. They probably realised then that, however hard the performers tried, nobody could replace Freddie.

The concert confirmed my view again that nobody in the rock world could, in any respect, really deliver the brilliant style, diversity, harmonious songs and exceptionally entertaining performance style of Queen. It's very difficult for anyone to compete with Freddie's voice and performance style, and if we add to that Brian's marvellously lyrical voice and Roger's rock vocals, which can't be mistaken for anyone else's, and the harmony of their three voices, we get the kind of combination that is unprecedented in rock history; a one-off, unrepeatable miracle.

The difference between Freddie and the other artists' productions – with the notable exceptions mentioned above – was about the same as between a spaceship and jet aircraft.

If anyone would think I am exaggerating please read the scientific study published in Logopedics Phoniatrics Vocology (via AlphaGalileo), in which a group of Austrian, Czech, and Swedish researchers proved that Freddie had an unparalleled singing voice.

(New scientific study confirms the obvious: Freddie Mercury had an unparalleled singing voice – consequence.net – Ben Kaye April 19, 2016)

I'm convinced it wasn't just me who would have needed a painkiller after the concert, but also Brian, Roger and John. It was the last time the three of them played together, and they had to realize nobody could replace Freddie. Much later on they have tried to replace him, and it seems the audience love it.

Even so, it was great that the artists performed because the income from the tribute concert went to the Mercury Phoenix Trust, which Brian, Roger and Jim Beach had set up in memory of Freddie, making a significant contribution to fund the fight against AIDS. Anyone can join the trust to support the cause of fighting AIDS.

50. The Hollywood Film: *Bohemian Rhapsody* (2018)

Fans worship the film and comment on parts of it on YouTube.

One critic wrote that they had whitewashed Freddie, in other words the film only covers areas that show what was nice and good instead of depicting Freddie's world realistically.

The film is fine just the way it is. It includes every important event in Freddie's life that he was ever willing to talk about, and whatever he didn't want to talk about, because he considered it a private matter, was treated by the filmmakers as Freddie's private business, or these matters are only briefly mentioned. However, some facts were unnecessarily distorted, and it's difficult to understand why they would do this. Freddie's personality only came across partly in the film, which wasn't Rami Malek's fault, but a result of the script.

I also read the book, *Bohemian Rhapsody – The Inside Story* (The Official Book Of The Film) because I was interested in how the film was made.

Graham King, the producer, wrote:

'This film is a celebration of the music first and foremost. It is about carrying on Freddie and Queen's legacy: these songs are larger than life, and put a smile on your face and bring people together.'

This is what Rami Malek said about Brian and Roger's collaboration:

'Having them involved was crucial. Their insight is immense, and no one knows their story and this band more intimately than the two of them. To be able to talk to them on almost a daily basis was invaluable, and they were so kind and so classy about the whole thing. This film is a credit to them.'

The actors, Rami Malek (Freddie), Joseph Mezzello (John), Gwilym Lee (Brian), and Ben Hardy (Roger) played their roles so well and the resemblance was quite surprising. So, if we lose ourselves in the film, we don't even think about the fact that they are not the guys from Queen in their younger days. The story had to be shortened to cram 20 years into two hours.

The film was very good at stimulating and maintaining interest in Freddie and Queen. It meets this goal perfectly and is entertaining, but the fact is, it's a condensed version. The difference between reality and the film is about as big as the difference between tomatoes and tomato paste.

Anyone who wants to know more about Freddie and Queen should read the books published about his life and the band. I've read them too, in four months, and then wrote my book. This is exactly why I found it easier to understand what went on in the film and why; and why it happened the way it did. The wonderful thing is that YouTube is full of interviews, so we can see Freddie's schoolmates, technicians, sound engineers and musicians, for example, including those who collaborated on his solo records. It's a fascinating experience.

A friendly word of caution before you read the last chapter. If you don't believe in reincarnation, it may be better to skip the next chapter. However, I do believe in reincarnation, as I believe in the traditional teachings of ancient Buddhism and the wisdom of Hinduism.

51. The Happy Ending

Freddie spent a lot of time in Jim's new house and hugged him tightly every night; he didn't give up, even when it seemed Jim was inconsolable. He loved being in Jim's garden; it reminded him of their own, with two cats and a few fish as well.

Freddie never went back to the area around Garden Lodge again. Who knows why? Perhaps he missed the piano too much; it hurt him that he couldn't play it, and only the angels could hear him sing.

When he sensed that Jim had finally found some comfort, he thought about the fact that so many people had been reincarnated; why not give it a try? He decided to be a singer again in his next life. He didn't even know when or how it happened, but on 24 May, 1994, he was born again and this time was given the name Dinmukhamed by his Kazakh parents. His mother is an opera singer and his father a composer. He started learning to sing and play the piano at the age of five, and took on the stage name Dimash when he began to perform. Some people say he has a five-octave vocal range, while others say it is seven octaves. He sang the 'Show Must Go On' in the Singer contest organised for professionals and held in China in 2017 in such a way that even Freddie would have been surprised. His first album went platinum in 16 seconds. A lot of people regard him as the world's best singer today. I can thank Dimash (Kudaibergen) for having gotten to know the real Freddie Mercury when I became curious about which of them sang this song better. My vote went to Freddie. Who knows why? Maybe it was because I loved his voice so much, and also Roger, Brian, John and Freddie himself. I can't get enough of him or them. I feel the same way as Jim did; I love Freddie for himself and his art, just as I love Brian, Roger and John for their music and themselves, for the way they stood by Freddie when he needed them. They are outstanding people and artists; they gave and continue to give a lot of pleasure to millions of people day after day. Thank you.

Freddie is delighted in his new body. He is successful and healthy. His parents and grandparents adore him, as do his fans. Whether he prefers boys or girls is not yet clear, but then who is interested in such a small matter? One thing is sure, he hasn't been sent to boarding school.

He has no idea who Jim and Joe were; they left us a long time ago, but if he did, he would always send fresh flowers to their graves. Peter is still alive and enjoying good health. If Freddie remembered him, he would send him postcards from wherever he went in the world.

He knows Queen well and it was certainly no coincidence that he chose 'The Show Must Go On', a Queen song. His English is not yet perfect, but he's learning the language. No doubt he is an admirer of his old self too. When he sang this song, he often had to listen to his own performance from his previous life.

So, the show does go on, until the end of time. Freddie is more than a legendary performer; he's a brilliantly shining star in the Heavens and on Earth. Dr Brian May could have written an essay about him as a special astronomical phenomenon, and everyone could have read it.

'You've never seen nothing like it, no, never in your life
Like, going up to heaven and then coming back alive'

This quote comes from Freddie's song *The March of The Black Queen*, in which he euphemistically describes the experience of orgasm.

Videos, the internet and film brought Freddie back to us as if he had gone up to the Heavens and then came back alive.

Special thanks

I would like to express my deepest gratitude and appreciation to all the authors who have written books about Freddie Mercury and Queen. Without them, I would never have been able to write this book, because it's impossible to interpret songs without biographical data.

I would never have had the opportunity to gather so much data and conduct interviews with anyone who knew Freddie, worked with him, or was friends with him.

I truly enjoyed your books, which proved extremely valuable to me.

A big thanks to Andrew Wild for his fantastic short summaries of the songs, which I never would have been able to write.

I would like to express my gratitude to my translator, David, who has been living in Hungary for 20 years as a dual citizen, and undertook the translation of the book.

I am also very grateful to Gabby,- who lives in Australia - for editing and contributing to the final content of the book, and for suggesting helpful ideas.

Select Bibliography

Books

Brooks, Greg & Lupton, Simon, *Freddie Mercury: His Life In His Own Words* (Omnibus Press, 2009).

Evans, David & Minns, David, *This Was The Real Life: The Tale of Freddie Mercury* (Tusitala, 2001).

Freestone, Peter & Evans, David, *Freddie Mercury: An Intimate Memoir by the Man Who Knew Him Best* (Omnibus Press, 2001)

Hince Peter, *Queen Unseen: My Life with the Greatest Rock Band of the 20th Century* (John Blake, 2011).

Hodkinson, Mark, *Queen – The Early Years* (Music Sales Ltd, 2004).

Hutton, Jim with Tim Wapshott, *Mercury and Me* (Bloomsbury Publishing PLC, 1995).

Jones, Lesley-Ann, *Freddie Mercury: The Definitive Biography* (Hodder Paperbacks, 2012)

Blake, Mark, *Is This The Real Life? The Untold Story of Queen* (Aurum Press, 2010)

Sky, Rick, *The Show Must Go On, The Life of Freddie Mercury*, Fontana, 1992)

Wild, Andrew, On Track: *Queen Every Album, Every Song (Sonicbond Publishing Limited, 2018)*

Jackson, Laura, *Queen The Definitive Biography (Judy Piatkus, 1999)*

Chapman, Phil, *The Dead Straight Guide to Queen (Red Planet Publishing Ltd, 2017)*

Bohemian Rhapsody The Inside Story

The Official Book of The Film (Carlton Books Limited, 2018).

Websites

www.icce.rag.nl

www.queenconcerts.com

www.queenarchives.com

www.queenonline.com

www.officialcharts.com